BORSTAL BOY

Brendan Behan was born in Dublin in 1923. A member of the I.R.A., he was sentenced to three years in Borstal in 1939, and to fourteen years by a military court in Dublin in 1942.

He became a dominant literary figure almost overnight with the 1956 production of his play 'The Quare Fellow', based on his prison experiences. This recognition was reinforced by the success of BORSTAL BOY and his second play, The 'Hostage'.

Brendan Behan described his recreations in WHO'S WHO as 'drinking, talking, and swimming', but no factual description could do justice to his flamboyant, larger-than-life character. Generally regarded as irreverent and unpredictable if not actually dangerous, there was nonetheless no publicity whch ever obscured his marked talents or his great understanding of human nature.

Brendan Behan died in 1964.

ALSO BY BRENDAN BEHAN

Confessions of an Irish Rebel

Brendan Behan

BORSTAL BOY

arrow books

Published in the United Kingdom in 1990 by
Arrow Books

19 20 18

Copyright © Brendan Behan 1958

First published in the United Kingdom in 1958 by Hutchinson & Co. Ltd

Arena edition 1990
Arrow edition 1990

Arrow Books
The Random House Group Ltd
20 Vauxhall Bridge Road, London SW1V 2SA

Random House Australia (Pty) Limited
20 Alfred Street, Milsons Point, Sydney, New South Wales 2061, Australia

Random House New Zealand Limited
18 Poland Road, Glenfield
Auckland 10, New Zealand

Random House (Pty) Limited
Isle of Houghton, Corner Boundary Road & Carse O'Gowrie,
Houghton, 2198, South Africa

The Random House Group Limited Reg. No. 954009

www.randomhouse.co.uk

A CIP catalogue record for this book is available from the British Library

Papers used by Random House are natural, recyclable products made from
wood grown in sustainable forests. The manufacturing processes conform to the
environmental regulations of the country of origin.

Typeset by JH Graphics Ltd, Reading
Printed and bound in the United Kingdom by
Bookmarque Ltd, Croydon, Surrey

ISBN 0 09 970650 4

Do Mo Bh.

'. . . One crew of young watermen or postboys . . . roared and shouted the lewdest tavern songs, as if in bravado, and were dashed against a tree and sunk with blasphemies on their lips. An old nobleman — for such his furred gown and golden chain of office proclaimed him — went down not far from where Orlando stood, calling vengeance upon the Irish rebels, who, he cried with his last breath, had plotted this devilry . . .'

ORLANDO: *Virginia Woolf*

PART ONE

Friday, in the evening, the landlady shouted up the stairs:

'Oh God, oh Jesus, oh Sacred Heart. Boy, there's two gentlemen to see you.'

I knew by the screeches of her that these gentlemen were not calling to enquire after my health, or to know if I'd had a good trip. I grabbed my suitcase, containing Pot. Chlor, Sulph Ac, gelignite, detonators, electrical and ignition, and the rest of my Sinn Fein conjuror's outfit, and carried it to the window. Then the gentlemen arrived.

A young one, with a blonde, Herrenvolk head and a BBC accent shouted, 'I say, greb him, the bestud.'

When I was safely grabbed, the blonde one gave me several punches in the face, though not very damaging ones. An older man, in heavy Lancashire speech, told him to leave me alone, and to stop making a — of himself. . . . There were now two or three others in the room, and this old man was the sergeant and in charge of the raid.

He took some Pot. Chlor and sugar out of the case, put it in the empty fireplace and lit it with a match. It roared into flame and filled the room with smoke. He nodded to me and I nodded back.

Saxonhead and another, a quiet fellow, had me gripped by the arms.

'Got a gun, Paddy?' asked the sergeant.

'If I'd have had a gun you wouldn't have come through that door so shagging easy.'

He looked at me and sighed, as if I had said nothing, or as if he had not heard me.

'Turn him over,' he told the quiet one.

Blondie began to search me with violence.

'No, not you,' said the sergeant, 'Vereker.'

Vereker searched me, quietly, and, even along the seams of my flies, with courtesy.

'Lift your arms up over your head. Put your leg up. Thank you.'

1

From an inside pocket he took my money, a forged travel permit, and a letter which happened to be written in Irish.

It was from a boy in Dublin who was sick in bed and wanted me to come and see him. He was a dreary bastard in any language, and I, a good-natured and affectionate boy, found him distressing to meet and embarrassing to avoid. I would have a good excuse for not meeting him for some time to come.

The blonde studied the Gaelic writing over Vereker's shoulder.

Disgusted, he turned to me and shouted, 'You facquing bestud, how would you like to see a woman cut in two by a plate-glass window?'

I would have answered him on the same level — Bloody Sunday, when the Black and Tans attacked a football crowd in our street; the massacre at Cork; Balbriggan; Amritsar; the RAF raids on Indian villages. I had them all off, and was expecting something like this. But the sergeant said in a reasonable tone:

'Well, Paddy, there are people gathered round this house, and I don't think they mean you any good.' He laughed a bit. 'But take no heed of them. We'll get you to the Assizes all right. Safe and sound.'

Vereker released my arm and went to the window. 'Uniformed men are making them move along.'

The sergeant told Blondie to let me go.

'We'll sit here a while,' he said, sitting on the side of the bed, grunting. He pointed and I came over and sat beside him.

'I wish to Christ I was your age, Paddy, I'd have something better to do than throwing bombs around. How old are you?'

'I'm sixteen, and I'll be seventeen in February.'

'So they sent you over here, you silly little twerp, while the big shots are in America, going around spouting and raking in the dollars and living on the fat of the land.'

Sean Russell, Chief of Staff of the IRA, was in the United States.

Vereker offered me a cigarette.

'Maybe he'd like one of his own. Give him them back. They'll take them off him soon enough in the Bridewell.'

He lit a pipe and Vereker and I smoked cigarettes. Blondie stood and did not smoke or say anything.

The sergeant pointed his pipe at the case. 'You're a silly lot of chaps, going on with this lot. You don't even know why you're bloody well doing it. It's supposed to be about Partition. About the Six Counties. Well, I've interviewed a lot of your fellows, and God blind old Reilly if one of them could even name the bloody things. Not all six, they couldn't. Go on, now, you. The whole six, mind.'

I began. 'Antrim, Armagh.'

The sergeant counted on his fingers. 'Right, that's two you've got.'

'Down, Derry, and Fermanagh and . . .'

'Right, five you got. Come on, the last one.'

'Down, Derry, and Fermanagh . . . and . . .'

'There you are, Paddy, what did I tell you?' He shook his head triumphantly.

I left out County Tyrone for he was a nice old fellow.

After a while Vereker had another look through the window and said that we could go, that there weren't so many people outside the house.

The sergeant undid the buttons of my pants, and I held them up with my hands in my pockets, going down the stairs.

Outside, as we got in the car, a few people shouted:

'String the bastard up. Fughing Irish shit-'ouse.'

It was an Orange district, but I think some of them were Liverpool-Irish, trying to prove their solidarity with the loyal stock.

In the car the sergeant said: 'That landlady of yours won't have a window left in her house tonight. They'll probably give the lodger a kicking and all.'

That was the least of my worries. The landlady was a mean woman from the Midlands. I don't mean that coming from the Midlands caused her meanness. You'll get good people from there, or from any airt or part of the world, but if Cockneys or a Siamese are mean or decent, they'll be mean or decent in a Cockney or a Siamese way.

3

This landlady was mean and as barren as a bog. Her broken windows would be a judgement on her for the cheap sausages and margarine she poisoned her table with, for she was only generous with things that cost little in cash, locking hall doors at night time and kneeling down to say the Rosary with the lodger and her sister, who always added three Hail Marys for holy purity and the protection of her person and modesty, so that you would think half the men in Liverpool were running after her, panting for a lick of her big buck teeth.

The lodger was a big thick from an adjacent bog. After the prayers for purity he had one of his own: that God would grant unto him strength and perseverance to abstain from all alcoholic drinks and to mortify the appetite, so gross a cause of insult to the most loving heart of Jesus, by partaking, but sparingly even, of innocent liquid refreshments such as tea, lemonade, herb beer, ginger pop, and cocoa.

The lodger had to say this every night, for he was a member of the Sacred Thirst, and went to their meetings on Friday night, directly after leaving the Post Office and putting his money in the Savings Bank. But the landlady told us that it would do us no harm to say it with him.

On the back of the hall door was a picture of the Sacred Heart, saying: 'God is here. Stand firm.'

'Yes,' said the sergeant, 'I shouldn't be surprised if they leave that house a wreck.'

I was brought to the CID headquarters in Lime Street. In accordance with instructions, I refused to answer questions. I agreed to make a statement, with a view to propaganda for the cause. It would look well at home, too. I often read speeches from the dock, and thought the better of the brave and defiant men that made them so far from friends or dear ones.

'My name is Brendan Behan. I came over here to fight for the Irish Workers' and Small Farmers' Republic, for a full and free life, for my countrymen, North and South, and for the removal of the baneful influence of British Imperialism from Irish affairs. God save Ireland.'

4

'Here, what's this about small farmers? It's your statement, Paddy, and you can put what you bloody well like in it, but I never seen a small farmer, Irish or English; they're all bloody big fellows with bulls' 'eads on 'em, from eating bloody great feeds and drinking cider.'

The left-wing element in the movement would be delighted, and the others, the craw-thumpers, could not say anything against me, because I was a good Volunteer, captured carrying the struggle to England's doorstep — but they would be hopping mad at me giving everyone the impression that the IRA was Communistic.

The 'God Save Ireland' bit made me feel like the Manchester Martyrs, hanged amidst the exulting cheers of fifty thousand fairplay merchants, and crying out with their last breath:

'God save Ireland,' cried the heroes,
'God save Ireland,' cry we all;
'Whether on the scaffold high,
Or the battle field we die,
Sure, what matter when for Ireland dear we fall.'

Blondie took the statement and looked at me with as much savagery as he could muster. I looked back at him, and he looked back to my statement.

Girt around by cruel foes,
Still their courage proudly rose
As they thought of them that loved them far and near,
Of the millions true and brave
O'er the stormy ocean's wave,
And our friends in Holy Ireland, ever dear. . . .

And all the people at home would say, reading the papers, 'Ah sure, God help poor Brendan, wasn't I only talking to him a week ago?' 'By Jasus, he was a great lad all the same, and he only sixteen.'

And Shiela would be sorry she did not let me thread her, the night we walked the canal.

Her cousin had been sentenced to fifteen years under an assumed name in England, and she was taking me up to his mother that I might break the news.

Shiela, when I tried her up against a telegraph pole on the canal bank, said that I should be ashamed of myself, and I a Volunteer, and especially at a time like that.

My statement was taken down, and I signed it. Again they asked me questions which I refused to answer.

I was a bit surprised to hear a chief inspector refer to '—ing old Roger Casement'. At home Casement was regarded as a Republican saint. Rory, my eldest brother, was named after him.

They gave me tea. Vereker said I was a well-read chap, and told me in a whisper that he himself did the competitions in *John O'London's Weekly*.

'Well, Paddy,' said the sergeant, 'we're taking you to Dale Street lock-up now. It's not going to be too nice there, but we'll have you in court Monday morning and you'll most likely be shifted to Walton in the afternoon. You'll get a proper bed there, with sheets. Come along, son.'

Dale Street was not so good. The station sergeant was an ignorant class of animal; he took my cigarettes and matches away from me, and told me he hoped I would get twenty years.

The sergeant and Vereker waved good night to me from the day-room, and I caught a last glimpse of them before I was taken along a dark passage and down a stair, where we stopped outside an open door.

A policeman said, 'This do, Sergeant?'

'Yes, shove the bastard in there. Hope he chokes during the —ing night.'

I went to the door.

'Eh, not so fast. Take off them bloody shoes.'

I thought they were going to beat me up, and wanted me barefoot, so that I would be less well able to defend myself.

'Come on, off with them.'

I bent slowly, my back to the wall, and undid my laces.

'Come on, look sharp. Don't keep us here all night, you sloppy Irish mick.'

I removed my shoes and left them at the cell door.

'Now, off with your jacket; undo your braces and give them to me.'

I gave them to him.

'You might decide to 'ang yourself in the night. Not that that would be any loss. Now get in that cell and if I 'ear one peep out of you during the night, we'll come down 'ere and we'll murder you.'

I went into the cell, holding my trousers up and carrying my jacket, shuffling slowly.

'Come on, get in there before I have to put my boot in your arsehole.'

They banged the door and went off up the stairs, their keys jangling in the distance. I looked around me. Bare concrete walls and floor. The door was a massive piece of timber and steel. The window was high up in the wall, below ground level and looking on to another wall. A bare electric bulb, over the door, shone through wire grating.

The bed was a wooden bench with a pillow of the same material, but I had three blankets.

I lay down, wrapped myself in the blankets, but the pillow was too much for me. I reversed, putting my feet on the pillow, with my head resting on my jacket. The pillow was too hard for my feet, and it strained my ankles, keeping them there. Then I wanted to use the lavatory. It was in a corner from the door. I stood over it, my bare toes on the cold concrete floor. As I stood, waiting over the lavatory, I heard a church bell peal in the frosty night, in some other part of the city. Cold and lonely it sounded, like the dreariest noise that ever defiled the ear of man. If you could call it a noise. It made misery mark time.

I got back on my bench, coiled myself up, so that my feet avoided the wooden pillow, in some comfort, and realized my doom. Even if I got away with a few years only, on account of my age, it was for ever. It wasn't even possible that Monday should come, when at least I'd get a walk up the stairs. The clock was not made that would pass the time between now and Monday morning. It was like what we were told about the last day, 'Time is, time was, time is no more.'

And Jesus Christ, even now, I was only locked up ten minutes.

I put my mind on other things. It was at least and at last permissible to a man in my position.

Then I settled myself more comfortably and wondered if anyone else had done it in the same position. I didn't like to mention them by name, even in my mind. Some of them had left the cell for the rope or the firing squad. More pleasantly tired, from the exercise, I fell asleep.

Waking, I felt the hardness of my resting-place. I didn't wonder where I was. I knew that all right. I looked up at the grey light, through the barred windows, and remembered it better. A blunt and numbing pain it is, to wake up in a cell for the first time. I consoled myself, comparing it to the greater horror, surprise and indignation of a condemned man waking up the morning of his execution.

I lay for a while, and wondered if they would take me to court this morning. Maybe I'd be shifted to prison in the afternoon.

There were noises of key-jangling and door-banging. I hoped they would open my door. Even if they were distributing nothing better than kicks or thumps, I'd prefer not to be left out, in my cold shroud of solitude. Fighting is better than loneliness.

He was coming down my way. He was at the door, looking in the spy-hole. Come in, we know your knock. For Jesus' sake, mister, don't go away without a word. Have a heart.

He turned the key in the lock, and, standing in the open door, said: 'Come on, out of it. Down for a wash. Look sharp.'

A big lump of a man and friendly, without caring much one way or the other.

'Can't keep you 'ands easy. What 'ave you been pinching now, eh?'

'I haven't been pinching anything.'

He noticed my accent, and the friendliness left his voice.

'Oh, you're the bastarding IRA man was lifted in Everton last night.' He was regretting the friendliness of his first remarks. 'Going to put bombs in the new battleships in

8

Cammell Lairds, was you?' He shouted down the passage. 'Larry, come down and see your bleedin' countryman.'

Another constable came and stood in the doorway of the cell. An elderly man, with a long Irish upper lip.

He shouted straight away, 'By Jasus, we didn't do in half enough of you during the Trouble.'

He had a heavy Munster accent, with an English one mixed into it. Probably, he had helped to murder people with the Black and Tans during the Trouble, and was afraid to stop in his own country or go near it since. I had him weighed up, all right.

I stood holding my trousers, and spoke up to him, 'I wasn't born the time of the Trouble.'

His voice screeched into the falsetto of hysterical laughter or rage. 'But I got my share of them, and as for you, you bloody swine, I know what I'd do with you.'

I looked up into his glaring red face, and shouted, myself: 'By Jasus, and they chased you out it, anyway. You haven't stopped running yet.'

'Be the living Lord Jesus,' he roared, aiming a blow at me.

The English turnkey intervened.

'Now, Larry, don't 'eed the dirty little ——er. 'E's not worth a kick in the arse-'ole.'

He turned on me, stern, indignant. 'Get on down to that wash-house and wash your bleedin' neck.'

Out of consideration for the other one, I suppose, he omitted the traditional jibe about Irish dirt.

I went down to the wash-house, if not in good humour, at least feeling more alive.

There were four bowls, all in use. A very old, or very down-and-out man, was replacing brown paper inside his shirt. A young man, in a bottle-green suit and a look of stupid conceit, was surveying his fingernails. There was a boy in a sailor's uniform, a little older than I, but lighter built.

I took my place behind him, innocently admiring the back of his neck.

The turnkey was in the passage, giving consoling chat to the Irish constable.

The sailor turned round. He had brown hair and long dark eyelashes. He rubbed his chin, and smiled.

'Could do with a rasp, mate,' he said importantly. 'Been here three days now. They won't let you have your bleedin' razor.'

'I only came in last night,' said I, rubbing my chin, 'I'm not so bad.' I had shaved four times in my life.

'You Irish?'

I nodded.

'Well, there's a lot of blokes round our way are Irish. Went to RC school and all, they did. We all used to sing Irish songs. Confidentially,' he lowered his voice, 'I don't like these Lancashire blokes myself. Bloody lot of swede-bashers. I'm from Croydon. Know where that is, Paddy?'

'Of course I do. It's in London, where the airport is.'

'That's it. Smashing place it is and all, Croydon. Not like this hole. I was picked up here for some screwing jobs. Here and in Manchester — another bloody graveyard. But some good screwing jobs to be done round there. What are you in for, Pad? Boozer battle or something?'

'No, I'm in over the IRA Explosives.'

'Are you—!'

'I am, though.'

'Straight up?'

'Straight up.'

'Cor, you won't half cop it for that lot.' There was no hostility in his voice but almost concern. 'Fix that vest, will you, Pad? Just shove it down a bit.'

He turned around, and I shoved down an inch of his vest that was showing above his blouse. 'There is a bit of soap behind your ear.'

He handed me a towel and I wiped, carefully, the back of his ears.

'Thanks, Paddy.'

The three others were finished and had lit cigarettes. The old man held a butt straight in front of his nose, staring into the smoke. The turnkey shoved in three others. He did not seem to mind the smoking. I remarked on this to the sailor.

'It's got bugger all to do with him,' he said. 'You can smoke your head off in here if you got any snout or the money to buy it. You can buy scoff, your breakfast, dinner and tea, chocolate. Any perishing thing. Except drink or a bit of crumpet, I suppose.'

'They took my cigarettes and matches away from me.'

'Oh well, Pad,' he said, seriously, 'it might be different for you. Being IRA, like. It's a sort of 'igh treason, isn't it.' But then, more cheerfully, 'But —'em all, china, you can have some of mine.'

I turned from the wash-bowl, protesting.

'Yes, you bloody will. I'll give you three snout, a card of matches, and a packet of chewing gum. I got stacks of that. And 'ave you got anything to read?'

'No, I haven't.'

'Well, I'll give you last week's *News of the World*.' He took it out of his pocket. 'Though maybe you saw that one?'

I said I hadn't seen that issue. I had never read the *News of the World* in my life. I was only forty-eight hours left Ireland, and it had been banned there since I was four years old. I thanked him again, and turned to finish my wash.

'Your hands are wet, Paddy. I'll shove them in your sky-rocket for you.'

I gave myself a final rinse, bent over the bowl. He put his hands in my trousers pocket.

'No bottle, Paddy, that one's got an 'ole in it.'

He tried the other side. 'That's all right. I'll shove the snout, matches, and chewing gum in here.'

I turned from the bowl, drying myself.

'And I'll put the paper inside your shirt, so's as that old bastard of a grass-'opper won't tumble it.' He put the *News of the World* next to my skin, putting his hand round me. 'He won't tumble it there, Paddy, under your jacket.'

'Thanks, kid,' said I.

'That's all right, kid. And, Paddy, my name is Charlie.'

'Thanks, Charlie.'

'That's all right, kid. And if I get any more stuff today, I'll work you a bit of snout, and chocolate, maybe, tomorrow. And I'll tell you what, Paddy,' he said eagerly, 'I know Irish songs. I'll sing you one when we get back to the flowery. Those other geezers are going to court today. All except you and me. We'll wait till the copper takes them to court. I'm on the landing over you. You'll hear me all right. I'll have my lips to the spy-hole.'

The door of the wash-house was unlocked, and the big turnkey came in. 'Right, all you shower. Puffed, powdered and shaved for his worship?'

The prisoners laughed and marched out behind him, and he locked up each one as he came to the cell door.

' 'Bye, Pad,' whispered Charlie. He tipped me with his elbow, and went into his cell.

'I'll put a double lock on you,' said the screw. 'You London blokes are so leery. Regular bloody lot of 'Oudinis, down there.'

I was left on my own.

'Now, Guy Fawkes, lead on to the dungeons.'

I went down the stairs.

'Plenty of accommodation 'ere. You've got an 'ole suite of rooms to yourself.'

I said nothing.

'And I bet you ain't satisfied. That's the Irish, all over. Never done cribbing.'

He opened the door. 'And fold up them bloody blankets. You ain't sleeping with the pigs now, you know.'

I collected my breath to speak without stammering, 'I don't know if that sort of abuse is provided for in the regulations, but, what's more to the point, I want some breakfast, and if I can't order it from outside I'm quite sure you'll have to provide me with something.'

There; it was done. I looked up at him. I'd often heard my father and uncles say that this manner of speaking worked wonders during the Trouble, soldiers, police, and warders being for the most part an ignorant body of men. But, then, that was a long time ago and the whole of Ireland was in arms against England and the sympathy of the world behind her. I watched his face, steadily keeping my anxiety out of my own eyes. But though he opened his mouth to roar, I knew, relieved, that he was a little bit puzzled.

'You'll order sweet fanny adams from outside, and never you mind the regulations, I'll regulate you, and give you a thick ear for your breakfast, if I get any more of your lip. Don't come the sea-lawyer 'ere. And, you —ing little bastard, you'll 'ave respect for Constable 'Oulihan and all.'

— you and Constable Houlihan, said I, in my own mind, and to the turnkey, 'and I'll complain to the magistrate about your bad language.' Now, you poxy looking ballocks, see what you make of that.

His wattles flamed in anger, and he banged the door and went off heavily up the iron stairs.

I thought it better not to smoke till he went to court. I put a bit of chewing gum in my mouth and walked up and down chewing in rhythm with my footsteps. Three chews a step. An advantage of my dungeon was that there was no one underneath to object to my walking overhead. Not that I'd have felt upset about disturbing him, but I'd heard a frightening shout from someone above to someone on the upper landings: 'Hey, you rotten bastard, for Christ's sake, kip in. Hey, you up there, get on your bloody bench and lay there, you —ing —.' Thanks be to God, there was nothing under me, only Australia, and I could take my morning walk in peace and dignity.

I heard steps on the stairs and stopped in mid-floor. They were coming down to me. Jesus, maybe I should not have said that about the regulations — or, worse still, told that old whore's melt that I was going to report him to the magistrate for his bad language.

They were in the passage. They could easily kill you. Say you cut up rough. It had happened before. Who would give a fish's tit about you over here?

At home it would be all right if you were there to get the credit of it. Give us back the mangled corpse of our martyr. Drums muffled, pipes draped, slow march. When but a lad of sixteen years a felon's cap he wore, God rest you, Frankie Doherty, Ireland's cross you proudly bore.

But the mangling would have to be gone through first.

The key was in the door. Into Thy Hands I commend my spirit, Lord Jesus, receive my soul. The door opened. The turnkey stood, with a prisoner who carried three slices of bread and a mug of cocoa.

' 'Ere's your bloody breakfast. —ing sight more than you deserve.'

I took it and would have thanked him if he had waited. It was just as well he didn't. I'd have nearly kissed him in relief.

They were going to court. The doors above were being opened and people were walking about.

I sat cross-legged on my bench, in some contentment, with my breakfast between my knees. The bread was thinly scraped with margarine. Previous occupants of the cell had only thought the cocoa good enough for decorating the walls with; but hunger is a good sauce, and I ate and drank, and opened my *News of the World* luxuriously, and read a consoling item. A magistrate of Hull had himself been sentenced to two years for offences against girls of eleven and thirteen, daughters of an unemployed man. The magistrate used to give them free vegetables from his greengrocer's shop. The older girl was noticed by her schoolteacher to be pregnant.

In Somerset, some farm labourers in a cider house fell upon one of their number, stripped him naked, poured paraffin on him, and set him alight.

When I'd finished my breakfast, I lit one of my Player's Weights and lay back to study the cross-word.

Then I heard singing. A young, clear baritone, not long in use.

'Oh, the days of the Kerry dancing,
Oh, the ring of the piper's tune,
Oh, for one of those hours of gladness,
Gone, alas, like our youth too soon. . . .'

I noticed Charlie's accent. How he sang, 'dawncing', and 'pipah', but he had his mouth to the spy-hole all right. I got every word.

Everyone, except Charlie and I, being gone to court, it was very quiet.

The morning is always a good time. Till about eleven o'clock when it begins to feel its age.

I was anxious about the lavatory. The seat was in a corner, in full view of the spy-hole. I wasn't shy in camp with the Fianna, or in the Tech. An apprentice sitting on the bowl would call over another boy to give him a light of a cigarette. Or pretend to be an old fellow after a night's porter and shout out, 'One of yous, which of yous, some of yous, any of yous, for Jasus' sake, come over here, and squeeze me head.' But if a master or building trade instructor came they'd shut over the door and be quiet till he left. I didn't like the idea of using the lavatory and that old John Bull's bastard of a copper looking in at me, so now was the time, while he was away at court with the others.

I sat reading the paper, ready to hide it behind the seat if I heard footsteps on the stairs. The serial was a full page. Not Hemingway or Liam O'Flaherty, I thought, settling myself in comfort, and inclining my head to condescension. It was entitled, 'No Star is Lost', and was a lot less interesting than the rest of the paper.

'Hey, Paddy.'

— you, Charlie, said I in my own mind, I'm not finished yet.

He shouted again.

All right, I'll be there in a minute.

The serial would do nicely, only ads. about lost relations on the back. I pulled the chain, and went to the spy-hole.

'Hello, Charlie.'

'Hello, Paddy, that you?'

Who, in Jasus' Name, do you think it could be?

'Like that song, Paddy?'

'Smashing, china.' I speak it like a native, English, in two days and a bit.

Our voices echoed through the lonely Bridewell.

'You sing one, Paddy. An Irish song.'

'In Irish?'

'Yes, "Mother Machree" or "Galway Bay".'

— 'Mother Machree' and 'Galway Bay'. I'll sing a song I learned at school. Ireland crying for the Bonnie Prince, not

that him or his old fellow or anyone belonging to him ever
did anything for us, but it was a good song.

'A bhuachail aoibhinn, aluinn-ó,
Ba leathan do chroí, is ba dheas do phóg . . .
　　. . . beautiful, lightsome, awesome boy,
Wide was your heart, and mild was your eye,
My sorrow without you, for ever I'll cry,
. . . Is go dteíghidh tú, a mhuírnín, slán,
Walk my love, walk surely.

White as new lime, your thighs and hips,
Your clustering hair, and your sweet-bitten lips,
My last blaze of strength would die well in
　　their kiss. . . .

Is go dteíghidh tú, a mhuírnín, slán,
Walk my love, walk surely . . .'

'Good old Paddy, but I couldn't understand it. Give us
"Kevin Barry".'

I sang up, slowly and mournfully, through the lonely corridors:

'. . . And before he faced the hangman,
　　in his dreary prison cell,
British soldiers tortured Barry,
Just because he would not tell,
The names of his companions,
And other things they wished to know,
"Turn informer and we'll free you,"
But Kevin proudly answered, "No" . . .
. . . Only a lad of eighteen summers,
Yet no one can deny,
As he marched to death that morning,
He proudly held his head on high . . .'

When the prisoners came back from the court I heard them
shouting to each other. Some had been remanded, and others,

16

on minor charges, had been sentenced to short terms. They all seemed anxious to get up to the jail before dinner. The food there, it seemed, was better than what we got here. Jesus judge the food that could be worse.

About two o'clock I heard the Black Maria back into the yard, and they were taken off, and the Bridewell was quiet again.

After a while I heard Charlie's door opened and shut again, and they came down my stairs. The door opened, and the turnkey handed me my dinner; three dirty and half-rotten potatoes on an enamel plate, two slices of dry bread, and a mug of water.

I looked at the plate.

'What's the matter,' said the turnkey, 'off your grub or something? You're bloody good soldiers and no mistake. "Up the Republic", and "Long live old Ireland", when you're outside a Scotty Road boozer on Saturday night, but you don't be long cracking up after a few hours in the old digger, do you? What'll you feel like after twenty year? That's if you're lucky, and they don't 'ang you. That scoff is good enough for you. Better than you got at 'ome, in 'ungry Ireland. —ing 'erring and an 'ot potato.'

I took the plate and mug, and he banged the door and went off.

I walked up and down in the cold light. It was already beginning to fade greyly from the window. I looked at the plate on the bench, and took a drink of the water. It made me colder, and the cold was gathering water in my eyes, and to try and warm myself or tire myself, I walked up and down a bit more, giving the plate an odd glance on my return journey from the wall towards the door. At last I sat down and ate the lot.

I had another chew of gum, a drink of water, and a smoke, and, revived, wrapped up in the blankets. Till it was time for walking till evening.

But there was an unexpected bit of diversion in the afternoon. In the middle of a walk I was taken to a room upstairs to be photographed. It was a different policeman opened my door, and this one said nothing to me one way or another.

The photographer was a young man with a pin head and a little moustache. He was wearing a sports coat and flannels. I could not imagine him laughing or being excited but at a cricket match.

In the hope of conversation I asked him the time. But he didn't answer and seemed to be professionally impregnable in his silence.

'Your head this way.' He hung a wooden label round my neck with the words 'IRA' and a number and my name chalked on it. I supposed this was like the pictures one sees of wanted men, and was interested in it, apart from wishing that I was wanted.

'Now, sideways.'

Sideways yourself, and take a running jump at yourself. Might put a bit of life into you.

When he was finished with me, I was brought back to the cell and walked up and down and drank water and urinated to pass the time.

The turnkey brought me a mug of cocoa, and my three slices of bread, and, sitting cross-legged on the bench, I pulled a blanket over my shoulders and had my supper. The light was switched on, and I fixed my bed and got into it. In the height of luxury, and hoping the turnkey would not come back, I lit a butt and read the half of the *News of the World* I had rationed for the evening.

'Good night, Paddy, good night.'

It was cold to jump out on those flags, but Charlie had got out. He was standing there, waiting, his face to the spy-hole in his shirt, and his bare legs as far as his thighs pink with the cold.

I jumped out in my shirt, and put my lips to the spy-hole.

'Good night, Charlie.'

' 'Night, Pad.'

Lying in bed, I could hear the trams far away in the distance. Turning the corners heavily, and gathering speed for the hills.

I used to hear them back in Dublin on the Northside when I was small, lying in bed, avoiding the eye of the Sacred Heart in the picture on the far wall. The house we lived in was a great lord's town house before it was a tenement, and there was a big black Kilkenny marble fireplace before my bed. If the souls in Purgatory really came back, it was out of there they would come. A Hail Mary was all right, but there was more comfort in the sound of the trams. There were lights and people on them. Old fellows, a bit jarred and singing, and fellows leaving their mots home to Drumcondra after the pictures.

The night was broken with shouts and thumps, curses and drunken singing. Some of the other prisoners shouted, 'Shahrap, you baa-a-stad,' in their English accents, but I think they were only shouting to show that they had the privilege of shouting and being on the side of the turnkey at the same time. I didn't mind the noise and the singing. It made me feel as if I was not altogether removed from Saturday nights. And I had the whole of Sunday to get through, and to have a bit of extra sleeping to do would be like having money in the bank.

In the wash-house Charlie and I met amongst the others. I was delighted to see him, and he was glad to see me. I don't know why he should not have been there. But I smiled with relief when I saw he was. We got bowls beside each other, and while we washed he said that those bastards didn't half make a bloody row last night. I agreed with him and said there was one bastard over me sang the same song over and over again, that's if you could call it singing. It was more like a death rattle.

Charlie said the turnkey had not brought him any more cigarettes or papers, though he had ordered them first thing yesterday morning, but he could let me have a butt and a bit of chewing gum. I refused, saying that I still had two snout left and a bit of gum, and was all right. He had brought down a paper for me, and I told him that was all I wanted. I put it under my shirt, and we said we'd see each other going to court in the morning, and after that we'd be shoved up to the nick together.

On the way back he tipped me with his elbow before going into his cell, and muttered, 'Cheerio, Pad'; and I went downstairs and was locked in my own cell and lay looking up at the window, till breakfast came round.

19

I wondered if they had Mass in this place. It would be great to hear an Irish accent, except Constable Houlihan's, and I felt more in a humour for the religion of my fathers than if I were outside and at home.

But they did not say anything about it, and, when the turnkey brought my breakfast, neither did I. He was quiet this morning, and I thought it best to let the hare sit.

Not that we were not reminded of Sunday in another way.
The bells of a hundred churches crashed and banged on my
ears all morning. It was not so bad then, because I like the
morning time, and the day did not begin to get gloomy till
the light faded from the sky in the afternoon. Then the bells
began again, and in defenceless misery I bore them.

I could not even walk, but sat huddled on the bed in my
blankets, with tears in my mind and in my heart, and wishing
I could wake up and find out that I had only been dreaming
this, and could wake up at home, and say, well, that's how
it would be if you were pinched in England, and not attend
any more parades, and drop out of the IRA and attend more
to my trade, and go out dancing or something, and get
married; and if, watching an Easter Sunday parade and listening to the crash of drums and scream of the pipes as the four
battalions of the Dublin Brigade went into the slow march and
gave 'eyes left', as they passed the GPO with their banners
lowered, and the crowds either side of O'Connell Street
baring their heads, I felt my blood go to my scalp — then
I could always remind myself of the time I dreamt I was
captured in Liverpool, and bring my blood back to my feet.

Dreams were often sent to warn people about the troubles
they were likely to bring on themselves if they didn't alter
their ways. Outside, I didn't think of such things, or, if I did,
it was only to laugh at them; but here it seemed very likely
that such things would happen and that it was better to be
quiet and good; and here being good meant not being a
Republican. Even Casement, that the loyalists at home
respected (every paper, including the *Irish Times* and the
Independent, joined in the demand for the return of his
remains, and W. B. Yeats wrote a poem about it: 'The Ghost
of Roger Casement is knocking on the Door'), was abused,
and called '—ing old Roger Casement' by the chief inspector
on Friday night.

Well, I was beginning to see the justice of that. He could do that here; and we could abuse the old Famine Queen at home, or the Black and Tans; and every man to it in his own country. And then to come over here and plant bombs in it, you couldn't expect them to love people for that. But, only to wake up and take the dream for the warning. Or to get out, anyway. Jesus, even to be let free and never to be let home again. Apart from anything else, wouldn't it save them money? Yes, that was a way of looking at it. Maybe, if I recognized the court and pleaded guilty, or said someone gave me the stuff to mind and I didn't know what was in it till I got back to my room, they might only deport me.

I heard steps on the stairs and the turnkey opened my door and brought me up the lighted passageway. My shoes and socks and braces were there, laid out on the floor.

'Put them on,' said he.

I will begod, sir, thanking you. Maybe something great was going to happen. Maybe they were going just to send me home, and say 'Stop out of here, in future.' Oh, and God knows I would, and thankful.

'Follow me; there's someone wants to see you upstairs.'

I kept up with him quickly and was shown into a room. My sergeant was there, and Vereker, who smiled at me. The sergeant winked, and pointed to a third man. A tallish, well-dressed man, and with a good appearance. The thin lips of an Englishman, and that was all right, too — wasn't it his country, to have any kind of lips he liked?

'This is Mr O'Sullivan, Brendan,' said the sergeant.

Better again, he called me 'Brendan', and the gentleman in the good clothes was Irish — maybe from the St Vincent de Paul Society or something, to bring me home. He smiled, even, a little, and said: 'I'm an Irishman, the same as you. I'm from Cork.'

'O'Sullivan's a Cork name, sir,' said I.

'So it is,' said he, 'but what kind of a name is Behan?'

'It's a very Irish name, sir. Literary family once prominent in South Leinster, Irish form, "Ó Beacháin" from "beach" a bee, meaning one who keeps bees, Anglicé, "Behan, Beggan, Beegan". It's in *Sloinnte Gael agus Gall*. That's Irish, sir. *The*

22

Names of the Irish and the Norman, it is in English, sir. Maybe you don't read Irish, but the English is on the opposite page. Your own name is there too, sir.'

'I don't read Irish, Behan, nor do I speak it. A lot of good it would do me if I did. What good is it anywhere outside Ireland?'

'Well in Nova Scotia, sir, in Cape Breton, it's the only language they use. They publish a daily paper in Gaelic.'

'That's Scotch Gaelic — a different language, different altogether.'

I knew it wasn't. The principal difference in saying 'it is' was that they said 'Thá' and we said 'tá', but it wouldn't do to act the know-all, or to downface the gentleman. 'I suppose you're right, sir, when you come to think of it.'

'How old are you, Behan?'

'I'm sixteen, sir.'

'I suppose you realize you can go to jail for the best part of your life over this business. The last crowd sentenced in London got a hundred years' penal servitude between five of them. Twenty years each. The sixth arrested with them is lying under sentence of death in Birmingham. For a cowardly murder.'

'It was no murder,' said I, off the tip of my tongue.

'It was no murder?' His lips tightened in anger. 'To put a bomb in a crowded street and kill five innocent people?' His indignation got the better of him, and his voice grated and his accent changed. 'You bloody little bastard!' he shouted, and rose his hand to strike me, as if he couldn't restrain himself, ground his teeth, and came forward. 'I'll give you murder!'

The sergeant restrained him with Vereker, and both of them looked reproachfully at me. I lowered my eyes and moved back a pace.

Mr O'Sullivan grunted as they held him, 'Let me go, ca-an't you.' His face was terrible to watch, the eyes bulging in anger from behind his glasses. 'Uh,' said he.

'Now, now, Inspector,' said the sergeant to pacify him.

'All right, Sergeant, all right,' said Mr O'Sullivan, in an easier tone. They took their hands from him, and he spoke to me more evenly.

'Don't you come that stuff here, Behan. You're not with your murder-gang pals in Dublin or Belfast, now.'

'Right, sir,' I said in a low voice, and a little bit dazed, wondering what to say that wouldn't start him off again. 'I only meant, sir, that that man had nothing to do with it.'

He looked at me incredulously, and Vereker and the sergeant sighed and shook their heads in my direction.

'I mean, sir, I mean—' I stammered.

'You mean that you are saying that the Birmingham police officers got an innocent man sentenced to death? Is that what you mean, Behan? Is it? Answer me.' His voice rose again, and the sergeant and Vereker moved towards him, but he waved them aside. 'Answer me,' he added in a lower tone.

I swallowed some spit and tried to collect my utterance. 'I mean, sir, there may have been a mistake, sir—'

'The English police, Behan, make no mistakes. In Birmingham — or Liverpool.'

'The man was arrested in London, with those other five fellows, and was in the custody of Scotland Yard before the bomb exploded in Coventry — an hour before.'

I got ready to shrink back, but he did not move.

'You seem to know a lot about it, Behan; maybe you were in that little operation, as you soldiers of the Irish Republic term your murders. How do you know all this?'

'I read it in the papers, sir, in English papers.'

'You were in England, then, when it happened?'

'No, sir, I was in Ireland, at home, but you can buy English papers in Dublin, sir.'

'I see; it's a pity you didn't learn a bit more sense from them.' He spoke very reasonably, and I breathed more easily. Then he put his hand in his pocket and took out a packet of cigarettes. He offered them to the sergeant and to Vereker, and then passed them to me. 'Have one,' he said.

'Thank you, sir,' said I.

Vereker struck a match and passed lights round.

'Listen, Behan,' said the inspector; 'you're only a boy, and your leaders are safe home in Ireland, or in America. We don't want to be hard on you, but the only one that can help you is yourself. You need not consider other people; they're

24

not considering you. But if you tell us where we can lay our hands on more of this stuff in England, we'll go and get it, and there'll be no questions asked or answered on one side or the other.'

'I don't know where is any other stuff in England, sir.'

'You're sure?'

'Certain, sir. The IRA does not let me into all its secrets.'

'Never mind that. If you did know, would you help us to find it?'

'Well, as I don't know where to tell you to find it, that does not matter, does it? I mean, I could tell you a lie and say I would, and then, for that again, if I did know I might not — and what difference would it make?'

'Do you know much about the organization of the IRA in Ireland? In Belfast?'

'Very little, sir.'

'How much?'

'Nothing that would be worth your while hearing about, sir.'

'We're the best judges of that. How much do you know of the IRA in Dublin? Who are the members of GHQ, as you call it?'

'I know something, of course, of the IRA in Dublin, but,' I smiled, 'I'm not a GHQ man.'

'Nobody said you were. And take the grin off your face. This is a serious matter, more serious for you than for anybody in this room.'

'Yes, sir.'

'Who gave you this stuff?'

'I didn't know his name, sir.'

'Who gave you the money you were found with, gave you your ticket, and your forged travel permit? I suppose you don't know that either?'

I said nothing.

'Listen, Behan, if you're afraid of what will happen to you when you go home, I can tell you this. If you help us, we can look after you. I'm sorry for you, in a way. You're only a foolish boy meddling in things that don't concern you. You owe these people nothing. They sent you over here, and now

25

you have to face the music, not them. Now, you know plenty about the IRA organization in Ireland. You've been connected with it since you could walk — you didn't get much chance, really — and you can be of assistance to us. You won't be the cause of anyone being arrested, because we can't make arrests in Ireland, but you'll help us in stopping this business, and, as I say, we'll look after you. You're a young man, not even that yet. We'll send you to the Colonies, Canada, maybe, put you on the boat with money in your pocket.'

He looked at me. 'Well?'

I looked at him, and something told me that he was not going to jump at me any more. I was glad of that.

'I can't help you, sir.'

'You mean you won't. However, you've a long time to go till the Assizes. Think it over when you're up in Walton, and when you change your mind let me know. I'll be up there, right away.'

He nodded to the sergeant and Vereker, and we went out, to the top of the stairs. The turnkey came up, and Vereker smiled at me. 'Good night, men,' said I.

'Good night, Paddy,' said Vereker.

'Good night, you bloody young fool,' said the sergeant. I followed the turnkey down the stairs, till we came to the cell door.

'Get them boots and braces off,' said the turnkey, 'before you go in there.'

Before I bent to untie my laces, I put the cigarette into my mouth to take a draw of it.

The turnkey put up his hand, and grabbed it from my mouth. 'What's all this 'ere,' he shouted, 'who told you you could smoke? Who gave you that?'

'The inspector,' said I, 'Mr O'Sullivan.'

'I don't care who gave it you,' said the turnkey, and flung it from him into the darkness, 'and get them boots and braces off.'

I took off my shoes and braces, and went into the cell. My cocoa was lying there and it was not too cold. I had my supper, and walked around for a bit, in some humour. I sang a bit of a song, at the top of my voice:

26

'Over hill, and through sands, shall I fly for thy weal,
Your holy delicate, white hands, shall girdle me with steel,
At home, in your emerald bower, from morning's dawn, till
   e'en,
You'll think of me, my flower of flowers, my dark Rosaleen,
My own Rosaleen,
You'll think of me, through daylight's hours,
My virgin flower, my flower of flowers,
My dark Rosaleen.
But the earth shall run red, with redundance of blood,
And the earth shall rock beneath thy tread,
And flame wrap hill and wood,
And gun-peal, and slogan cry, wake many a glen serene,
E'er you shall fade, e'er you shall die, my dark Rosaleen,
My own Rosaleen,
The Judgement Hour must first be nigh,
E'er you shall fade, e'er you shall die,
My dark Rosaleen. . . .'

'Good old Paddy,' I heard Charlie shout from above.
I went to the spy-hole.
'We're getting out of this drum in the morning anyway,
Paddy,' he shouted.
'Right, Charlie, smashing, ain't it?'

But in the morning I was brought away on my own, in a
police car. I wondered whether they had a special court for
the IRA till we got to our destination and I was brought into
a room and put in with a dozen little boys and girls.

There was a boy of about twelve sitting beside me,
smoking a cigarette which he put away every time the door
opened.

'Like a bash?' he asked.
'I would,' said I, 'very much.'
He took a packet from his blazer pocket and handed me
a crumpled cigarette.
'Thanks a lot,' said I. 'But what's this place?'
'It's the juvenile court, ain't it?' said he.

27

I was glad in a way. They could hardly give you twenty years' penal servitude here, but on the other hand, it seemed a funny place for a Republican Army man to be tried.

'It's for anyone under seventeen,' said the boy.

Well, that was why Charlie was gone to some other place. He was three months older than I, and a couple of weeks over seventeen.

I was brought before the court, and a lady on the bench told me politely enough that they had no power to try me on that charge in their court, and that, therefore, I was being sent over to the magistrates' court.

At the magistrates' court, it was a much more important business.

The police solicitor asked if they would try the case in camera, and the magistrate asked me if I had any objection.

I said I had, and that it was supposed to be a principle of justice that it be done in public.

Apart from anything else, I wanted my people at home to know where I was, to send me some papers or cigarettes, and to see that at least I was not done in at Walton Prison. Already there were stories at home of the warders having incited the convicts to attack our fellows on the exercise yard in Dartmoor. I did not want to die or be beaten silly, unknownst to anyone that would care a damn about me. But I did not say this to the magistrate, only the bit about justice being public.

He smiled at me, and so did other people in the court, and said that the police felt that it would hamper them, and give information to certain parties, if the case were not in camera; and in camera it was. I was remanded for a week, when he assured me the proceedings would be 'as public as one would wish'.

The sergeant came round to me afterwards and I asked him if he had a cigarette, and he had none on him, but went back to the police solicitor, who gave him ten Capstan for me, and I stuck one in my gob before I got rightly out of the court, and he told me for Christ's sake to wait till I got into the cells, or did I want to have them all sacked and get everyone in trouble as well as myself?

And in the cell, I saw, was Charlie, with the other prisoners waiting to go up to Walton Jail.

I took out the packet of Capstan, and we lit up and smoked, as Charlie said, 'like lords' bastards'.

Later in the afternoon, we were brought up to the day-room, and fell into line to have our possessions marked off and signed for. A policeman put them in a leather satchel.

When they had finished with me, the turnkey said, 'That's the lot, and keep a tight eye to this bleedin' Irish patriot 'ere.'

I looked at him steadily.

'And take that look off your face.'

'That's all right, Constable,' said the one with the satchel, ''e's going somewhere now, where they'll kick 'is arse into good manners.'

I sat beside Charlie. Opposite us, in the Black Maria, was a red-haired boy of my own age, and a small man with a broken nose, a cauliflower ear, and a begrudging look. He was going up for kicking his wife. He was not unfriendly, and told me his name was Donohoe. I said that by a coincidence that was my mother's name. It was not her name, but civility costs nothing.

The noise of the traffic, as we passed through the city, was a sad sound. It is impossible to see anything out of the Black Maria. There are slits along the top, but only for ventilation. Donohoe and the red-haired boy argued about the places they thought we were passing.

'We're going through such a street. I can hear so-and-so's mill whistle.'

'No, you can't. We're on such a road. That's not such a whistle, it's such another one's horn.'

Charlie and I looked at each other in boredom, but said nothing, only listened with respect when Donohoe gave his opinion.

'There,' said Ginger, 'what did I tell you? We're going up such a street; I can hear the railway yard.'

'No,' said Donohoe, 'that ain't the railway yard.'

Before Donohoe could say that it was the Black Maria pulled up with a crash that nearly threw us off our seats.

We could hear the driver arguing with someone on the

road. He turned in his cab, and shouted into the policeman: 'Bleedin bastard there, ran straight across me. I've a good mind to get him a summons. —ing coal lorry.'

The policeman turned to us. 'Could have killed the lot of us.'

Ginger said, '—ing bus drivers.'

Donohoe said, 'Was a coal lorry.'

'Well, coal lorries. Think they own the bloody road.'

We were patently delighted with each other, and all we'd suffered under this coal lorry driver, and the policeman cocked his head sympathetically, while Ginger told a story about a coal lorry he nearly saw knocking down a woman with a pram, and Charlie said it was the same in London with these bastards. I said that in Dublin they were notorious.

The policeman listened with judicious attention, and only turned the deaf ear when I mentioned Dublin. When I had returned humbly to silence, he was friendly and voluble with the others, and I at least was permitted to listen.

Yes, he agreed, we might have been killed, and some of the drivers nowadays should never have been let behind a wheel.

As far as the jail gate, we considered the position. Till the van pulled up, and the policeman closed up again. Ginger said the driver of the Black Maria must have been a good man, to pull up in time. The policeman said:

'When I open this door, hop out and stand in line in the yard, till I tell you. And no talking.'

'We know that,' said Donohoe, the begrudger. And to give him his due, they were the first and only words he addressed to the policeman.

We got out, and stood in the front yard of the prison. The outside gate closed on us. As it swung to, I saw the bit of road outside. There was an old man going past, shoving a handcart before him, his breath steaming in the cold air. As he looked in, I suppose he said to himself, 'You're never bad but you could be worse,' and pushed on in better heart.

It was a cold raw evening, and the light leaving the sky, wondering how it ever got into it.

The big main door of the prison had a decoration over it.

A snake in chains. Crime, strangled by the law. I knew what it meant. There was a similar piece of sculpture over Kilmainham Prison. I had often passed it with my father, taking me for a walk on Sunday mornings. It was where he had first seen me, from his cell window, during the Civil War. I was born after he was captured, and when I was six weeks old my mother brought me up to the jail and held me up, on the road outside, for him to see from the cell window.

A warder came over and chatted with the policeman.

Charlie whispered to me, wondering if we would get anything to eat.

The warder turned on us. 'Hey, you, cut out that nattering. You're in prison, now, and if you don't want to begin with a dose of bread and water keep your mouth shut.'

We were brought to an annexe of the prison; a single-storied building. Inside, a warder, wearing a white coat, stood by a desk, calling out names. As each name was called, the policeman took our possessions from his satchel, the warder listed them, and we signed the list, in our turn. When this was finished, the policeman went off, the warder and he smiling cordial farewells to each other.

'Now,' said the warder, 'if you've anything in your pockets, turn 'em out.'

I turned out my pockets. Except the one I had the cigarettes in, the Capstans I got off the sergeant.

'Will you turn 'em over, Mr 'Olmes?' said the warder to another.

Mr Holmes turned us over. He found a bit of shoelace on Charlie.

'Want to practise sailors' knots or something?'

Charlie said nothing.

'Why did you not hand it over?'

'I didn't know.'

'You didn't know — what?'

'I didn't know it was any harm.'

Mr Holmes roared, 'You didn't know it was any harm — what?'

'Oh, I didn't know, sir. Sir, I didn't know, sir, sorry, sir.'

The other warder come down, and looked at Charlie.

31

'Remember when you speak to Mr 'Olmes in future, you'll 'ave respect and haddress 'im properly.'

'Or,' said Mr Holmes, 'any other hofficer of the service, as Mr Whitbread will tell you.'

Mr Holmes and Mr Whitbread looked at each other, fine-featured.

Mr Holmes searched Donohoe, and found a piece of paper in his pocket. The begrudger looked at him.

'You won't want that, you know,' said Mr Holmes. 'We give you toilet paper, 'ere.'

'I know all about what you give 'ere,' said Donohoe.

Mr Holmes passed on to me. Oh dear dilapidated Jesus, why did I keep those bastarding Capstans?

He passed his hands over me and came to them in some excitement. 'What have we got 'ere, eh? What? What 'ave we 'ere? — Mr Whitbread, sir.'

Mr Whitbread came down and stood with Mr Holmes in front of me. Mr Holmes held up the cigarettes, and Mr Whitbread looked at them.

' 'Oo 'ad this little lot, then, Mr 'Olmes?' asked Mr Whitbread, who had just seen them taken from my pocket.

'This one 'ere, sir.' He spoke into my face. 'Tell Mr Whitbread your name, you.'

'Behan, sir.'

I put my first name first. In moments of stammering it's easier to pronounce.

'Tell Mr Whitbread your Christian name,' said Mr Holmes.

'Maybe you don't 'ave any Christian names in Ireland,' said Mr Whitbread.

'Br-Br-Br-Brendan Behan, sir.'

'Yes, Behan,' said Mr Whitbread, quietly, looking at his list, 'I've got you 'ere all right. IRA man, ain't you? Don't like us much over 'ere, do you, Behan? Pity, you know, seeing as you're going to spend a long, long time with us. About twenty years. That's what the last lot got at Manchester, wasn't it? And you was going to blow us all up, Behan? Weren't you, Behan?' My name seemed strange to me, the way he said it. 'Weren't you, Behan?' He shouted into my face. 'Weren't you?'

'Answer Mr Whitbread, Behan,' said Mr Holmes reproachfully.

'Not much of the old rebel in you now, Behan, is there? Thought you blokes would 'ave brought over your ox-guns with you,' said Mr Whitbread. 'Do you know what an ox-gun is, Behan? It's what they 'ave in Ireland for shooting bullshit out of.'

He looked at the others. Mr Holmes laughed, and the ginger boy, and Charlie's face was serious and troubled till he looked away from me and laughed with the rest.

'And 'old up your 'ead, when I speak to you.'

' 'Old up your 'ead when Mr Whitbread speaks to you,' said Mr Holmes.

I looked round at Charlie. His eyes met mine and he quickly lowered them to the ground.

'What are you looking round at, Behan? Look at me.'

Young Cuchulainn, after the battle of the ford of Ferdia, on guard the gap of Ulster, with his enemies ringed round him, held his back to a tree and, supported by it, called on the gods of death and grandeur to hold him up till his last blood flowed.

I looked at Mr Whitbread. 'I am looking at you,' I said.

'You are looking at Mr Whitbread — what?' said Mr Holmes.

'I am looking at Mr Whitbread.'

Mr Holmes looked gravely at Mr Whitbread, drew back his open hand, and struck me on the face, held me with his other hand and struck me again.

My head spun and burned and pained and I wondered would it happen again. I forgot and felt another smack, and forgot, and another, and moved, and was held by a steadying, almost kindly hand, and another, and my sight was a vision of red and white and pity-coloured flashes.

'You are looking at Mr Whitbread — what, Behan?'

I gulped and got together my voice and tried again till I got it out. 'I, sir, please, sir, I am looking at you, I mean, I am looking at Mr Whitbread, sir.'

'Well, Behan,' said Mr Whitbread, 'now you've learnt that lesson, remember this: We've only three sorts of tobacco 'ere.

Three Nuns — none today, none tomorrow, and none the day after.'

The others laughed, Mr Holmes, the ginger boy, and Charlie looking away from me. All except Donohoe, still begrudgingly eyeing the wall.

'Understand that, Behan?'

My face burned and I searched my aching head for my voice.

'Answer Mr Whitbread, Behan.'

'Yes — sir. Yes. Mr Whitbread.'

'Don't you forget it.'

'No, Mr Whitbread, no, sir.'

He stood away from me, and gave us all his attention, pointing to each one a cubicle.

'Go in there and take off all your clothes.'

Each of us went into a cubicle and he signalled a prisoner in grey clothes, who shut the doors.

It was a tiny place, not the size of a dwarf's coffin, with nothing but a wooden shelf to sit on, too small to stretch my legs in. I hoped in Christ this was not a place they kept people any length of time, and stripped.

The door of the spy-hole lifted and an eye appeared. I put my hands over my crotch, and sat shivering.

'Got your clothes off?' The prisoner in grey opened the door, and threw me a towel and a book. He was a short, tubby man; smiling, he looked me all over while he collected my clothes. 'You'll only be here a couple of hours. There aren't many receptions today.'

A warder shouted, Tubby winked, smiled, shut the door and went off.

The book was a volume of *Punch* for the twenties. Many of the drawings had to do with Ireland, and Irishmen, drawn with faces like gorillas, shooting Black and Tans who were all like the pictures of Harry Wharton you'd see in the school stories, usually in the back. I found it interesting, and there was easy two hours of pictures and reading if I took it carefully.

Charlie, in the next cubicle, slowly tapped on the wall. A bit timid, I thought. I tapped back, lively, and he answered with a more confident, a reassured rally of his knuckles.

34

Then I read on, in peace, till it was too dark and I could not even make out the illustrations. Besides, I was frozen with the cold.

At last the doors were opened, and we stepped out, holding our towels round us.

The fat prisoner led us to the baths, gave each one a compartment, and closed over the half-door.

Warm and soapy, I lay studying myself. I thought it would be pleasant to die, just there; weary of the struggle, to slip out of it.

But I stood up to soap my legs and looked over the half-door across at Charlie. He was rubbing his chest and under his arms. He smiled over at me. The red-haired boy in the next cubicle winked and smiled, too.

Tubby went round the cubicles, looking in at us.

'OK, Paddy? Like me to go in and wash your back?'

I smiled. 'No, thanks.'

He laughed comfortably, and went over and said something to Charlie, who indignantly told him to bugger off.

This made him laugh the more, and in great spirits he went into Ginger's cubicle. There were splashes and Ginger stood up again and put up his fists, 'Give over, you dirty old bastard.'

The warder shouted down to be silent, or he would do this and that. Tubby shouted back to enquire whether we were all remands wearing our own clothes. The warder said we were. Except for Behan and Millwall. This was Charlie. He was a sailor, Tubby explained, and the King's uniform can't be worn in the nick, only when he'd be going down to court.

The bath had so far revived me that I told Tubby that Behan wasn't a sailor, and why couldn't I have my own clothes like any other unconvicted prisoner?

He told this to the warder, who said I wasn't fit to be in the sailors, or even in the other Services, nor fit to wear the King's uniform one way or another, and that if I gave any more lip he would shove me into chokey, ballock-naked, wearing sweet fugh-all.

Tubby came back, mock serious, with shirts and underpants, putting them on Charlie's door and on mine.

35

I asked him to turn on the cold water for me to finish off with. He said I must be fughing mad, weather like this.

'I thought the cold tub was the hall-mark of an English gentleman,' said I.

'They're fughing fed for it. They don't do it on skilly and sea-pie.'

I was glad of a few minutes' chat, and asked him what was sea-pie.

'You'll see it often, before you go to Borstal. Sea-pie today, see fugh-all tomorrow.'

He laughed himself into a black knot over this. I'd to wait to ask him another question.

The police had told me that I would get twenty years. Borstal was for kids. Would I only stay there till I was old enough for a man's prison?

' 'Course you won't get twenty years. Don't 'eed those fughing bastards. They can't give you a lagging. You're too young. Can't do nothing but send you to Borstal for three years, and you won't do all that if you keep your nose clean. I'd send you to a fughing nut-'ouse, I would, and all your fughing IRA mates with you. I'd 'ave your brains tested. We 'ad some of your blokes 'ere.'

I asked him who they were. Most of them were Northerners, from Belfast or Derry, but one was a Dubliner called Jerry Gildea and I knew him well. I was trained with him in an old castle the IRA had taken over at Killiney, near Bernard Shaw's cottage, looking away out over the Irish Sea. Shaw said that no man was ever the same after seeing it at dawn or sunset. You could sing that if there was an air to it. I know a good many besides himself that are not the same after seeing it, and some of them hung or shot, or gone mad, or otherwise unable to tell the difference.

Jerry Gildea was a clerk in Guinness's brewery, and had volunteered to 'go active in England' for the period of his annual summer holidays. A fast whip over *via* the LMS, a time bomb planted in a railway or an incendiary package in a dock warehouse, and back to the office. 'Have a nice hols., Mr G.?' Smiles, little do you know. 'Yes, quite nice, Miss

X, thank you. Shall we do file Y, this morning?' Later on, when the history of that epoch came to be revealed . . . begod, there's many a man become a TD for less.

But the inscrutable ways of the Lord being what they are, the first day he was in Liverpool an incendiary primer exploded in his pocket, and he walking up Dale Street, and, with half his face burned off, he was savaged and nearly lynched by the populace, who apparently disapproved of having the kip burned about their ears. The accident happened just in time for the Autumn Assizes, and when the period of his holiday was over, he had been had up, tried and weighed off with fifteen stretch under the assumed name of Clarence Rossiter.

(The IRA mostly used Norman names that could be Irish or English, like D'Arcy, Reynolds, or Dillon. But some of them picked names for themselves. I knew a Connemara man who christened himself Thomas de Quincey. He could barely speak English.)

Jerry Gildea's mother, meanwhile, thought her darling boy was sunning himself and refreshing himself to invoice some more porter barrels in the coming year. When we read the news in the Dublin evening papers I was detailed to break the news to his mother that the Clarence Rossiter who had so bravely defied the might of an Empire that day at Liverpool Assizes, and drawn fifteen years for his trouble, was her son, Jerry, and that there would be a vacant stool in Guinness's counting house for some time to come.

His cousin escorted me to the house. A lovely girl, just a few months older than myself. My weight, in fact, if I could screw up my courage to try.

I did, going up the canal, against a telegraph pole, but it was no dice. She wasn't having any just then, and I have a stammer, and it made me worse and more nervous when I'd to meet the old woman.

I felt that if Shiela had let me, I'd have been so strong in myself that I could have split rocks with a kick, but she didn't and I was nervous and not very able to meet anyone, or break the news to Mrs Gildea.

When we met the old woman, she wanted to make us tea,

37

and all to that effect, but I made some excuse to refuse. She didn't even know that Jerry was in the movement at all.

'M-m-m-mrs G-gildea,' I began. 'Y-y-your son, J-j-jerry, w-w-was—'

In the manner most exasperating to stammerers, she proceeded to help me out.

'Ah, sure, God help us. Take your time, son. My son, Jerry, was—?'

'H-h-h-h-he w-was—'

'He was delayed be the boat, was he? Ah, sure you could expect that this time of the year. I'm told the crowds of the world does be in the Isle of Man.'

'H-h-he w-was—'

'Nice place, too, and a nice class of people, be all accounts. Talk Irish and all, some of them. More nor I could do. Though the cats doesn't have any tails.'

'He was s-s-s-sen-sen—'

'God knows they must be the queer-looking beasts. Still, everyone to their fancy, as the old one said when she kissed the ass.'

I caught her by the sleeve, beseeching.

'He-he-he w-w-was s-sent—'

'God help you, and such a nice boy, too. Maybe, it'd be God's Holy Will that you'd grow out of it. Sure, you're not finished growing yet.'

'He-he-he w-was sentenced—'

'Sentenced?'

I got it out with a rush. Now or never. 'To fif-fifteen years in Liverpool to-to-today.'

'Sweet Mother of Jesus, comfort me this night,' said Mrs Gildea and collapsed in a weakness.

'Don't you go believing anything a copper tells you,' said Tubby. 'It's their business, putting the wind up you when they ain't being sweet to you. Like fughing parsons, they are. You'll go to Borstal, and you'll 'ave a kip-in time, with football, concerts, swimming. Maybe you'll be sent to Portland, where I was. Drake 'Ouse, I was in, Good old Drake,' he sighed wistfully. 'You might even be sent to one of these open

Borstals. You give your word of honour not to scarper, and there's no lock on the dormitory door, even.'

He looked over at Charlie.

'He'll probably go to Borstal and all. Want to watch his ring, though. Hey, Jack,' he shouted to Charlie, 'ever 'ad a length of bo'sun's whistle? Any old three-badge stoker ever shown you the golden rivet.'

Charlie stood, holding the towel to himself, proud and fierce. 'I'll show you a knee in the balls.'

Tubby laughed and gave us the rest of our prison clothes.

' 'Ere you are, young prisoners. YP brown jacket, shorts, shoes, stockings and belt. Bloody 'ikers' outfit. Though you won't 'ike far in it.'

'Like a bleedin' Boy Scout,' said Charlie, putting on his shorts.

'Well,' said Tubby, 'just get bent over there, and do your good deed for the day.'

Charlie bit his lip in temper.

'Don't mind me, kid,' said Tubby. 'I just can't 'elp taking the piss. Still, there's no 'arm in me. Just a bit of clean fun.'

The warder shouted at him.

'Right, sir,' he shouted. 'Be right along, sir,' adding in a lower tone, 'you shit-'ouse.'

He turned to me. 'Ever 'ear of the screw married the prostitute?' 'E dragged 'er down to 'is own level.' He exploded, laughing at his own remark, and took a moment to uncrease his face into becoming gravity. 'Right, sir. Just coming, sir.'

He turned to us and said, 'Right, you receptions, 'op along.'

We were marched back to the cubicles, and locked in them again. I read some more *Punch* till Tubby came round and shoved in an aluminium can of cocoa, and a cob of bread with a piece of cheese the size of an oxo cube, but very nice with one bit of the bread, which was all I could eat. Tubby seemed glad to collect all our left-over bread when he came round again.

'I'll take your can, now, Paddy, and that bit of bread. This time next week you'll be offering me a Player for that much. And now, we're 'aving some more mannyquin parade. Get your clothes off again and put that round you.' He threw in a sheet and went off with the can and the bread. I did not begrudge it to him. He was a friendly sort of chap, even to me.

I took my clothes, and looked down at myself. My legs were glowing from the bath, and my hairs were curling and still a bit damp, and laziness and heat were coming back into my crotch after the cold water, and even when I bent forward there was no more than a crinkle on my belly. Jesus, it must be the terrible thing to get fat, I thought. Porter it was that fattened people in my own family, and it would be a hard thing not to drink porter with every other decent man, and maybe stand filling your pipe with your back to the counter, and maybe talk of the time you were in jail in England. Still that day was a good bit from us yet, but so thank God was the day of old age. I rapped into Charlie, and he rapped back, real lively, with a smooth rally of his knuckles.

They opened the doors and we were lined up outside the doctor's.

'You three YPs stand together,' said the screw to me and Charlie and Ginger. We shuffled over together in our sheets. It suited us.

Donohoe stood with some other men prisoners, and their bent old legs and twisted buniony toes on a line, the way, I thought, looking from the smooth neatness of Charlie, and Ginger and me, that God would have a lot to do forgiving Himself for sentencing us all that would live long enough, to get like that.

I was marched before the doctor and stood to attention before him as best I could, in my bare feet and holding up my sheet.

He sat in civilian clothing behind a desk, looked down at a form and up at me. He was a dark man, not very old, and very hard in an English way that tries to be dignified and a member of a master race that would burn a black man alive or put a pregnant woman out the side of the road in the interests of stern duty. Looking at him, I thought of the war, and hoped themselves and the Germans would keep at it.

'What's this, Mr Paine?' he asked the medical orderly.

'This,' said Mr Paine, 'is an IRA man, Doctor.' Then to me, and almost in the same breath, 'Leave off the sheet and let the doctor look at you, Behan.'

I let the sheet fall and stood naked. I felt puny and weak and miserable, standing there before them and different from when I was with Charlie or Ginger. My hands moved over to cover my lonely bush of hairs as they looked me up and down.

'You don't call that a man, Mr Paine?' said the doctor, from his desk.

'The best the IRA can do, Doctor. Scrapings of the man-power barrel, I suppose.'

The doctor came from behind the desk, and put a stethoscope to my chest and back, and put his hands under my balls, and made me cough. Then he sat me on a chair and tapped my knees. All this, I thought, was civil of him, for all his herrenvolk looks, and when he asked me whether I was sick or not, I replied, 'I'm great, thank you!'

'I don't care whether you're great or not,' he said sternly.

'Just answer the doctor,' said Mr Paine, 'he hasn't the time for any of your old blarney.'

The doctor set his lips and spoke through them, like an English officer in a film about the Khyber Pass. 'It is my duty to look after the health of the prisoners here, even yours, Behan, or whatever your name, but I'll stand for no familiarity, particularly from you. Understand, Behan?'

'Yes, sir, I mean yes, Doctor.'

'Come to attention when you address the doctor,' said Mr Paine.

I looked anxiously round for my sheet.

'Jump to it,' shouted Mr Paine.

I brought my two bare heels together and took my hands off my crotch and brought them to my side, and stood, naked, to attention.

Afterwards I heard the screws talk about the doctor and what a good man he was, and overworked, and he did go round looking like Lionel Barrymore, and sighing like the doctor in *The Citadel*, but I never heard of him actually doing anything for anyone. The prisoners said that he gave a man two aspirins for a broken leg, but that it was not really viciousness, only stupidity, and anyway, if he wasn't a prison doctor he'd have to go in the Forces.

When I got away from the doctor, I was sent to the reception screws to be weighed and have my height taken. I had to take my sheet off for this, and then I was searched. I had to lift my arms above my head, while the screw looked me all over. He put his hands through my hair, looking for cigarettes, though my hair was still damp from the bath, and, lastly, made me bend over while he held open my back passage with his fingers and looked up there, with a pencil torch. I had heard of this personal search in Fenian times, in a book by Tom Clarke, when he got fifteen years for the bombing campaign of the eighties, but I did not know before what it meant. It was a normal part of prison routine and the screw did it with the usual appearance of British official detachment. I noticed that he only searched Charlie and Ginger and me like this and did not bother with Donohoe, the begrudger, or the other adult prisoners.

Then we put our clothes on and at last were ready for the walk to our cells. I did not know what they would be like. Maybe, I hoped, they would be like the cells you see on the pictures, with two or three bunks — I wouldn't have minded being with Charlie and Ginger — and bars up the side, where you could look out and see the fellows on the other side of the cell block.

We walked through darkness, and doors were unlocked and locked after us, and we stood in a huge, high hall, dimly lit, gloomy and full of a heavy smell of well-washed stuffiness. It was like walking away from the world and back into the times of Charles Dickens. I was thinking about this and had not heard the screw tell us to halt, till he shouted, 'You boy, where do you think you're going?' I stopped and he said no more, but made us stand in the circle at the end of the wing.

Charlie and Ginger and I were stood together and Donohoe and the other adult prisoners were marched off, I'm happy to say. I could hear their feet echoing on the iron stairs and the lights being switched on and the doors of the cells banged to.

Then Charlie and Ginger and I were marched on again, till we came to a far wing, and there was more door unlocking, and we were told to stand in the circle. Here we were given our kit — pillowcases containing sheets and a towel and comb and a handkerchief, and cell cards. In the dim light I could see that Charlie's was white, Ginger's was yellow, and mine red; C of E, Nonconformist, and Catholic, which they called 'RC'.

We were walked in darkness through the hall, and first Ginger was called to stand to the door of his cell. Ginger moved around a bit. He could see no cell; neither could Charlie nor I for the matter of that. But the screw switched on a light and we could see a peep coming from the wall in front of us. Then the screw turned a key, and we were looking into the cell.

My Jesus, my heart fell into my boots. It was like a whitewashed hole in the wall, like a tomb up in Glasnevin.

'Come on, get in and get your bed made down,' said the screw; 'don't keep us 'ere all bloody night.'

Ginger nodded to us as well as he could and went inside. The screw took the door, slammed it over, then re-locked it, as if the door, which was really a piece of the wall, was not secure enough as it was, and walked Charlie and me upstairs to the next landing. He took the card from Charlie and stuck in into a slot beside the door and locked him up. Then it was my turn. We stopped at another place and he switched on the light, and opened the door. I stepped inside and he slammed the door behind me, rose the cover over the little spy-hole in the door, and looked at me again, and re-locked it, and went off down the stairs on padded shoes.

I looked round me. I could walk five paces from the door to under the window, which was too high in the wall, even if there was anything better than Liverpool to be seen or heard over the wall. There was a table and a chair, and a mirror, and a chamber-pot, and some bedboards, a mattress, and blankets. The floor was made of slate, and there were also the rules to be read. I decided they were better than nothing, and when I had the bed made on the boards, it was all right. I got in between the sheets, and, though it was only a few inches off the floor, when I took up the rules and started to read them, I felt as comfortable as ever I did in my life. I was dead tired after that plank thing, or hand-carved couch in Dale Street, and was drowsy and falling off to sleep when I heard the cover of the spy-hole being moved.

'You all right, there?'

'Smashing, mate,' said I in gratitude.

'What do you mean, "mate",' said the voice from the door; 'where the bloody 'ell do you think you are — *"mate"*,' he spat, vicious and indignant; 'and what do you think you're on putting those notices on the floor, eh?'

'I was only having a read of them, sir,' said I, sitting up anxiously in my comfortable bed.

'Read them where they're supposed to be read, on the wall, not on the floor. Come on, get up and put 'em back.'

'Yes, sir,' said I, got up quickly, in my shirt, hung the rules back on the wall, slipped quickly back into bed, lay there breathing quietly till the screw dropped the cover of my spy-hole and went on to the next cell.

I lay in the dark, and heard the sounds of outside, dim and mournful, away over the walls in the distance. A church bell rang out on the frosty air, and I got further down into the warm bed. Eight o'clock, it rang out. I'd have thought it was later than that, much later. It seemed like a year since I came from the court, but the bed was warm and comfortable after the bath, and I was tired after that Dale Street, and I was soon asleep, and half-eating the sleep till I got so far down into it I was unconscious.

44

Mornings, we were wakened at six and slopped out, throwing the contents of the chamber-pot into the bucket brought round by the prisoner appointed to this position. There was competition for the job because the same man brought round the breakfast and might nick a bit buckshee for himself. I nearly got sick looking at it, but the screws shouted briskly, 'Come on, sling it in, look sharp,' and if he was a decent screw he might even say, 'I've got to get my breakfast, too, you know.'

Then we went down to the recess with an enamel jug and got water for washing. There was only one lavatory on each landing, and it was impossible to get in and use it, with another thirty or forty fellows queueing for water for washing, and rinsing round the bottom of the chamber-pots to get out what had not gone into the big slop bucket. Some of the orderlies did get using the lavatories after they had emptied the slop bucket and while they waited on the breakfast to come up from the kitchen, and it was considered a great thing, because it gave the cell a chance of freshening itself a little during breakfast-time, with an empty pot.

The breakfast consisted of a tin of porridge with an ounce of sugar, six ounces of bread, and a tiny pat of margarine.

Our two landing screws, of whom we saw one or the other first thing in the morning, were Johnston and Mooney. These were in charge of the Young Prisoners because they had special qualifications in YP training. Johnston had been twelve years in the Scots Guards and Mooney had been middle-weight champion of India.

Johnston was cross-eyed. In the Guards they are made to wear their hats over their heads. It makes them keep their heads erect. Because if they don't, they won't see where they are going. He was over six foot, tall and lean.

Mooney was a chesty barrel of a man. He gave us PT every morning, in a Lancashire accent. He was a Catholic, 'RC' they called it. Catholic warders were the worst. Irish

Catholics, worst of all. They showed their loyalty to the King and Empire by shouting at me and abusing me a bit more than the others. The next worst were the Scotch and Welsh. The Cockney warders were very rare, and the least vicious of all.

One warder, who looked very young, with red cheeks and a happy rough North of England accent, used to smile and whisper 'Up the Republic', whenever he was on the locking or unlocking of the doors. Once or twice he gave me an extra slice of bread. He had an English name and I heard the other fellows say that he came from Durham, but maybe his mother was Irish, or his wife, or maybe he was just a decent man that didn't give a God's curse. You find an odd one everywhere.

All the time it was cold and black. In the morning the slate floor was freezing cold, and over the whole huge wing was a cold smell of urine and bad air, like a refrigerated lavatory.

It seemed to me the English were very strong on washing and cold, but not so much on air and cleanliness. Like the well-tubbed and close-shaven looks of the screws — cruel and foul-spoken, but always precise and orderly.

When breakfast was eaten, I had to clean the cell, or wash it. Every morning the bedboards and table and chair had to be scrubbed and the black slate floor rubbed with soap to make it blacker still. We were issued with two big bars of soap a week. It was the only thing we were not short of, and when the morning's cleaning was over, the blankets and sheets laid out for inspection, and the bedboard and plate and mug laid out in a special way on the newly scrubbed table, there was a shine on the cell furniture and the black glistening newly soaped floor and heavy smell of human excrement over the place that would make you respect the stern fishy eye and the stiff thin lip and the steady and high-purposed gaze of Englishmen doing their duty.

When all was ready for inspection you could have the morning bowel movement. Not before. Business before pleasure.

Unless it was a Chief 's Inspection. In that case you would have to wait a couple of hours, as no one could leave their cell, even to empty a chamber-pot, until he had gone round. Only once did it happen that a bloke couldn't stick it out and used the pot during breakfast-time. He had finished the porridge and tea and bread, and his stomach was loaded. The breakfast was the most likely meal to do this, because it was the only one that filled you. The dinner and supper were safe enough, and even if you did want to use the pot, you could as much as you liked, and empty it after dinner, or leave it in the cell till morning after supper.

This bloke couldn't stick it out this morning, anyway, and used the pot after eating his breakfast. The screw, when he opened the door and your man tried to get down to the recess to empty it, nearly died of shock and horror. Here was a prisoner with no pot to be laid out for inspection, and the Chief an ex-Navy man, so particular. He let the fellow go down the landing to try and smuggle it into the recess, and empty and clean the pot, but the PO was looking up from the bottom of the wing and let a bark up to the screw as to where that man thought he was going with that pot, before the Chief came round, and the fellow had to go back.

The screw got out of it as best he could by making it up with the medical orderly to say the man had medicine the day before. But it was a narrow thing for the screw, and the other screw, the medical orderly, was heard by a prisoner to say that he couldn't take the can back if it happened again.

The prisoner was a Channel Islander, from a place called Peter's Port, and the screw said he'd bloody soon cure him of his dirty French habits.

The screws were for ever telling each other they wouldn't take the can back. They hated each other's guts and all with good cause, but never gave us the satisfaction of hearing them saying anything abusive to each other, only an odd dirty look or a mutter. They shouted, 'mister' and 'sir' to each other all day. When a prisoner left their party or when they were telling another screw at the far end of the wing that prisoners were being sent down to them, they would shout, 'One on to you, sir', and 'one off, mister'. When the Principal Officer passed they would come to attention, so rigid with respect that you'd nearly think they'd burst from keeping themselves

47

tight. When the Chief passed through, which was more seldom, they shouted even louder and got even tighter, and when the Governor came through the wing, they shouted, 'Ill Kirr-ect, sir', so loudly and tightened up so much till he'd passed on, that I wondered what was left for a Prison Commissioner if he passed through — they'd have dropped dead from tightening their guts to attention and forcing a thinner but more concentrated 'Ill Kirr-ect, sir', from between their thin lips.

On my first morning, I was brought down to the end of the wing to see the Governor. He had an office in each wing on the left-hand side, looking towards the end, where the PO stood and looked out from his kiosk. This wing office of the Governor was a sort of viceregal apartment in each of the halls of the prison. His real office was somewhere in the main hallway of the prison, but only very important people were ever allowed or brought there — like a murderer coming back after being sentenced to death, who would be allowed to sign for his property and that there, instead of going through the reception where the other prisoners coming back from the court would see him. As regards his bath, they would give him a bath during the time he was waiting to be topped, all on his own, with a screw to turn off the water and turn on the water, maybe late at night, when nobody else would be going there.

The morning after I came in I got up and folded my blankets, and did out my cell, and ate my breakfast, and used the chamber-pot and slopped out with the rest, but was not opened up with the others when they went down to work. I thought it was something to do with being Irish and that, and in a way I was not displeased but a little bit frightened, till they came to my cell and opened the door and told me to put on my tie, for I was for the Governor.

I went down and stood with Charlie and some other fellows outside the office. The other fellows were wearing shorts and were YPs the same as us, but they looked very old to me. There were three of them and all of them looked as if they shaved at least three times a week. I was hoping to God I wouldn't be left among fellows the like of that, because apart from being big, they did not look too friendly. But Charlie and I and Ginger stood together, happy enough, and listened to the whispering of the others. They were there for extra letters and one fellow was there about a visit from his wife but they said we all would have to wait till the Governor was finished with some fellows that were being had up over having snout. One fellow was a remand but had brought in a butt, a dog-end they called it, off exercise, when he was supposed to throw it in the bucket which was there for that purpose; and another fellow, a convicted prisoner, had been caught with a dog-end which this remand had brought in for him for the day before, and which the remand fellow had told about when they caught him and asked him was he bringing in the dog-ends for himself or somebody else.

When the two fellows were brought out of their cells and rushed into the Governor's office to be tried and sentenced, the other YPs that were waiting with Charlie and Ginger and me just laughed and said they'd get Number One, the both of them. They whispered their laugh, but seemed really to enjoy it because they thought it was funny to be punished. For somebody else to be. They seemed to think the screws were better men than themselves, because they could do these things and get fellows put on bread and water and stand up in the circle when the Governor was gone and they were done saluting him, and bend their knees, belch, break wind, yawn, and shout at some fellow they caught talking a bit extra at his work, when he was supposed to be only asking for a loan of a scissors. The prisoners thought the screws were comedians when they caught some fellows like these two merchants and got them to inform on one another and then gave them both solitary confinement. They had a slang term for informing. 'Shopping', they called it. A nation of shoppers, and if that's the way they would treat one another, my Jesus, what would they do to me?

My name was shouted at last and I was rushed before the Governor. I was told to stand to the mat, state my registered number, name, age, and religious denomination.

I stood to attention and said, 'Behan, sir, sixteen years,

49

Catholic.' I did not know my number, but the screw standing beside the desk shouted it for me.

'Be-han, Bren-dan, three five oh one, sixteen years, YP, remand, RC.' Then he said 'sir' to show he had finished.

The Governor was a desiccated-looking old man, in tweed clothes and wearing a cap, as befitted his rank of Englishman, and looking as if he would ride a horse if he had one. He spoke with some effort, and if you did not hear what he was saying you'd have thought, from his tone, and the sympathetic, loving, and adoring looks of the screw, PO, and Chief, that he was stating some new philosophical truth to save the suffering world from error.

'You're—er—remanded—er—till Friday—er—I see—er. See—er—that you behave yourself—er—here and give no—er—trouble to my officers—er.' At this point the officers looked sternly, and almost reproachfully, at me, and so intense was their grateful look towards the feeble old face of the Governor that I almost expected them to raise an exultant shout of 'Viva il Papa!' 'If you give—er—us trouble—er—we'll win—er . . . we'll win all the time.' The officers' faces set in determination with him. 'We can—er—make it—er—very—er—bad for you—er, it's—er—all the same—er—to us, and—er—it's up—er—to you, whatever—er—way you—er—want it.'

I was marched out and told to wait outside. We were to see our clergyman and I was looking forward to meeting the priest. Maybe he would be an Irishman, and it would be like water in the desert to hear a friendly Irish voice again.

But the screw put me back in my cell while the others went to see the Protestant chaplain. The priest would not be in till Monday.

I was disappointed but thought that it would make a break in Monday morning, and this was Friday, so after tomorrow I would have Mass to look forward to on Sunday morning, and after the visit to the priest I would be well into the week till I went down to the court on Friday, and that would be that week over.

After a little while, I was opened up again from my cell and brought down to the hall of the wing where we sát on

50

our chairs in silent rows, about sixty of us, sewing mailbags. The class instructor they called the screw who went round showing the prisoners how to do the bags, and examined them or complained about the bad work when it was more or less than four stitches to the inch. That seemed to be the important thing, and most necessary for salvation.

He came over to me and sat down on a chair beside me and showed me how to wax the thread and put it through the canvas with the palm, which was a leather band with a thimble in the middle to save the skin of the palms, though sometimes even the most expert had to shove the needle through the canvas with their forefingers and thumbs, which in most of the prisoners were scarred like the hands or arms of drug addicts with the needle marks you would read about.

On Saturday afternoon we were locked up from twelve-thirty. The screw gave us a half-hour's exercise from twelve o'clock and remarked that it was handier than taking us out for exercise after dinner. It got the whole lot finished early, he said, and we could be left in our cells till morning. We all nodded our heads, and quickly, in agreement with him. It seemed the right thing to want to be locked up in your cell over the week-end, and I even felt my own head nodding when the screw said that it was better to get the exercise over with so that we would not have to be opened up again after dinner.

So locked up we were, and Charlie and I and Ginger smiled at each other, so that the others would not know that we were not used to being locked in a cell from half past twelve on Saturday morning till slop-out at seven Sunday morning, and in we went. The dinner was old potatoes, cold, and a slice of bully beef and a piece of bread. This was always the Saturday dinner and I heard a screw saying that it was like that to give the cook a chance to get off, and after all he wanted a rest, too, and when he said that we all nodded our heads, and were glad the screw was no nice and civil as to say it to us.

After breakfast on Sunday, I heard the C of Es being fell in and marched off to their chapel, and later I heard the strains of hymn-singing coming from a distance. I walked impatiently and happily up and down the cell, washed and with my hair combed, and wearing my tie, a brown piece of canvas, but still it fitted in with my brown frieze jacket and my brown shorts. I was waiting for our own turn to go to Mass, but the singing of the C of Es was good to listen to. They sang a hymn to the tune of *Deutschland Uber Alles*, which surprised me a little bit, till I remembered that the British Royal Family were all Germans and spoke German in their own palaces.

Then our own cells were opened up, and Mooney, the screw, stood in the hall, and shouted, 'RCs fall in for morning service, bring your prayer books and your 'ymn books.' I had not seen the priest yet, so I had no prayer book or hymn book.

But I did not want any prayer book to follow the Mass. That was the same the whole world over, from one end of it to another.

I had been extra religious when a kid, and the day I made my First Communion I had prayed to God to take me, as Napoleon prayed, when I would go straight to Heaven. I was a weekly communicant for years after, and in spasms, especially during Lent, a daily one. Then I had difficulties, when I was thirteen or so, with myself and sex, and with the Church because they always seemed to be against the Republicans. My father had been excommunicated in 1922 with thousands of others, and so had De Valera, and the Bishops were always backing the shooting and imprisoning of IRA men. I had been for the Republicans in Spain; and it seemed the Church was always for the rich against the poor. But I have never given up the Faith (for what would I give it up for?) and now I was glad that even in this well-washed smelly English hell-hole of old Victorian cruelty, I had the Faith to fall back on. Every Sunday and holiday, I would be at one with hundreds of millions of Catholics, at the sacrifice of the Mass, to worship the God of our ancestors, and pray to Our Lady, the delight of the Gael, the consolation of mankind, the mother of God and of man, the pride of poets and artists, Dante, Villon, Eoghan Ruadh O Sullivan, in warmer, more humorous parts of the world than this nineteenth-century English lavatory, in Florence, in France, in Kerry, where the arbutus grows and the fuchsia glows on the dusty hedges in the soft light of the summer evening. 'Deorini De' — 'The Tears of God' — they called the fuchsia in Kerry, where it ran wild as a weed. 'Lachryma Christi' — 'The Tears of Christ' — was a Latin phrase, but in future I would give Him less reason for tears, and maybe out of being here I would get back into a state of grace and stop in it — well, not stop out of it for long intervals — and out of evil, being here, good would come.

I fell in with the rest and noticed that there were a great number, more than half those I'd seen sewing mailbags in the hall, going to our chapel.

Nobody spoke, of course, but everyone seemed happy, and smiled a bit kindly at each other, like going on a factory outing, for even the screws seemed a bit relaxed and only said, 'Straighten your tie, lad', 'Tie up your laces, there, boy', and 'You put down for an 'aircut, Crapp, Tuesday, like a bloody poet going round there, you are', and we even laughed a bit, quietly.

We marched into the chapel and it was like any church at home, only for a wooden notice-board with numbers on it for the hymns. I'd seen such things in pictures of England. But everything else, the tabernacle, the lamp, the candles, and the Stations of the Cross around the walls, were the very exact same as at home, and when the priest came out, genuflected, and began the prayers before Mass, I blessed myself and happily whispered my prayers with him.

The Acts of Faith, Hope, and Charity and the Act of Contrition. . . . 'Oh, my God, I am heartily sorry for having offended Thee' . . . so I was too. . . . 'Who art worthy of all my love . . .' and that was the truth, and I promised 'never more to offend Thee and to amend my life' . . . and I would and maybe here I could get closer to God, and I was sorry it was only in a place like this you appreciated Him, but that's the way with human beings, and He'd know our weakness, and I'd make it up to Him, when I got outside, just to show that it wasn't only as a Friend in need I wanted Him.

The chapel held about four hundred men. The very front rows were occupied by forty thin, and haggard and frightened men and boys. They sat apart from each other and kept their eyes fixed straight ahead of them on the altar.

These were the prisoners from the punishment cells, from chokey, where they were on bread and water, Number One Diet, and others of them on Number Two Diet, bread and water for breakfast and evening meal, with a mixture of porridge and potatoes for their midday meal. They were in solitary confinement twenty-four hours of the twenty-four, and this was their only diversion during their time in chokey. They were doing from three days to six months. I noticed half a dozen YPs amongst them, dressed in shorts and coat, the same as the rest of us YPs. They sat apart from each other and apart from the other chokey merchants, at the end of the front bench nearest the door.

The priest was a fat man, and looked reassuringly like a country parish priest at home that you'd seen going to a greyhound meeting and wouldn't be afraid to have his ball of malt of an evening.

The server was a little thin miserable-looking Englishman.

I had often heard people at home, who had been to England, saying that you could tell an Irishman on the streets even if you were not personally acquainted with him.

I was beginning to be able to do this, and the priest looked like an Irishman and I was very anxious to meet him in the morning. I would be consoled by the sound of his voice, and whole Faith was a consolation, and I'd often heard the old people say that it was only in time of trouble we appreciated the Faith, and it was the truth — you could say, it was the God's truth.

I had often been impatient with the Church because the

Bishops attacked the movement, but still it was like being let to the warmth of a big turf fire this cold Sunday morning to hear the words of love and consolation:

> 'There in Thine Ear, all trustfully,
> We tell our tale of misery,
> Sweet Sacrament of Love, sweet Sacrament of Love.'

Then we went back to our cells and waited till the Methodists came out of service, when we all went to exercise together. Charlie and Ginger and I marched round behind each other, and even got in a few words of conversation on the way though the passageway from the exercise yard to the wing.

There was a great smell of dinner and the screws shouted, 'Come on, hurry up, the quicker you get in your cells, the quicker we get the dinner,' and happily we clattered up the iron stairs and into our cells.

They came with the dinner, and it was roast meat with baked potatoes and bread and cabbage, and I smiled at the screw, taking it from him at the door, and he gave me a knife and fork, too, from a box of them he had, and I slammed out my door and sat down to the dinner. I nearly spoke to it and said, 'Dinner, I shall never forget you,' and I didn't forget it either and never will.

It was cold sitting on the chair, after my dinner. I thought about dinners. Maybe, in a way, the best one was the pork and beans, though it did not taste as good as the Sunday one, with big lumps of pork fat in it, but it filled you better. You were not let make down your bed and lie on it till the bell went at eight o'clock, but Lord Jesus, I was perished with the cold. I sat on my chair facing the door and pulled my mailbag up over my legs, and put my hands down my shirt. Not too far down, though (save that for tonight), and besides it would be dangerous if a screw looked in the spy-hole at me. Not that that was against the rules — at least I hadn't heard it was — and even if the screws mentioned it, it was in a joke; but it would be embarrassing to have them see you, and they would more nor likely jeer the heart out of you for the rest of time. I wished I had something to read, though. At least, thanks be to God, the RCs got another service on Sundays. We'd be going to Benediction shortly, where the C of Es and the Methodists would be left in their cells. Poor bastards, the ministers were too bloody lazy to come in and disturb themselves by getting up from the fire this cold evening. But I had always heard of the priests and their devotion to duty (even Protestants gave into it) in the first war — priests like Father Willie Doyle, SJ, and Father Patrick Bergin that were killed along with the troops.

Sure enough, at about three o'clock I heard the doors being opened on the ground floor, and the screw coming up the stairs and he opened the door of a fellow opposite I had seen at Mass in the morning. I had left the spy-hole cover up before I came into the cell at dinner-time and I could see the boy opposite stretching himself contentedly and yawning, standing in the doorway.

My own door was unlocked and the screw said, 'Stand to your door,' and went on, opening the doors of the other RCs, anywhere he saw a red cell card.

Then he called us down to the ground floor. We straightened our ties and marched off to the chapel. I could see some of the other spy-holes and the glint of an eye looking out, wistfully, I suppose.

There was the same crowd in the chapel, only there were no chokey fellows. Us YPs sat in the two front seats instead.

The little rat-faced, severe-looking one was lighting the candles when we came in. The fellow beside me, a pale boy from Birkenhead, said the server was doing a five stretch for rape.

There you are again, said I to myself, our Church is not for hypocrites, it's for sinners as well as saints, and one mortal sin is as good or as bad as another, whether it was against the Sixth and Ninth Commandment or the Fifth or Tenth.

Ratface was about the ugliest server I'd ever seen, and a real cup-of-tea Englishman with a mind the width of his back garden that'd skin a black man, providing he'd get another to hold him, and send the skin 'ome to mum, but Our Lord would be as well pleased with him if he was in a state of grace as He'd be with St Stanislaus Kostka, the boy Prince of Poland, and race or nationality did not enter into the matter, either, one way or another.

We sang the Benediction hymns, and I had the fellows in my seat and behind me looking at me. The screw looked at me from where he knelt at the end of the seat. I'm a good singer, but you wouldn't know whether the screw was vexed or pleased by my voice rising over the rest. But rise it did, and fugh the begrudgers:

> '. . . et antiqum documentum, novo ce dat ritui.
> Salus honor virtus quo que sit et Benedictio. . . .'

Ratface swung the thurible with a will, till there was a cloud of incense you could hide yourself and go asleep in, and when it died down a bit the priest began the Divine Praises:

> 'Blessed be God, Blessed be His Holy Name, Blessed be Jesus Christ, true God and true Man, blessed the Name of Jesus. . . . Blessed be the Name of Mary, Blessed be Her Holy and Immaculate Conception. . . . Blessed be God in His Angels and in His Saints. . . .'

I was a bit disappointed to notice that the priest had an English accent of the 'Haw, old-boy' type, but maybe he had to speak like that to make himself understood, and anyway wasn't it English people he was ministering to?

And no matter what accent he had, wasn't there yet another pleasant surprise in store for us, when the Benediction finished?

The priest went in off the altar carrying the Monstrance and attended by Ratface, but even then they didn't bring us back to the cells.

The screws put the lights on, so that it looked real cosy in the chapel, and everyone looked round them a bit, and the screws never said anything but just gently rebuked an odd one that wasn't satisfied but had to start whispering too. And then the priest came out on the altar wearing only his soutane and biretta casually on the back of his poll and a Sunday newspaper under his arm.

Everyone's face lit up and he began to read the football results and make an odd joke about them, about Burnley and Everton and Liverpool, and the prisoners tittered and had to laugh aloud sometimes at his jokes, and even the screws couldn't repress a grin themselves, much less have anyone up for laughing.

And after that he went in, smiling himself at us, and we marched back, happy and still smiling at some of the things he said, and clattered up the stairs in the dark to our cells where the lights were on in each open door, welcoming us, and the orderlies came round with the supper, the cocoa, the bread, the margarine, and the cube of cheese, and I settled down contented over my steaming mug on the table, waiting for the bell at eight o'clock when I would make down my bed and go asleep.

There was a black dark frost outside, and the cocoa was smashing and warm. It was now four o'clock and the biggest part of the weekend punched in, thanks be to God.

On Monday morning we woke and it was almost a merry noise after the long week-end, though us RCs had a right to be thankful for our two services on Sunday.

I could hear the doors opening and shutting, and coming nearer and nearer, and I stood with my pot ready till it would be my turn and I could get rid of it.

Everyone tried to get a couple of shits in the daytime and during the time they were sewing bags, and only use the pot for pissing in, but it as not so easy when we only got out of the cell for a half-hour between Saturday noon and Monday morning, so most fellows had to use their pots for everything and the smell this Monday morning was so foul that I felt myself getting sick, when the door was opened, though I suppose my own cell added its quota to the general stench. I emptied my pot into the brimming bucket and joined the queue at the recess to rinse it clean at the tap. I met Charlie there, and while we waited we had a bit of a chat.

Everyone seemed to want to wait on everyone else so as they could whisper a bit longer.

'We get a smoke this morning, Paddy, and all,' Charlie whispered. 'We fall out, a geezer told me, with the other remands, and exercise smoking, going round the ring.'

'Come out of that recess, come on, 'urry up, get moving there,' the screw shouted.

'See you later, Pad,' whispered Charlie, waving his free hand and running up the landing with his pot.

When I came back to my cell there was a bucket of water, a dirty black mat for kneeling on, a scrubber and a bar of soap.

'Take that in,' said the screw, passing my door, 'and scrub your furniture and floor, and soap your floor when you've dried it. I want that furniture as white as snow, and the floor as black as soot — got that?'

'Yes, sir,' and I ventured a smile in honour of the poetry of the soot and the snow, but the screw meant it as serious wisdom, and only nodded.

'Take it in, then, and get crakin'.'

The breakfast came round before I had started and I ate it, and then, God of war, did I want a crap. I squatted down anyway, and used the pot. There was a lid thing for it and when I finished I put it on, and started to scrub the furniture; bedboards, table, chair, and wash-hand stand, and then started on the slate floor, to wash it first, and dry, and then I got on my knees and soaped it, and had to move the chamber-pot out of my way, like some covered dish of disgust.

When I had finished, the cell had the smell of shit and soap — the first smell I was conscious of, when I came into the reception, the smell of a British jail.

I finished my washing and made up the bed, putting the bedboard on its side against the wall, the mattress lying with it, and the bedclothes draped over it, blanket, sheet, blanket, sheet, blanket, the cover lying the length of the top of the mattress and board and the pillow on top. The table at the side, with my plate and mug flanked by my knife, the tin toy one we used except when we had meat for our dinner like

59

Sunday, and got a real knife and fork issued to us for the duration of the meal. I laid my spoon the other side of the plate and mug, and if I said so, myself, it looked real neat.

When the screw opened the door I looked at it, not ashamed of it.

He looked round him for a minute, and then at me. It was Mooney, the short, chesty, Catholic one.

'What the bloody 'ell do you think that is, eh?' he snarled at me. 'Come on, lad, come on, why isn't your pot laid out, with the cover off, eh?'

'I'm — I'm after using it, sir.'

'You're aaaf-ther using et,' he spoke in a mock Irish accent.

Johnston, the long skinny Birkenhead bastard, appeared in the doorway. 'What's to do now, Mr Mooney?'

'This feller 'ere was to clean out his cell and leave it ready for inspection and 'e 'asn't even got 'is pot clean and laid out. "I'm aaafther using et", 'e says. I suppose I can tell that to the Chief and all when 'e comes round. " 'E's af-ther using it, sir".'

'Stick 'is bloody 'ead in it,' said Johnston, and indignantly, 'don't stand there, you dirty Irish pig,' he roared at me, 'it's swine like you turn a good officer wicked. 'Ow can 'e be 'alf decent with bastards like you trying to get everyone in the shit? Come on.' He got me by the neck and shook me. 'Come on, get bloody well down to the recess and clean out that bloody pot of yours, get on with it!' He nearly flung me across the cell. I gathered the pot and cover and went down to the recess with it, emptied it, and cleaned it under the tap.

Coming back along the landing, I could see the glint of an eye from behind an odd spy-hole. They'd have been looking out wondering what the row was, and thankful that it wasn't them was involved.

Mooney locked me in the cell again, and I laid the pot in its proper place. The table was at the right side of the cell as you looked in. On it was my plate, flanked, as I said, by my tin knife and my spoon, and with my salt cellar at the back of my mug. On the left side, standing against the wall, was my mattress, and, lying against it, my bedboard with the bedclothes laid out along it. In the middle was my mat, rolled up to show there was nothing in the line of dust or dirt concealed under it. My mailbag of the cell task lay on top of that, with my needle, palm, and scissors laid out on top of that again. My chair was behind the mat, and in the centre of it all. My basin laid upside down on the seat, to show that it contained no dirty water, and my chamber-pot at one of its front legs, lying on its side, clean and decent for all to see, and at the other leg, to match it, the cover. I laid out my carpet slippers against the rung of the chair.

These were made out of pieces of old cloth, and were supposed to save you making a noise on the head of the fellow in the cell under you, when you were walking up and down.

But after you'd been in a day or two, you had no time to walk up and down, because you were doing your cell task, and in any event you got used to sitting on your stool, staring at the wall, and having a bit of a read now and again. The staring at the wall saved your library book, because only two a week were issued and the only fellow who couldn't read more than that in the time he was in his cell would be a fellow that wasn't able to read at all.

I had no books yet, so I'd been staring at the wall any time I was not in bed, or sewing the side of my mailbag, so I had not worn my carpet slippers.

The screw opened my cell with the others after breakfast, and shouted at me: 'What bloody way 'ave you your kit laid out? Get that bloody lot in shape before I come back or I'll get really angry with you — you sloppy Irish bastard.' He went off fuming to the next door.

I was miserable enough to myself, looking around hopelessly at the cell. I had washed it and laid out the stuff as best I could, and I was hopelessly looking at it, for I could do nothing else for the reason that I didn't know what else to do.

But when I heard him coming back, after he'd finished unlocking the doors, I bent over the bedboard and fumbled with the sheets and blankets, so as to be doing something, and not just standing there. He came back, and looked in the open door at me. 'You're a reception, and waiting for the RC

61

priest, so you won't be going down to work anyway, but before the Chief comes, by Christ, if you haven't got that lot straightened out' — he reached over and caught me by the hair — 'get on with it, you bastard, don't stand there looking at it!'

I was frightened and fumbled around with the bedclothes another bit, till I got hopeless and didn't know what I was doing.

'Christ!' said the screw, and I really thought I was for it, expecting a blow. I stood there with the bedclothes in my hand. He went out on the landing and shouted to someone. I sighed to myself, and waited.

God's help is never farther from the door, for the next thing was Charlie was in the cell with me, and the screw was showing him. 'Your cell is not extra good, but it's better than this Irish pig's pigsty, and you know how to make your bed up. Well, show 'im, and try and get some shape on this bloody lot before 'e goes down for the RC priest. You're a reception, aren't you? And you're for the doctor, aren't you?'

Charlie began helping me with the blankets and laying them out.

And a bad time was turned into a grand one, for he left Charlie there and went off.

We looked at each other, and smiled.

'This is a bit of all right, Pad, n't it?' said Charlie.

'Handy enough,' said I. 'That's an awful whore's melt, that screw, Charlie.'

'He is and all, china, there's nothing the matter with your cell furniture, the way it's laid out. It's just like it says on the card there — but the bedclothes could do with a bit of straightening out. But the screws just find fault with everyone. It's like in the Glass'ouse, they give a geezer a toothbrush and an eggcupful of soapy water and tell him to scrub the lawn, it's just to be bastards, that's all. Then he don't like Irishmen, that screw. According to what he was saying' — he lowered his voice — 'Pad, they got the dead needle for you, Pad, the screws; and, Pad, some' — he spoke as if embarrassed at having to mention something shameful — 'some of the blokes don't fancy you neither.' He spoke in his serious, concerned, boy's voice, and I felt older, and spoke to him reassuringly.

'They can go and fugh themselves, Charlie, I didn't expect anyone to lay down a red carpet for me if I was pinched over here.'

'I don't care, Paddy, if you were in the IRA or what you were bleedin' in. You're my china, Paddy.'

I looked into his serious eyes and smiled. 'I know that, Charlie.'

He smiled. 'That's stright-up, Pad.'

The screw came back. 'You should be finished now.'

'Yes, sir,' said Charlie, 'I've just shown 'im.' He turned round to the screw.

The screw looked at us sharply. 'Well, get back to your own cell, you, we've no married quarters 'ere.'

Charlie blushed and bit his lip. 'Yes, sir,' said he, and without looking at me went on back to his own cell.

'You get your tie on and be ready for the RC priest,' he said to me, and banged out my door.

I stood by my mat, not wanting to walk on the clean black floor, with my tie on and waiting to be called in. I also decided I wanted to piss and it seems to be always times like that when they can't that people want to. I was there a half-hour or so, when I heard the screw down below calling for 'Bee-hann'.

The screw on the landing came running up, opened the door, looked at me, and told me to hurry down and get fell in for the priest.

There was a small queue for him outside the doctor's room, and I fell in and waited happily. Every time a boy came out, a screw came out with a list and called a name till at last he called '3501 Behan', and I smiled and willingly hurried to his side. 'Go inside and stand to attention, feet to the mat.'

I ran in, and came smartly to attention at the mat, looking at the priest.

It was the same man, a stout block of a man, God bless him, that had said Mass. He was a bit bald and wearing glasses. I smiled at him and said, 'Good morning, Father.'

'When are you going to give up this business?' His two eyes glared at me from behind his glasses, and his accent was that of someone who had got a better chance in life, as they'd call it, than their parents. It was the accent of O'Sullivan, the detective-inspector from Cork — the Irish peasant's son trying to imitate the Lancashire lad's son whose dad 'as made a bit o' brass.

I shivered and hadn't been expecting this, but now it happened that this priest, too, was part of Walton Prison, I wasn't surprised. Tom Clarke saw Dr Gallagher in Portland with his lips a mess of raw meat, streaming blood where he had gone mad and started to chew glass.

He told the priest, and the priest told him to mind his own business. The priest had a bad name amongst Irish Republican prisoners, even the most pious of them.

'Haven't you any manners, Behan?'

'Answer Father Lane, Behan,' said the screw, who had shut the door and was standing beside me.

'I don't know what business you're talking about, Father,' said I.

'You know all right — your membership of this murder gang — the IRA.'

'The IRA is not a murder gang, Father,' said I. Grip tight and hold on, said Tom Clarke. I'd do my best. Clarke held on for fifteen years, and lived to fight the bastards on more equal terms in Easter Week.

'Don't answer Father Lane back, you——.' With difficulty the screw held back the low expletive, in deference to the man of God. The screw took a step half-towards me, but the priest put up his hand.

'It's all right, Mr Millburn,' he sighed, and they nodded to each other sympathetically. 'Cardinal Hinsley and the Hierarchy of England have issued pastorals denouncing the IRA, and while you're here I cannot let you come to the altar, unless you tell me once and for all that you're giving up having anything to do with this gang.'

His small eyes looked up at me, and his mouth closed tight in authority.

'Why should the Bishops of England be supposed to have

the right to dictate about politics to an Irishman, Father?' I asked, as steadily as I could.

Mr Millburn looked angry and indignant towards me, but the priest held up his patient hand. 'The Bishops of Ireland have denounced the IRA, Behan, time and time again, even early this year. The Church has always been Ireland's best friend, in Ireland, here in England, and all over the world. I must inform you that your own clergy and Hierarchy have excommunicated the IRA. You are automatically excommunicated till you repent of your sin in being a member of it and promise God in confession to sever all connection with it. Surely you can't set yourself up against the Bishops, an ignorant lad against educated men, who have spent their lifetime studying these matters?'

'I didn't spend a lifetime studying theology, but I know that the Church was always against Ireland and for the British Empire.'

Mr Millburn again looked angry, but the priest looked wise and tolerant, and indicated that I might continue.

'With no disrespect to you, Father. A synod of Irish bishops held at Drumceatt in 1172 decided that any Irishman that refused to acknowledge the King of England as his ruler was excommunicated. That was only three years after the Normans landed and held only a bit of country not the size of the County Louth, the smallest of the Thirty-two Counties. The O'Neills in Ulster even after the Reformation had to threaten to the Pope that they would burn the Catholic Archbishop of Armagh, Richard Creagh, out of the Cathedral if he didn't take Queen Elizabeth's soldiers out of it. In 'Ninety-eight weren't the rebels excommunicated and wasn't Father John Murphy, that was burned alive by the yeomen, excommunicated? Didn't Archbishop Troy issue pastorals condemning the 'Ninety-eight men, and didn't he have prayers offered up in thanksgiving when poor Robert Emmet was captured?'

'Look here, you,' said the screw, Mr Millburn, and Father Lane looked angry, through his little eyes, but a bit surprised. But I didn't care now. Me blood was up and me country in me knuckles.

'Didn't they condemn the men of 'Forty-eight and tell the people to give up their crops and die of the hunger in the ditches at home, with the grass-juice running green from the dead mouth of a mother clutching a live infant—!'

'Here, you,' began the priest, in a gathering roar, but I might as well throw the hammer after the hatchet.

'Weren't the Fenians excommunicated, and didn't the Catholic chaplains in Portland and Chatham join with the rest of the warders in driving Dr Gallagher mad with torture when the Fenians were doing their solitary confinement in Tom Clarke's time?'

Mr Millburn glared at me in amazed anger. The priest swallowed his temper and tried to speak, but rage got the better of him and he could only signal to the screw to take me out. But, be Christ, I wasn't done yet. Before Millburn reached for me, I said to the priest right into his seething little eyes: 'And excommunication is nothing new to the IRA. Didn't yous excommunicate De Valera and ten thousand others in 1922? Didn't Bishop Cohalan of Cork excommunicate the IRA and support the Black and Tans before that? Wasn't—' Millburn grabbed me but I finished what I had to say, eyes blazing and my heart in my ears — to hell with you, you fat bastard, to hell with England and to hell with Rome, up the Republic, lurry him he's no relation, the greasy fat bastard trying to show himself a Limey gent with the rest of the screws. 'Wasn't my own father excommunicated and him in Kilmainham Prison in 'Twenty-two?'

'Get out, you swine,' said Mr Millburn and threw me out of the priest's office. But I was quiet now. I had said what I wanted to say and would go peaceably to my cell. If I was let. But I wasn't.

'Mister Mooney,' said Mr Millburn to Mr Mooney, who hurried up the wing from where the rest of the Young Prisoners were sitting in rows sewing their mailbags. In indignation, 'This — Irish swine — insulting — the priest—' Mr Mooney nodded, shocked, and hit me a blow in the face, without taking his attention from Mr Millburn, and Mister Johnston came up as they shoved me towards the stairs leading up to the landing, and they told him, Mister Millburn

66

and Mister Mooney, 'This — Irish — insulted priest — bloody bastard' — not the priest, me, and Mister Johnston, though not a Catholic, but a Protestant and wouldn't bloody well stand for that all the same, insulting any clergyman, any priest even, and especially Father Lane, decent man beloved by all and spending his time working for the prisoners. 'You fughing shit-house, we'll teach you 'ow to be'ave, you dirty Irish fugh-pig,' and, grunt and push, I fell a couple of times on the iron steps on the way up to the landing. 'Wait till we get you up there in the cell — now by Christ we'll—ge-eh-t up, there, you bastard, you Irish—!'

They took me to the cell, and beat me in the face, slaps but not punches. The punches they gave me in the ribs, in the kidneys, and once or twice they hit me across the face with a bunch of keys, but concentrated mostly on the guts and a few kicks in my arse, when they sent me sprawling across the room and shouted all the time about killing me, and insulting the priest and me a half-starved Irish bastard, and they'd give me IRA, and the cell was in disorder with the bedboards and bedclothes scattered all over the place, and then they shouted at me to clear that bloody mess up and get that lot straightened out and went off banging the door locked, and left me alone, thank Jesus, and still breathing, though heavily, and getting back into breathing practice.

I fumbled around the cell as best I could. I had left the jug full of water in the cell in the morning and I took the liberty of bathing my face with the cold water, and had a look in the mirror when I was finished. My face was not too bad, nothing noticeable, though my lip was cut on the inside where I got the blow from the bunch of keys and I could feel the blood going down my throat and sickening me. I was also now being sickened, and a cold clammy sweat was coming out on my hands and on my forehead now in delayed action for the fright I hadn't had time to have when they were dragging me up the stairs and belting me in the cell. I wiped the sweat off, too, and then got a kind of sick bilious headache, and I wanted to have a shit, and so I did in quick time on the pot and wiped myself and had the cover on and was up

67

and about again in no time, when the door opened and a prisoner and a screw stood in the doorway. They had a parcel of books, and the prisoner handed me two and wrote my name on a card.

'Don't go swopping them now, you,' said the library screw. He had a Cockney accent and was a long, cadaverous-looking man with glasses. 'Unless you want to 'ave a little trip down to chokey.'

I took the two books in my hand. 'I will not, sir,' said I, 'and thanks very much.'

I spoke so fervently that he looked at me as he spoke. 'Don't thank me, thank the Lord. You're an Irishman, ain't you? I can tell by your brogue. I got a book about Ireland. Remind me about it or ask for it by writing on your slate for me when we come round Tuesday next week. Write on it, "Please leave *The Life Savers*, the Irish book".'

The prisoner was a small rat-faced man like a twin brother of the altar-boy. Maybe they had a supply of these merchants for library and altar work, all in for rape. But he nodded kindly to me, and I said, in his direction as well as in the screw's, 'Thank you very much, and I'll leave you the note if I don't see you.'

'Right, Paddy,' said the librarian, and 'Right, Paddy,' said the prisoner, and the prisoner I noticed banged out my door and I turned to lay the books on the table. Better than a dozen of stout it was to see them there, the books.

It didn't look like there was going to be anything more about this morning, and I could have a read tonight, resting my bruises for a bit before the lights were put out, and happy, I looked at the books and looked forward to the night, for all my mouth was raw and bleeding still a bit and painful on the inside, and my kidneys, if that's the things you have on your sides, were sore and maybe this bit of a belting they got would be a contributory cause of my early death in the years to come, but sure what matter of that? One thing at a time, and I looked forward to my read, and it was decent of that old fellow to call me 'Paddy' and say he'd give me a book about Ireland, though I never heard of anything called *The Life Savers*. Maybe it was one of those banned books by

Joyce or one of those fellows, in which case all the better as the old one said when she was told that there was no tea but only porter.

In any event I should have a read, and a read every week, and a kind of pay-day to look forward to when they changed the books; and, thinking these thoughts, I had the cell, between bedclothes and all, laid out and tidied up, and I gave myself another rub with the cold fresh water and had a look at myself in the mirror and I looked all right, except my mouth was a bit bloody with a thin red line around the edge of it, but I wiped that off too and then let myself have a look at the books.

It's a queer world, God knows, but the best we have to be going on with.

One of the books was *Under the Greenwood Tree* by Thomas Hardy, and the other was the life of General Booth, the founder of the Salvation Army. I looked at them a good bit, over and over, but did not open them except to look at the fly-leaves. I was standing on one leg leaning on the table and looking at them, without using up as much as a page of either one. I didn't notice time, till I heard them coming round with the dinner. A great smell it had too; coming nearer and nearer, till they came to my door and opened it the same as they did everyone else's and I took the dinner in; and in the afternoon I was opened up with the rest and got down and emptied and cleaned the chamber-pot and went out and sewed mailbags with the rest till four o'clock when they locked us up for the night, and gave us our supper till the night was in and the day over, and divil a much the matter with me, everything all right, thanks be to God and His Blessed Mother, only for my mouth being still a bit raw when I sipped my mug of cocoa — but I didn't mind that, looking forward to getting into my bed, being warm, unharmed, and with a book to read.

I was feeling my inside lip with my tongue, and being careful not to eat on it, when the spy-hole cover was lifted, and a voice said, 'Ahst ad tha cuckoo, Paddy lad?'

This was a Young Prisoner called Brown. He was a nice decent little round ball of a fellow about eighteen, and went round with the scoff and was an orderly. Everyone liked him, and called him Browny, and he smiled all the time, going about his work, and even the screws didn't seem to mind. He came from some old bog road part of Lancashire, and I think they liked him as a bit of Old England (for the English are very nationalistic). They smiled when Browny spoke in his funny dialect to them, and some of them even answered him in the same way, taking him off in a friendly fashion. He was a bit of a pet with everyone, and I think the screws looked upon his lingo in somewhat the same way as in Ireland they'd look upon the Irish of a lad from the Gaeltacht, in a tender smiling approving sort of way.

He was a good little fellow anyway, and I held my mug of cocoa up for him to see, and smiled in the direction of his eye and said, 'I've had my cocoa, thanks, Browny.'

The eye winked and said: 'That's a good lad, Paddy. Ah'll see thee tomorra; g'neet, lad.'

'Good night, Browny,' said I, and he scarpered off down the landing.

The bells out in the city range a quarter to five, and I sat with the bread and cheese and cocoa hot inside me till five o'clock, when I started my cell task.

I had to side three mailbags, and it was easy enough to do, now that I had done a few days at it (not that I was a natural sewer), and I was looking forward to *Under the Greenwood Tree*, when I would be done; so I was fairly quick and when the bags were finished I shoved my chair back from the door a bit and turned into the table, stuck my legs in the mailbag, pulled it tight up about me, and when I opened the book on the table I put my hands down under the bag and was warm all over, though the air of the winter night was black cold and blunt as metal.

The lad going home in the late Christmas Eve, and singing the bar of a song for himself:

> 'With the rose and the lily, and the daffodown dilly,
> The lads and the lassies a sheep-shearing go.'

I tried not to read any more than my ration. There were two hundred pages in the book — that was about thirty a night. The life and times of General William Booth wouldn't be much use. I had read a bit about him in a 'Penguin' by St John Ervine, a North of Ireland man who was manager of the Abbey Theatre when my uncle was property man there. He was in favour of the Salvation Army, but he said their enemies accused them of groping for Jesus in the dark. This book, though, didn't look it would have anything like that in it. Still, it would do for having an odd look at it at the weekend, and I could save a bit of *Under the Greenwood Tree* on it. It would be better than nothing, like my father's song about the small potatoes in the time of the Famine:

> Oh, the praties they were small over here,
> Oh, the praties they were small over here,
> Oh, the praties they were small, but we ate them skin
>   and all,
> They were better than fugh-all, over here.

We all used to laugh, only my mother, who said it was a disgrace and a shame to be making game of the poor people that died in Black Forty-Seven and the dead mothers that were found with the green grass-juice trickling from the sides of their mouths, and the babies crying and tugging at their dry breasts.

But honest to Jesus, you'd have to laugh at my old fellow, and he put in bits like that into national songs, and it was all equal to him, he'd nearly put them into hymns, only he was never much where they'd be singing any.

He was a great fiddler and so was my uncle, my mother's brother, who had a fiddle presented to him by the prisoners in Ballykinlar Internment Camp for writing the National Anthem. My mother was a good singer, and my stepbrother's aunts were pianists, and great nights we had in their big house on the North Circular Road. I could see my old man with the fiddle, standing beside the piano, and Aunt Emily playing the piano and this book in a way reminded me of them. All these old West of England men, with the cider barrel and mead and meat and cheese.

It was like that at home only, strange to say, we were all city people and these were countrymen. But even their speech when they said 'carrel' and 'traypsing and rambling about' was like Dublin speech.

And they went round playing their carols in the bright frosty night, and I had to go on reading after page thirty and up to forty to where it was Christmas Day and they were having the Tranter's party that night; I couldn't miss that, so when the bell went I got into bed and read on, warm and

72

enjoying myself, and Dick, the lad that was singing the song at the beginning, is trying to get off his mark with the new school-teacher, a nice little mot of seventeen or eighteen and just my own weight, if it went to that, and everyone is drinking and singing, till they come to the part where they're going to dance and I had to read on there, too, promising myself that I would read only fifteen pages tomorrow night, and make it up with fifteen of the Booth book, which more than likely would not be so quickly read, and the Tranter got the wife up to face him, in the dance.

'Reuben,' says she, 'was always such a hot man,' and she no way ashamed of it, and maybe she ought. It put me in mind of my mother and father, and he getting her up to take the floor in 'Haste to the Wedding', and the two of them singing:

'Twas beyond at Macreddin, at Owen Doyle's Weddin',
The lads got the pair of us out for a reel,
Says I, 'Boys, excuse us,' says they, 'Don't refuse us,'
'I'll play nice and aisy,' says Larry O'Neill,
I looked at me woman, the song she was hummin',
Was ould as the hills so I gave her a *póg*
'Twas like our ould courtin', half-serious half-sportin',
When Molly was young and hoops were in vogue. . . .

Says herself to meself, 'We're as good as the rest,'
Says herself to meself, 'Sure we're better nor gold,'
Says herself to meself, 'You're as wild as the rest of them,'
'Kathy,' says I, 'sure we're time enough old. . . .'

The next morning I was brought before the Governor and told that I could use the money that had been found on me to buy food, cigarettes, and papers.

But I knew no one in Liverpool to get me the food, and the Staff did not want to help me to get food (they thought they were treating me well enough in letting me buy cigarettes and papers, and according to the Governor they were not required even to do that — 'to fetch and carry for me,' he said).

I was glad to be let have a paper, and I put down for the *Daily Herald*. I asked for *Reynolds's News* for Sunday, and the Governor said I could not have *Reynolds's News* which was not an approved paper but I might have the *News of the World* which was.

Years and years ago, when I was a child, my father used to get the *News of the World*, and said it was for the sheet music on the back he bought it. I used to wonder why he laughed, and why my mother said, half-laughing in spite of herself, that he was a terrible man, because it was banned at home, before I could read, and I only saw it once or twice in the Tech., when some fellow sneaked it out of his house where it had been posted from England, and on building jobs I saw it an odd time.

It was a very interesting paper, mostly about *that*, and I had enjoyed Charlie's copy in the Bridewell, and I was looking forward to seeing it every Sunday; with that and the *Daily Herald*, and a smoke every day, my standard of living was going up with a bang.

That day I started the life of Reilly, as you might say.

I went to work as usual in the wing on the bottom floor, sitting on my chair in line with the other prisoners. Then the screw called out 'Remands and awaiting trials for smoking', and I fell in behind Charlie and the other remands and we went out to the yard.

We fell in in front of a cabinet, and when the screw unlocked it there was a drawer in it with a number corresponding to each cell in the YP wing. There was a drawer with 'C.2.26' on it and in it were kept my cigarettes.

The screw struck a match, and we each went up in turn to get a light. Then he warned us not to try bringing a butt into the wing, and that if we did we'd get Number One. 'And no talking,' he shouted; 'now get spread out.'

We walked round the ring in single file, smoking like lords' bastards till the frosty air had a great smell of smoke in it, and a kind of an outside smell.

For fifteen minutes or so we walked around and then an

orderly came to the gate from inside the prison carrying a bucket. The screw opened the gate and he came out and left the bucket on the steps and stood beside it.

The screw then called us up, and in turn we dropped our dog-ends into the bucket. We marched back again to our seats in the hall and took up our sewing again, while the screw went off down with the orderly carrying the bucket to the recess, where it would be thrown down the lavatory and the chain pulled out by the screw.

Twelve o'clock was not long coming round and I had my paper to read. When I got up to my cell, there it was waiting for me on the table. It was great to see such a thing, although it was a lonely thing in a way to be reading only about things and places I neither knew nor cared about. But it was something to read, and secondly it saved the *Greenwood Tree*, and it couldn't be denied that it was a great and a notable thing to be able to sit there with the day's paper spread out while I leant over my dinner. I could see myself getting through all this, even through a long sentence, and still coming out alive and kicking, even though at the very least I would be over twenty years of age. Still, there were Young Prisoners here that were twenty-three, for I'd seen it on their cell cards, and they looked it.

There were three of them that were fairly old. Two of them were Licence Revokes, fellows who had been in Borstal, and released on licence and brought back to the nick. Dale and James. Dale was a big, Spanish-looking fellow and he told me one day, and I sitting near him, that he was Liverpool-Irish and that his mother was from Westport, County Mayo. He was a bad bastard for all that, and told me in a hurry that he didn't like Irish people, that he was an Englishman himself, and that Irishmen came over to Liverpool to work for scab wages.

I tried to whisper to him in an urgent stammer that that was wrong, that the wages of a Dublin building worker, painter, plumber, carpenter, bricklayer were the highest in Europe, as they were for bankers and printers and most other trades, and that the wages in Liverpool in the painting trade were so low that a fourth-year apprentice in Dublin or Cork or

Belfast or Derry or Limerick would get a bigger rate per hour.

He didn't listen but turned on me and, as if I had done something on him and he was only restraining himself from giving me a belt, he said, half aloud, 'Just shag off, you Killarney bastard, or I'll 'it you.'

The screw looked down and said angrily, 'What's to-do down there?'

'It's this Irish bastard, sir,' said Dale, ' 'e keeps talking all the time — I just told 'im 'e'd get me in trouble.'

I looked up at the screw and was trying to tell that Dale had spoken to me first, telling me that his mother was from Westport, County Mayo, and that I didn't care where she was from, nor was I asking any of these bastards to be Irish, but I couldn't, and anyway the screw looked down at me and shouted in a even more venomous way than he had before:

'I'm just about browned off with you, you gabby Irish bastard. Move over your chair there and get on with it. I shan't warn you again, I shan't. I've warned you before and this is the last time.'

I moved over my chair, and kept my head down so as the others looking at me couldn't see my red face, but I looked up again when I had my face set right and went on sewing the canvas, staring straight ahead. I could see from the corner of my eyes fellows in the rows in front of me, letting on to reach for their wax or their scissors on the ground beside them so as they could give a quick glance at me from under their arm. I just stared ahead and hated, fixing my eyes on the British coat of arms on a fire-extinguisher on the wall behind the screw.

And for the rest of that morning and other mornings following, I sat by myself on the edge of the row and kept my head down and was ready when the time was up to get my chair and go up to my cell without having anything to do with anyone.

But Dale was promoted, when another fellow got sentenced, to go on the table. James went with him.

On the table they collected the work for the screw when it was finished and they could call him to reject the work if they didn't like it. On siding the seams of the canvas, which was what I was at, the stitches were four to an inch. I was not a very good sewer, but after a week I was able to do it properly, and God knows there was little enough to it, but every time I went to the table to give up finished work they called the screw and he gave it back to me and called me a 'stupid Irish bastard'. Dale laughed at this a lot, and so did James.

Then I stopped bringing up my finished work, and kept it beside me, waiting for the day the instructor would come round and collect it, but then when I went up for another canvas Dale said I couldn't have another one till I brought up some finished work.

I went back to my chair and sat down. Dale and James were jeering at me, and calling me names in a low tone of voice that only the other fellows at the back rows could hear, and they were looking at me and laughing, too.

Jesus, if they'd only let me sit there and sew away, I could be looking down at the canvas and watching my stitches and seeing them four to an inch, and passing the time myself by thinking about Ireland and forgetting even where I was, and, Jesus, wasn't that little enough to ask? What harm would I be doing them? If any of them was in Mountjoy, say, and I was there with a crowd of Dublin fellows, I wouldn't mess them about, honest to Jesus Christ I wouldn't, no matter what they were in for. And that James, that was a proper white-livered whore's melt.

He had whitey-coloured hair and a sharp little nose, and though he was about twenty and maybe a little bigger than myself, I was not afraid of him. I couldn't say that I was not afraid of Dale because I was. He was a big well-set-up man and James only trailed after him, like a bully's labourer. But, by Jesus for that again, if I was afraid of the engine-driver I was not afraid of the oil-rag. No, be Jesus, and I twisted the palm round in my hand. I'll James you, you foxy-faced drippings of a cankered—, you poxy bastarding whore's melt, I put it to myself, and thought it worth it to hit him a belt; but, when all is said and done, I was but sixteen and he was a grown man and had come through Borstal institutions, mostly, I would say, by sucking up to bullying big bollixes the likes of Dale, not by letting his backstraps down — he was too ugly for that, but maybe some of these bastards would get a bit of a drop. I was no country Paddy from the middle of the Bog of Allen to be frightened to death by a lot of Liverpool seldom-fed bastards, nor was I one of your wrap-the-green-flag-round-me junior Civil Servants that came into the IRA from the Gaelic League, and well ready to die for their country any day of the week, purity in their hearts, truth on their lips, for the glory of God and the honour of Ireland. No, be Jesus, I was from Russell Street, North Circular Road, Dublin, from the Northside where, be Jesus, the likes of Dale wouldn't make a dinner for them, where the whole of this pack of Limeys would be scruff-hounds would be et, bet, and threw up again — et without salt. I'll James you, you bastard.

Then the smile had to fade and the joke was rejected and the gentleness refused, never a better nor my own sweet self, and it wasn't off the stones I licked. The old fellow would beat the best of them round our way and him only my height now, though fully grown a hell of a long time. James, be Jesus, prepare to meet thy Jesus. And I just stood up, held up a bag and said, 'Finished work,' and the screw nodded, though I hadn't said 'sir' because I hadn't time.

I walked up to the table and stood there till James stood up. That was as well; it would never have done if it had been Dale that stood up. It was James, and I held out the bag to him.

'Finished work,' said I.

'Oh, is it?' He put on his sneer, too thick to notice any difference in me. He looked at it in great annoyance, no less, but glad, as I saw by his lips settling for more sneering, to have another bit of diversion at my expense. The more fool you, you bastard, said I in my own mind. He looked at me and took up the bag. 'What's to do with you? You Irish bastard, that's one of them you 'aven't done right. 'Ere, take it back and do it again, cop.'

He flung the bag in my face, and Dale laughed, and so did the fellows turning round in their seats, pleasurably, as when the curtain rises on a play.

I took the bag and laid it on the table and looked sorrow-
fully at James, miserably like Oliver Twist, to meekly and
hopelessly enquire: 'Please, oh, please I did nothing to you.
Why are you so cruel to me?'

I led with my right and came up with my left, but my open
palm with the metal thimble, right up into James' face. He
went down and tried to hold his face down and I caught him
by the hair with my right hand and held back his face while
I rammed him in the face with my palm, the metal one I
mean, and his blood was pouring over my hand, and the
screw came rushing down; but I was more afraid of Dale,
who'd got up from his seat, and I pulled James still by the hair
farther down the table so as the screw would get me before
Dale could get over the table and give me a few belts, free
gratis and for nothing, saying he was stopping Young Prisoner
Behan from taking the life of James, Young Prisoner.

And, dear dilapidated Jasus, was I going well at it till the
screw caught me and pulled me off James and he went
blinded and moaning and holding his hand to his face and the
pouring blood.

He went round in a circle of blood, and it dripping from
him, holding his hands to his face and moaning words and
music.

The screw came down and I thought he was going to start
battering me there and then, but he didn't. Johnston, the long
skinny ex-Guardsman it was, and he looked at me from his
coffin face, and said quietly, 'Stand there a minute, you,' then
he turned and shouted down the wing to a screw who was
going round searching the cells, 'Here a moment, Mister
Thorne, will you, sir?'

The screw, Thorne, came running when he saw the cut of
James.

'Been a bit of bother 'ere, Mister Johnston?'

Johnston nodded and said, 'Will you take James over to the
hospital while I take Behan up to his cell?'

'Right, come on, lad,' said Thorne to James, 'and take your
'and from your eyes, if you don't want to trip over yourself
and do yourself some more damage. You are a proper bloody
mess, as it is.'

79

I stood and waited for Johnston to bring me up to my cell. He was waiting for a few more screws to come up and give me a battering, and for the PO to come up and supervise it, I supposed, but I didn't care. I had a look with great satisfaction at the other bastards sitting in their seats and looking round at me. There was no laughing or grinning or jeering or jibing with them now, the shower of shits.

I caught Charlie looking down at me and he gave me a kind of a good-bye look, sad and friendly. That cheered me up a bit, and I looked back at him as much to say: 'It'll be OK, kid. I'll be seeing you again, won't be both returned for trial to the Assizes till the end of January, and that's still nearly two months away. They'd never give me that much Number One.'

I supposed wrong about the battering, too. Johnston just took me to my cell and said, 'I suppose you know you'll be for the Governor in the morning, Behan?'

'Yes, sir,' said I.

He nodded and shut the door, and I heard him taking my cell card out of the holder outside to make the report. Then he went back down the stairs.

I was delighted, thinking of James, and him going round a walking advertisement to the other bastards to leave me alone.

I took my book and started celebrating with a bit of a read extra. I might as well read as much as I could because they'd more nor likely take it away from me in the morning anyway.

Bejasus, and no one could say that Dick Dewy wasn't getting every chance of a running leap at Fancy Day. He brings over her furniture up to the new house where she's to set up as the village school-teacher; and there he was sitting on his hunkers trying to get the fire going till she'd make the first cup of tea in the house; but by the way they were 'Yes, Mr Dewying' and 'Do you think so, Miss Daying?' they'd be there till the Lord would call them before he'd get down to introducing Fagan. And a bed and all in the house. — I heard tell the bed was a gift, far and wide in front of the standy-up job. Bobby Hamill, on our corner, got married to Gloria Carmody when he was only sixteen, and he said there was no comparison. I was sorry over that. That I regretted, and if the judge was to get up at the Assizes and say, 'You silly young eedgit, you're not going to get a chance of chasing a mot now till you're no longer a youth, and you can pull your wire now till we let you out,' and it's a very well-known sociological class of a phenomenon that, after a long number of years in the nick, men coming out are not able to do anything else. God between us and all harm.

Ah, but Dick wasn't as green as he was cabbage-looking. 'Dick, Dick, kiss me and let go instantly — here's somebody coming!' — it's me, Brendan Behan, 3501, HM Prison, Liverpool, Vol Brendan Behan, 2nd Battalion, Dublin Brigade, Irish Republican Army. But I didn't, only started thinking about my cocoa and cheese tonight, maybe the last meal I'd eat for a while, and a man needed all his strength in the times that were in it. Not to be thinking of things like *that*.

In the morning I was left locked up when the others went down to work and until they went out to exercise.

Then the screws shouted 'Behan' and rushed up to my door and opened it and said, 'Quick, you, put on your tie,' though I already had it on, and we rushed down the stairs to the bottom floor and up to the Governor's office, where the Chief looked out at us, the PO flung open the door and shouted, 'Stand to the mat, and state your full name, number, age, religion, and sentence.'

I went in and stood to the mat, and said, 'Behan, Brendan, sir, three five oh one, age sixteen, Roman Catholic, awaiting trial.'

The old Governor sank back in his chair and didn't look up, but read a sheet of paper in front of him.

Johnston stood, cleared his throat and looked at the PO, and the PO looked at the Chief, and the Chief looked at the Governor, and this time he nodded his old head, and Johnston read off a paper about my assaulting James; and when the PO nodded to the Chief and the Chief nodded back to the PO, the PO looked at the Governor, who looked up slowly and said:

'You — er — heard that — er, Behan? That charge that the officer has just read?'

'I did, sir,' said I, with my hands at the seams of my trousers and looking manly, admitting my fault to this tired old consul, weary from his labours amongst the lesser breeds, administering the King's justice equal and fairly to wild Irish and turbulent Pathan, teaching fair play to the wily Arab and a sense of sportsmanship to the smooth Confucian. In my ballocks, said I in my own mind, you George-Arliss-headed fughpig, dull scruffy old creeping Jesus, gone past the Bengal Lancer act now back to where you started, like a got-up gentleman with his Curragh cap. Bejasus, any decent horse would drop dead from the shame if he managed to get up on its back. 'I did, sir.'

He screwed up his keen eyes, which you'd know had been used to gazing over wide open spaces from the gate to the hang-house, and said: 'There is no need to call the other prisoner. I would warn you that for this offence I could have you charged in the magistrates' court, and I must take this opportunity of warning you that if this assault had been carried out on one of my officers' — the Chief, PO, and Johnston, the screw, gathered themselves up off the sands of the desert and looked at him, proud and grateful, and looked at me — 'or even a lesser sort of violence offered them, you would most certainly have been flogged.'

I looked at him and merely nodded, to show my com-miseration with him for the trouble I gave him in belting Marsh, but also my horror, at the thoughts of doing anything so awful as striking or offering to strike one of his officers. I had no wish to commit suicide, and secondly I wasn't fed for it.

The old Rider Haggard head of him shook, and he said, 'I sentence you to—' What the vicious old cur would have sentenced me to, I'll never know, for the Chief leaned forward to tell him that I was going to court the day after tomorrow. The Governor nodded and said, 'And remember this is only a warning to you—'

I nodded my head and looked at him as earnestly as I could. I'll go straight, Gov, strike me pink if I don't.

'— to one day's cellular confinement, one day's deprivation of mattress, and one day's Number One diet.'

Well, good old Rudyard, what an escape, I'd be out and about in three days' time. I looked at him and moved my Adam's apple or where it should have been, to thank that good old man — for bugger all. But the Chief roared and the PO opened the door, and the screw shouted to me to about-turn, and I was marched off at a hell of a lick up the stairs and back along the landing to my cell.

'Now,' said Johnston, 'go inside and take out your cell furniture, your table, chair, wash-stand, wash-bowl, jug, knife, spoon, plate, mug, mattress, bedboard, everything except your chamber-pot, and leave them on the landing outside your cell. Come on, boy, look sharp.'

I brought them out, one after another. Johnston was not hostile, and even helped me drag out the mattress and bedboards. My two books were on the shelf, and I had a great hope he would not ask for them. He didn't, but when I had everything else out of the cell, he said: 'Now, take off your stockings, your shoes, your belt, your tie and your jacket, and put them outside here. You can take back your slippers and wear them.'

'Thank you, sir,' said I.

Johnston said nothing; only nodded.

I went into the cell and he banged the door, put another card over my ordinary card, pulled down the cover of the spy-hole which I had left open on purpose to have a window on the world and a view of the two doors within my range on the landing opposite, and went off down the stairs.

Then I settled down to my Number One and solitary. Number One, I knew, was eight ounces of bread and a pint of water, and I wondered when I would get it. Would they give it to me at dinner-time, for the rest of the day, or would they leave it till supper-time? The next day I knew I was off the diet, but still on the deprivation of mattress, but the day after I would not give a God's curse, because the solitary would be the only thing, and that would not mean a lot because I was going down to the court, and I would have my mattress back that night.

83

And I still had *Under the Greenwood Tree*, not to mind the book about the old Salvation Army sawdust pocket.

I walked up and down in my slippers and was not in a bad humour, but whistling softly to myself the songs that many an Irishman had whistled or whispered to himself in those kips. And I'd have sung it out and not given a God's curse for no one, only they might hear me, and it was better to be defiant in a quiet sort of a way. These sportsmen would be serious men if it came to kicking the shit out of you. A desperate thing for the Germans or the Russians or the Fuzzie-Wuzzies to do as much to one of theirs, and a crime against humanity, but a far different thing it looked to them to do the same to someone else — and you couldn't blame them. Everyone has their own way of looking at things and you couldn't blame them for taking a favourable view of their own kicking once they were kicking you in their country and not they being kicked by someone else in someone else's. But still a little whistle was in order, once I kept it low.

> In boyhood's bloom and manhood's pride,
> Foredoomed by alien laws,
> Some on the scaffold proudly died,
> For Holy Ireland's cause;
> And brothers say, Shall we, today,
> Unmoved by cowards stand,
> While traitors shame and foes defame,
> The Felons of our Land. . . .

By Jesus, I could hear the blokes being marched in, dismissed, and then sent hurrying up the stairs, and rattling along the landings, and their doors being banged out, one after another. And I could smell the dinner.

Would they ever give me my bread and water, now? No, the boards went past me; I could hear them; so another bar of the whistle was indicated, to keep my heart up.

That it choke you, you shower of bastards!

> Some of the convict's dreary cell,
> Have found a living tomb,

84

> And some unseen untended fell
> Within the dungeon's gloom,
> But what care we, although it be
> Trod by a ruffian band,
> God bless the clay where rest today
> The Felons of our Land. . . .

The dinners went past me, I could smell. Wasn't it the great pity that the fellow that was doing the suffering couldn't be where the singing was to get the benefit of it. Mother of Christ, wasn't there a thousand places between Belfast and Bantry Bay where a fellow would be stuffed with grub, not to mind dowsed in porter, if he could only be there and here at the same time? But I supposed that would be like trying to get a drink at your own funeral. Make way there, you with the face, and let in the man that's doing jail for Ireland, and suffering hunger and abuse, let him up to the bar there. Oh, come up at once, the publican would say, what kind of men are you at all? Have you no decency of spirit about you, that wouldn't make way for one of the Felons of our Land? Come on, son, till herself gives you this plate of bacon and cabbage, and the blessings of Jasus on you, and on everyone like you. It's my own dinner I'm giving you, for you were not expected and you amongst that parcel of white-livered, thin-lipped, paper-waving, key-rattling hangmen. And, come on; after your dinner there's a pint to wash it down, aye, and a glass of malt if you fancy it. Give us up a song there. Yous have enough of songs out of yous about the boys that faced the Saxon foe, but bejasus, when there's one of them here among you, the real Ally Daly, the real goat's genollickers, yous are silent as the tomb. Sing up, yous whore's gets.

> Side by side for the cause when our forefathers battled,
> When our hills never echoed the tread of the slave,
> On many a green field where the leaden hail rattled,
> Through the red gap of glory, they marched to the grave,
> But we who inherit their name and their spirit,
> March 'neath the banner of liberty then,
> Give them back blow for blow,

Pay them back woe for woe.
Out and make way for the Bold Fenian Men. . . .

' 'Ello — 'ere, Paddy.'

I turned on my heel to the spy-hole. It was Browny.

'I'll 'ave your cob and your water up shortly, Paddy.'

I smiled in the direction of the spy-hole. 'Good man, Browny, thanks.'

When all the dinners had been given out and all the doors were locked, my door was opened, and Browny came in, with my bread and water. It was the usual two-tiered aluminium diet can with solids in the top shallow can, and liquids in the bottom long can. In this case a cob of bread and a pint of water.

' 'Ere you are, Paddy, lad,' said Browny in his soft voice. 'It's not much, but it'll keep your guts together till tea-time.'

'Do I get more then?' I asked.

' 'Course you do,' said Browny. 'There's eight ounces of bread in that, and you get a six-ounce cob tonight, and a four-ounce in the morning for your breakfast. Then your Number One is up.'

'Only for the mattress and the solitary!'

'He'll give you your mattress all right tonight, and you're out then at dinner-time tomorrow and all's well again.'

'I thought it was three days — one day's Number One, one without the mattress, and one in solitary.'

'Nay, you silly feller,' said Browny, ' 'tis all one day. Pad, I 'ear screw coming back. I'll slip along landing later this afternoon and 'ave a bit of chat to cheer y'up like, if I can make it. I 'ear 'im coming.' He gave his soft smile and winked, and went off down the landing.

Johnston came up and looked in round the cell. 'Got everything?' he asked.

'Yes, sir,' said I, holding my can and my cob of bread.

He nodded, banged out the door and went off down the landing.

I had nothing to sit on but my mat, so I sat there and broke the crust of my cob of bread. It was a new one, and washed down with the cup of water, I wasn't long finishing it. It was great to think, I thought, that I would be getting more bread at supper-time, and that the whole thing was over tomorrow. I had only two more meals of bread and water before I went back on ordinary diet. It was well worth it, to give that James bastard a trimming, though for that again I hoped he wouldn't be needled enough or have guts enough to go for me over it. But then I knew that was not likely to worry me much, for it couldn't last long. The screws would see to that. The only thing to be afraid of was him coming at me all of a sudden, like I did at him. And I'd look out for that. Get my chair in against the wall, when we were at labour, and keep a good eye round the exercise yard as we walked round the ring.

I got up and did not wipe the crumbs off me, but gathered them and went for a bit of a walk up and down the cell in my slippers, thinking about Ireland and the suffering for her and all the starvation — in particular of Terence MacSwiney, seventy-eight days with no scoff at all, and my own father on hunger strike with ten thousand others in the internment camps during the Civil War, but that was a different thing, with ten thousand others. MacSwiney had the eyes of the world on him, and knew that it must be driving these bastards mad from the publicity it was getting. They were up and offering him every conceivable delicacy, chicken, ham, turkey, roast pork, steak, oh for the love of Jesus, give over, me mouth is watering.

If Johnston came up and said, 'Here you are, sing two lines of "God Save the King" and I'll give you this piece of round steak,' would I take it? Would I what? Jesus, Mary and Joseph, he'd be a lucky man that I didn't take the hand and all off him.

And sing a High Mass, never mind a couple of lines of 'God Save the King', for it, aye or for the half of it.

After I stopped for a minute or two and allowed myself a bit of a read at *Under the Greenwood Tree*, and had a look at the bit early on where they have a Christmas carol, I started to put an air to it. That's a thing we're all very well able to do in my family. On my mother's side, my uncle was one of the best song-writers in the country, and one of the best known, and others of them were in the variety business, so it wouldn't take me long looking at a poem or a song to put an air to it.

So I put the air of the 'Famine Song' to this carol, my situation being more like Famine than like Christmas:

> Remember Adam's fall,
> O thou Man:
> Remember Adam's fall
> from Heaven to hell.
> Remember Adam's fall;
> How he hath condemned all,
> In hell perpetual
> There for to dwell. . . .

So I was walking up and down the cell humming this carol of Thomas Hardy's and I never felt the time going till I heard the cell doors being opened and the cans being left out — door open, clang can, door open, clang can, and then a bit of walking up and down to and from the recess with their pots and the water they had washed their plates and knife and spoon with, and the screw shouting, 'Stand to your doors,' and they getting ready to go down to work for the afternoon, and I had my humming over by this time and my face serious again because it does not look the thing not to look unhappy in the nick, especially and they going to the trouble of putting you on Number One.

The screw then opened my door, and Browny came in for my containers.

' 'Ow goes it, Pad?' he smiled. 'You'll be getting a dinner tomorrow. A good one and all, beans and bacon.'

I looked sad at the water. 'I'll finish that water, Browny, in case I get thirsty later.'

Browny laughed. 'You can 'ave all the water you want, Paddy. Wait till I tell screw!' He spoke to the screw, who came up and looked in. He was a big old Cockney. He wasn't small and wiry the way they are supposed to be, but he wasn't a bad old bastard for all that.

'You can 'ave all the bleedin' water that's in the tap. Go

dahn, Browny, and fetch 'im up that diet can full!' He muttered in the door: 'Water. No one's deprivin' you, Taffy.'

'Paddy he is, sir,' said Browny, 'from Ireland.'

'Well, Paddy or Taffy or Jock is all bleedin' one to me. Go down and get him the bleedin' water.'

Browny came back and left me the diet can, the long bottom part, full of water, and I said, 'Thank you, Browny,' and, 'thank you, sir,' to the screw.

He just said, 'Don't thank me, thank the Lord,' and gave a bit of a laugh and banged out the door.

I drank a sup of the water when I heard them gone off down the stairs. I was going to have a walk up and down again till it was time to have a piss, and in that way make a break in the time till they come round with my tea-time bread and water. I had nothing to sit on, only the mat, and it was cold, with no jacket on, only my shirt, shorts, stockings, and slippers. It was dark and bleak and the bit of sky I could see was a dirty grey and that nearly dark, with a dead cold.

I walked up and down, and went back to putting an air to the whole carol and getting the other verses off by heart. I did, too.

> Remember God's goodnesse,
>   O thou Man:
> Remember God's goodnesse,
>   His promise made.
> Remember God's goodnesse;
> He sent His Son sinlesse
> Our ails for to redress;
>   Be not afraid!

I had a few drinks of water and pissed three times, and walked up and down, and though the cold was sharp, I'd have been colder if I'd not kept walking up and down. The light was dying, but not the day, more was the pity: the cold, black, hungry day stretched forward, and it was only four o'clock when the night came down and the cell was in pitch darkness.

Then I heard the chairs being shoved back and the fellows coming up the stairs from exercise. At least, I sighed, it was a good thing about getting another bit of bread at tea-time. But, Jesus, it was cold and dark, and my mind even was gone numb from the cold, and I couldn't think myself away any more for this December day. But I did another turn and walk up the floor, to keep things going some way.

'Paddy!'

There was a whisper at the spy-hole and I rushed over to it. Charlie had the cover up and his mouth to the glass.

'Hello, Charlie,' I whispered, 'how are you?'

'Not bad, kid, and yourself?'

'All right.'

'I'd 'ave worked some scoff for you, but I couldn't get near when Brown was bringing your bread and water.'

'I know that, kid. I'll take the will for the deed.'

'Old James ain't 'alf carved up. Those bastards will be dead frit of you. They won't take no liberties when you come out. James got seven stitches.'

'That was a pity — a pity he didn't get seventy bloody stitches.'

Charlie's lips parted in a smile at the spy-hole glass. 'You're a lad, Paddy, you are. See you tomorrow, kid.'

' 'Bye, Charlie.'

He whispered soft against the glass of the spy-hole, his lips close to it, ' 'Bye, Paddy,' then put his eye to it, winked, and slipped down the landing towards his own cell.

So I walked up and down again with more spring in my heel, and when Browny came with my four-ounce cob, the screw let me go down to the recess, where I used the lavatory, emptied my pot, and refilled my diet can with water for the night. Which meant that I would not have to shit in the cell, a thing to be feared between half past four in the afternoon and seven the next morning.

The screw switched my light on and I walked up and down, feeling better, while I ate my bread and took a drink of the water.

At eight o'clock the screw came and opened my door, and Jesus be praised, told me to take in my bed.

I got in the boards and mattress and blanket, and he banged out the door.

When I had the bed made down and got into it, wasn't I as good as anyone, tired from the walking and warm after the cold, and my day's chokey over me only for the breakfast, but, sure, wouldn't I appreciate the beans and bacon all the more?

I celebrated with a read of the book. I was well on to the end of it now, but I decided it was worth being reckless for once and read on, warm and happy, where they are all at the wedding and poor Thomas Leaf, an amádan, comes up and asks to be let in to the hooley. 'I washed and put on a clane shirt,' says Leaf, pleading like, not to kept out of the diversion.

'Let the poor bastard in,' says the Tranter, 'he's a bit silly-looking but I never heard he was in jail.' Sure, if he was itself, there was as good as ever he was in it.

But they let him anyway, and he tells a story, about a man that got a pound and then he got another pound and another one and another till, before Jesus, he had a thousand pound and such a half-arsed class of a story I never heard, but sure he was doing his best to oblige the company, and I fell asleep.

In the morning I ate my four-ounce cob and drank some water, and waited till dinner-time for the end of my sentence. I walked up and down the cell and was thinking of my beans and bacon when, at eleven o'clock or so, the screw came, opened my door and told me to bring in my furniture and put on my clothes. He asked me if I wanted to slop out and I went down and emptied the pot and had a shit in the recess, as I was there, and got a basin of water.

The screw banged out the door and I had a wash after I had put back my furniture. It was only when I had put out the furniture that I noticed how desolate the cell was without it.

At dinner-time I heard them marching in and clattering up the iron stairs and the next thing was the screw coming round with my *Daily Herald*, and in a minute or two I smelt the dinner, and heard the doors being opened again.

This time my door was opened like anyone else's and Browny handed me a hot diet can, with a grand smell off it.

'There you are, Paddy, lad.' He smiled like you'd think it was himself was getting it. The screw banged out the door and I put it on the table, and spread my *Daily Herald* back of my plate along the wall and got into my beans and bacon.

The beans and bacon were in the bottom long can of the diet cans and there was a cob of bread in the top shallow part. I ate it well, and it was salty and thick, and I drank more water after it.

I thought of going down to work after my dinner in the hall with the others. I did not think James would have the guts to say anything to me nor did I think that Dale would have the decency to do anything to me on James' behalf. Not for fear of me, but for fear of the screws. They would not be acting for love of me, but simply to keep the law. The others, Scouse bastards, would be frit of me, Charlie said, and that was a relief. Bigger and better IRA men than I had got very bad kickings in Dartmoor and Parkhurst when they were there in very small numbers, so it was no harm at all, at all, but a good investment of a day's Number One to scare these sportsmen.

I washed up my plate and tin knife and spoon, and was ready when they came round and opened my door for my descent to the hall.

I went down the stairs carrying my chair and got in a little before the rest, to a place beside the wall, where I could see all round me and where there was no one sitting in front of me.

Dale came on down the stairs and passed me, but didn't take much heed of me one way or another, beyond a look.

Then up the wing came James all dressed in white.

He had a bandage plastered to his cheek, and the two of his eyes were bruised and discoloured, I was happy to see. He looked over at where I was sitting, and I looked back, to be as good as what he was and not lose my hard-earned advantage.

Then he looked away from me and sat down beside Dale, at his usual place at the table.

Then the others came down and sat in their rows, and what happens but Charlie comes and puts his chair beside me.

' 'Ello, Pad.' He smiled and whispered.

'Good on you, Charlie,' said I, 'sit down. You're welcome.'

So the afternoon passed from two till a quarter past four, and we working off the one-hank of waxed end, and I was content enough, and better again when Charlie reminded me we were both for court in the morning.

I had *Under the Greenwood Tree* finished, but after doing my bit of stitching I had another look at the carol and muttered it to myself, and hummed it till the bell went and I got into bed and read over it again till they put the lights out, and I lay in the dark, happy and thinking about my trip to court in the morning, though too excited about it to go asleep till well after an hour, for I heard nine o'clock strike on the church bells in the city.

In the morning I was rushed down the stairs with my kit, my sheets and my towel and handkerchief, and told to stand at the foot of the stairs. I waited in line for the others. Two were fellows that were going out after doing a six months' and a nine-months' sentence, three were going to court, in Birkenhead and Preston; and there was Charlie and Ginger and myself going to court in Liverpool.

We came out of the reception in our own clothes, and stood at the Black Maria which was drawn up in the yard. But I was not put into this but brought away from Charlie and Ginger outside the gate and put into a police car on my own.

I was driven down to Dale Street, Bridewell, and locked in a cell there to wait for the court, but it was not like being there the first night I was brought in.

My sergeant came down and gave me a cigarette and introduced me to a chief inspector.

The chief inspector brought me out right into the street and, it dazes me to tell it, through the crowds and into a snack bar where he bought me a pork pie and a cup of tea.

He was called Chief Inspector Haines, and after I finished the tea and the pork pie we had another cup of tea and I smoked two cigarettes.

He told me he was in charge of my case, and then I remembered him. He was the one that did not like Roger Casement. I did not refer to this, however, and we hardly mentioned my case at all. He certainly did not ask for information. I think he gave me the tea and the pie and the bit of a walk up the city because he was a decent man. That it may be before him.

He brought me back to Dale Street and then I was taken out of my cell again and brought up to the court. The judge remanded me for another week and I was brought back to the cells.

In my cell I still had a smoke and walked up and down like a gent. Then others were brought down and I could hear doors opening and being banged locked, and Charlie shouted to Ginger and they both shouted at me, and we passed a couple of hours smoking and shouting till they came and put us in the Black Maria, to bring us back to the nick.

Charlie and Ginger and I were three chinas in the wagon and two other new kids even asked us what it was like in Walton, and though Charlie told them they'd bloody well find out when they got up there and nodded to Ginger and me, and we three nodded like old soldiers together at the new kids, I told them that it wouldn't be too bad, they'd get used to it.

And this time when the fat orderly came round the baths even Charlie laughed at his jokes and he gave us a bit of bread each off what the new receptions couldn't eat, and when we came back to the wing, dark and black as it was to us, it wasn't so dark or so frightening as it was to the new kids.

In the morning we saw the doctor and the Governor and the priest, like the other receptions, but they didn't delay us long. The Governor didn't even glance up at me. He only said, 'Remanded again.' And I said, 'Yes, sir,' and went out. The doctor was just as brief, and the priest didn't even glance at me, but nodded his head in a surly fashion, and then I went back to sit with the others sewing, my chair against the wall and Charlie sitting beside me.

The days were the same except Friday night, when the RCs had a religious instruction in the doctor's room. This was at half-past five in the night and everyone looked forward to it. Despite being excommunicated, I half-hoped I would be let go to it, and, sure enough, when they unlocked the doors on Friday night they unlocked mine with the others.

'Right, bring down your chair to the doctor's room,' said the screw without looking at me but going on to open the next door where he'd seen a red card.

I brought my chair down, and when I went to the doctor's room, there was a blazing fire in the grate, and the fellows all sitting with happy smiling faces round it. They moved their chairs back, quite friendly even to me, and a weedy-looking man with a mournful face came in. I heard the fellows say he was from the Liverpool Archdiocesan Legion of Mary.

I sat with the rest looking up at him and delighted to be there, and saying that maybe the priest wasn't such a bad sort after all, and was only trying to do what he thought right, when a hand tapped me on the shoulder and a screw spoke to me.

'Take your chair and get back up to your cell, Behan,' said he.

I looked at him and he said, 'Come on, look sharp, and get up when I tell you.'

I saw the others looking at me, took up my chair, put my head down so as they couldn't see my face, and went quickly from the room.

When I got into the wing I saw the priest looking into the room. I looked at him, stared at him, as I went past.

'Get on,' said the screw.

I went up the stairs and into my cell, and the screw banged out the door and went off down the stairs.

I sat down on the chair and leaned my head in my hands. I felt like crying for the first time in years, for the first time since I was a kid of four or five. I had often prayed after Mass at home that God would not let me lose the Faith. I thought of Sister Monica, the old nun that prepared me for my first Confession and Communion and Confirmation, and

Father Campbell, the old priest in Gardiner Street that I went to Confession to, and Christmas numbers of the little holy books we used to have at home. Never, never no more.

It was all ballocks.

One of the Fenian prisoners said the things you missed most in jail were babies, dogs and fires.

Wasn't I the soft eedgit all the same, to expect anything more off that fat bastard of a druid? Weren't the priests famous for backing up the warders even the time of the Fenians? When Dr Gallagher was driven mad in Chatham Prison.

But I wouldn't always be inside, and if I could do the like of Father Lane an ill turn in my turn, by Jesus and I'd be the boy to do it.

Let them come to me some time at home with their creeping Jesus old gab, I'd say to them: what about this night in Walton Jail, you bastards?

Twice more Charlie and Ginger and I went down. We enjoyed the run down, and the smoking in the cells and in the Black Maria coming back, and telling new blokes what it was like, and being welcomed by the fat bloke in the reception and slipping him a dog-end and getting a bit of extra bread off him that the receptions couldn't eat, and looking over at each other and laughing as we soaped ourselves in the bath standing up, and then lying down full length in it, and resting ourselves, and coming up and going straight into kip, till at last we were all returned for trial at Liverpool Assizes, and it was the week before Christmas and we had six weeks to wait, till the first week in February.

The librarian was not an undecent sort, and brought me books by Dickens that I had asked for. It was not much good asking for modern authors because they did not have any. It was my belief they bought the books for the prison by weight. I once got a *Chums* annual for 1917 and a Selfridge's furniture catalogue for my non-fiction or educational book. But when I explained to the librarian that I could not read the Selfridge's furniture catalogue and that I had had the *Chums* before, which was not true, he changed them for me. He gave *The Mayor of Casterbridge* by Hardy and *The Moonstone* by Wilkie Collins.

'Irishman, eh, Paddy? Ever 'ear of Michael Collins?' asked the screw. Michael Collins gave my mother a five-pound note on O'Connell Bridge, a few months before I was born, when my father was locked up by his government. But I didn't tell the screw that. I only smiled, and nodded. 'And this 'ere book — by an Irishman — Ballock is 'is name — must say they got funny names in your country, Paddy — well I couldn't find *The Life Savers* so I brought you another one of 'is.'

I thanked him and when I was locked up, had a look at the book. It was by Shan F. Bullock. 'Shan', I supposed, was some gammy way of spelling 'Seán — like Shaun and Shane. But it was Irish all right.

'Aw, ay,' he said and slouched up wiping the wet from his hand on his corduroys; 'aw, ay; it'll follow ye safe to Clogheen anyhow. Good-bye and God speed you!'

At home on the corner of the North Circular Road we used to make a jeer of that Abbey Theatre bogman talk. 'Oh, woman of the roads, be not putting it on me now.' 'With your long arm, and your strong arm, be after pulling me a pint of porther.'

But I was delighted to read it here, in this cold kip.

The book was short stories and called *Ring o' Rushes*, and was all about the North of Ireland. The other book when I got it, which I did, was called not *The Life Savers* but *The Loughsiders*.

I went out every day and Charlie and Ginger and I walked behind each other at smoking exercise, and worked near each other at labour. I got my paper every day and the *News of the World* on Sundays. James said nothing to me (his face was a bit scarred where it was completely healed), and neither did anyone else say anything to me. I was brought down once more to the instruction on Friday night, but it was a mistake again and I was brought back to my cell, and then I saw a notice in the office at the top of the wing saying that 3501 Behan was not to attend the RC religious instruction on Friday nights. I still went to Mass and Benediction on

Sundays because it was compulsory and because it passed the time.

The smoking was the big part of the day.

We remands and awaiting trials were called out from the others, the convicted boys who looked at us, licking their lips, and sometimes signalled to us to try and bring in a butt for them.

This was nearly impossible. Though a couple of times Charlie and I got in a little dimp for Browny. He was out of his mind for a smoke all the time. But it was very dangerous and difficult.

Sometimes, though, we succeeded in breaking a bit off the top of a cigarette, and then, instead of getting a light off the screw, we got our light off one of the boys who was already lit, put the bit we'd broken off in our handkerchief and had the end of the cigarette to hand up when we had it smoked. These butts were put in a bucket of water, which, when we were finished exercise, was brought into the wing and flushed down the lavatory. Sometimes the cistern did not flush properly and the butts floated back on the surface.

Dale's cell was just beside this recess and it was understood that he got these butts. He was the daddy of the wing and what he claimed was his. He collected these butts when we finished labour and put them on the sill of the window where there was a little hole, and left them there to dry.

Sometimes if a fellow went to fall out in the middle of labour, after the screw had emptied the dog-end bucket into the lavatory, and saw them floating, he would whisper to Dale when he came back, and Dale would fall out himself a minute or two later and go down and collect them and put them out to dry.

The orderly on the bottom floor used to watch out for the screw leading in the bloke with the bucket and he'd nip in and flush the lavatory, and slip out again, so that when the screw came up, and told the prisoner to empty the butt bucket into the lavatory and flush the chain, the cistern would be empty. Sometimes the screw would come back and flush it when it had refilled but, for that again, he'd sometimes leave it go with the butts floating there. Then the orderly would nip down and tell Dale and might be rewarded with one himself when the butts were dried. In any event Dale was the daddy, and blokes would like to be doing things for him, to keep on the right side of him.

One morning Dale's butts were knocked off. When he got down to the window and put his finger out of the hole they were not there. The word went round the mailbag class as we worked, and everyone shivered a bit. I was even glad that I was a remand and that Charlie was one. Everyone wondered who'd taken the dog-ends.

The orderly came down from his cleaning to whisper and swear before Jesus as he stood at Dale's table, letting on to be sweeping up bits of canvas, that he did not and he knew not.

I had a good idea who did. There were four orderlies who were working in the wing all day; one on each of the four landings. The only one of them that did much wandering in a general way was Browny, and the day before when Charlie and I told him we were sorry we hadn't been able to nick a bit off the cigarette for him at remands smoking exercise, he only smiled and said it was all right, thanks, that he'd got a bit of snout.

Where did he get it? I looked over at Dale's glowering face, when I stooped to pick up a bit of wax-end, and shivered a bit myself. Poor Browny. It could be worse. It could be me. But still, poor little Browny. He was like a little Teddy Bear, and as innocent.

When we finished at four o'clock I saw Dale pack up his things at the table very quickly and go up the iron stairs to our landing. I went up the stairs just after him. I always made to get locked up in the cell since I had the bundle with James, but I thought too that I might have a chance of warning Browny that Dale was going to put it on him, but I was too late.

I heard a commotion from the recess, and I heard Browny's voice, pleading and then crying. I stood with my chair and my cell-task canvas and didn't know which to do first, but went on to my own cell and left in my chair and canvas and wax-end, and then came down towards the recess; and before I got there I saw Dale come quickly down the landing towards the stairs.

I went into the recess and it was dark and I couldn't see Browny, but then I heard his moans coming from the lavatory, from behind the half-door. I swung it open and there he was, trying to lift his head out of the lavatory bowl. His shorts were all slashed to ribbons and covered in blood.

Ah, Mother of Jesus, I was sorry I went up first with my chair and canvas to my cell, that I had gone up there first and not come down and done something to save him. That was the time he was carved up, and I didn't come down, but waited till I'd left my chair into my cell because I was afraid I'd be carved up. There's a fearless rebel for you.

I lifted him, put my arms under him, and carried him out to the head of the stairs, where the screw would see me without having to shout for him, or interfere in the matter any more than I could help.

Johnston came up the stairs and we carried him to the doctor's room and laid him on the couch, face downwards.

We took off the seat of his pants in blood-soaked strips and the blood still pouring from him.

He kept his hand over his face and moaned. It was trying to protect his face he was, and stuck it in the lavatory, and Dale just slashed away with a razor blade wherever he could.

When the medical orderly arrived and took over, Johnston asked me what I knew about it.

I said I knew nothing; I heard screaming, ran down to the recess and saw Brown lying there moaning.

Johnston nodded and said he would see about that, whether I was telling the truth. The others were all in their cells, locked up for the night, and he came outside with me and saw me go up the stairs into my cell and bang out my door.

The next morning I was brought before the Governor as a witness.

Dale was standing in front of the desk and it was easy to see that the night had not passed easily over him.

I still swore holes through pewter pots that I had not seen

the attack on Browny, and knew nothing about it beyond finding him with his head in the lavatory pan and his backside all blood.

The Chief Officer, from the far side of the desk, nodded to the Governor and roared at me to get out. I marched outside and waited till I was told I was not required any more and sent back to my place sewing mailbags.

Later we all looked up and from under our eyes saw Dale marching between two screws down to the punishment cells.

Johnston came back in charge of the mailbags, and after the Governor had gone we heard thumps and moans coming faintly from below stores, from chokey.

The Principal Officer, a thin wafer-shaven man, erect, slim and spotless and beribboned, turned his old eyes to Johnston, cocked his ear to the moaning with the air of a connoisseur, smiled and murmured appreciatively, 'Someone getting a clean shirt, Mr Johnston?'

A clean shirt was the beating they sometimes gave a prisoner beginning his punishment. They told him to strip and then when he had his clothes half-off, they would accuse him of resisting the search, beat him, baton him on the kidneys, and on the thighs.

Our PO was most feared. Now that he was no longer young and active enough to lead the fray, he waited till the prisoner was stripped naked by the other screws. Then he would catch him by the ballocks and twist and pull on them. Putting his weight and swinging down out of them, not abusing the prisoner or angry but rather the reverse, grunting and saying softly, 'All right, all right, now, it will be over in a minute.' Grunting and perspiring with the effort. 'There, there, it will soon be over.'

It usually was — the bloke passing out. They never hit a prisoner on the face, but on the rest of him which would only be seen by the prison doctor. Extras such as our POs performance were reserved for people with a good long bit of time to do. Even if the prisoner was ruptured, nobody would know, except prison officials, warders, prison doctors, and clergymen.

The moaning from below grew fainter, and then stopped.

The PO smiled, and the prisoners smiled to see the old man in such good humour.

James smiled at his new companion on the table.

During the morning, Johnston called down to me, 'Paddy, come up and collect a letter.'

I smiled and was as delighted to be called 'Paddy' as to get the letter.

Charlie and Ginger and I went out with the others to smoking exercise.

Charlie got his light off mine and I reddened it to give him a better light, and he looked up at me, smiled and said, 'Thanks, Pad.'

'That's OK, kid,' said I, and when we marched round, I went behind him studying the back of his head where the hair finished on the smoothness of his neck.

Now I began to get letters from Ireland wishing me a 'happy Christmas'.

It was coming up to that in a hurry.

There was a blizzard in Christmas week and on the Saturday afternoon, I was sitting in my cell after exercise trying to keep myself warm with my legs in a mailbag. They served the supper early on Saturday, at three-thirty sometimes, and you would be in two minds about it. It was great to get it as soon as possible because you were ravenously hungry, not to mind cold, but for that again it meant that by seven o'clock you were starving again, and by eight you were that bad that it was hard to sleep.

There were some blokes that didn't read much or didn't know how to, and they passed the time as long as there was any light at all in the sky looking out their windows. They had to stand up on their table to do this, the window being that high that they couldn't have seen out of it otherwise.

If the screw sneaked round in his slippers and caught them, they might get a report and a day or two on Number One. But most of the screws did not bother much and sometimes the prisoners at the windows carried on shouted conversations with each other.

Some of the prisoners would interrupt these conversations by shouting, 'Can't you blokes never quit nattering?' as if they were genuinely annoyed by people shouting, which I do not believe they were. Even when I was reading myself, I enjoyed the noise of voices, and listened sometimes to the conversations. It saved a couple of pages of book anyway.

I never went in for conversations myself, even with Charlie, who was only beside me because my accent stuck out and the others would shout, 'Kip in, you dirty Irish bastard,' as they did once or twice.

Besides, if I had a book at all, I'd sooner read.

Sometimes two chinas from the same district or town

would start off a conversation and get really into it, and as they knew the same places and even the same people, it was worth listening to.

But then some fellow was sure to shout out, 'Kip in there, you bastards,' in an angry tone, and the conversation would be spoiled and end up in an exchange of abuse with the interrupter. 'Kip in yourself, you bloody puff,' one of the conversationalists would shout and the interrupter would answer, 'I'll do you, you bastard, at exercise, see if I don't, you shit'ouse.'

'Get stuffed, you bloody puff.'

Compliments pass when the quality meet.

The interrupter would be only shouting to hear his own voice and also there were prisoners who seemed to delight in hearing of other prisoners being punished, and would shout as if they agreed with the silence rule. In another way it was a safe way of breaking the silence.

The rows carried on from the windows were never even remembered when we all came out again, to work or exercise.

This blizzard went on all during Christmas week, and on Saturday the place was under a deep fall of snow and we could not use the exercise yards.

We were glad of this because it was torture to walk round with only a jacket and shorts.

We were wondering up to this what we might get for Christmas, and some fellows thought we might get a concert or something but we began to understand that it would be nothing but a hell of a long weekend. There was to be duff on Christmas Day, but that did not make up for a weekend of one Saturday, a Sunday; a Christmas Day, and a Stephen's Day, all days when we would be deprived of getting down to work in the hall, which to us was like a busy street in the city with people going up and down to Governor's and doctor's, and doors with people going up and down and fellows coming in and going out to court and being brought up before the Governor and down to chokey and fellows being called to the doctor, and you could look up from your sewing and, provided you didn't start talking, there was no law against you enjoying all this, and a bit of noise of doors opening, and screws shouting, 'One away, sir.' 'two on to you, sir,' unlike these dreary four days, which stretched in front of us like a jail sentence, as a person might say outside.

They only gave us half our usual exercise time, walking round the landings, and then we were locked up for the day, at dinner-time. The dinner was the usual Saturday's dinner, a piece of bully beef, which we liked, two cold, bad potatoes, and a piece of bread.

I ate mine. The potatoes and bread didn't go well together, so I ate the potatoes first, and then put the piece of bully beef on the bread and ate that with a drink of water.

It was dark in the cell, and after I washed up, I sat at the table and listened to what few noises there were going on. The fellows had not got up to the windows yet, because a screw was going round the RC's cells and seeing if they wanted to go to Confession.

I'd have liked to have gone on account of Christmas-time, even apart from the walk with the other blokes to the chapel, but being excommunicated I could not.

Nearly all the others went, and the screw came round to all the cells with red cards, and when he came to mine he looked in and said, 'Going to Confession?' but then he recognized me and muttered something and went off to the next cell with a red card at it.

That fat bastard of a priest. I chewed my lips to myself when I heard the others all going down the stairs like free men.

Then the blokes got up to the windows.

It was too dark to read and anyway, I wanted to save all the reading I could for these four days, and there was a bit of white light in the sky and the snow coming, and I decided the screws might be a bit easy on us even if they caught us, it being the day before Christmas Eve, so I pulled over my table and got up.

And as well that I did.

Our Chief Officer, the stocky cruel-faced turkey-toed bastard, walks out with his glare and his strut, looking round and down at the snow, and up at the windows, five tiers of them in a square round the yard, in dead silence, and he knowing we were looking at him, and he glaring up at the barred windows, and some near me, though they must have known he could not have seen them at that distance, got down in fear. But I did not, thank God that I did not, and those that got down must have been cutting their throats a minute later, for the next thing is, the Chief Officer, with his red-faced glare and his strut, walks clean off the steps and into six foot of snow.

He floundered and was lost in it, there was even hope he'd smother in it, and oh, Jesus, what a shout went up from all the windows. What delight, what joy, and as a bonus on it, didn't the old bastard, when he struggled up a step, shake his fists in anger and fall down again, and the boys roared from the windows so that the screws came rushing out, thinking we'd all broken loose, and they shouted at us to get down from the windows, even as they helped the Chief up, covered in snow, and brushing himself while we roared, till the screws came rushing into the wings and round the landings, and we jumped down double-quick before they'd look in our spy-holes and catch us.

I sat down again at my table, and was thankful to God and His Blessed Mother for this.

If I had gone to Confession, I'd have missed it, and I was consoled. God never closes one door but He opens another, and if He takes away with His right hand, He gives it back with His left, and more besides.

The next day we went to Mass and had our exercise walking round the landings, and had our usual Sunday dinner, which was good, and the fellows talked a lot up at the windows but the screws did not bother them, and they talked away till they heard the supper coming round at half three.

It was even a bit earlier than usual, I heard an orderly saying, to give the screws a chance to get off early.

The RCs had no Benediction in the evening on account of having it the next day, and it made that Sunday a bit long.

I got a bit hungry at six o'clock or so and drank some water and walked up and down till eight o'clock, when I went to bed with the bell.

I had a bit of a read till they put the lights out, and then, thinking that at least half the four days were over, went asleep.

I met Charlie in the recess and we wished each other a 'happy Christmas'.

All the blokes wished each other a 'happy Christmas', quiet-like so as the screws wouldn't hear them talking; it would not do to go too far on Christmas morning.

We banged out our doors and washed ourselves, waiting for the breakfast being brought up.

When they came to my door, I heard one of them saying that I was an RC and would not be getting my breakfast till after church service. This was on account of most of the RCs going to Communion, and I was going to say out through the spy-hole that I was not going and was to get my breakfast in the usual way, when I heard the screws saying to the orderly that I was not allowed to go to anything like that and that I was getting my breakfast with the rest.

He opened my door and asked, 'You're not for Communion, are you?'

'No, sir,' said I.

'Well, 'ere's your breakfast then!' He was a nice old bloke for that morning anyway and added, 'anyway, Paddy, you get your scoff now and don't 'ave to wait an hour and 'alf for it.'

I took it from him and thanked him and he banged out the door. I always like breakfasts and I always like mornings, and the old screw trying to be nice to me and put me in good humour.

When the RCs fell in for Mass, the boy beside me whispered that we would see Dale that morning. Be God and so we will, said I to myself, sitting up with the chokey blokes in front, and I heard the boys saying along the line that he would be there to be seen and we'd see how the chokey was affecting him.

We marched out of the wing and had to cross a yard but the snow was glittering white in the sunshine and the sky was blue.

We went in our seats and sat down while the rest of the chapel filled up. At the back of us were old men and younger ones, doing every sort of sentence from seven days to fifteen years, and they all kind of smiled at each other, for it being Christmas.

When all the other seats were filled up and five or six hundred men in the chapel, the chokey merchants were marched into the very front seats and separated from the ones behind them by an empty row. They were all on either Number One, bread and water; or Number Two, bread and water with porridge and potatoes at midday. They had been in chokey, some of them, for five months, and some of them had not been out of the punishment cells to Mass during that time. They seemed to appreciate being brought out today, and looked neither to right nor left as they came in but sat right down and looked straight ahead at the altar.

All the prisoners looked white by comparison with the screws, but these prisoners from chokey were Persil white by comparison with the other prisoners.

The YPs gave each other tiny nudges when we picked out Dale amongst the other prisoners from chokey. He seemed to have forgotten us, or how he'd sat back in the seat previous Sundays, and just looked straight in front like the others from chokey.

The priest came out and the chokey prisoners were the first and quickest on their knees. We all got down to it, and knelt till the sermon, when we stood for the gospel and sat down to listen to the priest.

He started off telling us that the greeting was not peace and goodwill to men on earth, but peace on earth to men of goodwill, and went on to say that Christmas was a time of prayer as well as a time for enjoying yourself.

'It is not for us, as it is for thoughtless people outside the Church, or for those who have forgotten the very significance of Christ's Mass, just a time for feasting, a mere Bank Holiday. True, we rejoice, as Christians should, at the birth of our Divine Lord, and welcome Him, with the gifts of a good Confession and Communion, as did the Three Kings of the East. I mean they welcomed Him with gifts, too. Not with the Sacraments, which were yet to be instituted, but with gifts. I use the word in its symbolic sense. And while not as the lantern-jawed Calvinist, that tried to eradicate from this England of ours the very memory of the feast, that generation of gloom, as the great Chesterton called them. Himself, Chesterton, a great man in all senses of the word, a fat man, jolly in God, as sound a judge of beer as he was of theology. We make rejoicing, and think with love all the time even as we break the crackling of the goose, even as we savour the tender white meat of the turkey.'

The chokey merchants in the front seats never took their eyes off the priest, and he looked kindly back at us all, and went on with the sermon.

'As we pour the sauce over that homely symbol of our own dear Christian land, the plum pudding, heavy, dark, rich and laden rarely with fruits of sunnier climes, Spain usually, and Italy, and while we enjoy the wine, as Christians should for, as I think it was Belloc remarked, it was given us in the first miracle, and liqueurs are to this day made by Carthusians, Dominicans, Benedictines and if I may mention, in this our own dear land, at Buckfast, the monks make a good wine, but, here he smiled and we smiled with him, 'in accordance with what I suppose is the traditionally more austere tradition of this, called by William Shakespeare, whom, as you know, lived and died in the Old Faith, "sceptered isle" for medicinal purposes only. Or as we pour ourselves a foaming glass of ale, and draw on our cigar—'

The prisoners drew their breath in unison with the preacher, and some of the fellows on punishment swallowed and rubbed their mouths with the backs of their hands.

'—we do so, remembering the great love God bore us, love that brought down this day to Mary, ever blessed Virgin, conceived without sin, and to Joseph, her most chaste spouse, a little child to die for our salvation on a wooden Cross, nailed and crucified to show His love for us.'

He looked serious here and we looked serious with him.

'Love as deep as the deepest ocean, as wide as the farthest horizon. Many of you have been mariners and you know how wide that is.'

We all looked round, and the screws did too at prisoners nodding in agreement all over the chapel, even some of the chokey prisoners nodded. They didn't nod to the rest of us, but only to each other, who had been mariners, and up at the priest, who nodded back, and went on with the sermon.

'A tender love, a forgiving love, the love of a father for his children, the love of brother for brother, and in that spirit and in that love, to those of you who are of goodwill, I wish a holy and happy Christmas.'

The organ struck up a hymn, then, and we all joined in:

> 'See amid the winter's snow,
> Born for us, on earth below,
> See the tender Lamb appear,
> Promised from eternal year.'

The chokey merchants left the chapel first, filing out of the door, looking neither right nor left, for their morning bread and water. The rest of us waited until they were gone and then we went back to our wings.

It was still very cold and the snow heavy on the ground but bright and clean to look at, just for the minute we were marching across the yard to our wing.

We got our smoking exercise in the end of the wing away from the others. There had been rumours that everyone was getting five Woodbines to smoke that day, the convicted and all, but when the convicted saw us remands and awaiting trials being called away to smoke separate from them, they knew that they were getting no smoke.

I walked round behind Charlie, and we smiled at each other, and when he got a chance to whisper he said that maybe next month we'd have been weighed off at the Assizes and be in Borstal.

Well, we had the Assizes to look forward to. It was a big day out, sometimes a couple of days, if your case went on, or if you were not called the first day, and you got tea and bully sandwiches. Sometimes they made a kind of pasty made with the bully and it was called Sessions' Pie.

Yes. I smiled a bit and whispered to Charlie that from this

good day it would be getting better, instead of worse, and we could smell the dinner coming up, and it smelt great.

It was as good as its smell. Usually the screws shouted out, 'Bang out your doors' the minute we took the diet can off the tray, but this day I took my diet can into the cell, put it on the table, and banged out the door.

In the top shallow tier of the can were three lovely golden-brown roasted potatoes with chopped green vegetable and in the long part was roast meat, a piece of Yorkshire pudding, at least that's what I thought it was, and gravy, and all roasting hot with steam running in pearls down the side of the can.

I was looking at it with delight and already had it eaten with my eyes when the screw came back to the cell.

'Don't you want your duff?'

He turned to someone else on the landing outside and said, 'Paddy, 'ere, 'e doesn't want 'is duff,' and went to walk off.

'I do, I do,' I shouted, and hoping to Christ he would not go off.

But he'd only been joking, and opened the door. It was the old Cockney, and there was a great smell of beer off him. He smiled as he handed me my duff and poured custard on it from a ladle.

'There you are, Paddy. That'll put 'air on your chest. We was forgetting all about you, we was.' He smiled again and nodded to the orderly to take up the tray and can of custard.

'A happy Christmas to you, sir,' said I, on an impulse of liking.

He looked at me for a second and then said, 'And the same to you, son, and many of 'em.'

I banged out the door and got out the dinner on the plate. It lay hot and lovely, the roast potatoes, the Yorkshire pudding, the chopped greens and the meat, and a big piece of bread to pack up with, and it wasn't long before I had it finished, and the plate clean (not that I left anything on it) for the duff and custard.

And then the door opened again and the screw gave me the *News of the World*. I'd forgotten that the day before was

Sunday. He just threw it in the cell to me, and banged out the door again.

Ah, better again, said I to myself, opening the paper; this is making a good day yet.

But after I heard the bells of the city strike three I knew we were not getting any more exercise, and I put down the paper to save a bit of a read for the night. It was getting too dark to read anyway, so I put down the paper and thought I'd walk up and down for a bit. But it was so cold that I didn't want to take off my shoes, so I just sat there crouched up on the chair leaning on the table, hugging into myself to get a bit of heat.

They brought round the supper about a quarter to four and it warmed me up for a while, and I decided I'd go to bed, for they'd hardly come round now till eight o'clock. I lay in bed after I'd eaten my supper and drunk my cocoa, and was warm, anyway.

I thought of home and my family sitting round the fire in Dublin, where there were forty hearths that would welcome me but, to tell the truth, I only thought of them because I thought it was what I should do, in my situation; and it was only for a moment I went on thinking of them, and then I came back here to my cell in the cold, and at least they had put the light on at tea-time so I had another read of the *News of the World*, but the light was in my eyes, and it was cold on my arms outside the blankets, so I put the paper down, and my hands inside the bedclothes, and must have fallen asleep, for the next thing I remember was doors opening and being banged out and the prisoners shouting.

Jesus, they must be making all the fellows get up till eight o'clock, I thought, and that maybe the bastards would report me to the Governor if I was caught in bed. The screw, whoever he was, was coming nearer and, by Christ, the fellows were getting very defiant all of a sudden, shouting and cursing: 'Fugh off, you rotten bastard.' . . . 'Fugh off . . .'

Jesus, what was happening? I struggled, standing on the cold slate floor, to get my shorts on. I'd never get the bed up in time. But if the others were ballocking the screw, I'd be as good as the rest anyway.

Charlie's door I heard being banged, and he shouting, 'Arn
. . . you bastard . . .' and then my own door opened.

Christ, what's this? A small, rat-faced screw never said
yes, aye, or no about the bed being made down or anything
else, but he handed me an envelope and looked at me, with
little nervous eyes, and banged out the door and went on to
the next cell.

I opened the envelope and found in it a card. It was not
personally addressed to me but 'a prisoner', and wished me
a happy and holy Christmas and blessings in the New Year
from the General of the Salvation Army.

'Ah, you bastard,' I shouted after the screw, 'stuff you and
him,' just in time to hear the next fellow let a roar and a string
of curses after the screw, while he went on his rounds
delivering his greetings.

Nearly every cell that he threw a card into, he got shouts
and curses from it in return, a thing I had never heard in
Walton before, but sweet Jesus, the dirty little bastard, was
it coming to make a jeer of us altogether he was?

I put the General's Christmas card convenient to where I'd
be using it in the morning and got back into bed again.

For there was no reason to believe that that screw would
be coming back to get us out of bed, barring he was coming
back to case us all for the Governor in the morning, so fugh
him and his happy Christmas. I'd have committed a sin with
myself, only I was too indignant to get my mind concentrated, so I just lay in bed and fell asleep again.

The next day, Stephen's Day, or Boxing Day as they called
it here, we had no church services but, in compensation I
suppose we had work in the afternoon, and went down and
sewed mailbags in the hall together, till four o'clock just as
any other day. So we went into our cells that night and ate
our supper and drank our cocoa, glad to know that this
bloody Christmas lark was over and next day was an ordinary
day, with blokes going up and down to court and all.

And the next day was an ordinary day like any other, and
we passed on to New Year's Day without noticing it.

New Year's Day everyone was in great humour for one
reason and another. Some of the convicted because they could

say 'I'm going out this year,' others because they could say 'I'm going out next year,' and Charlie and I were glad because we would be going down to the Assizes and be in Borstal in a few weeks' time.

One of the LRs was a fellow called Littlewood. He had been in chokey since shortly after Charlie and Ginger came into the nick, and we had no chance of seeing him till the day after New Year's Day when he came up.

I had often heard the others talk about him.

Dale, or that other bastard, James, or any of the other LRs, if they were asked what it was like in Borstal, they'd try and frighten us with stories of what the screws would do to us, and worse still, with stories of the way receptions were 'salted', with their shorts taken down and all manner of stuff rubbed on or poured over them.

Littlewood didn't tell us anything like that. We had a great chat with him, on bath-day, the week he came back to the wing.

Littlewood was twenty and married. We thought he was as old as the Hills of Tullow. The screw hated him because, in a quiet way, he mucked them about. He had been in jails all his life and didn't like coppers or screws.

He started knocking off because he had no work, and then, even when there was, he didn't like work, never having had the habit of it. Dale and James and the other LRs were kind of afraid of him and they would try and speak to him but he'd only smile and make no answer.

Dale came back up from chokey the day after Littlewood and didn't look any the better of it. It was too good for him to be looking, the bastard, if he looked twice as ill. He wasn't finished with the charge of slashing Browny. It would be brought up when he went before the Commissioner about his Borstal Licence being revoked. He and James got together again at the table, but had not got so much impudence and making little of the rest of us, as before.

Charlie and Ginger and I were getting used to the nick and as leery as anyone, now, but we listened to Littlewood with interest when he told us about Borstal, in the bath-house.

'Littlewood, can you talk in Borstal?' he was asked.

' 'Course you can talk in Borstal. Talk your bleeding 'ead off if you want.' Except, he said, for the Silent Hour, when you had to sit in the dining hall reading a book or writing a letter, or else doing nothing but be quiet. Littlewood laughed and said that even at this period you could shove your head in your hands and think about the last bit of crumpet you had outside. That was, he added, if any us pink arses had ever had a bit, which he doubted.

Littlewood laughed again. I suppose because he was married at sixteen and had two children. He had been put in chokey for throwing a can of porridge at a screw that got leery with him, but to the rest of the prisoners, especially the younger ones like Charlie and Ginger and me, he was always decent and good-humoured.

Towards the end of January, there was an appeal by the two Irishmen that had been sentenced to death at Birmingham before Christmas. I knew the man that had planted the bomb and it was neither of the men that had been sentenced. But that would not matter very much to the English. The men that had most to do with it were back home in Ireland, but all would happen would be that the judge would say that all prejudice must be put out of your mind to the jury and after informing the men in the dock that they were getting justice in England the like of which you would get no place else, they would be sentenced to death, as they were.

I could see the logic of saying to any IRA man, 'You may not be the one that planted this bomb, but you have planted others and anyway you are all in this conspiracy together and if we can't get the ones that caused this explosion you'll bloody well do as well as the next, whether you knew they were not going to let this bomb off at such a time and at such a place or not.'

I could see the logic of it, even if they applied it to myself, which God forbid — I considered my present ration of suffering quite adequate — but where any country might do that — and the Irish in the Civil War had no room to talk about death sentences — only England would shove on all this old insulting hypocrisy and tell you in the next breath that they were desperately careful that every foreigner the world over should know that justice had been done according to law.

Their appeal was dismissed and the screws were more barefaced than the judges.

'We're going to top those two bastards in Birmingham all right,' said Johnston one morning when he opened my door.

I didn't answer him. The prisoner carrying the slop bucket came up behind him.

'You know — your two pals,' said Johnston. 'Old Pierry will give them harps and shamrocks.' He looked round at the orderly and laughed. 'Another martyr for old Ireland — eh?'

I just emptied my slop into the bucket and stared straight into the prisoner's eyes. He was a fellow called Shaw from Cheshire and I know he didn't fancy me much, so I stared at him for a minute, daring him more or less to join in a free laugh with Johnston. But the bastard didn't, but just looked down and said nothing.

The belting I gave James was the best day's work I'd ever done. These grey days of the New Year were getting longer and brighter and I was like a man gaining money with each day that brought me towards the spring, towards the Assizes and towards Borstal, where I would get leave to talk, work in the fields, and see the sun and the sky.

I was getting more independent of the shouts of the screws, and they were getting more used to me, and the prisoners were easy in their mind that if they got it up for me too much, I'd carve them up just as quick as I did James.

James now got nearly polite to me, though his face was scarred faintly from where I'd caught him with the palm, and I was polite enough to him when I had to go to the table.

Dale sat with him just as before and said nothing to me either. He was a quiet man since he came out of chokey and was waiting now for the Borstal Commissioner who would take his attack on Browny into account when he appeared before him to see about finishing his licence period.

Browny we had not seen since. He was still over in the hospital and would be there till he went to Chester Assizes. He was already returned as recommended for Borstal and when he was formally sentenced he would be transferred straight from the hospital to Borstal.

I sewed on at work-time and we had started to go out in the yard for our exercise. Charlie and I were contented enough, and so was Ginger. But to save myself trouble and not embarrass Charlie, I kept my head down these last days of January and did not say much, or put myself forward in any way.

Since the appeals of the two men at Birmingham had been refused there was a lot on the papers about it. It was on my *Daily Herald* and on the *News of the World*. They had begun sending the Irish papers from home, but I got a couple with mention of the condemned men and then they stopped.

There was great agitation in Ireland, with marching and demonstrations, and in America the Irish were furious and had asked Roosevelt to intervene. But here they were regarded as worse than murderers and it was the best of my play to keep easy and say nothing.

The screws started at me about them, and saying that every IRA bastard should get the rope, that it was too good for them, and that they should be given out to the people of Coventry. The screws began saying, too, that the lags in Dartmoor had kicked the shit out of IRA men, and were nearly telling the prisoners here that they would not mind if they gave me a kicking.

So I looked round me carefully at exercise in case they'd jump on me and give a kicking, and Charlie still walked in front or behind me, though they said things an odd time to him, too, and not very choice things either, but as much as to say that there was more in it than us just being chinas. He just walked round near me and at smoking exercise smiled quietly at me when we went for a light. Ginger said nothing one way or another.

There was one thing. That I was safe inside the wing. Old Dodd the PO would never let them give me a kicking. Not because for the pain it would cause me but for the pleasure it would give them.

On the 29th of January we were brought down to the Assizes. There was a whole crowd of us in a bus, handcuffed

117

and chained, on two long chains that ran the length of the bus. Ginger and Charlie and I were in a back seat squeezed up together. I was wearing the blue suit I'd been arrested in, and Ginger was wearing his sports coat and flannels and Charlie was wearing his sailor's uniform. He looked real grown-up and more sure of himself in it. I suppose we all did in our ordinary clothes. The shorts in the YP wing made us look like kids; like Boy Scouts.

One of the grown-up prisoners heard my accent and asked if I knew Mountjoy Jail in Dublin. I said that I knew plenty that had been in it, but had never been there myself. This man was Irish, and said he knew some of our blokes in the jail. I thought he was friendly but then he said: 'A miserable lot of bastards. They had plenty of snout and scoff but never gave us poor bleeders any of it. They wouldn't parade with the ordinary prisoners — thought they were too good for us.'

I did not believe what he said about the IRA prisoners not giving any cigarettes to the others, for it was notoriously well known that they were very generous in that way and, in fact, it had been argued by the Minister for Justice in debates in the Dail that their generosity to the other prisoners with tobacco was an excuse for not letting the politicals have any.

As an Irishman I'm quite sure he understood their position in demanding separate treatment from ordinary prisoners. I was certain he was only saying these things to keep in with the other prisoners and with the screws, and so as they would not hold it against him for being an Irishman.

I turned back to Charlie and Ginger and didn't answer him or have anything further to say to him. I could understand why he didn't want to suffer for Ireland or the IRA, but I did not see why the yellow-born bastard should use me as a sort of sounding board for his hunker-sliding to the English.

In the coach it was like an excursion. The screws gave out their cigarettes to the prisoners, and even gave me a packet of twenty Gold Flake out of my property. We smoked and talked as the coach went down to the city. The screws smoked with the adult prisoners and gave them lights, and were as friendly as a crowd of men on a building job or in a factory.

They didn't address any remarks to us YPs, but let us smoke and we talked amongst each other. I talked to Charlie and Ginger.

Nobody was saying anything to me one or another till this shoneen — Irish bastard — brought it up about the IRA. Then the screws and the adult prisoners began talking about the two men under sentence of death at Birmingham and all found it a great point of agreement that they should be hanged, and every other IRA prisoner with them. I pretended not to take this as a personal matter and said nothing but went on talking to Charlie and Ginger. Ginger went on talking to me, as well as Charlie.

'Bloody lot of murderers,' said one of the YPs. I looked over to see who it was, and saw it was Shaw. He was a shrivelled-up-looking bastard from outside Birkenhead and was appearing on different charges at two Assizes, this one at Liverpool and another at Chester Castle. The principal charge against him was stealing his dead mother's insurance money. I saw it in the *News of the World* that his aunt said that he put his hand on the corpse and swore he had not touched it. 'You're lucky you're not down in Birmingham with your pals, Paddy,' he said across to me.

You skinny-looking whore's melt, said I, in my own mind. Jesus look down on you, if I ever get you in a place where I can give you a kicking. All the other prisoners looked over at me and one old fellow angrily said: 'Woman cut in 'alf. I'd give 'em bloody bombs, the Irish bastards, I would.'

He glared at me with his mad old eyes, but I said nothing. Shaw, though, I promised myself, I'd be like God, and pay my debts without money, with a good kick up in the balls, for a beginning, what they called in the slums at home 'a Ringsend uppercut'.

The other prisoners and the screws all looked around at me and, for a moment or so, I did not like it and wished they'd get back to their own conversations, and forget about me, and so they did, for the next thing was the coach pulled up in the middle of the city and we were told to get out. God's help is never farther than the door.

We were in a big square, and were being brought across

to the building opposite — a big place like the Four Courts at home, but not so genuine — more Victorian than Georgian. Like everything else in Liverpool, I'd say.

They got us out and marched us across the square to the court. The ground was covered in dirty snow and the people stopped to have a look at us, some of them coming nearer across to the middle of the road to get a better look — two lines of prisoners on two chains.

The prisoners gave out about the crowd as we trudged into a doorway in the base of the building and down a long tunnel with bare electric bulbs lighting it. I didn't mind about the people looking once they were not looking at me specially as an IRA man, but I suppose it would be different if you were a local of the place and someone that knew was to see you going over the street on a chain, to the court to be tried for robbing or rape. Anyway, the best thing about it was that it kept them off the subject of IRA men and hanging and beating-up.

We were locked in the cells but in two lots together. The grown-up prisoners in one cell and the YPs in another. Charlie and Ginger and I stood talking in a corner and someone said we were not going to be tried that day. Well, I had not thought the judge would get through the whole lot in one day but I thought he would make a start and, taking the shortest cases at the beginning, might try me amongst the first. It would not mean I would go to Borstal any the quicker, but maybe the other prisoners were wrong, and I might get sent down for about fourteen years, ps. The screws said I would, and though I'd sooner believe Littlewood or the little fat prisoner in the Reception, both of whom said I could only get Borstal on account of my age, how did I know, maybe, that they were wrong and the screws right, and that I would get fourteen stretch? But at least if I did I'd be along with some of our own fellows.

I'd like to know anyway, to be out of pain, one way or another, but I was a bit ashamed in a way that I was worried over going to ps for fourteen years or to Borstal for three and ashamed, too, because it was not really the length of the sentence that worried me — for I had always believed that if a fellow went into the IRA at all he should be prepared to throw the handle after the hatchet, die dog or shite the licence — but that I'd sooner be with Charlie and Ginger and Browny in Borstal than with my own comrades and country-men any place else. It seemed a bit disloyal to me that I should prefer to be with boys from English cities than with my own countrymen and comrades from Ireland's hills and glens.

But no one had really expected the judge to do much business that day and we were not disappointed. At about four o'clock we were chained and taken out of the cells and brought through the tunnel and back up the steps to our coach. We stood together in the shadow of St George's Hall and it was great for a minute even to stand there and hear the traffic and see the darkened cars and buses move slowly through the black-out, and feel the thousands of free people about us, going home for their tea, or maybe in for a quick one into the pub, warm and bright behind the darkness.

It was sad too, and for the moment we all stood together, united in sadness, in the dark cold night.

Then the door was opened and we got back into the coach and the prisoners had a quick smoke, though this time the screws did not light up, but gave orders to put out them bloody dog-ends when we came to the corner of Walton Road.

We waited for the Assizes; we counted the days. We were all for Borstal. That we knew and we listened only half believing to the whispers of Littlewood on the way to the bath on Wednesdays, or going to the exercise yard, turning the corner of the next wing, and for a moment out of the screw's sight. These were the times for questions and Littlewood was well interrogated.

The screw would shout automatically when we passed round the corner from his sight: 'Hey, cut out that nattering in front. What do you bastards think you're on, eh?'

Get stuffed, you old bastard. We'll have another few words on the way back.

'Right, lead on to the yard. Get spaced out there and cut

121

out that whispering. Come along there, well behind each other. You, there, come off his neck. Get spaced out. And not a bloody word from you, unless you want to go before the Governor in the morning. He'll give you something to bleedin' natter about. Quiet.'

Round and round in the cold. Dear Jesus, except for this bit of a whisper on the way there and back going round the corner of 'D' wing, you'd be better off in your cell. Where you could freeze on the slate floor, in shorts and thin shirts and jackets that were only good for creating a draught up your back. The hands were the worst. Round and round, slip your hands in under your belt. Warm against your stomach. Over your Jesus, it's shrivelled to nothing.

'Hey, you, take your hands off your brains. Come on, give over nursing it. That's what has you looking so bloody dossy. Get them hands out of them belts, and swing 'em up.'

All right for you, you big-bellied bastard. Standing up there on the steps in your fughing overcoat, muffled up to the cap.

Charlie is ahead of me and smiles as he goes round on the bends. There are three Polish kids and they smile at me too. Charlie looks cold but rosy-cold like an English boy in a soap advertisement. The Poles are refugees because they are Jewish. Out of the frying-pan into the refrigerator. They look frozen. But then for that again, Warsaw is north of Liverpool and they must have been in worse winters than this. But then, for that again, I suppose, they were fed for it. The biggest Jewish boy is about ninteen, and has an ugly strong face. The next fellow is a stocky, hardy-looking youth and I'd have said he was the toughest of them. One of the YPs said something insulting to him, and though he could neither understand English or reply in that language, he gave the English fellow a look as good as a summons and yon Englishman looked away first. The third, and youngest Jewish boy, is slim with a jaunty head of close black curls and blue eyes like a garsun from Connemara.

He smiles but the poor biggest fellow is frozen blue. I suppose it's because he's more face than the other two.

122

Ah well, God is good and His Mother is very decent, and it won't be long before the three of yous are burning your bellies beneath the sun of David.

The buildings on the four sides of us are like a sooty grey monster with five rows of eyes. They say that at night time with the lights on in the cells the jail looks like a set of huge tram cars.

I got paper for the purpose of preparing my defence and wrote on it:

> 'My lord and gentlemen, it is my privilege and honour today, to stand, as so many of my countrymen have done, in an English court, to testify to the unyielding determination of the Irish people to regain every inch of our national territory and give expression to the noble aspirations for which so much Irish blood has been shed, so many brave and manly hearts have been broken, and for which so many of my comrades are now lying in your jails.'

Outside the doctor's one morning I met another Irishman. He was from Monaghan and I am ashamed to say that he might have been from the moon as from Monaghan for all I had in common with him, outside of being for Ireland, against England. By God he was that, all right. Callan was his name and he was a mad Republican. Not that he was in over the IRA but was in over his own business, which was stealing an overcoat from Sir Harry Lauder's car outside the Maghull Alhambra. He gave out to me from between set lips about the two men that were under sentence of death in Birmingham.

But in two months Walton Jail had made me very anxious for a truce with the British. I had come to the conclusion, not only that everything I had ever read or heard in history about them was true, but that they were bigger and crueller bastards than I had taken them for, lately. Because with tyrants all over Europe, I had begun to think that maybe they weren't the worst after all but, by Jesus, now I knew they were, and I was not defiant of them but frightened.

Pay them back, blow for blow, give them back woe for woe,
Out and make way for the Bold Fenian Men.

Yes, but for Christ's sake not here. Not here where they
could get you kicked to death for a Woodbine, or an extra
bit of bread, if they didn't want the trouble of doing you in
more officially.

This goddamned Callan though nearly seemed to like the
idea of being a martyr. He had been to the great annual
procession to Wolfe Tone's grave at Bodenstown, County
Kildare. I had marched there myself, first as a Fianna boy
since I was able to walk, and later in the IRA, and more often
than Callan, but I had to admit that he had the order of the
parade and the drill off all right. Except that he gave a whole
impression of the procession while were were walking round
the exercise yard, I'd have enjoyed it.

He was able to roar in a whisper. When we'd go on the
exercise yard, he'd start: 'First Cork Brigade, fall in, by the
left! Belfast Number One Brigade! Quick March Third
Tipperary Brigade, by the left! Third Battalion, Dublin
Brigade, South County Battalion, Dublin Number Two, dress
by the right, eyes left Clan na Gael contingent Camp Number
One, New York City . . .' By the time the screw was standing
on the steps and scratching his head and wondering where
the muttered roars were coming from, Callan had finished
drilling the entire Irish Republican movement from the thirty-
two counties of Ireland, Boston, New York, Liverpool, and
London and had them on the march to Tone's grave, to the
stirring scream of the war-pipes proceeding from the side of
his mouth.

He did it so well that the others started marching round the
exercise yard in step to his piping, even despite themselves.

> Proudly the note of the trumpet is sounding,
> Loudly the war cry arise on the gale,
> Swiftly the steed by Lough Swilly is bounding,
> To join the thick squadrons by Saimear's green Vale,
> On! every mountaineer, stranger to fright and fear!

125

Rush to the standard of dauntless Red Hugh!
Bonnoght and gallowglass, rush from your mountain pass,
On for old Erin, O'Donnell abu!

He didn't sing the words of course but made a noise like the
pipes playing them that went like this:

Burp burp buh burp burp bee burp burp beh burp burp,
ur ur uh hur hur deh dur dur duh dur,
Birp birp bih birp birp bir birp birp bih birp birp.

which went just to a steady sensible marching noise, till he
got to a frenzied screech of the pipes at the end:

. . . Miaow aow aow aow aow aow, miaow yaow yaow awo,
haow yaow,
Yaow aow aow aow aow, yaow aow haow yaow yaow!

For a time the screw stood on the steps in amazement
looking round and straining his ears to catch the faint but
rhythmic and persistent drone of Callan's piping. Then he
screwed up his eyes and spoke through his teeth.

' 'Oo's making that bleedin' noise, eh?'

We all looked around to show him our mouths and to show
it wasn't us. Callan did too, and I was the only one to know
that it was him was making the noise, and I wouldn't have
known it but I'd already heard his preliminary drilling and
ordering of the troops.

The other prisoners were terrified of getting into trouble
over the noise and would have stopped whoever was doing
it double quick, and Callan or me quicker than anyone, but
his mouth never moved. It's ventriloquism Callan should have
gone in for, in place of patriotism and overcoat-robbing.

The others did not know in the name of God where the
noise was coming from, and were getting as worried about
it as the screw.

He was doing his nut, standing up there on the steps. He
stared at each face in turn, in a quiet frenzy, but still the
piping went on. He came down off his steps and stood on

the edge of the ring as we passed him, and looked into each face.

Callan came up in his turn and just stared quietly and passed on after the others. I was following and opened my mouth so that at least he'd be certain it wasn't me. . . . The piping had ceased, and the screw went back on his steps, and the piping started again, resolute, though quiet. The screw stared about him, and cocked his ears to see if he was imagining the noise, and then nodded his head slowly and looked about him in horror. We looked at him in horror, Callan looking at him in horror, even while he went on with the march.

Then the screw fixed his eyes on one of us. I hoped to the dear Christ it wasn't me. He took a run down the steps, and Callan stopped his music. The screw came forward and I ducked with the rest. He made a dive on a boy from Glasgow that had hardly ever been heard to open his mouth in the place, even to ask you to pass the wax-end at labour.

'Aaarh, you Scotch bastard. Want to play your bleedin' bagpipes, do you?'

He caught a hold of poor Jock and beat him up the steps, to the gate, where he shouted through the bars for the screw on duty inside in the wing to come and take control of Jock.

'Playing the bleedin' bagpipes through 'is bleedin' teeth, 'e was.'

The other screw gave the usual reproachful look one screw gave when you were accused to having talked or broken any rule while in charge of another screw. As much as to ask how could you find it in your heart to do anything that would make life difficult for such a good kind man. Then he gave Jock a routine blow into the face and took him by the scruff of the neck, and nodded reassuringly to the exercise screw as much as to say that he wouldn't let these bastards take advantage of his good nature.

When Jock had been dragged off to his cell to await the Governor, the screw came from the gate and stood on the steps, shaking his head with satisfaction, while we all, myself included, more shame to me, breathed easier, and plodded round in our less martial and more resigned gait.

And then, in despair, because we couldn't help it, our steps tramped in unison and our backs straightened and our heads went up. Callan was at it again. This time it was drums and trumpets that blared discreetly out the side of his mouth, as he crashed into the old Republican march with a warning roll of the drums:

Burump de dumpiddy dum, burump de dumpiddy dum,
Step together, boldly tread, firm each foot, erect each head,
Fixed in front be every glance, forward! at the word advance!
Noise befits neither hall nor camp,
Eagles soar on silent feather,
Proud sight, left! right! steady boys, steady boys!
   and step together
Steady boys! and step together!
Bardiddly bardiddly bar bar bar bar!

The screw looked down at us and said the exercise was over and all inside, and up to our cells. While we passed him on the steps into the wing, he kept his ears cocked to each prisoner's face. But Callan was not as green as he was Irish and we broke off and went into our cells without his musical accompaniment, though I thought when we halted in the YP wing before falling out that he was going to shout in a whisper, 'Irish Republican Army, dismiss!'

Safely in the cell I was pleased with Callan's performance. I had never seen anyone get the better of the screws before. It was hard luck on poor Jock, though. If it had been one of the English bastards I wouldn't have cared a God's curse, except for Charlie or Ginger, of course.

In the first week of February, the snow was over and there were birds of some dirty colour singing on the window-sills. But whatever their colour, we were glad of them. They were like the spring and a change from the pigeons that sat grunting on the windows all during the winter.

The first of February is the first day of spring and the ninth is my birthday. And the old saying has it, 'If we live through the winter the divil wouldn't kill us in summer.'

Well, I was after living through the winter and on the ninth I would be seventeen.

The first of February is St Bridget's Day. She was from the County Kildare and is called the Mary of the Gael, being very beautiful and a great friend to the poor.

Raftery had a song about the springtime and it went, 'Anois, teacht an Erraigh, beidh an la dul chun sineadh. . . .'

> Now, in the springtime, the day's getting longer,
> On the feast of Saint Bridget, up my sail will go,
> And I'll not delay, but my step getting stronger,
> Till I stand once again in the Plains of Mayo . . .

Every day except Sunday, Charlie would be saying that we might be going to the Assizes that day.

On my paper it said that the two men sentenced to death at Birmingham were to be hanged on the seventh. On Ash Wednesday.

The screws started again to make jeering remarks about them. So did some of the prisoners. Dale didn't nor James. I'd given the latter bastard something to cure him the time I belted him but I could see the pair of them were delighted with the screws getting it up for me. And one of the prisoners was constantly joining in when the screws were willing to let him, which was any time the PO was not there to spoil the fun.

His name was Shaw, the same shrivelled-up seldom-fed bastard that had stolen money from under his dead mother's body and then put his hand on her and sworn he hadn't. He was about twenty but looked as if he had never been that young in his life. Like a little man, he was. I could have beaten him up about three times as easily as I had done James, but I was afraid, not of him, but of the whole lot of them.

Again they were muttering, and I had to sit every day beside the wall at the back when I could, where I could not be attacked from all four sides at once. Charlie sat beside me or behind me and walked in front or behind me at exercise, and Ginger still saluted me.

Callan, thank Christ, was working in the carpenter's shop with the convicted prisoners, and I didn't know, at that, whether to be glad or sorry he was on a different labour to me. Looking at it one way, I was glad, because he'd start them off by answering them, screw or prisoner, and looking at it the other way, if a mill did start, he'd be there to make two of us anyway. I was hoping Charlie wouldn't join in, if there was a heave, and whispered that to him, on the way to the baths, on the Monday.

'I'm your china, Paddy,' was all he said, and went on down the passage.

On Tuesday I heard that Callan had nearly started a riot in the carpenter's shop. They'd started at him over the executions on the next morning, and he'd gone for someone with a wood chisel, and when we were going to our cells that evening, I noticed that his cell which was on the ground floor and under me was locked, so that he must have been there before the others. Going up to my cell I hoped that he would keep easy till morning, and then in my cell and I drinking my cocoa, I was ashamed of myself for hoping that, but it didn't change me from hoping that Callan would keep quiet. It only made me ashamed as well as being afraid.

They were two innocent men and one of them was arrested in London within half an hour of the explosion which happened in Coventry.

They were brave men. One of them before he was sentenced to death said that he would walk out smiling, thinking of all the other men that had died for Ireland.

And when he was sentenced to death, he'd said as good a thing.

The judge said, 'May the Lord have mercy on your soul,' and he replied, 'You too.'

The humour of that would be appreciated in his part of Ireland, where it was a reply to such commonplace greetings as 'Hello', or 'Good health'.

Still and all, I was here, on my own in this place, thinking of them, and even thinking of them having to face the rope in the morning didn't inspire me. It would inspire the crowds at home and in Madison Square Garden, where they would burn Union Jacks and curse the British Empire into hell and out of it back into it and think with pride and the blood surging through their veins of these brave men. The song of the Manchester Martyrs to the air of the American Civil War song, 'Tramp, tramp, tramp, the boys are marching', would roar from ten thousand throats:

> 'God save Ireland,' cried the heroes,
> 'God save Ireland,' cry we all;
> 'Whether on the scaffold high,
> Or the battlefield we die,
> Sure, what matter when for Ireland dear we fall.'

It didn't inspire me. I thought it better to survive my sentence and come out and strike a blow in vengeance for them, than be kicked to death or insanity here.

And even that was not the truth. I only wanted to survive the night. I sat with my legs in my mailbag sewing my cell task, and thinking of sadness and sorrow and shame, and hoping that my demeanour was a peaceable one, and that the book I was going to read was a very meek one. Not that that would count with the screws. Most of them couldn't read anyway. Well, not books. My book was *Cranford* by Mrs Gaskell.

I got into bed when the bell rang, thankful that Callan had let the night go past without starting a heave, and comfortable and warm, opened my book.

It was a very comfortable class of a book. I'd never heard of it before, and when I saw it lying on my table with my other library book, I didn't think much of the look of it. It was in a heavy old cover, from the times of Queen Victoria, and I only knew of one class of book like that that was worth a God's curse, and they were by Charles Dickens. When I didn't see his name on it, I thought it wouldn't be worth opening and when I saw it was written by 'Mrs' Someone, I said good night, Joe Doyle, this is a dead loss.

All that class of book was about little sweeps' boys that

131

saved up money to buy their mothers' cloaks or little girls going out to put on the light in the lighthouse when their fathers were not able to do it. They were probably lying some place pissed drunk, I thought to myself, but that wasn't in those books of course.

So I took no heed of this *Cranford* other than to read it in bits, for a throwaway, like, in the middle of the day, after dinner, when I would be going out of the cell again and only wanted to look at something besides the bare whitewashed walls of the cell for a while. I reserved any good or readable books for the night, when I would want something to read at my real read in bed. I could read when I was four years old, well in a kind of a way, and was always very fond of reading, but every one of the prisoners was the same with regard to their books, which were the principal and only thing we enjoyed; well the only thing we enjoyed with official permission. They could hardly stop us dreaming or thinking bad thoughts. We all kept our best book for the night, and read or looked at the worst rubbish at dinner-time.

I started this *Cranford* in the dinner-time, but after I got into it a bit, I promoted it to the night time, and even had to ration myself to twenty pages a night, which would leave forty each for Saturday and Sunday.

This night, I decided, I could lawfully allow myself a few pages extra, as a matter of that, and as much as I could read before I went asleep, and forgot everything.

'For Miss Baker had ordered (nay, I doubt not, prepared, although she did say, "Why, Peggy, what hev you brought us?" and looked pleasantly surprised at the unexpected pleasure) all sorts of good things, for supper — scalloped oysters, potted lobsters, jelly, a dish called "little Cupids" (which was in great favour with the Cranford ladies, although too expensive to be given except on solemn and state occasions — macaroons sopped in brandy, I should have called it, if I had not known its more refined and classical name). In short we were to be feasted with all that was sweetest and best; and we thought it better to submit graciously, even at the cost of our gentility —

132

which never ate suppers in general, but which, like most non-supper-eaters, was particularly hungry on all special occasions.

Miss Barker, in her former sphere, had, I dare say, been made acquainted with the beverage they call cherry-brandy. We none of us had ever seen such a thing, and rather shrank back when she proffered it us: "Just a leetle, leetle glass, ladies; after the oysters and lobsters, you know." We all shook our heads like female mandarins; but at last, Mrs Jamieson suffered herself to be persuaded, and—'

There was an unmerciful roar from a cell beneath me: 'U—u-u-u-up the Rep—u-u-u-u-u-ub—lic!' roared Callan.

That the devil may choke you and the Republic, I snarled to myself, and why the fughing hell isn't he satisfied with his own exclusive martyrdom without dragging me into it. You're not much good alone and unarmed, are you? I said to myself and answered, No, by Jesus, I am not; not worth a light. But maybe with the help of the Holy Mother of God, he'll carry on his Plan of Campaign by himself, all honour to him, of course; I'll never deny it to him, but tell them at home how all alone he stood and shouted for the cause all on his own. If he only leaves me out of it.

'Be—eee-han. Bren—daaaaaaaaan Be-ee-haaan!'

You lousebound bastard, said I to myself, putting down *Cranford*.

'Uu—uuuuu—up the Rep—uuuuuuub—lic!'

Answer you better, you whore's melt, to give the man back his overcoat and leave the Republic to look after itself.

'Breeeeeeeeeeennnnnn—daaaaaaaaaannnn Beeeeeeeee—hann! Get up and give a shout—a sh-oooooouuuuuuut!'

A kick up in the ballocks is what I'd like to give you, said I resentfully, getting out of the bed. I stood for a moment in my shirt, wondering what to do. May God direct me, said I to myself.

'Uuuuu—uuu—uup the Rep—uuuub—lic, Beeee—haaaaan!'

All right, all right. I gave a discreet shout down the ventilator of 'Up the Republic'.

'I caaaaaaaa—n't heeeeeeer youuuuuu riiiiiightly,' answered Callan.

'I'm shouting,' I said in a low tone down the ventilator, 'the walls here are three feet thick.'

'All right. Gooooood maaaaaan. Up the Reeeeee—puuuub—liiic!'

'Up the Republic,' I said, but in a lower tone down the ventilator. 'We defy you. To hell with the British Empire,' I added in a hurried whisper, for I'd heard voices down below, and the noise of keys at Callan's door.

I jumped back into bed. Callan was getting done. They'd burst open his door and were on top of him. They'd be round to my door in a few seconds, for a look in the spy-hole. And where was I, when they did come round? In bed reading *Cranford*.

'What are you doing in there, Behan?' they shouted in from the spy-hole.

I put down my book and looked up at the door. 'I'm reading, sir.'

He snuffled something of a threatening nature, and went off. I heard Callan's door being opened and heard moaning. They were after finishing with him, and were carrying him down to the chokey cells.

I went back to *Cranford*.

' ". . . It's very strong," said Miss Pole, as she put down her empty glass; "I do believe there is spirit in it."

"Only a little drop — just necessary to make it keep," said Miss Barker. "You know we put brandy-paper over preserves to make them keep. I often feel tipsy myself from damson-tart."

I question whether damson-tart would have opened Mrs Jamieson's heart as much as the cherry-brandy did; but she told us of a coming event, respecting which she had been quite silent until that moment.

"My sister-in-law, Lady Glenmire, is coming to stay with me." '

Lady Glenmire — Glenmire, that was the name of the Cork City railway station, I remembered, before I fell asleep.

'Cahm on, cahm aht of it,' I heard a voice shout in at me.

I jumped out of bed remembering it was the morning of the executions at Birmingham, and then about Callan last night, and I was a bit alarmed, but it wasn't that at all. I was going to court.

I got dressed quickly and emptied my slops down at the recess, went back and collected my kit. The screw hurried me down the stairs and through the prison to the Reception. I looked at the clock there, and it was a quarter to eight. They were going to be hanged at nine, I knew.

When I was bathed and dressed in my own clothes, I was told to stand in line with some prisoners. They were all grown-up men and I did not know any of them. I had been there only a few minutes when I was brought by two screws in civilian clothing to the yard, where they told me to stand a minute.

A car came into the yard and I was handcuffed to the two screws and put into it. As we drove down the road from the prison, I saw a newspaper placard; 'Irish Murderers To Die'.

A church bell rang out a little later. They were beginning to die now, said I to myself.

As it chimed the hour, I bent my forehead to my hand-cuffed right hand and made the Sign of the Cross by moving my head and chest along my outstretched fingers. It was the best I could do.

The screw who was handcuffed to me on my right looked at me and I looked back at him. If he was going to say anything, he changed his mind, and we both looked ahead of us again, towards the windscreen.

I was the first to be tried. The proceedings were short and sweet like an ass's gallop.

The stuff had been caught with me, and as a soldier of the Irish Republican Army I refused to recognize the court. This made the clerk enter a plea of 'Not Guilty', after it had been established that I was not a deaf mute, but mute of malice.

The judge asked me had I anything to say. I delivered my speech which I had off by heart.

After I had said, My lord and gentlemen; it is my

privilege and honour and all that effect, he very rudely interrupted me to say, as casually as he could, though he was a ham actor, and in a temper, that he and the jury did not wish to listen to a political speech.

I waited on him to finish and went on with my speech, in a louder voice. I have a sense of humour that would nearly cause me to burst out laughing at a funeral, providing it was not my own, and solemn speeches are not easily made by me. I can't keep it up. But when I'm speaking to ignorant people I will use any and every means to needle them as best I can according to their particular brand of insolence. For instance, I was at the races one day, and a very wealthy citizen made some indulgently funny remark to me. I pretended to think that he was touching me for money, and handed him a shilling, and said, 'Excuse me now, my good man, I've a bet in this race.' Another time I was singing double-meaning songs in a public house in the country and a lady was shocked and complained to her husband who complained to the management. My friends and I pretended to believe that she was a prostitute, and convinced the publican that she was, and that she was doing business on his premises, and we had her thrown out.

So as this judge was in a vicious and not very judicial temper, I decided to put him in a worse one.

'. . . and this to a proud and intelligent people, who had a language, a literature, when the barbarian woad-painted Briton was first learning to walk upright.

'By plantation, famine, and massacre you have striven to drive the people of Ireland from off the soil of Ireland, but in seven centuries you have not succeeded.

'Many times have you announced that you had stamped out the rebels, that "you had terrorism by the throat", that you had settled the "Irish Question".

'But there is but the one settlement to the Irish Question, and until the thirty-two-county Republic of Ireland is once more functioning, Ireland unfree shall never be at peace.

'God save Ireland. No surrender.'

The two screws looked at me, and the judge had given up his pretence of boredom, and settled himself to sentence me.

136

He stated, which was a lie, that I had taken advantage of the mildness of British law in regard to the punishment of persons under eighteen. He also expressed his regret that he had to give me the benefit of this mildness, and that he could not sentence me to fourteen years' penal servitude, which he would have, if I had been eighteen years of age. He also said that he thought that the law should make allowances for people like myself, who though young in age were mature of purpose. He could only sentence me to three years' Borstal Detention.

I shouted 'Up the Republic!' across the court and right into his face, and went down the stairs in good humour, because I had needled the ill-mannered judge into admitting that he was nearly cutting his throat that he couldn't give me fourteen years, and also because I had only got three years.

I did not know enough about Borstal to be glad that it was Borstal Detention I was sentenced to, and if he had given me the choice of three years' Borstal Detention or two years imprisonment, I'd have taken the imprisonment.

I got down the stairs, well satisfied with myself that I had given that judge as good as I'd got, and also that the world would know that my two comrades now lying in the clay this few hours past were not so soon forgotten.

Thousands had marched in mourning all over Ireland and in the United States, but I was the only one priviledged to stand up for the cause ennobled by these humble men openly and defiantly in the midst of our enemies — great as they were, with their money, their Army, Navy, and Air Force, their lions, unicorns, and ermine robes to hide their hangman's overalls.

I got down to the door of my cell and waited for the screws to open it.

'Hey, you,' a woman's voice shouted at me. I looked around and it was a policewoman or wardress with a young weeping girl. 'Dry your tears, dear, and 'ave a look at the 'ero. 'Ere's a poor girl got in trouble, and is up over doing away with 'er baby, though of course it will only mean she'll be bound over,' she put in quickly, 'and you young pup 'ave nothing better to do than coming over 'ere making trouble for everyone and your poor Dad and Mum worried to death, I'm sure, over in Ireland, and, you young pup, give you three years' Borstal, did he? I know what I'd have done, tan your backside for you, that's what I'd have done; taken down your pants and given you a good tanning and sent you back on the boat tonight. And this poor girl 'ere—' She glared at me, and I didn't know what to say to the old bitch. I only wished the screws would open the cell and let me get to hell away from her.

But under the court the cells are not like prison cells of solid wood and steel, but gates with bars, the same as you see on the pictures, so there would be no escape from her there. At least she could have the decency to go away and let me have a piss.

' 'Ere,' she came over to me and handed me a package, 'you don't deserve them, but Elsie 'ere can't eat them. We'll be 'aving a cup of tea afterwards.'

I looked at the screws. One fellow was standing smoking a pipe and said, 'Go on, take them, they're sandwiches.'

Well, to get rid of the old whore, I took them, and muttered thanks. Elsie was called then, so I shouted 'good luck' after them as they went up the stairs to the dock. After all, it wasn't Elsie's fault that old one had given out to me, and I ate the sandwiches and also Session's Pie, which the screws gave me with tea. They were very good sandwiches, and after the humiliation I had undergone from that old screwess I might as well eat them. The tea was very good, too, and so was the Sessions' Pie.

When I finished eating, I looked round for something to put my mark up on the wall.

It is surprising what people will find to do this with. There were inscriptions all over the walls. Even from men sentenced to death. One had a man's name, and then the words, 'sentenced to death' and a date, and then 'for killing my dear wife, with a hammer I am innocent of as a new born baby'.

Others read: 'Six months for larceny ladies watch I only took to keep it safe.' 'Jesus and dear God help a wicked sinner. Oh, if I get out I will go straight.'

There were defiant ones that read: '— 'em all—bar one —
he can — himself.' 'The Preston Jacks are all bastards and
perjurerers.' 'To h— with everyone and — the rest.' The 'h—'
was spelt like that but the '—' was spelt in full.

There were a few from Irishmen, and three from the
Irishmen sentenced at the last Assizes. I decided to stick mine
up there between a Corkman's name and a Dublinman's:

> Breandán Ó Beacháin, Óglach,
> 2adh Cath, Briogaíd Atha Chliath,
> IRA. An Phoblacht abu!

which means,

> Brendan Behan, Volunteer,
> 2nd Battalion, Dublin Brigade,
> IRA. The Republic forever!

I wrote 'IRA' in English so as they would understand it that
read it.

When I was sitting down, having a smoke, they brought
another kid into the cell. He was a Liverpool-Irish boy called
Patrick George Hartigan. His father was a Catholic from the
West of Ireland, he told me, and his mother a Protestant from
Cheshire. They had given him his two Christian names to
give the Catholic Church and the Protestant religion fair play.
He was a very hungry-faced boy with puffed eyes and white
jaws stretched on his peaky face, and though he said he was
twenty he was smaller and much lighter than I. I have never
seen anyone so young rely so much on a cigarette which he
hung on to, and drew smoke out of, and carried it down into
his guts, and kept it there before he blew it out as if he was
doing it for a bet.

'I didn't like my old man,' said he, 'because he used to bash
my Mum, but I'm half-Irish just the same, Paddy, and you
and me will be chinas, getting sentenced and all the same
day, what?'

'Yes, sure we will,' said I, though I didn't want the poor

139

bastard for a china. Besides, what would Charlie say? We were chinas first.

'We might get sent to the same Borstal, Paddy, and do our bird together.'

May God forbid, said I, treacherously, to myself. 'Yes, we might, on account of being sentenced the same day, what?'

'They call me "Harty", Paddy, that's what all my mates calls me outside, like.'

'And a good name, too, Harty,' said I, and we laughed together.

' 'Ere you are, Paddy, 'ave a Senior Service. They'll be taking them off us up above, in the nick. A bastard 'ole.'

'What part of it were you in up there?'

'What part was I in? What wing, do you mean? I was in the YP wing same as you. But I went out a couple of days before you was picked up. I saw your case in the papers. It said you was going to blow up Cammell Lairds' shipyard over in Birken'ead.'

'They said that,' said I, 'and they'd say Mass if they knew the Latin.'

'Well, I was let out on bail — to get married.'

'To get married?'

'Yes, my Judy's 'aving a nipper, that's why they let me out.'

'Oh, I see, good man, yourself.' I didn't know whether to say congratulations or what. Harty didn't seem that pleased about it.

'She was in court, and all, and pleaded and all. But 'e wasn't 'aving any.' Harty got indignant. ' 'E said Borstal would make a man of me and I'd be a better 'usband when I came out. I'd too much form anyway. Remand 'ome, approved school, six months up 'ere with the YPs. I been screwing since I was ten year old. I 'ad to. I wouldn't 'ave eaten if I didn't. 'Course it's different now, a bit more work starting. Funny thing, I didn't mean it any other time when I said I'd go straight, and they believed me a couple of times. Now I do mean it, they won't bleedin' well believe me. I'd go to work I would, if I was out. Always would, if I could have got any other job but shoving a bleedin' messenger boy's bicycle about with two 'undredweight of stuff on it for ten bob a week.' He drew on

140

his cigarette, shook his head, sighed and blew out a lot of used smoke.

'That's the way with the world, Harty,' said I.

'And I 'ate the nick, I do. Lot of bleedin' sex maniacs, most of them.' He spat with geniune disgust. 'Filthy bleeders. You keep yourself to yourself, Paddy, and don't listen to them, because I can tell you, their talk is mostly filth, and in those Borstals I believe they're a bleedin' sight worse.'

'I can imagine it,' said I.

Up in the Reception they changed me into blue convicted clothes, but the same shape, jacket, shirt and shorts. Harty looked miserable in his shorts, and shook his head when we were going up to our cells.

He looked down at his bare knees when we were going up the stairs. 'Like a bleedin' Boy Scout,' he muttered. 'Ah well, Paddy, that's one day of it up 'is arse. Only one thousand and ninety-four to go. Roll òn death.'

We stopped at my door, while the screw unlocked it and put on the light, and Harty wished me 'good night' and said he'd see me in the morning during the slop out.

The next day I didn't see Charlie or Ginger because they were gone down to the Assizes, but the day after we were all on the convicted exercise together, and though we didn't get our smoke any more we looked with condescension and pity on the remands that did. To us they were new kids. Another thing they brought a few of us, Charlie and Ginger and me included, out to shovel coke into heaps for the prison boilers, and it was out in the open air. Though there was still snow on the ground we weren't perished with the cold like we were on the exercise yard but as warm as toast, and sweating because we were shovelling and using our muscles. Harty wasn't allowed on it because he wasn't allowed on that labour. The doctor had marked him 'No 2' labour.

He let on he didn't mind, and laughed at us, going out like bleedin' 'alf-pay navvies, he said, but I think he was disappointed.

His jaw dropped a bit when I fell in with Charlie and Ginger on the day after they were sentenced. I had gone round with him on the first day because they were down at

141

the court and Harty fell in beside me and seemed to think I'd be with him.

I was sorry for him but then there was nothing I could do about it since he seemed used to being miserable, and just went round with anyone that was handy, at exercise.

Charlie and Ginger and I were in great humour, waiting to go to Borstal, though we were a bit impatient, wondering when we were going to be sent there.

PART TWO

We were sent down one week after we were sentenced, and I heard said that we were very lucky to be sent there so quickly.

Charlie and Ginger were put into one car and Harty and I in the other, but when we got to the railway station we were all put together in a reserved compartment.

Being in the train was smashing, but the best was the last look at the gates of Walton opening, and a last look at its huge, dirty red walls in the morning fog when we sped down the road towards Lime Street.

Harty hardly spoke to me at all, but I didn't care much because when we got in the train the eight of us were together; Charlie and Ginger handcuffed together and their two screws, and Harty and I handcuffed together with our two screws.

The screws got newspapers, and gave us all the cigarettes we wanted and in great excitement the train pulled out for London. The screws, I think, were in good humour because it meant a trip to London for them, and they were very friendly with us.

Harty talked to one of them, a Liverpool man like himself, and they talked together like two old working men about their wives and the screws' kids, and Harty's wife and kid to come, and complained about their in-laws, and talked about how hard it was to get a house and all to that effect, just as if they were two ordinary hard-working men looking after their families and trying to get the price of a pint besides, instead of a screw and a criminal.

In his ordinary own clothes, Harty got back his serious middle-aged manner along with his gloom, and drew with firmness on his cigarette. The only attention he paid the rest of us was an impatient glance at me when I leaned across to join in Charlie's and Ginger's excited chatter.

After a couple of hours we got a bit tired, and Charlie and

Ginger asked the screw if they could fall out. He brought the two of them to the toilet next door and I heard the three of them laughing and joking when they pissed in their turns. The toilet only held one at a time, and being handcuffed made it a tight squeeze.

I wanted a piss, too, and I was half-afraid our screw would ask Harty and me if we wanted one and more afraid that he wouldn't. For I was handcuffed to Harty and I would feel embarrassed doing it with him standing beside me. If it was Charlie or Ginger I wouldn't have cared but would have made a joke of it, the same as they did. All the same I badly wanted one, so when the screw nodded to me and said, 'Want to fall out, Behan?' and on second thoughts to Harty, his travelling companion, 'Or you, Hartigan?' I waited on Harty to answer.

'I suppose we might as well. Come on, Paddy,' said he, and the screw took us to the toilet. When we stood in the corridor, I said to Harty: 'You first. Age before ignorance,' making a joke of it. He got in, used the toilet and came out again.

'Right there, Paddy,' said he soberly, making way for me at the door.

I tried to let on to myself that it was an everyday thing to piss and someone handcuffed to me, but it didn't work. The more I tried, the more I got embarrassed and I was in a panic even sooner than it would have taken to have a piss in the ordinary way. At last the screw said, 'Whistle for it, Paddy.'

I had to say to him, and my face red as fire, 'Could you take off the cuffs for a minute, sir, please?' Harty looked at me, and at the screw patiently.

'Well,' said the screw, 'I'd never have given you the credit for being so self-conscious.'

But he took the cuffs off, and I went in and shut the door, but didn't lock it, because he might think I was trying to jump out the window and scarper, and even at that it was a fair while in coming, but at last it did, and I went out, and was grateful to the screw and got back in the carriage.

He put the cuffs on Harty and me again but said nothing, only that he wanted to go to the jacks himself. Which he did and the other screws in their turn, and then we had more tea and sandwiches, and Harty and our screw got into a deep conversation again about wives, money, in-laws, greyhound tracks, beer, the price of things, and well-known people in Liverpool and thereabouts, mostly crooks and bookmakers and boxers and landlords of pubs.

I was looking at them and thinking that in a way they'd be very well-behaved customers in a pub and well liked by ordinary citizens as decent chaps that only went in and spent a night, talking as they were talking now, over a few pints. For some reason I doubted if either of them ever tasted whiskey.

Charlie was showing Ginger all the places he knew when we passed Watford, till at last we pulled into Euston Station. There was a car waiting for us, and they drove to a place a long way from the station which was called Feltham Boys' Prison. Our own screws parted from us, and said 'Good-bye, now,' and handed us over to a fat man in civilian clothes, who spoke with a Scots' accent. We were sorry to see we were in a wing of tiny cells.

Harty looked after the Liverpool screw as if he would have sooner gone back to Walton with him; the rest of us were a bit disappointed when the Scotsman asked us to hand over any cigarettes we had before we were searched.

'You're not in Borstal yet, you know,' he told us, 'this is an allocation centre where they'll keep you till they decide what Borstal Institution you're suited for. I tell you what, stick a dog-end in your pocket, and when you're changed after your bath you can have a bash after your supper — but take no snout over to North House with you. You'll get plenty of snout in a month or five weeks when you go down to a BI and can earn it. You won't find this place too bad — though it's a bit of a bloody mad-house at the moment. This here is the remand place. You'll be in dormitories in North House and we have a Borstal Institution of our own in South and West House. We have to run a remand prison, a BI, the Allocation Centre, and a Boys' Prison. I don't want to threaten you fellows, but I want to tell you we also have a chokey department. Most of the lads that come here behave themselves all right, and we seldom get anyone in chokey,

147

except for trying to scarper. That's another thing I want to tell you; the electric railway runs outside these walls and we've had fellows electrocuted when they tried to get across it. Now, down to the baths and when you get back we'll feed you and put you to bed. Your kit will be left down in the baths as soon as you've stripped off your civilian clothing. Right, sir.' He nodded to another screw and this one marched us down to the baths, which were showers.

Harty scowled when we were taking off our clothes. 'Call this a bleedin' Borstal — and the first thing 'e does is tell you he's going to take away our snout?'

' 'E seems a decent bloke to me,' said Charlie, ' 'e's letting us 'ave a burn after our supper, and then we go on smoking when we're sent to a Borstal. This ain't proper Borstal yet.'

'Oh, stuff Borstal,' said Harty, slowly removing his clothes.

Charlie and Ginger and I were already under the showers, and larking about, naked and ruddy from the steaming hot water.

Harty stood, skinny and white, modestly covering his crotch, and got under a shower on his own, and just looked at us, shaking his head, sighed and came out again and, putting on his kit, looked at the shorts miserably and muttered, 'Like a bloody Boy Scout.'

When he was dressed he stood impatiently, shook his head. 'Look sharp, there, you bleeders, can't you? I want some scoff before we go to bed.'

We looked over at him and went on soaping and rinsing ourselves. Harty was impressive in his suit and collar and tie talking to the screw on the way down, man to man, but when he took his civvy clothes off he lost his shoulder padding and he was like a little old man dressed up like a Borstal Boy.

We were brought back to the Reception by the Scot's screw and he gave us our suppers.

'Bloody great plates of stew,' said Charlie.

They were so big that a thing that I did not think possible in a jail happened. I was unable to go a second lot. Then he gave us a mug of tea and a slice of bread and margarine each, and told us we could smoke our dog-ends and hand the rest over to him. We each of us selected what we thought was

148

the best dog-end in our collection, the leavings of the cigarettes we had smoked on the train journey, and handed the Scot's screw the rest.

We smoked away after our meal at the table, and even Harty seemed in a good humour for a moment. We were collected by a screw with a good-humoured cynical manner and a limp.

'I'll take you over to the dormitories,' said he and led us through endless dark-lit corridors, till we came to the dormitories. In through the glass partitions we could see heads bobbing up and down to have a look at us and they'd bob down just as quickly from the eye of the screw.

I noticed that the blokes inside seemed to be wearing pyjamas, and when we stopped outside our own dormitory the screw went to a cupboard in the corridor and handed us a set of pyjamas each.

'You're lucky there are vacancies in this dorm,' said the screw, 'we sent a batch today to North Sea Camp, and another lot to Portland. Otherwise we'd have had to stick you in cubicles.'

'I'd sooner be in a cubicle, sir,' said Harty.

'Would you?' said the screw, 'most fellows prefer the dormitory. You see the officer tomorrow and put your name down.' He opened the door and we went in. He pointed to four beds in the corner and said: 'You can get into one of them for tonight. Now, hurry up and get in bed. Good night.'

'Good night, sir,' said we, and a whole lot of blokes round us whispered, 'Good night, sir.'

'Good night, good night,' said the screw, 'now kip in, the lot of you.'

The moment the screw's steps ceased on the corridor outside there was a sort of silent riot. Fellows jumping out of bed in their pyjamas and running over to us, to ask where we were from. Some of them had bits of cigarettes, and asked us if we would like a 'spit'.

I didn't but I enjoyed the company and all the attention we were getting and took a spit from a thin cigarette, while the other fellows sat on our beds and asked us who we were, and what we were in for. They didn't seem interested in my being

149

in over IRA activity but were very friendly to all of us. Even to Harty, who was bad-tempered and complained about having to sleep in a dormitory.

' 'Aven't they got no floweries 'ere?' he asked, looking round at the row of beds. 'This is like a bleedin' lodgin' 'ouse — or like the bleedin' snotty orphans.'

'He's twenty years of age,' says Ginger in a kind of apology.

'And he's married,' said I, so they wouldn't think bad of him describing them as snotty orphans.

'They'll give you a cubicle if you want,' said a fellow sitting on Charlie's bed. 'Anyway, most old blokes, nineteen and that, they put them in cubicles anyway. They probably didn't think you were that old. I wouldn't have took you for more than sixteen when you came into the dorm tonight.'

Good on you, said I, to myself; nothing like getting a bit of your own back. Harty said nothing.

When we settled down for the night, the other boys said, 'Good night' to each other in whispers. Ginger leaned over and said, 'Good night, Paddy,' and I said, 'Good night, Ginger,' and I turned to Charlie, and said, 'Good night, kid,' and he answered, 'Good night, Paddy.' I could just see his eyes and the tip of his nose over the blankets.

Ginger and Charlie and I, in our turn, all said, 'Good night, Harty,' but he never answered us, only muttered something from his sleep.

The next morning I woke up and the screw was outside rapping the partition and kicking the door and shouting, 'Rise and shine.' The boys shouted, 'Rise and shine,' too, and it echoed all over the place and some added to it, shouting, 'Rise and shine, the day is fine,' and others added still more to it and shouted, 'Rise and shine, the day is fine, the sun will scorch your balls off.'

Charlie threw a pillow over at me, and shouted, 'Up, Paddy, 'it the deck,' and Ginger and he and I hopped out of bed in our pyjamas, and called Harty. He struggled up in bed, and reached for his shorts, and put them on very carefully under the bedclothes, without putting his bare legs out of the bed till he had them on. Then he reached for his shoes and socks.

Charlie asked a bloke were we to dress now? and he said that usually most fellows went down to the ablutions in their pyjamas. I thought I'd go down that way. I'd never had a set of pjyamas before and rather fancied them.

Our days in Feltham were the same every day except Sunday.

We got up at seven, washed, and went to a big hall with tables each seating about twenty where we had breakfast. This was a great and happy surprise to us after Walton. It consisted of any amount of bread, a piece of margarine, and wonder of God! a rissole, and a big bloody rissole at that. There was a big pot of tea to each table, and you could usually get three mugs, if you wanted them.

After that we cleaned up the place. There were orderlies selected for it but most of the others joined in, to pass the time. To tell the truth, I've never had much difficulty passing the time, and I usually stood over looking out of the window.

After that we were brought up to a bag-shop to sew mailbags. So long as you didn't exactly shout the place down, the screw didn't mind you talking. At twelve o'clock we went down to this hall again for dinner and a good dinner it was too. This usual prison stuff, sea-pie, stew, and shepherd's pie, except that there was as much of it as you could eat and there was never the Saturday prison cold dinner of bully beef and cold bad potatoes. They sometimes gave us bully beef at breakfast in place of the rissoles.

After dinner we sat around till it was time to go to work again, and sewed more mailbags for a couple of hours. We came down and sat or walked round the hall till tea. This was good and substantial. With plenty of bread, the same-sized piece of margarine each that we got at breakfast and the same big pot of tea for each table and some fried stuff usually made up of what was left over at dinner.

Then after tea, from seven o'clock till eight, we had the famous Borstal 'silent hour'. This meant you had to sit at the table, write a letter home, if you hadn't already written your fortnightly letter, or else read your library book. If you didn't do that you had to sit there, anyway, and just sit, but not talk.

Well, we had a good library and most fellows had got into the habit of reading while they were in the remand nick and they didn't mind; anyway, it was only for an hour and even if it seemed a bit balmy, they were decent in Feltham with scoff and the screws were decent and the boys were that surprised to get enough to eat and be treated so well, after their remand prisons, that they did not mind the silent hour.

After the silent hour we got a supper of cocoa and a couple of slices of dry bread, and went up to bed, to dormitories or cubicles. The only thing we did not get was exercise, except on Sunday mornings. We only got one hour's outside exercise in the week. That was because the place was so over-crowded and was catering for more prisoners and more sorts of prisoners than it did normally, because of the war.

In ordinary times the Allocation Centre for newly sentenced Borstal Boys was in Wormwood Scrubs Prison, and the remands would have been in Brixton. There were also, with us, fellows called Judges' Respites.

Besides the Allocation Centre and the remand wing they called Scrubs House, they still ran, as a strictly separate concern, their own Borstal Insitution at Feltham. We often saw the BIs, as we called them, walk past the windows and going about their work. They sometimes came into our part of the place to do building repair work, or to deliver stuff, and we were as interested in them as if they had come from the outside and tried to get talking to them, but they were not interested in us and hardly spoke to us.

There was a certain amount of monotony about our days, but you'd get that in any nick, only more of it, and there was always a certain amount of diarrhoea amongst new arrivals, due to getting too much food all of a sudden.

Charlie, Ginger, and I suffered in our turn, like everyone else, but I can't tell how Harty got on in this matter because after his first night in the dormitory he asked and got moved to a cubicle and we saw him at bedtime no more, though we were all together during the day.

Most of the older fellows we only saw during the day, because they were in cubicles. Many of them were Licence Revokes, that is, fellows like Littlewood in Walton and Dale and James, the bastards, that had done Borstal and had been let out on licence and had broken the conditions of their licence and been brought back. It was just as well these LRs were kept in their cubicles at night because they were older than the rest of us, and terrors.

One fellow was called Dick Hanson and he was nearly twenty-three and married with three children. He was smaller than I, old as he was, but neatly made. The second or third night Charlie and Ginger and Harty and I were there, he came out of the kitchen and threw bits of bread dipped in cocoa at the fellows. One landed on Charlie and Charlie shouted, 'Turn it —ing up, can't you?' in a very angry tone of voice.

'Oh, kip in,' said Hanson, hardly bothering with him.

'I won't bloody kip in,' said Charlie, 'you little short-arsed bastard.'

Hanson went over to him in a bad temper and drew on him.

'Leave him alone!' I shouted. To tell nothing but the God's truth before I even knew I had shouted anything.

'Oh, so you want to bundle, you Irish bastard?' said Hanson. 'Come on, then.'

I got up from the table, and went towards him in a rush. I moved quickly, I suppose, but I remember everything as I went the few paces towards him, in slow motion, till I found myself on the ground, and Hanson standing over me, laughing, 'Get up, you silly old sod, I could 'ave booted the head off you.'

So he could too, and he laughed again as I picked myself up, but not a jeering laugh, but almost a fatherly laugh.

'Come on, you silly old silly,' said Hanson, 'and I'll take you down the cawsy and throw some water in your face.'

He brought me down to the lavatory and splashed water in my face, and wiped it with his handkerchief. He lit a cigarette with a flint and tinder and gave it to me. 'Take a spit, Paddy.'

I did so, and said, 'Thanks very much, Dick.'

'You're a good boy, Paddy, and the boys like you. The London boys do, and they're the only ones that matter. I don't mind you 'aving a go at me but you want to be more careful.

153

Box clever, you know, and find out who you're having a bundle with before you go for them. I could 'ave done you proper, Paddy, apart from the knee and nut. I suppose the boys told you about me, and you, being an Irishman, thought you'd 'ave a go at a professional boxer.'

He smiled and I smiled, deprecatingly.

'I admire you, for sticking up for your china, Paddy, but don't let that old Irish temper of yours run away in future.'

I did not know anything about Hanson being a professional boxer but I found out that he was, and a very famous one, and for some years was one of the best fly-weights in Europe.

I certainly did not go for him because I knew that about him. In the first place I did not know it, and in the second I'd not have gone for him, except in a much more extreme case, and then only with a weapon of some description, or I'd have put my arms round his neck and twisted his head round his little body a bit.

It might be thought that I went for him over him going for Charlie, my china, but was not altogether true, either.

My main reason for going for him was, I think, that I was trying to build up, in a small way, of course, a reputation as a terror, so as blokes would have heard about me before I got to Borstal and would leave me alone. I attacked him through fear, which is the way of the world. Not fear of Hanson, but as an insurance against the future. Also, I thought Hanson was a soft mark. He looked one but, like everyone else, he thought he looked more impressive than he did, and never dreamt that, far from knowing anything about his record in the ring, I thought he looked like a midget from the Fun Palace.

The fact, as it turned out, that he was a boxer who'd topped the bill at Blackfriars, would do my reputation a lot of good in the future — like laying up store for the future, as the Church says.

I also heard that he'd fought in some Baths or other. Lambeth Baths, I think they said. I did not know how you could have boxing in a Baths, unless it was a kind of swimming boxing, like water polo, but I made up my mind to find out before I left Feltham, so as to casually introduce it into my conversation, for the Baths seemed to impress the Cockneys.

The other terrors were Flash Harry Lewis, Sammy Curtis, Lovely Ball, and Denis Manning. The daddy of them all was Doug Murray.

Lewis was a tall fellow of about twenty-one, and I don't think he was much good to bundle, considering his size and age, but he was counted in with the terrors because he was clever enough to get them to do the bundling if anything started and, anyway, it was realized that he was one of the terrors, so it would not be much good any of us new chums trying to fight him. But even with us he was careful who he messed about and mostly tormented the life out of a poor kid who was college educated and was doing His Majesty's Pleasure for running a motor-car over his father.

Lovely Ball was the ugliest human being I've ever seen in my life. He was twenty-three and had a wife and children outside. I told a geezer one day that, for the children's sake, I hoped they took after her people, while this Lovely Ball was looking down at us, when your man was laughing at what I'd said, and he glared a bit suspiciously, as if he knew we were talking about him, but thanks be to Christ that's as far as it went.

Denis Manning was about nineteen and he was London-Irish.

The daddy of them all, Doug Murray, was about twenty years old but had a pair of shoulders on him like a bull. I'd say he could have bundled anyone in the place with one hand tied behind his back. But, and just as well, he was a very good-humoured class of a fellow and, apart from the respect due to his strength, he was very well liked.

There was the youngest terror, a London-Italian bloke called Joe Da Vinci, but he was only seventeen, the same age as Charlie and Ginger and I, and as he started to go round with us he didn't count as a terror any more. He started sitting beside us at meal-times and during the silent hour.

One day, Dale and James, the bastards, arrived down from Walton, and that other get, Shaw, that I had it in for, for abusing me on the bus and drawing attention to me the first day we went down to the Assizes. I said nothing to any of them, one way or another, but I wasn't long about remarking to Charlie and Ginger that Dale had not so much mouth out of him since he'd come down to Feltham. They went round very quiet men for fear of Murray and Lovely Ball and the terrors.

The great excitement of our days in Feltham was the visit of the Commissioner. In preparation for this we were examined by the doctor and questioned by the Lady Visitor.

The Lady Visitor was sent to ask us a lot of questions and all the time you were answering she was writing down. Some of the fellows laughed at the idea of the Lady Visitor being able to find out so much about them, and thought it was all ballocks but I, though I laughed with the rest, had an idea that the Lady Visitor could tell as much from lies as from truthful answers to questions. Unfortunately, I came to this conclusion after I'd told her some lies and it wasn't that I thought they would do me harm with the Commissioner as that it made me look a bit of a fool before the Lady Visitor herself.

But when she saw me again and I went to correct my lies, she said that I was not by any means the biggest liar she had met amongst the Borstal Boys, nor even in the first three, and that on the whole she rather enjoyed Lady Visiting me.

Though they gammed on not to take them seriously and said that they were asked questions like, 'Has your mother ever had a baby?' most fellows liked their Lady Visitors and respected them as sensible people who were interested in them for their own sakes. Parsons, nor priests, never got the same respect, nor any sort of religious official.

The doctor was a stout busy-looking man, and grumbled over me telling him lies. These lies were not over sex or anything like that, because neither the Lady Visitor nor the doctor asked questions about sex and I don't see why I should have told them lies about such simple matters, for instance like the names of the members of my family. I listed by name and age a family of about ten brothers and sisters that I did not have.

156

Later, when I listed the proper names of my family, the doctor was very cross and said he had communicated with my parents and also discovered that I had told him a lie about something else. That I told him I was getting one pound two shillings a week as a painter's apprentice when, according to my father, I was only getting ten shillings. Now, I was not wrong there, but my father was. He forgot that I was a third-year apprentice and that my wages were as I stated — sixpence an hour — twenty-two shillings for a forty-four hour week, because I had told the doctor the other lies about my family he would not take my word about this.

'No, Behan, it was just lies, that's all,' said the stout doctor crossly, 'and giving me more trouble, when I'm working a twelve-hour day as it is.'

'Maybe I should have been sent to Borstal, sir, anyway.'

'Let me tell you, you're a perfectly healthy young man, and you should not be taking up my time and attention when so many others need it more. I suppose this is all jolly good for your election manifesto when you want to enter the Irish Parliament, but it's damn' well not fair to me, wasting my time. I am not appointed or paid by the unfortunate taxpayers of this country to settle the Irish Question.'

He looked at me, and I looked at him, and both of us laughed. 'Get out of here, Behan,' said the stout doctor, 'and send in the next man.'

He laughed, shook his head, and sighed to himself, as he put away my file.

We waited for the visit of the Commissioner with as much importance as we waited for the Assizes. And, for the matter of that, his verdict on us was a very important one.

There were six Borstal Institutions, to any one of which we might be sent. They were Portland, and Sherwood, all cells, and regarded as tough places; Feltham and Rochester, dormitories and some cells, walled institutions; North Sea Camp and Hollesley Bay, where the boys lived in buildings which were never locked, all dormitories.

Many fellows like Harty preferred cells, and some fellows that had been at Portland seemed to think it was all right, but nobody had a good word for Sherwood and, as a rule, it was only Licence Revokes that went there.

The majority of us wanted to go to North Sea Camp or Hollesley Bay because they were on the sea and were famous for freedom, the open air and hard work, which were all regarded as advantages by the boys.

Rochester was said to be a good place too. I heard them saying that the name 'Borstal' came from the village near Rochester where the institution was situated, and that its official address was, 'HM Borstal Institution, Borstal, Rochester, Kent.'

All day we talked about where we would be sent, or where we hoped to be sent. I hoped I'd be going with Charlie and Ginger and Joe Da Vinci and so it seemed I might, because we were all seventeen, and a lot of it went by age, though I was in for a very serious offence and Joe had previous form and, as a rule, first offenders only were sent to the 'open' Borstals. Still, live horse and you get grass, and there is no harm in hoping. Harty gave me great hopes of going to an open Borstal, in his dismal way.

This morning we were all brought down too early for dinner from the bag shop and we were standing and sitting around talking about this and that and Harty said mournfully:

'You're going to a bleedin' 'oliday camp, Paddy, like 'Ollesley Bay, for trying to blow up Cammell Lairds' shipyard or summat, and I'll get sent to a bleedin' ole like Portland for a little bit of screwing. Couple of ware-'ouses and a lock-up shop in West Derby, and I got bugger all from that lot. Old cow used to bring it 'ome with 'er.'

Said one of the blokes, 'She probably kept it up the chimney.'

Said Harty, 'She might 'ave kept it up 'er shop-front for all I know.'

'I thought you liked sleeping in a cell, Harty,' said I, 'on your own?'

He never answered, but I knew what was wrong with him. All the terrors would be going down there.

Murray said, 'We'll be all down to Portland together, Harty.'

'Yes,' said Harty, 'and this bleedin' IRA man will be going to the Bay, or North Sea Camp. Bleedin' 'oliday camp, I'd call it.' He grunted to himself, and set his peaky white face. 'Please, sir, I give my word of honour not to fugh off if you leave the cell door open. Only there's no cells, only dormitories.'

'Nothing wrong with that,' said Murray, 'I'd kip in the next bed to you, Harty. You know, Harty, I might even have you when we get to Drake House.' Portland is named after admirals: Drake, Benbow, Rodney, and Nelson.

Harty's face twisted with disgust. 'Why does a grown-up bloke like you talk like that? Disgusting, the way you bleeders talk.' He looked round at everyone. ' 'Ow are you going to face your tart outside, talking like that?'

Dick Hanson came out from the kitchen. 'Still talking about ring, Harty?'

'All the bastard ever thinks of,' said Murray. 'He says I fancy him and will I give him a 'alf-ounce of snout for it when we get down to Portland.'

Harty scowled. 'Oh, turn it up, Murray. Don't take the piss.'

Then a Black Maria pulled into the yard, and we ran to the windows.

'Receptions,' said a bloke.

'No, you silly twot,' said another, 'receptions come by coach. That's for the LRs that's going to Sherwood today. Look round you, and you'll see they're missing. They ain't been brought out to work today.'

Amongst those missing was Dale and James, the bastards.

'They'll be going to Sherwood Forest today.'

'With Robin 'ood and 'is merry men.'

'They'll be double merry,' said Murray seriously, 'when they get inside that nick. First thing when the gate shuts behind you, you get a poke in the mush from a fughing great screw. You wipe the blood off and ask him what that's for. He'll tell you that that's for fugh all, but just see what you get, if you do fugh about.'

I was thinking of Dale and James, and hoping that big screw was in good poking form, when it came to their turn to go in the gate. That's all the sympathy they had from me, though I felt sorry for the other prisoners, though most of the LRs seemed to be liberty-taking bastards. With an odd exception, like Littlewood.

A screw shouted at us to come away from the windows. We went back to our tables and someone said that there was a rumour that fellows were going to North Sea Camp, soon. A boy called Knowles, that was in for rape, said: 'Wouldn't fancy that drum. Diggin' bloody ditches. Like King Canute 'olding the sea back.' He had a soft voice and a mouth like a girl's.

'It's good work,' said Harty, 'land reclamation.'

'And stacks of land girls round the place, Knowlesy,' said someone else.

'Oh,' said Knowlesy, quietly, smiling with his mild eyes, and moist red lips, 'I shouldn't mind digging them.'

'Too bloody right, you wouldn't. You want to shove 'im under the coldwater tap, now and again, Knowlesy.'

'He doesn't mean no 'arm,' smiled Knowlesy.

'They didn't think so at the Assizes.'

'It's only that you're so sudden like, Knowlesy.'

'Bloody good job she 'ad the presence of mind to open 'er legs, or she'd 'ave been stabbed to death.'

'The course of true love never runs smooth,' said I, affably, not to embarrass poor old Knowlesy any more.

'It were all a mistake,' said Knowlesy, thoughtfully.

'Just what I said to Recorder,' said a Manchester kid, 'but he weren't 'aving any.'

'Which Recorder?' asked a bloke.

'Salford 'undred Sessions,' said the Manchester kid.

'Oooh, 'e ain't 'alf a bastard, that one, ain't 'e? Weighed off about twenty blokes all the one afternooon, when I were there. Laggin's and 'andfuls. 'E'd give you five year like five bleedin' minutes, 'e would. Geezer of nineteen, a squaddy, 'e was, 'e give 'em bang, bang, seven stretch and eighteen strokes of the cat.'

'The squaddy jumped a schoolteacher — I seen a picture of 'er, diabolical-lookin' old 'ag — in a park.'

'Oh, a bushranger, 'e was.'

'Like Knowlesy.'

Knowlesy smiled. 'No, no schoolteachers.'

'I don't believe this squaddy done 'er at all,' said the Manchester kid. 'At least she went in the park with 'im at twelve o'clock at night. She must 'ave fancied it summat. A bleedin' prick teaser, she were, I reckon.'

' 'E just stood there in 'is uniform when 'e was weighed off, came to attention and saluted the judge.'

'I'd have saluted the fugher. With my bloody boot between 'is mincepies.'

'You would!' scornfully. 'Would you—'

'Quicker than you, I would, you dossy—.'

'You'd bloody shit yourself, you would, if you got seven stretch, leaving out the cat.'

'I'll do you, you leery bastard.'

'Kip in, kip,' said Murray, with authority. With no prospect of a fight, we all found them a bit monotonous.

Then a fellow said, 'You were dead lucky you wasn't eighteen, Knowlesy.'

'I just missed it. I was seventeen and 'alf when it 'appened and just coming on eighteen years old when the Assizes came round. The judge, the old bastard, said 'e were sorry I were under age for penal servitude and a flogging.'

'Probably the old perisher was jealous,' said I, 'that he couldn't get a stand-on himself.'

Some of the fellows didn't approve of Knowlesy's offence — I didn't myself, but I didn't approve of the judge either — so to mark their disapproval without embarrassing Knowlesy they turned on me.

'You're a bloody good one to talk, you are. Putting bombs in railway stations and post offices.'

' 'Ow about the poor bleeders working there, and their wives and kids?'

'Why didn't you do in some of the big pots?'

'Like that old Lady Astor?'

A reedy but persistent voice came from the crowd. 'Tried to blow up a ship in Lairds' shipyard, in Birken'ead, 'e did.' It was Shaw, who had robbed the money from under his mother's dead body, the shrunken-looking old man of twenty winters. He looked at me from his old dead eyes. 'What about the men working on it, and the—'

'You, you grass-hopping bastard, is it?' I shouted, and caught hold of him by the throat. 'You shit-house, you grass.'

'Grass-hopper' was the best thing to call him. Nobody loves a spy, Irish or English, and the boys shouted, 'That's right, Paddy, give him the nut!'

I was trying to pull his head back by the hair to hit him in the face with my head. And his face was grey and sick with fright, the bit I could see of it. The boys shouted, as loud as they could without bringing the screws on us.

'That's it, Paddy, give 'im the nut.'

'Give 'im the loaf of bread, Paddy.'

'Carve 'im up, the bleeding grass-'opper.'

Shaw was muttering distracted appeals. I pulled his head back by the hair, and aimed for his nose with my head, cursing and almost frothing at the mouth with a heavy Irish accent:

'Jasuss! Be the livin' Jasuss, I'll bejasuss—'

Shaw's eyes widened in terror.

'Nick, nick!' someone shouted. The screw was coming back. I let Shaw go; I was glad.

The screw walked down, and looked at us keenly. 'What goes on here?' said he. 'All lost your tongues?'

'They're weak from the 'unger, sir,' said Dick Hanson from the kitchen door.

'Ah, well, grub will be up in a tick,' said the screw, going into the kitchen, where it seemed he was going in the first place.

'You don't shop old Paddy to the screw,' growled Murray to Shaw.

I was a made man, for as long as I'd be in Feltham.

'Fughing grass-'opper. I was in Walton with 'im — biggest nark in the nick, 'e was.'

'Bastard 'ole, Walton.'

'Not worse than Strangeways.'

'Nor Armley.'

'A bloody sight worse than any of 'em. Bleedin screws in the YP wing there would bang you, as quick as look at you.'

'Good enough for you bloody swede-bashers,' said Murray. The London boys are getting fed up with all this talk of Lancashire and Yorkshire nick.

The Richardsons, two blocky, squat brothers from Newcastle-on-Tyne, quiet in a ferocious way, like broad, narrow-browed, broad-shouldered apes, shoved in a remark about their native prison, in their own dialect.

'Shude 'ave bayne in Durham,' said one Richardson. 'That's a bastard owl, ent et?' He looked over at his brother, who nodded back, and grunted.

'Oh, stuff you and Durham,' said Murray, 'where the 'ell is it anyway?'

'Up in fughing Geordie-land,' said Charlie, following Murray.

But if the Richardsons would not offer fight to Murray, he was about the only one they would not offer it to. 'What's the matter with fughing Geordie-land?' asked the smaller Richardson, adding, in case Charlie might give him a reasonable answer, 'you bloody Croydon bastard.'

'Who's a bastard?' asked Charlie.

'You're a bastard and a double bloody bastard,' said the smaller Richardson, confident and ugly.

'Go on, 'ave a go, your muvver won't know,' all the boys shouted, but in a low shout, not to bring out the screw from the kitchen.

I looked at Charlie, and he looked at Murray, but Murray only announced his neutrality, telling Charlie and the smaller Richardson, 'Now, no knee and nut stuff and no catching by the cobs. And break up quick if we give the nick.' He looked around at the other Londoners. 'And no team-handed.'

The Richardsons had no team, thank Jesus. The two of them was team enough. Pressing in to see it, I bumped against Shaw.

'Sorry, china,' I muttered. Not so much in apology, as thanksgiving that it was him I'd taken on, not this bullet-headed coal-block of a Richardson.

And Shaw was delighted at being forgiven so soon, and said, 'It's OK, Pad.' Jesus, I could have hugged him, yellow teeth and grey jaws and all, for not being this half-animal of a Richardson.

Poor Charlie was a silly-born bastard to have taken a liberty with him. But Charlie stood there, putting on a brave face, in his open-necked shirt and blue shorts, like a typical English boy in an advertisement, just come from the football field to wash himself with Lifebuoy soap, only his cheeks weren't so rosy.

His face was good for hardness, but bad for colour.

The stocky, smaller Richardson had no stance, but stood facing Charlie with his paws raised up like Jem Mace or John L. Sullivan or one of those drawings you'd see in the *Ring* of boxers in the year of One. But Richardson would have frightened the Jew Jesus out of anyone. If I'd have had a bundle with him, God between us and all harm, I'd have gone in straight with the boot, right up into his marriage prospects.

But then, God be merciful to us, what about his kennel companion?

'Give 'im one, henny,' said the taller Richardson.

' 'E won't, you know,' said Charlie. His voice was steady enough; condemned man's last words.

All the boys were getting impatient.

'Come on, get cracking,' said Murray.

'Like a pair of old Judies,' said Harty, from the sensible comfort of the back of the crowd.

'Come on,' said voices from the crowd, 'less natter and more batter.'

The smaller Richardson looked at his brother, then at Charlie and made a determined rush. Prepare to meet thy God.

'Nick, nick!' I shouted, in an urgent whisper.

The crowd milled in between Charlie and the smaller Richardson and we all let on to be casually talking.

Murray looked around. 'I see damn-all screw,' he said.

'There,' said a bloke, pointing through the window. 'He must 'ave let himself out of the kitchen by the other door. There 'e is, coming from the quarters, from 'is 'ouse, I suppose.'

' 'E's after 'aving 'is morning bunk-up,' said Knowlesy.

Murray shook his head impatiently. 'It's 'im all right. Who gave the nick, then?'

Nobody answered but a fellow said, 'Was it you, Paddy?'
' 'Course it bloody wasn't,' said I.

'No. He wouldn't,' said another bloke. 'An Irishman would never stop a bundle. Nothing an Irishman likes better than a bundle. You've got the wrong Irishman, mate, at least when it comes to that Richardson. I 'eard my old man say that the Irish will fight till there's only one left, and 'e'll bleedin' well commit suicide 'cause there's no other fugher left to fight with.'

But at that moment the screw did come in, and shouted: 'Right, grub up, stand by the 'atches!'

We collected our dinners and sat down at the table.

'Sea-pie,' said a bloke, and another, of course, added the remark usual in such cases, 'Sea-pie today — see fugh all tomorrow.'

Sea-pie is a kind of Irish stew with suet instead of potatoes in it, and though it may not sound so delicate, it's great food for the appetite.

'I was thinking of sea-pie at the silent hour last night,' said a bloke. 'Ain't that funny?'

'I was thinking of a set of tits and a juicy pair of legs,' said Knowlesy. 'Ain't that funny?'

'No, it's not funny,' said Harty, indignantly from the other end of the table. 'You never think of anything else.'

'Well, during the silent hour, when I can't get a good library book, I try and get 'old of a picture book, and see if there's any girls, in swimming togs, like, and then I keep a good look at them so as I can remember them when I'm in bed, and it 'elps me to plan me wank for the night. Don't you never do that, 'Arty?'

'No, I do not. I don't be thinkin' of muck like that. I think of me Mum, or me wife, or I do plan screwing jobs on ware'ouses I remember or shops, for when I get out, but I don't think that kind of filth.'

'Well, I was only rememberin' last night,' said Knowlesy, 'there were this young judy lived opposite us, and she were only all sixteen but she 'ad a pair of—'

'Oh, shut up for Christ's sake,' said Harty, flinging down his knife and fork. 'You're turnin' me bloody stummick.'

'Well, all right, said Knowlesy, and quietly bent to his dinner.

Murray turned to me at the table. 'Listen, Paddy, did you give the nick that time?'

'I did not, Doug,' said I, looking him straight in the face.

'Well, there must be a bleedin' ventriloquist in this gaff. It seemed to come from near you.'

'Well, what would I want to do a thing like that for?'

'Because that Charlie is a china of yours.' Murray smiled, but I just repeated:

'I didn't give the nick anyway, and he's got other chinas besides me.'

'It's all right, Paddy, don't do your nut over it,' said Murray, and smiled again, but friendly and amused at my moment of temper.

'OK, Doug,' said I, 'smashing sea-pie, isn't it?'

'You're dead right, kid.' He sighed and said seriously, 'We'll 'ave shifted a couple of ton of it before we finish this lot.' He moved his huge form around him and looked over the tables. 'It's all right for you, you're only a kid, and anyway, what you did is for your country — but what am I doing 'ere? Perishing King of the Kids!'

I muttered in sympathy, 'Ah well,' and we went on with our dinner.

When we finished, Charlie smiled over the table, and beckoned, 'Come on down the cawsy, Paddy.'

I put my hand up and shouted, 'Fall out, sir?'

'Right, Behan,' said the screw, 'don't spend your youth in there, and wait till Millwall comes out. No married quarters 'ere.'

Everyone laughed, which pleased the screw.

When I got down to the cawsy, Charlie was standing at the urinal, as if he were having a piss.

'I've got a dog-end, Paddy,' said he, raising his hand and taking a drag from a bit of a cigarette and passing it to me.

We smoked in silence for a while, passing the dog-end between each other.

'You know, Pad, I'd have messed that Geordie about today. I'd 'ave done 'im good and proper.'

You would, Charlie, if he was tied hand and foot, and under ether.

'Yes, I know, kid. Too bad. Someone gave the nick, and the screw miles away. You'd have had plenty of time to carve that Geordie up.'

'I don't like them Geordie liberty-takers, Pad.'

'Nor me, kid.' Like Lanty MacHale's dog, I'd go a step of the road with anyone. 'Give me a Londoner any time. I never fancied those Geordie bastards, that I must own up to.'

'The screw was miles away, Paddy. Slipped over to the quarters. To 'is wife, I suppose — for 'is morning cup of tea.'

'For 'is morning blow-through,' said Knowlesy, coming in behind us. 'There you are, always talking about football.'

'I thought you were the screw,' said Charlie, 'stuff me!'

'Get in the queue,' said Knowlesy, 'and I'll consider your application.'

'I thought you were the bleedin' screw,' said Charlie, again, 'and me with a lighted dog-end in my hand. My heart near stopped.'

So did mine. I thought it was one of the Richardsons.

During the next fortnight the Commissioner came and saw us. He sat in a room over the office block behind a big desk. He was the Prison Commissioner that dealt with Borstal. With him sat the Governor of Feltham and another, the Governor of Hollesley Bay.

The Commissioner was a tall man with a high forehead, very impressive eyebrows and an Irish name. The Governor of Hollesley Bay was a stout gentleman with his hair split in the middle like an English Soccer player, Hapgood or Bastin, and the look of a British Army officer about him. The Governor of Feltham was a quiet, sad man that I'd often seen before, going about his three jails, with a raincoat draped over his shoulders.

His own Borstal boys said that he was an ex-submarine commander. I didn't know whether this was true or not, but it was a good means of knowing that they liked and respected him, even if it was a lie. For if they didn't like him, they would have made up a different kind of lie about him. About the Chief Officer in Walton, they said most awful things, and they could not have been true for he was too old.

The Commissioner asked me to tell them what I was brought in front of them for and I answered, 'You are trying to see which Borstal Institution you should send me to.'

The Governor of Feltham looked in his quiet way at the others and the three of them smiled.

'That's right, Behan,' said the Commissioner.

'That's all, Behan,' said the Governor of Feltham.

'Good night, Behan,' said the Governor of Hollesley Bay, 'send in the next man to us.'

'Good night, gentlemen,' said I, and went off. I hoped I'd be sent to Hollesley Bay, and the next man in was Charlie. Ginger and Joe sat there, in the line too, so maybe we'd be all sent to Hollesley Bay together — with God's help.

In the next week groups went off to different institutions; to Portland and Sherwood in Black Marias and to North Sea Camp in coaches.

Murray and the other terrors were very cheerful, and very friendly to me the morning they went off, but Harty who went with them was miserable and had me nearly as miserable as himself, when he was leaving us.

I said that I had heard that Portland wasn't a bad place at all, amongst other things you could swim in the sea there during the summer, although what poor old Harty would be doing in the sea, summer or winter, I do not know.

He shook his head. 'It isn't that so much, Paddy,' he said, shoving up his pale eyes from his peaky face, and an expression on it like a condemned man's, weary of everything, except the bitter truth, 'but you don't care a fugh where I go, so long as you and that Croydon geezer get sent to the same place.

'I thought we'd be chinas, on account of coming down from Walton together and all. I thought maybe the other geezers wouldn't reckon on you, with you being an IRA man and all. I thought the Cockneys wouldn't reckon on an Irishman and I thought you and me would be chinas, on account of me being from Liverpool. Being a Scouse is like being an Irishman, in a kind of way.'

He drew his breath, bit his lip, and got on with it.

'And I thought we'd be chinas. I didn't care if you was an IRA man, though my old man was Irish, and I hated him. He was a big cruel bastard, and he used to beat our Mum; she was a nice clean woman from Cheshire. He used to beat her if we missed the Mass on Sundays. She told us they worshipped the Devil, but she got on 'er knees to us to go because he'd give 'er a kicking if we didn't, so we went because 'e'd kick 'ell out of us, too and all, if we didn't go.'

I muttered something in repudiation of Harty's father.

'But I still thought we'd be chinas down 'ere, but you hardly walked round with me once since we came. The first Sunday the screw fell us in for exercise, 'e asked me who I wanted to go round with, and I says, "Paddy", and when I looked round you was going round with that Croydon geezer, and didn't even see me, and talking away with 'im, like two bleedin' gramophones, and I didn't 'alf look a — before the screw and I was odd man out, and 'ad to walk round with a bleedin' 'alf-wit from the 'ospital, till 'is clickety-clack bleedin' natter nearly drove me bloody barmy and I was near asking the perishin' screw to let me to buggery out of it, that I didn't want fugh-all exercise.'

Then, thank God, the screw called on them to line up and get ready and I took the opportunity of shaking hands with Harty and saying, 'Good luck, now, Harty.'

He shook his head, caught my hand for a moment and walked in his blue suit, with a mackintosh over his arm, to the Black Maria, where I heard him telling someone to bleedin' move up there, or did 'e want the whole bastard lot for 'imself?

Doug Murray, Flash Harry Lewis, Sammy Curtis and Denis Manning passed out, and all shook hands with me, and told me I wasn't a bad old bastard, and to come round the Elephant sometime and meet all the boys.

The doors of the Black Maria clanged over, and away they went, out of the yard, and at a spanking pace south-west from London.

169

Charlie and Ginger and I were impatient to get going to some place. They treated us all right in Feltham and the scoff was good and plenty of it, but it was very monotonous, up there in the bag-shop everyday. Joe Da Vinci, who thought at first he'd have been sent to Portland, being a young terror, went round with us, and though he was glad at first that we all seemed to be going to Hollesley Bay together, after another week, without anyone going anywhere, he was cheesed off like the rest of us and said he'd sooner have gone down to Portland with Murray and the others.

Then we were told at Mass on a Sunday that next week was Holy Week and that we would have a service every day till the next Sunday, which was Easter Sunday.

We were all delighted and when we came back and met the C of Es after their service, they said they had no service during the week, only the usual one on Sunday.

Charlie said: 'You lucky bastards will be going down every afternoon from the bag-shop. You and Joe.'

'That's right,' said Joe, 'you can stop up there and carry on with the seaming and bottoming and siding and roping, while we'll be down there going to the RC chapel and back, and 'aving our service in between. It's your own fault you're not coming. It's because you're a bloody 'eathen.'

'I'm not a bloody 'eathen,' said Charlie, with indignation, 'I'm a C of E.'

'Don't mind Joe,' said I, 'he's only taking the piss.'

' 'E's got no call to go calling me a bloody 'eathen, even if 'e is only taking the piss,' said Charlie.

'Anyway,' said Joe, very generously, 'I don't see why you shouldn't come if you want.'

'How can I, when I'm not an RC?' asked Charlie. 'The screw will only fall in the RCs.'

'The screw won't know,' said Joe, 'what number 'e's to get the first day and after that, once he gets the same number, 'e won't care.'

'That's right,' said I, 'they're going in and coming out here all the time, that once you fall in the first day, he'll be expecting you every other day.'

'Can I — can I come too, Paddy?'

I looked around and it was a bloke that was called 'Two-lips' by some, and 'Chewlips', by more. He was a London boy and in some villainy where they had pinched lorry-loads of tulips, and sold them in the markets.

Chewlips, which was how I pronounced it, was not as green as he was cabbage-looking, for he got an awful lot of money out of this villainy, and was believed by the police to have a lot of it stacked away.

It was not because the blokes believed this that I believed it, because most of them would believe anything, but the police said so in court, and we saw it in the paper.

Chewlips himself didn't boast about it and hardly ever spoke about his villainy. He often mentioned his business, which was flower and fruit selling at which he helped his father and mother, but the only thing I ever heard him boast about was the fact that his grandmother had a cauliflower ear.

His lorry-loads of tulips, the ones he'd pinched, only seemed a part of his business to him, and as he couldn't read nor write, but only count, he was very surprised to see them mention them in the papers.

He used to go to race-meetings on the family business and he was very interested when I was telling him about the people from the Coombe in Dublin going down to the meetings at the Curragh and Leopardstown and Faireyhouse, and the family I knew that lived in our street that used to shove their barrow up on the Liverpool boat and go across the Irish Sea to sell apples and oranges at the football matches in Goodison Park and Anfield.

He asked me what prices they charged and how much they paid for their stuff in the markets, and he wasn't long before he found out that I didn't know much about it, but only what I'd heard.

He told me the way he shouted his stuff, 'Foh-pance a pahnd pehhs!' and asked what they shouted in Irish. He meant English, I suppose. The fruit-sellers don't shout in Irish, and, though I didn't know what the fruit-sellers shouted, I knew what the newsboys did, 'It be the ha-ha doe-eeee!' and he said that he couldn't make out what that meant and I told him that neither could I, nor anyone else for the matter of that.

171

I liked listening to Chewlips, for he was a rest from all the liars that would be telling you about the jobs they did and the suits they had and the girls they had, and every bloke telling the same sort of lies.

I don't know how he managed it, but he'd never gone to school in his life, only helping his people in the fruit and flower business and going all round the country, to race-meetings and fairs.

He was ignorant about everything except money, and he was the only ignorant person I ever met that was interesting to speak to. Most of the ignorant people I met would put years on you listening to them, but Chewlips was well worth listening to.

Chewlips was a fairly big lad of eighteen, and he had dark hair, well oiled with margarine off his bread, and a gold filling in one of his teeth. He had a serious face and listened with great attention; like when a bloke was saying that the sun was made of burning gas. When Chewlips heard this, which the bloke was telling from a book he'd been reading, Chewlips went over at dinner-time to look through the window and up at the sun, as if he'd never seen it before.

'You want to come to the services every day?' I asked him.

'It'd be smashing, Paddy,' said Chewlips anxiously.

'You don't want to ask 'im,' said Joe; 'what do you think 'e is — the fughing Pope?'

'Well, I'd just like to,' said Chewlips, looking anxiously from Joe to me.

'Don't mind this eejit,' said I, 'certainly you can come.'

'That's right,' said Joe, giving his permission, too, 'all you do is fall in, you and Charlie, and the screw will count you in, and just make sure to fall in each day and nobody will say a dickybird.'

'Smashing, mate,' said Chewlips, gratefully, 'I'll be looking forward to it. I never been to church much outside. Matter of fact, I think I was inside a church only once, before I came in the nick. It's very interesting, I think.'

'And this is different to the one you go to on Sunday,' said Joe, proudly, 'it's got candles, and — and incense, and — the lot.'

172

'What's incense?' asked Chewlips.

'It's a kind of smoke with perfume in it,' said I.

'Cor, smashing,' said Chewlips. 'Like the Jews.'

'I used to go round lighting fires for the Jews on Saturday mornings — they're not allowed to light their own,' said Joe, 'and I knocked on this 'ere door and an old girl came out and I said: "Want your fires lit, lady? Only cost yer a bob." So she looked at me and she was a fat old girl in a dressing-gown and she says, "Come in," so in I goes, and looks round the parlour, to set the grate, and blimey, 'ere she's got a picture of Jesus up on the wall. "Oh, I'm sorry, ma'am," I said, "I see you're a Christian." "That's all right, just come in, just the same," said she, and grabbed 'old of me, and puts two bob in my 'and. "I'm an old maid," she said, "and I live 'ere all alone," and blimey, she drags me upstairs and rapes me, 'eaving and moanin', "Lovely, mate, it's lovely, if I'd known it was like this, I'd 'ave done it years ago".'

'Blimey,' said Chewlips.

'You lying sod,' said Charlie.

I burst out laughing thinking of it. Chewlips, like most people that don't tell lies or stories themselves, saw no reason to disbelieve it, and Charlie, who wasn't sure whether to believe it or not, laughed, and said again, 'You lying sod.'

'And she told me,' said Joe, 'not to forget and call every Saturday afterwards.'

'Cor,' said Chewlips.

Everyone in the nick looks forward to a religious service and in the afternoon in the mailbag shop, we all sat up, all the RCs and Charlie and Chewlips, when a screw would come in, till at last the right one came in, and shouted, 'Right, fall in, the RCs!' and we flung our bags on the floor, our palms, and our needles in the box and had our scissors counted, and fell in, looking satisfied at the others, non-Catholics, who had to go on sitting there, sewing.

Charlie and Chewlips stood in line and some of the blokes looked at them curiously, from having sat beside them in the C of E maybe, but no one said anything. The screw just counted us, and said to the mailbag instructor, 'Thirty-eight, off, sir,' and they saluted each other and we marched off,

173

down through the corridor and chatting away, the screw opening the doors in front of us, till we got to the chapel, where we slowed up before we went into our seats.

Like every prison congregation, we were seated according to the amount of tobacco allowed the different sections. The front rows of seats were occupied by the remand prisoners from Scrubs House, who wore their own clothing and were permitted to receive up to twenty cigarettes a day, their own food, and to buy chocolates and newspapers and were also allowed to receive parcels.

There was an empty row and then came the Borstal Inmates from Feltham Borstal Institution. The BIs could earn Borstal wages of between sixpence and one and sixpence weekly, with which they could buy shag tobacco and cigarette papers from their own shop. They were also allowed to receive a weekly newspaper.

There was another empty row, and there we sat; Allocations, Judges' Respites and Licence Revokes.

And behind us, with two empty rows between them and us, sat the blokes from chokey.

These were fellows doing a couple of days' solitary, a few days' bread and water, or Penal Class till Further Orders, which meant getting their ordinary three meals a day and supper, but working for a couple of hours a day, in a silent row outside their cells, scrubbing buckets to make them shine like silver, till it was evening and they went back inside.

There were not as many chokey merchants as there would be in Walton and not many considering the number of prisoners in Feltham, but still, I don't suppose the few that were there liked it any the better for that. And they must have done something to get put down there, because in Feltham they would not put you there for nothing. I heard that most of them were there for trying to scarper. One fat fellow that was pointed out to me by Joe was a London bloke who'd scarpered and been out for three months, all over London, dodging here and there everywhere, in the streets and in the traffic, reading about himself in the papers. But most of them had only got as far as the yard or over the wall, and on to the railway.

All these diversions were strictly maintained and it was, as in Walton, a punishable offence for any prisoner to attempt to communicate with any prisoner not in his class. So after a half nod and wink towards the chokey blokes behind us, we turned our faces to the altar, Charlie, Joe, Chewlips, and myself.

We were whispering together before the priest came out and Joe and I were trying to show Charlie and Chewlips how to bless themselves.

I never realized it was a difficult thing to do offhand for the first time, but somehow Charlie didn't look right doing it. He seemed to be looking at his right hand all the time, and then didn't seem to know what to do with his left, while he was moving the right.

It didn't matter this first day very much because none of the screws were RCs to know the difference, but it would make them a bit conspicuous just the same, if they didn't do it properly and casually.

When we were getting into our seats, Joe and I automatically genuflected, going down on one knee in the aisle before the altar, and Charlie and Chewlips tried to imitate us and nearly tripped over themselves.

When we got knelt down, after looking round at the chokey merchants in salutation, Joe and I told Charlie and Chewlips not to be so ambitious for the rest of the week, but only bless themselves when they saw everyone else doing it.

Joe told Charlie, when he'd tried it a few times, that he'd give him a bit of practice that night in the dorm.

Chewlips managed all right after a couple of attempts, and after I'd told him not to use his left hand at all. He seemed to be using them in turn.

'I got the old tic-tac right now, Paddy,' he whispered, 'and I'll only use my right German band, right?'

'Right,' said I, 'now get your head down, here's the druid.'

The priest came in the door behind us, and up the aisle. He was a small man, with eyes like two blue buttons stuck on his face. Joe whispered that he was an Italian. He was followed by two altar boys, wearing soutanes and lace surplices over their Borstal shirts and shorts. They were

175

Feltham Borstal boys. Joe made a remark about the smaller one, a boy of about seventeen, with dark hair, ruddy cheeks and great reverence. When they bowed going up towards the altar, Joe pretended to put his hands up this altar boy's surplice.

I laughed. I would have been very angry and violently angry about such behaviour in a Catholic church before my time in Walton, but why should I be angry, and stick up for them, who wouldn't stick up for me, but hounded and insulted me worse than the English Protestants? What the hell did I care about them or their service, except to pass an hour and enjoy it, like anyone else?

Anyway, I was a non-runner at the proceedings, not allowed to go to the Sacraments, and only allowed into the service because it was one of His Majesty's Rules and Standing Orders that a 'prisoner must attend the services of the denomination to which he belongs', just as he must get a bath once a week, so why shouldn't I enjoy the service as well as the bath?

So I laughed at Joe gamming on to put his hands up the altar boy's surplice.

But Charlie didn't laugh, and whispered angrily that he didn't like jokes of that sort, in church or anywhere else.

Chewlips was too interested in all that went on to take any notice of Joe's antics and just smiled faintly out of politeness, and kept his eyes on the priest going up to the altar.

The altar boy caught Joe at this lark, and before he went on up the aisle, he turned and muttered angrily at Joe, asking whether he wanted a belting, in a rage and an Irish accent.

I was interested in him and looked at him, wondering who he was and where he was from, and he looked back at me, as if he wanted to say something to me.

I hoped he wouldn't hold me responsible for Joe, for even though I enjoyed anything that made the service more enjoyable, I did not want to hurt the chap's feelings.

A thing I had never seen before; they had the Benediction first, before the sermon.

The altar boys were swinging the incense and bending low to the priest. Joe made more funny remarks. I nearly burst out laughing, but Charlie whispered to Joe to kip in, to perishing kip in or he'd get us all cased, if the screw caught him.

Joe and I joined in the singing of the Benediction. Joe was very solemn and serious at some bits, and I sang them because they reminded me of being at home and being a kid again, and because I liked singing anyway.

Charlie was very impressed with us all singing in Latin together, and Chewlips was looking about him, maw-mouthed at everything, sights and sounds.

Then we said the Litany: 'Blessed be God, Blessed be His Holy Name. . . . Blessed be His angels and His saints . . .' and I caught myself saying them, through force of habit, and forgetting that I was drummed out of the Church, so I decided to talk to Joe, for Chewlips was dumbfounded.

But Joe was muttering away with a serious face on him, and Charlie was the far side of him and staring silently up at the altar so I shut up until they'd finished, brassed off and wishing for something to pass the time.

Then the priest went in and came back, having left off his vestments and wearing his cassock and biretta.

The priest spoke in a foreign accent about the Passion, and what Christ was to suffer during the week. He spoke very sadly but in resignation, because there was nothing he nor any one of us could do about it, except suffer a bit too.

If Christ as God Almighty couldn't do anything to prevent it, well there wasn't much we could do except resign ourselves to it.

'Thees week,' said the priest, 'from now till tree o'clock Friday, all, all, ees sorrow, sorrow, suffering . . . suffering.'

He sent his little bright blue eyes, like glistening diamonds, all round the chapel, and we all looked up at him in silence. It was a serious matter.

'Cor,' said Chewlips, when we marched out, 'that little bloke in the robes, 'e don't 'alf take it to 'eart. You'd think it was 'imself it was all going to 'appen to.'

The next day we went down and, as we expected, once the screw got the right number, the same as he got the day before, he included Charlie and Chewlips along with the others, genuine RCs and myself, excommunicated RC, and off we went to the chapel.

There was Benediction the next day and a sermon from the priest. It got better again because the screw told us in the bag-shop when we went back after the service that it wasn't worth our while to start work for the few minutes before tea-time and he said that for the rest of the week we needn't take out our scissors and palm and wax and needles at all in the afternoon, but were just to sit there, till the other screw would come to call us for the chapel.

On Spy Wednesday, Chewlips and Charlie were so confident that they fell in before Joe and myself and down we went to the chapel. The little Italian priest gave us a long and sorrowful account of the agony in the garden and of our Lord's betrayal by Judas.

Chewlips followed this with breathless attention, and muttered some comments about Judas.

'—ing grass-'opper, —ing bastard, just like me.'

'And Jesus said to him, "Judas, dost thou betray the Son of Man with a kiss?"'

'Just like me,' whispered Chewlips, '—ing bastard, we're going round in to Russell Street—'

'Kip in,' said Charlie, in a fierce whisper, 'you'll get us done.'

'And,' went on the priest, 'they that were about Him, seeing what would follow, said to Him: "Lord, shall we strike with the sword?"'

'That's it,' said Chewlips, 'carve the bastard up. Do the—'

'Shahrrapp!' said Charlie. 'That screw has you copped!'

He had, too.

I looked round under my joined palms, and saw this screw giving us very hard looks. He was a Catholic himself, too, for I saw him blessing himself and muttering responses. He looked over threateningly at Chewlips.

And on the way out he pounced on poor Chewlips, caught him in the corridor, and held him against the wall. Charlie and I marched on to the bag-shop with the others, but he called me, 'Hey, you, Behan,' in an Irish accent.

I did not know how he knew my name, because he was

a screw from the Borstal Institution, but I went back and stood beside Chewlips.

'Two off, sir,' he shouted to the screw that was marching us back, 'I want these two for a moment, sir.

'Now,' he said to Chewlips, 'when were you converted?'

'Eh, wot, sir?' asked Chewlips, in fear and puzzlement.

'You're not an RC,' said the Irish screw.

'No, sir,' said Chewlips.

'And you knew he wasn't a Catholic, Behan,' said he to me.

'It's all equal to me what he is. I don't own the Church. I'm only let into the chapel myself, because it's prison regulation.'

'I know all about your prison regulation, Behan, and I don't want any of your old buck, but you'll behave yourself in church and not to be talking and whispering and laughing, whatever you're there for.'

He turned to Chewlips. 'You,' he said, 'don't come down here tomorrow, and I'll leave you to explain yourself to the officer that falls in the RCs for chapel in the mailbag class tomorrow.' He turned to me. 'I'm not on the service tomorrow, but I'll see you when you come out of the chapel on Good Friday.'

He spoke in a paternal kind of way, and almost as if he was a relation of mine coming to visit me on Friday.

Chewlips made Charlie and Joe and me promise to tell him what went on, while we waited for the screw to fall us in, on the afternoon of Holy Thursday.

He fell out and stayed in the cawsy while the screw fell us in for the chapel, and though the screw was a bit puzzled with his tally, there had been Receptions come in the previous night, two of whom were RCs.

'I thought I should have one more, apart from these two new 'uns,' said the screw.

'Maybe it's that bloke that's fell out,' said the screw.

'Oh no, sir,' said Knowlesy, who was sitting getting on with his sewing with the other non-Catholics, ' 'e's a C of E, that bloke. 'E was in church last Sunday with the rest of us.'

Chewlips had Knowlesy put up to say that and of course a lot of other blokes joined in, all saying: 'He was sitting

179

beside me at church, sir,' 'He wouldn't be with that lot.' 'My old man says the RCs—'

'That's all right what your old man says, kip in, the lot of you,' said the mailbag screw.

They went silent again. In a way calling it 'the mailbag class' wasn't such a bad name for it. They were like a lot of kids in a class at school the minute the teacher gives them any chance of talking about something besides their lessons.

'Right,' said the mailbag screw, 'that's your tally now, sir,' and they saluted each other and we marched off down the corridor.

'I see old Two-lips never came back from the cawsy till we were gone,' said Joe.

'No, bejasus,' said I, 'that fellow's as cute as a shit-house rat.'

Charlie smiled and said, 'You 'aven't 'alf got some comical expressions, Paddy,' as we went along the corridor.

'He is though,' said I, 'he'd mind mice at a crossroads.'

Charlie burst out laughing.

' 'Ow is it you never laugh at my bleedin' jokes?' said Joe.

'You've only got one bleedin' joke,' said Charlie.

'I 'aven't got a thick way of speaking,' said Joe, 'like this Irish —'

I let on to make a belt at him, and he said, 'Nark it, Paddy, we're just at the chapel.'

When we got back to the mailbag shop, Chewlips said we could tell him about it at tea-time.

So we told him all that went on, and he said: 'That bloody screw. I got a good right to be there. My gran she was RC and always ate fish on Friday.'

'And taters,' said Knowlesy. 'Our granny, she'd eat buckets of fish and taters but she were never RC. Anyway, you'll 'ear the 'ole lot on Sunday in your own church. And in English.'

On Good Friday we sat, Charlie and Joe and I, in our seats and turned our faces to the altar, after a hurried glance and a wink and a nod round at the chokey merchants behind us. We had got to know some of them by appearance, apart from the fat scarperer.

Though he was doing the longest term in chokey, having

got the most value of it, going round London for three months on the run, he looked the most cheerful of them, and every day at the service he folded his hands across his lap and sat looking to the priest with a mild and sympathetic eye.

The little Italian was even more worked up than we expected, even though we knew he was not a regular prison chaplain.

He got so upset over the Passion and Death of our Lord that after he announced the Stations of the Cross, he instructed us all to go round with him to each Station.

We looked round at the screws, for it was a sore thing in any nick for one class of prisoner to get mixed up with another, but there was no RC amongst them and they did not know what to do.

Then the priest signalled to us again, impatiently, thinking that we didn't understand his English, and moans once more about the Crucifixion and calls on us to go around with him.

Still, we didn't know what to do and we were in confusion, looking over at the screws. But the screws themselves didn't know what to do. They never like to get the wrong side of a clergyman, so they signalled to us to do as the priest told us.

So off we went, in great confusion. Remands loaded down with snout, Borstal Boys from Feltham with some snout, ourselves, the Allocations, Judges' Respites, and Licence Revokes with no snout and the chokey blokes behind us, with no scoff but bread and water some of them, not to mind snout.

The screws just gathered at the door looking as if they were going to go mad any minute.

Round to this Station we went and the priest giving out about Our Lord's Holy Passion and how He was taken in the Garden of Olives by the other crowd on information received, having-been shopped by Judas and then taken off and most cruelly scourged and even the chokey blokes were mixed up in the crowd milling round the Station and waiting to go on to the next one.

The chokey blokes were delighted to get to the chapel out of their solitary confinement, and now this arising round the

181

chapel is as good to them as a trip to Switzerland or a cruise in the Mediterranean, out of the cell and the silence.

Joe Da Vinci is in there in the middle, shouting the Stabat Mater and whose sorrow is like unto mine? And his hands deep in the overcoat pocket of a remand, standing in front of him, and he comes up with a whole cigarette and a big dog-end, and there is another bloke in front of me exploring a bag he's just taken out of a remand's pocket and he hands me a piece of jelly from it, which I stick into my mouth and swallow, in one delicious gulp. Joe gets a light for his dog-end off a bloke and there are plenty of fellows in the middle of the congregation smoking but the screws can't tell cigarette smoke from incense; and there is another geezer leaning against a statue of St Jude, the Patron of Hopeless Cases, reading a *News of the World* he's after getting off a remand, and two of the chokey blokes, on the far side of the crowd from the screws, and they savaging the sandwiches the remands had given them, and one of them for a dessert eating a Mars Bar and looking over at the priest and the crowd round the picture as if they thought very well of them.

'What do you think of it, Tosh?' says Joe to one of the chokey blokes.

'Smashing, ain't it?' says the chokey bloke.

'Ah doan't know,' says his china in a miserable North of England accent, ' 'twill make it all worse when Ah'm back, sad and lonely in me flowery dell. And 'aving bread and water for me supper, after these lovely sandwiches and chocolate. Bread and water won't taste so good, and I was just getting used to Number Two and all.'

'Well,' said the first chokey merchant, 'I'll be back in the flowery and 'aving bread and water meself, but stuff me, it wouldn't do for us all to be so bleedin' miserable.' He took another bite of a sandwich.

'Come on,' said Joe, 'next Station.'

The priest and congregation went to stand before the next picture and we moved on with them, the chokey bloke with his sandwich in his hand and taking admiring bites of it as we moved over.

'Tenth Station, Jesus is nailed to the Cross,' moaned the priest.

'Of course,' said the chokey bloke, settling himself against a pillar, and finishing his sandwich, 'there's some bastards couldn't be 'appy no matter where they were. If they was in the Ritz Hotel with a million nicker and Rita Hayworth, they'd find some bloody thing to moan about.'

'Well,' said I, 'you better make the most of it, only three more Stations to go.'

'I'll say one thing,' said Joe, topping his dog-end and putting it in his hiding-place a piece of mailbag canvas sewed to the tail of his shirt, 'you don't get this in the C of E.'

'You're dead right, you wouldn't,' said the chokey bloke, turning to this china, 'think of the other poor sods back in chokey that never got out to this.'

'And why should they get out to it?' said the North of England bloke. 'They're C of Es and Methodists and Yids and such like. Why the 'ell should they get out to our church? If they was 'aving a bit of a do, do you think we'd be let out to it?'

'Well, when the Sally Army came and played the band in Strangeways, we got out to that.'

'Those sods. With their card on Christmas Day, and each bloke lying in the dark, alone in his bastard flowery, and one of them ——s shoves in a card from the Salvation Army bleedin' general wishing us a 'appy Christmas — the perishing bastard.'

'They came round Walton, too, on Christmas Day,' said I. 'The screw that put them in the cells was in the Sally Army.'

'This screw,' said the chokey bloke bitterly, 'was a fughing cornet player in the band, and I 'ope 'e blows 'is fughing brains out, I do.'

' 'Course,' said Joe definitely, 'the Sally Army's got damn-all to do with us RCs.'

'I reckon he's nearly finishing up now,' said Charlie from behind us.

'So he is,' said I. The screws were advancing round the congregation to put us back into some order.

'We better scarper back,' said the chokey blokes. 'Ta for now.'

'Ta,' said Joe.

'Ta,' said Charlie.

'We'll see you tomorrow,' said I, 'with the help of God.'

'Ta, Pad,' said the first chokey bloke, and the sad North of England one gave a shade of a smile and said, 'That's right, Pad, ta for now.'

'Ta,' said I.

When we were marching back to the bag-shop the Irish screw came from behind and caught me by the arm, signalling to the other screw that he would pass me through after the others in a minute.

'Wait there, Behan,' said he, 'there's someone wants to see you.'

Charlie and Joe and the others marched off and I stood there wondering who it was that wanted to see me, and then I saw, coming out of the chapel, the altar boy Joe had made the remarks about. Jesus, says I, I hope he is not going to hold me responsible for Joe's carry-on.

I noticed, too, that he wore a little silver star on his jacket. He had left off his canonicals and was in his ordinary Borstal jacket now. I knew that the crown meant he was a house-captain.

He spoke to me in a Belfast accent. 'I want you a minute,' and caught me by the arm.

'Here,' said I, 'what do you reckon you're on?'

'I'll tell you what I "reckon I'm on",' said he, mimicking the Cockney expression. 'I'm an Irishman,' said he.

'A Northern,' said I.

'And is a Northman not an Irishman?'

'I didn't mean that,' said I, and I didn't either. 'I only meant I could tell by your accent.'

'I saw you today taking very little notice of the Stations, and you were with a fellow that made some remarks of a filthy nature.'

'You should tell him that, Mac, not me.'

'I'm not interested in him. If he was stopping in Feltham for long, he'd know all about it. I can tell you that. I'm not interested in him, I'm interested in you. You're from the second battalion, Dublin Brigade, aren't you?'

'The what? Oh, sure, you mean the IRA.'

'And what else would I mean? You've nearly forgotten what you're in here for.'

To tell the truth when he sprung that question on me about the second battalion of the Dublin Brigade, he might as well have been asking me about the fire brigade, but I assumed a soldierly demeanour, and asked sternly, 'Do you think I discuss the business of my unit with anyone?'

'You were trained in Killiney Castle,' said he, 'with Seumas MacIlhenna and Tommy Gunn.' His face softened in a reminiscent smile. 'Tommy was great fun, at a party or a ceilidh.'

'He was,' said I, remembering the great fun Tommy was, reciting 'The Memory of the Dead', or 'Our Hero, Noblest of Them all, Took Seven Weeks to Die'. He'd keep a wake going.

'A wake is right,' said I. 'You were in the Army in Belfast?'

'What do you mean,' said he, 'you were in the Army? I was in it, and am still in it. The same as you are still in it. Or maybe you've boggied up.'

'I haven't boggied up.' I hadn't either, and didn't. 'I don't know who you are or what you are, or whether you're an Army man at all. You could be working for MI5 for all I know.' He flushed at this, though I didn't believe he was anything else but a genuine West Belfast IRA man. 'I didn't boggy up, nor have I any intention of boggying up, and I told them as much at Liverpool Assizes.'

He smiled reassuringly. 'I know you did. That was a great speech you made altogether. I saw it in the papers. That's not really what I wanted to see you about — they expect an awful lot from an Irish Catholic here in the chapel.'

'They expect a lot,' said I sincerely, 'and give nothing; except abuse. I'm excommunicated and not allowed to go to the Sacraments unless and until I declare that the IRA is a murder gang, and some of the priests would nearly expect you to give information and get some other poor bastards caught. Older fellows than us that would be sent to the Moor for twenty years.'

'I know,' he said, with a sigh, 'the same thing has happened

185

to all of us. But the priests here are good. We serve Mass, even though we can't go to the Sacraments. It's not the priests' fault here. The Cardinal and Bishops won't let them. My name is Lavery, from Belfast.'

'I saw about you in the papers,' said I, 'and I heard the lads talking about you in Killiney.' He was a good IRA man this Lavery, I'd heard them saying.

'Well, you know who I am, then, and you won't mind me giving you a bit of advice. The officers and staff in Borstal are all right.'

'Agreed,' said I; 'from what I see of them.'

'The prisoners, though, though they're all right in their own way, they have as much respect for themselves, or for one another, as a bloody animal. They talk about things, aye, and do things,' said he, fearlessly, 'that the lowest ruffian in Ireland, Catholic or Protestant, wouldn't put his tongue to the mention of, things that you could be born, grow up, and die an old man in our country without ever even hearing the mention of.'

I nodded, but what I was really thinking about was, that in Dublin no one ever heard of Protestant ruffians. At least not on the north side. All the Protestants I ever heard of were rich people in the city, and the poorest ones we knew were clerks in builders' offices who sang hymns on the street in their spare time. They were appointed from Merrion Hall where the master builders read the lessons, with no clergy only themselves, and the clerks were taken on, on condition that they sang their hymns. I'd have liked to have seen a Protestant ruffian.

I suppose Charlie and Knowlesy and Chewlips were Protestant ruffians, Joe was a Catholic ruffian, and poor old Harty was a sort of mixed ruffian.

'You know,' said Lavery, in his northern drone, 'what they talk about in the dormitories, and you can't go and take a shower but there's some fellows making filthy jokes that you have to listen to. You know,' he said very seriously, in his mournful Ulster accent, 'I can see a joke as well as the next sod.'

You could, be Jesus, if it was two feet from your nose and

written as high as the neon sign over Larne Harbour, 'Welcome to sunny Ulster, the wages of sin is death'.

'But thon talk and jokes of theirs is animalism. A Presbyterian minister that comes in here is a Derry man, and although he digs with the other foot, he's still an Irishman and he says he thinks it a disgrace to put Irish lads in here with them. Catholic or Presbyterian, the Irish are reared the same, he said, and I agree with them, though it's only when you're listening to the English that you realize it. Now, you don't have too much to say to those fellows and never get into their dirty way of speaking. Remember that you're not a cat burglar or a — a — ponce, but a Republican soldier, and carry yourself as such.'

Then he handed me a book. 'Take this. It won't do you any harm to have a look at it, now and again.' It was a prayer book. 'The priest gave me that for you, and here's something from myself.'

I nearly fell out of my standing for he handed me a large packet of Players, a box of matches, and six bars of chocolate.

'Go on,' he said, 'take them. I suppose you haven't had a smoke in months. I've some more for myself. I'm allowed parcels, and a girl that lives here in London comes to see me every month.'

'Did you live with her outside?' said I.

'Of course I didn't,' said he, annoyed.

'Oh, I didn't mean that. I only meant did you live in the same digs.'

His annoyance softened. 'Oh, of course. I took you up wrong. I've lived in London since I was fifteen. This girl went to the Gaelic League in Hammersmith and sometimes I used to leave her home.'

'Go raibh míle maith agat (that you may have a thousand thanks),' I said and with sincerity.

'That's all right, Brendan, tá fáilte romhat (you are welcome),' said he, adding an IRA farewell, with a smile. 'Keep in touch.'

'I will, Harry, and thanks again.'

'Here's the screw now, slan leat.'

187

'Slan a't.'

He shook my hand and went down the corridor.

The Irish screw came up and said, 'Finished your visit?'
I smiled and said, 'I have, sir, thanks.'

'Don't thank me,' he said, 'unless you want to get me
sacked. Come on, now, and I'll pass you back to your own
lines.'

When I got back they were already in the dining-hall, sitting down and waiting for their tea.

'Where've you been, Pad?' asked Charlie.

'That altar boy,' said I, 'he's an Irishman.'

'Oh, so you been with 'im, 'ave you!' said Joe. 'You've been
at 'im.'

'He's an IRA man,' said I, 'and he worked me some snout.'

'Oh, 'e was at you, then,' said Joe, ' 'e rung the changes.'

'All right,' said I, 'I'll tell you no more.'

'Kip in, you,' said Charlie to Joe.

'I was only 'aving a joke,' said Joe.

'Don't you never 'ave a joke about anything else?' asked
Charlie.

' 'Course I do,' said Joe indignantly, 'what do you take me
for — think I'm King Lear? But it's no 'arm 'aving a lark.
Go on Paddy, tell us.'

'I don't know whether I bloody will or not.' But I did, and
told them about him having the visit with me.

'Cor,' said Chewlips, 'the IRA must have worked the snout
and chocolates in for you.'

Charlie and Joe even were very much impressed and
nodded their heads.

'We'll split the stuff in the dorm tonight,' said I.

Then the tea was up and we started talking to everyone
else, because they'd been looking at us while we were talking
together. Chewlips gave me a wink across the table and
started a conversation with another London bloke about
pomegranates.

But it had got round before we got into bed.

That night in the dormitory they were whispering.

'Old Paddy's got snout. Geezer from the Feltham BI. 'E's
another RIA man worked it to him.'

' 'Tain't "RIA". It's "IRA", ain't it, Paddy?'

I'd have answered them, but Charlie was giving them hard looks for ther impudence.

'Wohzamarafawgwohihis, if it's —ing "ARP" man or "RIP" man so long as 'e's got the snout. Don't forget us with a spit, Pad.'

'Dog-ends on you, Paddy.'

'Hey, — off. I was dog-ends on 'im first.'

'— off, you —s,' said Charlie indignantly, ' 'is chinas come first.'

'Don't tell me to — off, you silly-born bastard, or I shall go over there and bloody pop you one.'

'You —ing won't, you know,' said Charlie.

'For the love of Jasus,' said I, lapsing into the speech of my homeland, 'keep easy, or none of us will get a bash; the screw will be round.'

' "Fur de luv ah Jaysuss." ' Someone was imitating my accent, and getting great gas out of it, for he could not continue his impersonation for the laughing.

'Right, so,' said I, gamming on to be needled, 'you piss-taking lot of —s. I won't light up at all. I'd dump the lot down the cawsy first.'

'Listen, you bastards,' said Joe, 'kip in or I'll get up and do someone.'

'Good old Paddy,' said the impersonator, in his natural accent, such as it was, 'go ahead and light up. We'll kip in.'

'All right,' said I.

'We won't say a dicky-bird, Paddy.'

'You better not,' said Charlie.

I turned to him. 'For Jasus' sake, you kip in, now, and don't start them off all over again.'

'All right, Paddy,' he said, hurt and angry, 'you work your snout, that's what you'll do, bloody work it!' And he turned on his side and shut his eyes.

I let on to take no notice of him and asked Joe, 'How many have we in the dorm?'

'I'll count them.' He looked around. 'Hey, you —s, what was the check last night?'

'Seventeen, Davvy.'

189

'And that geezer that went to North Sea Camp this morning. That leaves sixteen.'

'Yes, but there was a geezer came over from Scrubs 'Ouse tonight. Got done at Kingston Sessions — case of rape.'

'It wasn't, you know,' came a sad voice from a corner. 'I was done for screwing — same as everyone else.'

'Speak for yourself,' said Knowlesy, who *was* in for rape.

'Knowlesy,' said I, 'the very man. Come over here a minute.'

Knowlesy jumped out of bed in his pyjamas. 'So long as it's not for owt of a questionable nature, Paddy. I'm leery of you and that Wop— you have with you.'

'Ar, you perishing swede-basher,' said Joe.

I divided cigarettes with Joe and Knowlesy, and they went round distributing them. Anyone that didn't smoke got a bit of chocolate.

When he came back to Charlie's bed, Knowlesy held out a cigarette. 'Wake up, kid, 'ere's a bit of snout for you.'

'Sod off!' said Charlie, his voice muffled and offended.

'That's all right, Knowlesy, I've got some for him,' said I, going over and shaking Charlie by the shoulder. He shook me away. 'Honest to Jesus,' said I, telling a lie, 'I didn't know that was you I was talking to that time. I can't see behind me.'

'That's right,' said Joe, ' 'e ain't a bleedin' caterpillar!'

'You mind your own bloody business,' said Charlie, sitting up.

Joe started to say something, but I looked over at him to be easy. 'Here you are, kid,' said I to Charlie, 'want a light?'

He took a cigarette from me. 'Here's another two snout,' said I, 'and a bar of chocolate on account of us being chinas.'

I had given Joe the same but I didn't tell him that. 'OK, Charlie?'

'Right, Pad, thanks.'

A bloke gave the nick that the screw was going round putting out the lights, so we all hid our snout, till he'd gone.

Then in the dark you could see the glow of the lighted cigarettes from each bed.

There was a blue pilot light from outside the glass partition, and I could see Chewlips drawing with great enjoyment on his cigarette. Their faces looked strange in the blue half dark. It fell on the face of the new bloke, and he looked over at me, and said in a whisper, 'Thank's Taffy, for the snout.'

'Paddy, 'e is, not Taffy,' said someone.

'Paddy, I mean,' said the new bloke.

'That's all right, kid, you're welcome,' said I.

Some others thanked me, and Joe said, 'Good night, Paddy.'

'Good night, Joe, good night, Charlie, good night, Knowlesy.'

'Good night, Joe,' said Charlie. ' 'Night, Paddy.'

'Good night, Paddy,' said Chewlips, topping his cigarette, 'and Up the Hey R Hey, or whatever they call it.'

Fellows laughed in the dark. It was the first joke Chewlips had ever attempted.

'Good night, Chewlips,' said I, 'good night all.'

I sat looking round me in the dark. Soon they were all asleep, and where the blue light dimly lit their faces, innocent they looked.

I thought, in gratitude for the feast, the least I could do was to look at the prayer book Lavery had given me. Anyway I wanted to go to the cubicle in the corner, where the light shone down on the cawsy.

I held the book up to the light, and some fellow said, 'That's a code book Paddy got from the IRA.'

I turned round and said, 'Kip in, you'll bring the screw down.'

And he said, 'Only geeing you, Paddy, good night.'

'Good night, kid,' said I, and screwed my eyes into the book.

I thought of the little priest's comic diamond eyes and his moans at the Stations:

> *'Quis est homo, qui non fleret,*
> *Matrem Christi si videret,*
> *In tanto supplicio?*
>
> *Quis non posset contristari,*
> *Christi Matrem contemplari*
> *Dolentum cum Filio?*

191

Is there one that wouldn't weep.
With Christ's Mother's inner grief,
Staring up there, tearless, dumb?

Where's the man that wouldn't share
Her sorrow that she couldn't bear
A torture for her dying Son?'

On Easter Sunday the little priest skipped round the altar like a spring lamb and gave a triumphant sermon in gleaming white and gold vestments and the sun shining through the window on him.

PART THREE

At last on Tuesday morning there was an empty coach drawn up in the yard when we went down to the dining-hall for our breakfast, and there was great excitement amongst the blokes wondering who was going where. They lined up and tried to shove each other and get a look out at the coach as if they were going to learn anything from looking at it.

The screws told us to get to hell away from those windows and said they'd be reading the list after breakfast.

At last the screw called for silence and read from his list: 'The following will go to their dormitories and collect their small kit. . . . 3425 Thorogood, 3892 Marshall, 3461 Balham, 3743 Tonks. . . .' Charlie and I looked at each other and Joe looked at us and I looked at him, and Knowlesy looked a bit sad for the first time since I'd seen him. For it was known that this bunch were for the Bay and there was little chance for Knowlesy going there, whatever chance there was for Charlie and me, or for Joe, and even though Joe was a ponce and a thief and one of a family whose normal business was poncing, seeing as they hadn't sent him to Portland, they must be keeping him for some place else.

But in open Borstal Institutions they didn't fancy rape cases, for they might get them in bad with the local people, if they happened to have young daughters going along the country roads.

Ponces were not that bad, and also they didn't mind carnal knowledges, for that could happen a bloke with his own girl friend, so Knowlesy looked very sad, till his name was called. Our names weren't and it looked as if he might be even leaving us behind but, on the heels of the hunt, Charlie, Joe, Chewlips, and I were all called out and, in great excitement, ran up to the dormitory to pack our small kit, take it down the reception and get bathed and changed into our civvies, or, in Charlie's case, into his uniform.

When I got into my own clothes I nearly tripped over my

long pants. Joe looked older and stylish in his own clothes, and feeling the cloth of his sleeve, said to me, 'Good bit of cloth this, Paddy,' and when I agreed that it was, he praised my trench coat. 'That's a real IRA gunman's coat, Paddy, like what you'd see Victor McLaglen wearing on the pictures.'

It had been sent to me since I'd come inside, for they were forbidden wear by the IRA, though in Ireland it wouldn't matter, because all sorts of fellows, University students and the like, wore them.

Charlie came out in his sailor's clothes and I must say fresh and well he looked in them. He met another bloke who was wearing sailor's uniform and they stood together talking importantly. There were two soldiers, and a RAF kid, and the soldiers looked at Charlie and the other sailor and at the RAF bloke and said, 'Thank Christ, we have an Army,' but even Charlie didn't take offence at this, because it seemed to be the thing to say.

We were handcuffed in pairs and the cuffs were attached to two long chains, one for each side of the coach. Charlie and I got ourselves handcuffed together and Joe and Knowlesy and Chewlips were on the chain beside. 'So we all travel,' said Joe, 'nice and cosy and team-'anded.'

Everybody was in great humour, and the only irritation caused the screws was when some fellows wanted to fall out, before we started the journey.

When they were unmanacled some others, myself included, decided that we might as well have a piss before we started, and Charlie, who had to be unmanacled, decided he might as well come down to the cawsy with us too.

'Why don't you blokes put a washer on it?' said the Principal Officer. 'Look sharp, we can't wait here all bloody day. Oh, what you blokes want is a couple of bottles of gin for your kidneys. If you're not back here in three seconds we're going off in the coach and you can bloody well walk to Hollesley Bay.'

But at last we stood in line for the start and were chained up again, shipshape and Bristol fashion, and seated clean and decent in the coach, and the coach moved off out of the exercise yard and the blokes we left behind us waved from the windows and we waved and cheered and, in short order, we were out on the open road and speeding from London.

Some fellows had got streamers, from where I do not know, and we had them flying out of the window, as if it was an excursion we were on. The PO went to the parcels containing our property, and distributed our cigarettes.

After a while they started singing.

There were three blokes from Feltham Borstal Institution who were being transferred to Hollesley Bay. One was a bloke of eighteen with a heavy mass of curly hair, and they called him 'Shaggy'.

The others were a boy called Ickey Baldock and a Canadian called Mac Stay.

Shaggy was, it was plain to be seen, the daddy of the three of them, and would probably be the daddy of the Bay, for he was ex-feather-weight champion of the British Army, and though sometimes a fellow could be a good boxer, but not so good in a bundle, I knew by the looks of this Shaggy that he had it in every way.

Ickey Baldock was a bit younger than Shaggy and was small, but very well developed, and had gone in for Physical Culture by the looks of him. A small and dangerous little bastard, I'd have said, that was conscious of his smallness and made up for it by aggressiveness. The sort of fellow that, in Dublin, liked to hear himself described as a 'great little bit of stuff'. He could probably box with great science, and I thought if ever I had a bundle with him, I'd bundle with great science, by twisting his scientific little head round backwards to front a couple of times.

From a mixture of cowardice and laziness — two parts cowardice to one part laziness — and the fear of not being sure of winning, I don't like tangling with anyone, but Ickey Baldock was the sort of little bastard that would pick a fight with you until he lost and the best thing to do with him was to make sure that he lost the first time.

Mac Stay was a sort of fellow that would go anywhere he could get his head in and was probably with Shaggy for the good reason that Shaggy was a good boy to bundle, and with Ickey Baldock because Ickey was a Cockney and also a cute little bastard that could be relied upon to be on the right side anyway.

Shaggy told me that his mother was an Irishwoman from Belfast and his father was London-Irish, and he had joined the Northamptonshire Regiment because they were stationed in Northern Ireland. He was sent over there and asked me if I knew Ballykinlar Camp.

I told him I had never been there myself but I knew where it was. My uncles and many of my parents' friends were interned there during the Trouble, and my uncle had written a song called the 'Ballykinlar March':

Listen ye nations of the world, to the message of the free,
Ireland stands with flag unfurled, sword in hand for liberty,
Ever shall her voice be heard, amidst the nations of the free,
Ireland stands with sword in hand, redeemed, erect and free. . . .

In some way, my uncles being interned there, and the First Northamps having been stationed there and even the IRA having raided there a few months earlier, all seemed to add up to Shaggy being Irish. His mother being from Ireland, the IRA, and the British Army, leaving out officers, of course, or conscripts, all seemed to add up to something Shaggy and I had in common. It wasn't all that extraordinary either, for there was something else besides my IRA relatives being there as prisoners, and my friends having raided it so often for rifles any time they were short of equipment, that the Belfast IRA called Ballykinlar Camp, 'the Stores'. My Uncle Jim, who was killed in Belgium with the Royal Irish Rifles and had his name on the Menin Memorial Arch, had been stationed there in the First War, and my younger brother, Seamus, a regular soldier in the Royal Irish Fusiliers, was stationed there in the Second. I did not know what song could contain all this, except a song about the County Down where Ballykinlar was situated, and I sang it with great feeling, with Shaggy very visibly affected, thinking of his mother, which English people go in for a lot, unlike the Irish or Scots, who sing about her on Saturday night when they are drunk and leave it at that.

Shaggy fixed his eyes on me while I sang, and I got great silence for my song:

'There's a rocky old road I would follow, to a place that is
 heaven to me,
Though it's never so grand, still it's my fairyland, just a
 wonder world set apart,
In my island of dreams you are with me it seems,
And I care not for fame nor renown — like the black sheep
of old — I'll return to the fold—
Little town in the Old County Down. . . .'

There was great applause for this song of mine led by Shaggy, and the PO took the pipe out of his mouth and said: 'Good boy, Paddy. Give us one of the old ones, you know, "The Long, Long Trail", or "Roses of Picardy", or "Tipperary".'

'Yes, yes, Paddy,' they all shouted. ' "Tipperary".'

All these songs I'd gained the knowledge of in the street, from the other kids or listening to the old ones on pension day in the pub, for I would certainly not have heard them in my own home, but I knew them all sang 'Tipperary' properly, with my own lone voice leading the verse:

'Paddy wrote a letter to his Irish Molly-oh,
Saying if you don't receive it, write and let me know,
You can sing your songs of Piccadilly, Strand and Leicester
 Square,
Until Paddy got excited and he — shouted — on —
the — air,'

Then everyone joined in, screws and all, with the PO waving time with his pipe:

'It's a long way to Tipperary,
It's a long way to go,
It's a long way to Tipperary,
To the sweetest girl I know,
Good-bye, Piccadilly, farewell Leicester Square,
It's a long, long way to Tipperary,
And my heart lies there.'

199

Charlie was delighted and sang like a lark, and Knowlesy sang up and Chewlips, and Joe made some sounds, though he didn't know the words. Chewlips didn't seem to know many words either, but kept up a happy whine, 'eeeeerrrrrrrr', and or course all the other blokes sang away.

When I finished my recital a bloke called Charlie Garland sang the 'Blind Boy', and we had solos from a good few blokes. In between two singers, Shaggy said, 'They were smashing songs you sang, Paddy,' and even Mac Stay said they were, only that little speedioch bastard, Ickey, shoves in his sharp ferrety voice:

'You shouted "Up, Down", Shaggy. 'Ow the bloody 'ell could that make sense, "Up, Down"?'

Shaggy looked at me to answer him and I said, ' "Down" means a fort in Irish. It doesn't mean down like—'

'Now,' said Ickey, 'I suppose it means —ing "Up",' and everyone laughed and I laughed myself, but said to myself I'd have an eye out for that begrudging little whore's melt.

When we passed Chelmsford Jail, this Charlie Garland said his father was in there doing a ten stretch, so we had a kind of a two-minutes' silence for Charlie Garland's father.

But it's hard to keep easy for long when everyone is in good humour, and we started singing again as soon as Chelmsford Jail went out of sight.

Anyway, Charlie Garland himself said: 'I've never seen my old man even once that I can remember. He's either been in the shovel or on the trot, and I only know what he looks like since I been pinched myself — a copper showed me his picture in the *Hue and Cry*.'

So they sang 'Roll Out the Barrel,' 'Wish me Luck as you Wave me Good-bye', and 'The Woody Woodpecker Song':

> 'Hear him peckin' at the same old tree,
> Peck, peck, peckin' out a melody,
> He's as happy as a bumble bee all day long.
>
> You've got to swing your lady,
> Where the trees are shady. . . . '

When we got into the countryside again the PO said we could all out; the coach halted, and we got out on to the road.

Then we were marshalled in our chains behind the hedges and the PO told us that there was an ATS encampment nearby, but if any of the girls passed up the road we were not to pass any remarks to them.

Some of them, he said, could take a joke but there was always a chance that one among them might resent us and would report us to her officers, who would complain to the Prison Commissioners.

Sure enough, while we stood behind our hedges half a dozen girls in uniform came down the road and, to their astonishment, were stared at by twenty pairs of eyes from each side of the road, in silence.

They glanced nervously at each other, and at us, whose faces were fixed on them and our eyes going over every inch of them, and every feature of their faces and figures.

One of them nodded and gave a weak smile in our direction but when she got no response, except the same intense stare, she hurried after her comrades, and another of them looked round, as they all hurried on, and said, 'Blimey, girls — loonies!'

I must admit that Ickey Baldock was not a bad singer, and Shaggy and Mac Stay and him sang songs about Feltham that we all joined in with, wherever we could pick up the words.

We passed over wild moors like the Dublin mountains, only low and flat, and the boys all agreed it looked a wild place. A Viking ship had been found on the moors and there wasn't a sinner to be seen anywhere, except a few sheep, but there was heather and fresh air.

The PO said we would come out of it as strong as bulls, and all the boys sang; one of the songs we'd picked up from Ickey and Shaggy and Mac Stay:

'Oh, they say I ain't no good 'cause I'm a Borstal Boy,
But a Borstal boy is what I'll always be,
I know it is a title, a title I bear with pride,
To Borstal, to Borstal and the beautiful countryside.
I turn my back upon the 'ole society,

And spent me life a-thievin' 'igh and low,
I've got the funniest feelin' for 'alf-inchin' and for stealin',
I should 'ave been in Borstal years ago,
Gor blimey!
I should 'ave been in Borstal years ago.'

One of the screws pointed along the road to some buildings in the distance. 'There you are,' said he, 'that's it,' and everyone was silent.

I looked over the moors and marshes, and saw again the sea and saw the gulls again, wheeling in the air and screeching, and I sang out for myself:

'The sea, oh, the sea, a ghradh gheal mo chroidhe,
Oh, long may you roll between England and me,
God help the poor Scotchmen, they'll never be free,
But we're entirely surrounded by water.'

Everyone looked at me in surprise and Shaggy laughed and said, 'Good old Paddy,' and the rest of them laughed and Charlie and Joe nodded proudly, and Chewlips said proudly, ' 'E's a comical bastard, 'n't e?' And the PO laughed and took the pipe out his mouth and said, 'You'll get sea all right, Paddy, here — right boys, we're nearly there' — and the coach turned into a yard and stopped.

The buildings were big, rambling and timbered like the head-quarters of the Horse Show or the Phoenix Park Racecourse buildings in Dublin. There were dormer windows and a clock tower. They were built about 1880 or 1890, I'd have said, to imitate a Tudor great house.

I'd learned about building, all my people being in that industry, and I was not reared to that style of building at all. I was reared to Georgian, Regency or modern, but I liked these buildings because they were more unlike a jail than any place could be.

It was two o'clock by the tower and there were groups of BIs standing around, digesting their dinner and smoking, before going back to work. They were wearing overalls and heavy boots. Some wore mechanic's blue bib and brace but most wore smocks and their Borstal shorts and gaiters. They all had the appearance of hard work, and walked methodi-cally, saving their energy for the job. They took no notice of us; after a glance in our direction they went out of the yard on their way.

The handcuffs and chains were taken off and we were lined up in the yard. Then the two screws led us into the building and upstairs to the Part-Worn Stores; the Principal Officer went off with our files in two big bundles under his arms and to get body receipts for our safe delivery.

The screws gave a list to the Part-Worn Stores Officer and he compared it with a list of his own. Then he called over our names, and when we answered them the Feltham screws went off, giving us a civil good-bye when they went down the stairs.

'Good-bye, sir, good-bye, sir,' we shouted after them, and we shouted 'good-bye' to the PO from the window, for they weren't bad blokes. The Part-Worn screw told us to take off our clothes and make them into parcels.

The Part-Worn screw was a man about thirty-five with a

thin face and big head of hair going grey. The Borstal boy assisting him was a tall boy of nineteen with a fresh complexion and, just now, looking very sulky.

We began to take off our clothes and the screw shouted to the orderly: 'Hey, Geordie, hurry up with those bloody kits, will you? They can't stand here ballock naked all day.'

He didn't seem in any way upset by our nakedness himself. Most of us didn't give a God damn one way or another; we were by this time used to living with one another, but the new fellow, the boy who'd been done at Kingston Sessions, was a bit shy and held up his pants with one hand while he tried to get his shirt off with the other.

'You can let them drop, kid,' said the screw, 'we're all cocks here.'

We laughed at this, but Charlie, too, held his hands over his crotch and stood crouched at the window.

At last Geordie came round with the kits — blue jackets, shorts, shoes, shirts, underpants, and stockings.

'Fine body of men, ain't they, Geordie?' said the screw, looking at us shivering and getting into our clothes.

Geordie refused to answer, but continued to look sulky.

It was almost as if the screw was trying to make up a quarrel they'd been having earlier in the day, before we came. It seemed a funny position, a screw trying to coax a prisoner into good humour. I said this to Joe, and of course he had his answer straight away.

'The course of true love never runs smooth,' said he, giving his views on the matter.

'I wouldn't doubt you,' said I, laughing. We were bent tying our laces, so as we couldn't be overheard. 'You dirty-minded old bastard.'

'He is that, and all,' said Charlie, 'and you're a fughing sight worse than he is. You've got a bit of education,' said he.

'Well, you must admit,' said I, 'it does look a bit like that.'

'Damn-all to do with me,' said Charlie, 'once the sod doesn't try that lark with me. Or any other bastard either.'

'I'll consider your application,' said Joe.

'Take your towels and fall in for showers,' said the screw.

'Right now, in the showers,' said Joe, bending low and

holding his hand over his mouth, as he always did when anything amused him.

'Gerch you!' said Charlie, and down we went after Geordie and all in good humour, for Geordie had passed the word round that when we came back from the showers we were all to be issued with a half-ounce of snout and a packet of cigarette papers.

There were ten showers and some fellows waited standing in the steam, while the rest of us stripped and got under.

Joe ran naked round the place in great delight, splashing and smacking rings round him, and curses were showered on him by all concerned. He was told to get to hell out of it, till at last he retired to his own shower laughing himself sick.

'Hey, Paddy, sing up there,' he shouted over to me, ' "The Boys from the County Cork".' He pronounced it 'Coke'.

'Paddy,' Charlie shouted from next door, 'come in and soap my back, will you?'

'I will,' shouted Joe, 'I'm good at that, I am.'

'You stop where you are,' said Charlie.

He stood under the water, the light down his back muscles faintly gleaming.

'OK,' said I, taking the soap. He straightened and stood gravely while I rubbed the soap over him. 'Right, kid?'

'Right, Paddy, thanks.'

When I was back in my own cubicle Joe shouted over: ' 'Ere, what about the "Boys from the County Cork", Paddy? Sing up!'

I sang that:

> 'Some of them came from Kerry,
> Some of them came from Clare,
> From Dublin, Wicklow, Donegal,
> And the Boys from old Kildare,
> Some from the land beyond the sea,
> From Boston and New York,
> But the boys that licked the Black and Tans,
> Were the boys from the County Cork.'

'You don't want to let old Forrest hear you singing that, Paddy,' said Geordie.

He was sitting on a bench having a rest and a smoke for himself while he waited on us to finish our showers.

'How's that?' I asked him, rinsing my legs. 'And who the —ing hell is this Forrest, that I mustn't let him hear me singing?'

'Oh, he wouldn't mind you singing,' said Geordie.

'That's terrible decent of him,' says I.

'But he wouldn't fancy that song. He doesn't fancy Irish people, neither.'

'Then it's a desperate bloody pity about him,' said I. 'Maybe they don't fancy him.'

'Well, I'm only telling you, Paddy. Forrest was in the Black and Tans himself.'

'Was he, bejasus?' said I, turning on the cold shower. 'Well, I'll have to give a serenade of this:

'On the eighteenth day of November just outside the town of Macroom,
The Tans in their big Crossley tenders, they hurried along to their doom,
For the boys of the column were waiting, with hand grenades primed on the spot,
And the Irish Republican Army made shit of the whole —ing lot!'

'Good old Paddy,' shouted Joe.

'Go it, Pad,' said Charlie.

'Foggem all,' said Chewlips, rubbing himself hard with his towel.

After the showers, Geordie led us back up the stairs to the Part-Worn Stores. The screw and Geordie appeared to have settled their difference in the meantime and while Geordie lined us up, the Part-Worn screw gave each of us one half-ounce of Ringers A1 Shag tobacco and a package of AG cigarette papers each. During this time we were also collecting the rest of our kit, our working clothes, our sleeping clothes and our underpants.

A couple of the fellows could roll cigarettes but most of

us could not. The screw sat up at his desk and showed us how to do it. He, himself, could roll them with one hand, like a cowboy.

Geordie was very much improved in his humours, and told us we would be sent out to work in the morning on the gardens.

We thought this would be great, to be out in the open air, but Geordie said we would not be long getting brassed off with it, doing the spring digging. He said it was all right in the picking season. There were plums, apples, and all manner of greengages, even tomatoes and cucumbers and grapes and peaches.

But he said we would never get near the tomatoes and cucumbers; the only vegetables we would get at would be leeks and carrots and a bloody cold and horrible job it was, pulling them on a frosty morning and your hands numb with cold. And as for the grapes and peaches, they were the Governor's and if he caught anyone as much as looking at his peach wall or his hothouses he did his nut and no one with any sense would even think of them.

'Well, we'll 'ave to make do with the apples and pears and currants,' said Joe.

'And very nice, too,' said Chewlips.

'They might give you a barrow,' said I, 'and you could go shouting the way you told us.'

'Give us a bit of a shout,' said Charlie, 'go on, Chewlips.'

'Foh-pance a Pahnd-Pehhs!' roared Chewlips.

A boy walking across the yard outside and carrying a ladder nearly dropped it and recovering, looked around him for the noise.

'Turn it up,' said Geordie, 'they'll 'ear you down below.'

'Reckon they've heard him, in Petticoat Lane,' said the screw, but with a smile, so that Chewlips put down his head and blushed with pride.

'Reckon they should 'ave a wall round this bleedin' drum,' said Joe, 'to stop sods trying to get in. Plums and apples and currants.'

'It's like that song was made about the Christmas cake,' said I.

207

'What song was that, Paddy?' asked Geordie.
I sang:

> 'There was plums and prunes and berries,
> Oranges, lemons and cinnamons, too,
> There was nuts and almonds and cherries,
> And the crust it was nailed on with glue,
> There was caraway seeds in abundance,
> 'Twould give you a fine headache,
> 'Twould kill a man twice, to be after eating a slice,
> Of Miss Houlihan's Christmas cake.'

'Well,' said Geordie to me, 'you're a funny sod, and no mistake.'

Said Charlie, 'He's an Irishman.'

'Oh,' said Geordie, 'I see. I sometimes get taken for an Irishman, though I come from Newcastle. It's on account of talking Geordie.'

'To tell the truth,' said Joe, 'when I first 'eard Geordies talk, I thought they were some kind of bleedin' foreigner.'

'I couldn't bleedin' make 'em out, neither,' said Ickey Baldock.

Mac Stay nodded his head, but before he could say anything I said, 'Well, everyone is a foreigner out of their own place.'

Him being a Canadian, and from farther away than myself even, that shut *his* bloody mouth on the matter.

'The Geordies is very honest people,' said a bloke.

Charlie said nothing, but I suppose he was thinking of the Richardsons, though he didn't let on.

'They can't be all that honest,' said Geordie, 'you see plenty of them in the nick.'

'Well,' said Joe, 'you see blokes in the nick for other things besides knocking off. I reckon most of the Geordies are in for fighting and suchlike.'

'Welsh are the most honest of the lot,' murmured Knowlesy, 'you never see a Taffy in for knocking off. Only sheep-shagging.'

'That's not so,' said the kid who'd been done at Kingston Sessions, 'I got done for sheep—'

We all nearly burst from laughing, for he'd got himself mixed up in what he wanted to say, but the poor kid was that embarrassed and blushing that we stuffed our laughter back and let him get on with what he had to say, for, after all, it wasn't often he opened his mouth.

'Kip in, kip in,' said the screw, lighting a cigarette.

'I was going to say that that's not true about the Welsh not being in the nick for stealing but only for—'

We nearly burst out laughing again, but the screw looked at us sternly and we kept our faces straight.

'— sheep-shagging, because I got done for screwing and my mum came from Swansea.'

'Well, she shouldn't 'ave done,' said Joe, 'she should 'ave bleedin' stayed there.'

'That's right,' said Ickey Baldock, 'London for the bloody Londoners. We don't get a chance in the bastard place with Welsh and Scotch —.'

'And Wops,' said Knowlesy.

Joe took it in good part and only pretended to go for him, saying, 'Bleedin' Lancashire swede-bashers, you mean.'

'And Irish,' said Ickey Baldock, 'going round with bleedin' time-bombs.'

'Paddy 'ere was only fighting for 'is country,' said Charlie.

I said nothing, but Shaggy said, 'My mum was Irish,' and that little bastard Ickey Baldock smiled as if he had only spoken for a joke.

'You in for the IRA, Paddy?' asked the screw.

'Yes,' I said.

'You must 'ave been barmy,' said he, blowing smoke down his nose. 'There's no percentage in that lark. I was in India in the Army from the time I was old enough to go overseas and saw plenty of it there.'

He said no more than that, but nodded to us. 'It's time now for the Governor. Take them down, Geordie, will you, and don't lose any of them.' He smiled at Geordie and Geordie smiled back and when we went out of the room I heard the screw humming to himself. We went down the stairs, taking

209

a last drag from our cigarettes before putting them in our top pockets.

While we stood outside the Governor's office, I read the notices on a board outside the orderly room.

It announced a concert which was postponed from Easter due to flooding at that time on the land and was to be held on the next Saturday night. It was described as a 'Heinz' concert of fifty-seven varieties and the notice also said that the entire Easter programme was being gone through. On another sheet it announced a sports day and a cross-country run. On another sheet the religious services announced. High Mass for the Church of England and for the Catholics. This surprised me, for I did not know the Church of England called it 'High Mass', but they did.

There was another holy bit on the board in a permanent frame, with flowers round the borders, and it contained a poem by Rudyard Kipling called 'Eddie's Service'.

The Chief came down. He was brisk and trim, wearing a suit of plus-fours and the look of an ex-Regular Army man about him.

'Come on, you fellows,' he said, stroking his clipped moustache. He went over to one bloke and said, 'Are you not able to do a tie yet?' and undid it and fixed it for him.

The bloke had tried to tie his tie in a Windsor knot, which is a double knot one over the other, but the thick Borstal tie did not allow for this.

'What way is that to go before the Governor?' the Chief asked another bloke who hadn't got his hair combed properly. 'Look lively there, you fellows, and get yourselves right. Pull up your stockings here, you, there.'

I think he was mostly doing it to impress us with the importance of the occasion, for when he did throw open the Governor's door for us to go in, he shouted: 'Right! Stand in front of the desk and give your number, full name, religion and sentence!' and though that was the form always used by the Chief or the PO when he sent you into the Governor, it would have been impossible for a score of us to have given the Governor these details all at the same time, and impossible for him to have understood them if we did.

The Chief didn't wait for us but saluted the Governor, who smiled from behind his desk and said, 'Thank you, Chief.'

The Chief shut the door and went off and the Governor smiled at us and said, 'Gentlemen, you are very welcome.' While we were getting over this he added: 'You may sit down. I'm afraid I've no chairs but park yourselves on the floor as best you can.'

We sat down on the floor, those at the back kneeling with their hands on the shoulders of the ones in the front.

'You got an issue of tobacco from the Part-Worn Stores officer. You may smoke.'

We rolled cigarettes or continued our dog-ends. The Governor took a cigarette from a box on the desk in front of him and lit it.

'While you are here, the first thing I ask of you is courtesy to each other, to the staff and to myself, and in other matters I must have your co-operation.

'For instance if, as we all do, no matter where we are, or under what circumstances, you find life unbearable, I ask you to come and see an officer or your housemaster or the Padre or myself about it. It may happen that the working party to which you have been sent does not suit you. I can't always guarantee that I can transfer you to work to which you would be better suited. Obviously, though some of you may be good sailors, I can't put you on a ship.'

The blokes laughed at this.

'A man came here today and I see he is by occupation a taxi driver.'

The boy who had been sentenced at Kingston Sessions looked up at the Governor, who looked down at him. 'It's you, is it?' asked the Governor.

The boy nodded and muttered, 'Yes, sir,' and went red in the face when we all looked round at him.

The Governor went on, 'Well, it stands to common sense that I can hardly give this man work at his trade.' Again we laughed. 'But we have tractors here on the farm and I do not see why, if this man got a recommendation from his working-party officer, and after some time of course, for we have a waiting list, and we haven't tractors for everyone, well I think he could have a go at driving a tractor on the farm. And so on. If possible we will make use of your talents in whatever way we can.

'Again, it may happen that you may get the notion that the officer in charge of your party is sorting you out. It may happen that the officer has lost his temper with you. It might even happen that the officer has been impatient with you. He has his own troubles like everyone else and sometimes gets out the wrong side of the bed just as you do. Maybe it will happen that the two of you have got out the wrong side of the bed the same morning.

'It may happen that you do not at first get on well with the men working with you, or the men sleeping either side of you in the dormitory may get absolutely on your nerves. This is a common occurrence.

'This happened to me at school and it's certainly no good just saying "grin and bear it, that you will have to put up with it, like everyone else, that maybe you're getting on someone else's nerves". Maybe, nothing can be done about it, but it's always worth having a talk with someone about it. More than likely, you will find out that your differences with staff or other men will straighten themselves out after a time, but it's always worth having a chat with someone if you feel your troubles are getting beyond you.

'In any case, do not leave this place without notifying me. We shall discuss the matter, and I know I'll be able to prevail on you not to take a step that will keep you away from your parents, girl friends, wives, and families. A few of you are married, I know.

'As you know, nobody ever succeeds in stopping out of these places. From this place, however, you won't even have the glory of a well-planned scarper, because there is nothing to plan about. All you have to do is to walk out at night-time, or even in the daytime. The officer in charge of your party may send you on a message miles away and I cannot very well have people holding your hand all the time.

'But if you run away it makes things difficult for everyone.

'Some of the local people did not want us here at all at the beginning, and it's taken some time to gain their goodwill.

212

'But an absconder cannot get far without breaking in somewhere for clothing or money. I, of course, get told off by the people round the place — you'd think I'd done the stealing.'

He did not seem to think it a laughing matter so we did not laugh and he went on, 'Also, from your point of view it means that I must close in the bounds on everyone and restrict your movements a great deal — so don't sneak off without telling me.'

Blokes nodded and said, 'No, sir.'

'The work will keep you fit, and if you like you can go to PT in the morning. It will be good for you all the days of your life, but some of you may find it difficult to worry about the latter days of your life just now. I could have had PT when I was your age and I didn't, and I'm sorry. It's a matter for yourselves.

'When men are doing a hard day's work in the fields or on the works, eight, nine, ten hours a day, I cannot find it in my heart to make PT compulsory, particularly' — he drew on his cigarette and smiled at us — 'when I was never overgiven to that sort of thing myself.'

We burst out laughing and Joe whispered in delight. ' 'E's a bleedin' rogue, 'n' 'e?'

'As regards other classes they are nearly finished now till the autumn. We have a great deal to do in the gardens, in the farm, and keeping the sea back, or we won't have either. Tomorrow is Saturday and you may have the day off—'

'Thank you, sir,' we said though we would sooner have gone to work, from curiosity and from the novelty of working outside.

'—and walk around and try not to get in other people's way till Monday, when we'll find jobs for you. Good afternoon and good luck to you.'

'Good afternoon, sir,' said we, getting up to our feet. The Chief opened the door and shouted, 'Right, put on your caps and march out!'

We had no caps but we knew what he meant and we went out and up the corridor back to the main building.

213

The Chief gave us in charge to a big screw called Hill and he allocated us to our places.

Most of the fellows were allocated to the new houses, St Andrew's and St Patrick's. These were modern camp-style buildings, one-storey structures of timber, corrugated iron, and plaster-board interiors. It was said that they were very comfortable, with a billiard-room, games-room, wireless-room and thermostatic showers. The dining-hall and dormitories were centrally heated.

Charlie and Joe and Knowlesy and Chewlips and I were staying together in this main block which was big and quaint, though some fellows said a bit too near the orderly room and the Governor's house and the Chief's office for their comfort.

It had the same recreational amenities as the others, with the library and gym for the whole place as well, but it had no thermostatic showers and no heating except for a fire in the library.

Still, I had a kind of liking for the old kip, and anyway, as Joe said, we were all being left together team-handed, himself and Charlie and me, and now Chewlips and Knowlesy, who were also in the team.

Shaggy and Ickey Baldock and MacStay were also in St George's.

We went back up to the Part-Worn Stores and the screw and Geordie gave us the rest of our kit, including our sheets. We were in 'B' dormitory, which was on the bottom floor, which was a big place with timbered walls and ceiling and timber pillars in two rows along the middle of the floor.

We dumped our kits till we would be shown to our beds and went back through the corridor to look for the housemaster's office, which we were to go to next.

A lightly built, fine-featured man, in a cassock, passed us while we were looking for the housemaster's office.

'Good evening, men,' he said, and smiled at us.

'Good night, sir,' said Joe and Chewlips.

'Good night, Padre,' said Charlie and Knowlesy.

'Good night, Father,' said I.

'Good night and God bless you, Paddy, whoever you are,' said he, and went on, smiling.

'Needn't 'ave called 'im "Father",' said Joe.

'Well, I could hardly have called him "Mother",' said I.

'He's the Padre,' said Charlie, 'the C of E bloke.'

' 'E's not the priest,' said Joe.

'I've as good a right to ordain priests as the Cardinal,' said I. 'It's only a difference of him getting paid for it.'

There was a bloke of about twenty or twenty-one going by, and he laughed and said: 'Marlowe said he had as good a right to mint money as the Queen of England. Did you know that?'

'I did,' said I, 'and I'm glad to see that someone else knows it.'

The older bloke laughed a bit more and went on.

We got in a queue. 'That's Rivers you've been speaking to,' said a small fellow at the door. 'He's your dormitory captain.'

'Seems a good bloke,' said I.

'Are you a reception too?' asked Charlie.

'Am I —!' said the small bloke, pointing to a badge on his jacket pocket. 'That's a discharge badge. You get that three months before you go out. I'm on discharge. Only eight weeks to go. Long time before you'll be wearing one of these.'

'Stuff me!' said Charlie. 'You'll be out for ages while I'm still in.'

The small bloke looked round in anger for support from the other blokes standing there before us.

'Well,' said I, to make matters more easy, 'you were out for ages when this bloke was in, weren't you? You weren't bothering much about him then, were you?' No more was I, if it came to that, but I had to say something to humour the small bloke. He looked like a kind of little get, that would rise a row and go down on his two knees in gratitude, like that other little bastard, Ickey Baldock, for the excuse — once he could get other people to do the battling. We didn't want to get into a bundle, our first night in the kip.

But the small fellow was soothed. 'That's right, mate,' he said to me, 'comes to everyone's turn. But that bloke you been

215

speaking to, 'e's on the same discharge as me, in eight weeks. 'E used to be 'ouse-captain over this 'ouse. George's this is.'

'We know that,' said Charlie.

' 'E was the 'ouse-captain of George's until 'e turned it up a few weeks ago. 'E handed over the job to 'Eath. 'E's 'ouse-captain now, but Rivers is still dormitory leader over "A" dormitory. That's the one you Receptions will be going into.'

'He's a nice bloke, Rivers is,' said another fellow, 'though 'is folks is toffs.'

'Yes,' said the small fellow, 'he is a good bloke. He was in a college before he came inside.'

'Oxford College, wa'n't it?'

'No. It was 'Arrow. I remember 'im saying one time it was 'Arrow. He'd sooner be 'ere though, 'e says. 'E says the grub's better.'

'What was 'is lot then?'

'Old toffs of ladies used to bring the college boys to dances in London when they were on their school 'olidays, along of all the other nice college boys and girls and, while they was down below dancing, Old Rivers would slip upstairs pretending 'e was in the Double You 'scuse Me, and 'e was going round the bedrooms casing the gaff for any odds and ends of stuff they might leave round in the way of rings or bracelets or watches and suchlike. And a few nicker, too; 'e didn't object to ready cash, neither. No way proud. He'd come back and screw the gaff after the ball was over. The old lady would tell the butler to give the young gentleman is 'at, and good-bye now, and call again, and 'e'd say, don't worry, I will, *au revoir* but not good-bye, and the next thing when they were all asleep 'e'd come back and do a creeping job and screw the gaff and that was that.'

'A judy got 'im done, wa'n't it?'

'That's right, 'e used to go out at night to this judy near 'is college and she kept the stuff for 'im. But 'e was followed there one night by one of the masters and she got frit and shopped 'im.'

'Bleedin' grass-'opper, like all judies.'

'Well, she didn't exactly mean to shop 'im. The old schoolmaster, 'e didn't tumble anything about Rivers being a

216

tea leaf, but she thought the master was a copper, and 'ad come after the stuff Rivers 'ad pinched. She didn't know that it was only a schoolmaster and that all they could 'ave done was get Rivers and throw 'im out of the college for going case-o with a judy. They didn't like bad boys that couldn't sleep by themselves. They didn't know nothing about the screwing jobs or the stuff being in the judy's room. They might have only caned 'im.'

'Or given 'im lines,' said Knowlesy, from behind me. ' "You bad lad, write out three 'undred times, 'I must not be getting out of the old school at night-time to look for a blow-through'. " '

' " 'Aven't you got your fag like everyone else?" ' said Joe, in an imitation public-school accent.

The queue shortened and it came to my turn. I knocked on the door and was told to come in.

I went into the room and stood before the desk. The housemaster, Mr Davis, was a well-set-up man and very well-dressed in a grey check jacket. He had a cheerful face and a clipped moustache, and was about thirty-six. He looked the sort of man that would shave every morning and again in the evening, if he was going out.

He looked up from his papers, smiled and said, 'What's your name?'

'Behan, sir,' said I. '4738 Behan, age seventeen, religion RC.'

'So's my stepsister,' said Mr Davis, smiling more broadly, so that I had to smile too. 'And when did you become seventeen, Behan? It only says sixteen on your file.' He looked down again at his papers.

'I was seventeen the ninth of last month, sir,' said I.

'And your number here is not four-thousand whatever you said it was. It says here that it's 537.'

'That's right, sir. I forgot,' said I.

'I've been reading your file here. I've been reading a lot of files. Twenty-eight of you came down from Feltham today. Did you have a nice trip?'

'It was great, sir. We had a ding-dong and all, sir.'

He smiled again, and rubbed his moustache. ' "Ding-dong",

217

eh? You haven't been long picking up the rhyming slang. You weren't long in this country, were you?'

'I was two weekends and a whole week and once overnight. I've never lived here ordinarily, sir, and I have no relations in England, sir.'

'You've only lived here extraordinarily, what?' He smiled again. 'However, you won't be without friends.'

'Yes, sir.'

'Well, I only want to tell you that there is a good library here and also that the Padre is getting a branch of the County Library here. We are entitled to it. His Majesty's Prison Commissioners pay rates on this place just like anyone else. Do you agree?'

'I do, indeed, sir. Good night, sir.'

'Send in the next man, will you?'

'I will sir, and thanks.'

He smiled and waved his hand. 'You're welcome.'

Joe was next and I sent him in. Charlie and Knowlesy asked me what the housemaster was like and I said he seemed a decent bloke.

A strongly built bloke of twenty or so came up to us, and said to the little fellow, 'Are there any Receptions here?'

Seeing as he was looking at us and had never seen us before, I thought he must have known that we were receptions, but the little fellow only said to us, 'This is Heath, the house-captain,' and turned to Heath and said with respect, 'here's three of them.'

Heath asked our names and compared them with a list he was looking at.

'I see. Now, let's get you blokes sorted out. You're all in my house.' He wore a silver star on his jacket. 'Which one are you?' he said to Charlie.

'I'm Charlie Millwall,' said Charlie.

'London, too, I'd say,' said Heath.

'That's right,' said Charlie, 'Croydon.'

'Well, you'll have plenty of company here, Charlie.' He turned his mild look in my direction.

'My name is Behan,' said I.

218

He smiled and said in a mock Irish accent, 'An' it's aisy to say where you're from, Paddy.'

I smiled too, because it seemed to be meant as a kindness.

'Phwat paart of Tipperary, Paddy?'

'I'm not from Tipperary,' said I.

'Are you not now?' said Heath.

'I'm not,' said I, 'I'm from Dublin.'

'Fair enough, Patrick,' said he, turning to Knowlesy.

He spoke to Joe when he came out of the housemaster's office, and then to us all.

'You blokes are sleeping in the same dormitory and you'll see your house numbers on the lockers beside your beds. These are the numbers you'll use while you are here. Your numbers are, from 533 Millwall, 534 Knowles, 535 Callaghan — who is he? He's not here — sounds another Chinaman like yourself, Paddy.' I smiled back at him.

'There were blokes transferred from Feltham BI,' said I, 'It must be one of them.'

'That's right,' said Knowlesy, 'the one they call "Shaggy".'

'Well,' said Heath, 'to get on with you lot. 536 Da Vinci, and 537 Behan. I have you all here. 'You're all in "A" dormitory. Got that? You'll collect your small kit and take it down there. Your towel, soap, razor, shaving brush and blades. You only get four a month, so look after them. Though I suppose four would do some of you for a year.'

We all smiled and relaxed.

'And sort out your beds, and get them made up and get the stuff into your lockers and keep it tidy.'

Joe said, 'I'll get kipped in beside you, Charlie, and don't scream in the night, it'll only be me.'

'Oh, sod off!' said Charlie. 'I wouldn't sleep in the same bleedin' field as—'

Heath looked up from his list, and spoke evenly to Joe, looking him straight in the eye.

Joe looked back at Heath, waiting for him to speak.

'Look here, cock,' said Heath, 'as long as I'm here, you keep that kind of talk to yourself. I won't wear it, and if I get you or any other filthy bloody swine talking like that he'll know all about it.'

'Got bugger all to do with you,' said Joe, who was hurt, and maybe a little scared for once in a way. Still, he would offer battle if the argument wasn't controlled.

'Ah, sure, it's only a manner of speaking he has,' said I, 'there's no harm in it. There's no harm meant,' I added quickly.

Heath turned to me and said kindly: 'That's all right, Paddy. Maybe it is only a joke. But we can joke without those kinds of jokes, can't we?'

'It's only a lark,' said Charlie. 'He goes on like that all the time but we're used to him. It doesn't mean anything.'

'Divil a bit,' said I affably.

'Well, we'll forget it this time,' said Heath and nodded to Joe. 'But remember not to let us have any more of it. Good night.'

'Good night,' said I.

'Good night,' said Charlie.

'Good night,' said Knowlesy.

' 'Night,' said Joe.

Our dormitory was a huge long timbered room with great beams and wooden pillars supporting it.

There was no heating and it was very cold undressing. Most of the blokes were half asleep in bed before the bell went, and I heard one of them saying to Knowlesy that after we'd been there for a while, the cold wouldn't trouble us going to bed; we'd be so tired from work that getting up would be our trouble.

Charlie was a bit put out when he found his bed was away from Joe and Knowlesy and me, who were all in a row beside each other. But Charlie had been put with the London blokes from Feltham, and in no time at all he was talking away to them about London.

The Callaghan Heath was asking about, was Shaggy, the Feltham transfer, and the daddy of them, and Charlie's bed was beside his, with Ickey Baldock, the little bastard, the other side, and Charlie and them were nattering away about London, till further orders.

220

Steps were heard in the corridor outside and Rivers shouted, 'Top those dog-ends.'

We could not see him, because he slept in a cubicle at the top of the dormitory. I thought it was sort of a place of retirement given to him since he handed over his house-captain's job to Heath, but I was told that every dormitory captain had the right to use this cubicle during his term of office. There were two beds and two lockers and he was also allowed to have his china in with him, if he liked.

All the blokes that were smoking topped their dog-ends quickly and carefully took up the ashes.

A big screw came down through the dormitory. He was a red-faced man, very stout and tall, like a farmer. He had the accent of an English bogman and shouted while he checked us against his notebook.

Then all of a sudden he stopped, and pointed to a bloke lying fast asleep in the bed. We all stared at him (and at the bloke who was covered up with the blankets over his head), wondering what was up.

The screw stood at the foot of his bed and shouted, 'Hey, you?'

The figure stirred under the bedclothes and groaned.

'Hey, you!' the screw shouted again and went over to the bed and shook the sleeper and let a roar in his ear that would wake the dead. 'Hey, you!'

The bloke struggled a bit and sat up, looking all round him and yawning.

'Ah, Jasus,' said I, 'it's Chewlips.'

So it was, too, the poor decent old bastard.

The screw turned in my direction. 'Any of you say anything?'

None of us spoke, least of all myself.

By this time, Rivers had got up and came down the dormitory in his pyjamas.

'Who is this fellow?' asked the screw. And not waiting for an answer he said, 'Get him out of it.'

Rivers went over to Chewlips and shook him in the bed.

'Come on, out of it, throw him out of it,' roared the screw.

221

At last Chewlips came to, and slowly and fearfully got out and stood on the floor.

'Come on,' said the screw, 'get them off. I can't stand 'ere all night.' He pointed to Chewlips' feet which were still wearing stockings pulled up over his pyjamas like a cyclist.

'Nice thing,' said the screw, 'and a bloody 'ouse-captain in and I 'ave to come in and find a fellow with 'is socks on in bed.'

'I'm sorry, Mr Carswell,' said Rivers.

'Well, anyway,' said Mr Carswell, 'I 'ope now you'll let these Receptions know that as long as I'm Principal Officer over St George's, I'll stand for no man going to bed with 'is socks on, winter or summer. I don't care 'ow cold it is. It's not a 'ealthy 'abit, and I'll get the man out of bed fifty times in the night, if I suspect 'e's got anything on besides 'is pyjamas. Now, you,' he said to Chewlips, 'remember that. And next time I'll send you up to the 'ousemaster. Got that?'

Poor Chewlips nodded his head fearfully, and as the screw walked off again with Rivers he got slowly back into bed and covered his face again.

The screw walked up the stairs and said, 'Right, Rivers, tell them to kip in.'

'Yes, sir,' said Rivers, 'good night.'

'Good night, Rivers, good night, you blokes.'

There was a chorus from the beds, 'Good night, sir.'

The lights were put out and I lay back. In the dark I could see the red end of a cigarette being drawn back to life.

The bloke beside Chewlips called him and said that Carswell was dead nuts on anyone trying to sleep with their socks on.

'I wondered 'ow 'e knew I 'ad them on,' said Chewlips mournfully.

'Why, you silly born bastard, w'en 'e didn't see them in your shoes under the bed, 'e knew, di'n't 'e?'

'I never thought of that,' said Chewlips. 'But if I did 'ave a pair under me bed, 'e wouldn't bother, would 'e?'

'You want to put a sock in your bloody great mouth,' said a peevish voice. 'I'm on with cows at six in the mornin'.'

Another voice sang softly, ' "To be a bleedin' farmer's boy. . . ." '

'All right,' Rivers said from his cubicle, 'turn it up, you blokes, and kip in.'

'Good night, Rivers,' the boys all said.

'Good night, you blokes.'

'All the same,' murmured Chewlips to the silent dark, 'if I 'ad a pair of socks under the bed with my shoes, it wouldn't matter what pair they were.'

'So long as you 'adn't bleedin' pinched mine,' muttered the bloke beside him, and settled down to sleep.

And so it was, I noticed a couple of nights later. Chewlips had his stockings in the shoes under his bed, and when he rose in the morning he shoved them in his pocket, for he had another pair on his feet.

In the morning we were sent to the Garden Party. We were given forks and told to fall in and go up to Small Acre. Charlie and I were on this party but Joe was put on the Works' Party which did building jobs.

Small Acre was a big field with trees in regular rows that seemed to stretch for miles. They were beginning to get back their leaves after the winter.

The ground was frosty underfoot; the screw gave each of us a row to dig between the trees and stood at the top of the field looking down the rows, telling us to get cracking.

I dug a field once with my father, the time of a strike, when the Dublin Corporation gave the men plots of one-eighth of an acre out on Dean Swift's in Glasnevin. My old man dug a good bit of the field, with great function, and talked about the land and how our ancestors came from it and how healthy it was, and saying that we could easily find relics of Swift or Vanessa and Mrs Delaney and Stella as we dug but, after a while, he got bored, and the next day he got a countryman to dig the plot in exchange for my father doing two turns on picket duty.

I asked my grandmother about our ancestors and their land, and she said she was my ancestor and she was no bogwoman but a qualified printeress and had been all her young life and that our family's land was all in window-boxes.

And I'd heard my father saying that Larkin aimed to abolish the village idiot, but as I stuck my fork into the ground I thought of all the great songs that were written about the fork and its stable companion, the pike:

'"I'll forge bright steel for liberty",' said Paud O Donaghue, the rebel blacksmith. Me life on him; and the one about the Fenian times:

'That rake up in the rafters, mother, why hangs it there so long?

Its handle of the best of ash is smooth, and straight and
    strong,
And mother, will you tell me? Why did my father frown,
When to make the hay in Summertime, I climbed to take it
    down,
He swung his first born in the air, while his eyes with light
    did fill,
"You'll shortly know the reason why," said Rory of the
    Hill.'

I dug and threw over the sods and there was a great sharp
clean smell from the earth, and I singing to myself, or grunting as I dug, all sorts of songs about forks and pikes and other
agricultural implements:

'I bear orders from the captain, "Get ye ready, quick and
    soon,
With your pike upon your shoulder at the Rising of the
    Moon . . ."'

While the screw stood at the top of the field, a free labourer
came round the party giving instructions in an accent that I
could not understand too well. I was not the only one that
found difficulty in understanding him, for his was an accent
and a dialect none of us was accustomed to.

Besides, as the fellow in the next row to me said, he was
a stupid old sod.

This was a boy called Ken Jones and he wore an outside
tie. He told me that everyone was allowed to have two ties
sent in and to wear them on Sundays or in the evenings, but
he wore his all the time and the screw never seemed to notice.
His whole appearance was very neat and he spoke with a
middle, or upper-class accent. He was very fastidious at the
digging, but he was an easy-going fellow and we talked as
well as we could, turning over the frosty clay, till the screw
shouted down at us to get a move on and we had to save our
breath to get up with the field.

I liked it there in the orchard. It was dark and damp, but
not the dark or the gloom you'd have in the halls of Walton

sewing those bloody mailbags. There were gleams of sun coming through the trees and it was sensible work, with a meaning to it. It was tough at first, after being so long without exercise, I suppose, but after I began to sweat I worked more freely and could have gone to the front and nearer the top of my row, but I didn't like to go too far past Ken, for politeness sake.

And besides, the old free labourer brought me back once or twice, to shake out my sods. He did that with a lot of the blokes, explaining that we weren't only to turn them over but to shake them out and get the air into them.

He was an irritable old bastard and, like all countrymen, he was contemptuous of the man that couldn't do the work as well as he could.

'Sure, we're only after starting at it,' said I, 'and every beginning is weak. It was one after another they built the castles.'

'Wen oy was yewer edge, I'd 'ave 'ad that deer roew dung long semce,' said he.

'Would you, bejasus?' said I. 'And when if I was that length of time at the business, I'd be digging them that quick that by now I'd be meeting myself coming back.'

'Good old Paddy,' shouted some of the blokes, looking up from their forks and laughing.

The old man, who was not so good at backchat, went off to the screw muttering.

The screw came down the row between the trees. Jesus, said I in my own mind, can't you keep your bloody trap shut? Now the screw will bring you back to the building and you'll be banged in a cell and spend at least a day there waiting to go before the Governor. I looked round at the trees and at the red sun, now getting a warmer colour, smelt the ground and looked at my fork and dug on, in sadness, till the screw stood beside me.

He grunted, and I looked up at him.

He had red hair, and was wearing a thick leather coat, a check suit, a muffler and gum-boots. He had a slight squint, a cross face, and the look of a boxer.

'Name. Number. House.'

'Behan, 537, sir, St George's House.'

'Oh, you're the Irishman.'

'That's right, sir.'

He had, I noticed now, a very pronounced Lancashire accent. 'What part of Ireland do you come from?'

'From Dublin, sir.'

'Do you know Mayo?'

'I was never there, sir; it's in the West of Ireland. I knew fellows from there, of course.'

'What did you think of them?'

'Good men, sir. "The Men of the West".'

'You're a lucky bugger, Paddy, you said that. My old man's from Mayo, and me mother's a Sligo woman. That's in the Province of Connacht, too, isn't it?'

'Yes, sir.'

'They're Catholics, and good ones. I suppose you're an RC?'

'I am, sir, of course.'

'Well, my dad 'e's an old man but 'e go round garden at 'ome, quicker than this.'

I looked round and saw that I was well in the leading half of the party.

'Don't mind looking at these other fellows. You're an Irishman.'

I am, said I in my own mind, but I'm not from Connacht.

'That's right, sir.'

'And I was in the East Lancs, and done me full time, though I'm not an old man.'

'Bedad, and you're far from it, sir,' said I, indignantly.

He laughed and said: 'Give me none of your old blarney, Paddy. I can do a bit of that myself. The name is Sullivan. That's Irish enough, isn't it?'

The only person of that name I knew of was John L., the Boston Strong Boy, but I said:

'As Irish as the County Mayo itself, sir.'

'Now get and dig a bit more and don't give Mr Vanwank any more lip. If you do well this morning, I can still give you two marks. I'd have given you three maybe if I didn't have to come down to you. You get five a day as maximum and, maybe if you work very hard this afternoon, the officer

227

may be able to give you three marks. That's if you go all out. If you get less than twenty-two marks a week, you'll get a housemaster's report, but I know no Irishman would be that bad — not even if he was a crippled one, much less a fine lad like you. For twenty-two marks you get fivepence and a ha'penny more or less for every mark over that. For sevenpence you can get a half-ounce of tobacco and a packet of cigarettes. I suppose you like a smoke as well as anyone else. Lady Nicotine, the Borstal boys' god.'

'Begod, and that's a hot one,' said I, with a laugh.

'So get moving there, Paddy, we've lost enough time, nattering. We can't waste that much time every day, neither.'

'No, sir,' said I, and got back in action with my fork.

He went under the trees and into the next row, and took the fork from Ken, to show him how he could do better.

I was delighted to be left in the field and not brought in for giving the old bloke lip, and I dug on with a will, taking in the air, and the sun, and smell of the fresh earth, and working like a Connachtman, as the saying has it. The sweat came from me, easy and freely, and I breathed with my stroke like a swimmer.

Then, on a turn of a sod, my fork uncovered a golden apple as hard and as fresh as the day it fell there. I held it up and showed it to Mr Sullivan in the next row and he smiled with his narrowed eyes and told me to go ahead and eat it.

I took a few hurried bites from it and, with the juice sharp on my tongue, put it back in my pocket, and got on with the work, with the morning well advanced and the springtime steaming off the trees and the grass.

By God you weren't that blind, Raftery, that you didn't get the smell and the feel of it:

Anois, teacht an Earraigh, beidh an la dul chun sineadh,
is tar eis feile Bride, ardochaidh me mo sheol. . . .

. . . Now, in the springtime, the day's getting longer,
On the feastday of Bridget, up my sail will go,
Since my journey's decided, my step will get stronger,
Till once more I stand in the plains of Mayo. . . .

228

At ten o'clock we knocked off for ten minutes and had a smoke. We sat round the screw and he asked if any of us were soldiers. Charlie said he was a sailor and the screw asked him what ships he'd been on, and didn't give him much chance of answering, but began telling stories of his own soldiering in the East Lancs.

This was all pre-war but he was proud of his adventures and what the Provoke Sergeant said to him, and what he had said to the Provoke Sergeant.

One of the boys had been in the East Lancashire Regiment and had known, if not that particular Provoke Sergeant, at least another one very like, so they got into conversation and the rest of us listened with attention with the hope that it would extend our break beyond the allotted ten minutes.

I had some of my tobacco left over from the night and the rest of them had a bit left, or a couple of dog-ends they broke up and re-rolled. The screw gave us a light but didn't smoke himself. Some of the boys said he was a Black Sash man at the judo and he also talked about that, when he was done with the Provoke Sergeant for a while.

Ken didn't have anything, and I gave him the makings.

'Didn't you get no snout this week, then?' asked Charlie.

'I bought ten Woodbines,' said Ken. 'I don't like them much, but at least they're tailor-mades. I don't fancy these things' — looking at the rake-up, the makings of which I had just given him — 'I'm not a cowboy.'

'None of us aren't cowboys,' said Charlie, 'but if we're only getting fivepence or sixpence a week, the half-ounce snout lasts longer.'

'I 'eard my old man saying,' said another bloke, 'that the Woodbine is the dearest smoke there is — and the most expensive tobacco.'

'I knew an old bloke where I come from and he won fifty thousand nicker on the pools, and he tried every kind of smoke there is; American, French, Rhodussian, Turkish — every bleedin' kind of smoke, but 'e went back to the Woodbines in the finish — said there was nothing to equal 'em.'

'I remember, sir,' said the bloke who had been in the East

Lancs, 'one evenin' we was going down to town, like — we were just coming out of gate—'

'At Fulwood,' said the screw knowingly.

'That's right, sir, tha knows it all,' said the bloke quaintly, and laughed.

'Should do,' said Mr Sullivan, 'Ah was in Fulwood Barracks before tha dad and mum were married, and Ah know where tha was goo'in' and all, Ah do.'

'Suppose tha does,' said the bloke.

'Ah, ta "Naked Lady" — best pub in Preston. Ah'd good times there, though I never supped beer myself — but with other owld sweats — talking about this and that. I remember one evening . . .'

And they were off again.

We got at least three minutes over the time, and it was with regret the screw shouted 'break up' and we got back to our work.

I knew Ken was a kind of an upset bloke so I didn't mind him so much insulting my bit of tobacco and my paper but I was glad when he said to me, and we crossing under the orchard to our own row, 'Thanks for the smoke, Paddy.'

'You're welcome,' said I.

'I'll send you in some from the outside, Paddy, when I get out.'

'Sure, kid.'

'I know how I can get stuff into here, Paddy.'

'Sure, kid, that'll be great.'

'You think I'm jeering you, Paddy, and that it'll be a long time before I'm on discharge — but I'm not going to wait for that.'

'No?'

'No. I'm not stopping in this place. I got it all worked out on a map I got in the library. My brother would come up here and pick me up in a car. He's a smashing driver, Paddy.'

'I'm sure, Ken.'

'He's a smashing bloke, in every way, Paddy. He's eighteen; more than a year older than me, Paddy, and he's

230

as broad as what you are, but taller. He's a good boxer, too, and a swimmer, and he won the school's championship in the eight hundred yards for St Paul's.'

I thought to tail off the conversation neatly with a complimentary remark about Sir Christopher Wren, but Ken kept on about his brother and how the brother would do the Scarlet Pimpernel and help him vanish from our midst.

Now, I was stopping a bit longer, and decided I might as well do another bit of digging, so I suggested to Ken that if we each dug the half of our row nearest each other, we could talk, and when the screw came near us we could work over the offside of our rows.

'But it doesn't look too bad here,' said I, 'could you not try it a bit longer?'

'I can't afford to wait — my brother is a lieutenant in the Marines and he could be ordered abroad with his regiment any day — probably to Africa — what should I do then?'

'No, begor, you have a point there all right,' said I.

'Anyway, think I'm going to wait another week even listening to that silly old bastard up there nattering about the bloody army? Or to that other yokel telling me "You bain't be a digging right, nor turning your sods right?" Old sod himself.'

He looked down at the fork and turned it over in the earth, listlessly.

'Well, of course, if you could do it,' said I, 'if you could get away with it.' You might as well rave there, as in bed.

'Certainly I could do it. My brother will meet me, just at the road there, I showed him the place when he was on a visit. My brother will be waiting there in a Jaguar — it's his own and was a birthday present from my father — and he'll let her in and we'll be fifty miles away before they even start looking for us,' and then eagerly he asked, 'Like to try it with me, Paddy?'

Not just now, I wouldn't. The place seemed all right. The Governor seemed a decent sort with a bit of humour to him. The screws were all right, and I liked the other blokes. It wasn't like Walton and lastly, although I didn't like saying it to Ken, I didn't like double-crossing the Governor.

'Whatever chance you'd have, Ken, I'd have none. I'm in

231

over the IRA and you know what that would mean. They'd have every bogey in England on the hunt for me. And all the Western ports watched before I'd even get near them. And it would spoil your chances.'

'I suppose you're right, Paddy. But I'm going. You don't think I'm kidding, do you?'

'No, Ken, I don't; of course I don't.'

And I didn't. His eyes were too troubled and his mouth curved too sadly for me not to think that he was in real earnest.

He was dead lonely; more lonely than I and with more reason. The other fellows might give me a rub about Ireland or about the bombing campaign, and that was seldom enough, and I was never short of an answer, historically informed and obscene, for them. But I was nearer to them than they would ever let Ken be. I had the same rearing as most of them; Dublin, Liverpool, Manchester, Glasgow, London. All our mothers had all done the pawn — pledging on Monday, releasing on Saturday. We all knew the chip shop and the picture house and the fourpenny rush of a Saturday afternoon, and the summer swimming in the canal and being chased along the railway by the cops.

But Ken they would never accept. In a way, as the middle-class and upper-class in England spend so much money and energy in maintaining, the difference between themselves and the working-class, Ken was only getting what his people paid for but, still and all, I couldn't help being sorry for him, for he was more of a foreigner than I, and it's a lonely thing to be a stranger in a strange land.

He dug moodily on till lunch-time.

'Right, grub up,' shouted the screw, and Ken threw down his fork and smiled at me, sad and defiant.

'See you after lunch, Ken,' said I.

'You will, Paddy, for a while anyway,' and he gave me a kind of a mysterious grin.

I nodded and joined the rest of the party going up to George's.

Charlie grumbled at me. 'What did you give that bloody Kensington puff a bit of snout for?'

'Because he hadn't anything to smoke, and I was reared that way by me mother, who would never see anyone without a smoke.'

'He got the same as we did, didn't he?' said Charlie, passing no remarks on my mother, for to Londoners all mothers are sacred. 'If he took it in ten Woodbines instead of a half-ounce of snout and wanted to be a lord's bastard for five minutes, instead of having a smoke for tomorrow, that was nothing to do with you.'

When we got into the dining-hall we sat four at a table. A table of polished wood and with cups and saucers instead of mugs. We got a Cornish pasty and cocoa. Our main meal, the orderlies said, we would get at five o'clock when we finished for the day.

'Well, I reckon this is a bit of all right,' said Joe, opening his pasty. 'Reminds me of being at 'ome in a caff.'

'Yes,' said Charlie, 'it would, wouldn't it?'

I said that it would too, but Charlie did not answer me. He had not yet forgiven me for giving Ken the bit of snout, and he told Joe about it and called Ken 'that —ing college boy.'

'Well, sure he has to do his bird like anyone else,' said I, 'no matter what he is,' and I went on with my lunch and left it at that.

No wonder for the poor bastard to scarper.

He did scarper, too.

In the morning he was working beside me again — for we were now kind of graft chinas and would have grafted together every working day, but I could see it on his face, and knew he was dead nervous over something.

'I've a pair of overalls planted and I'm going to fall out just before break. That will give me ten minutes extra.'

I thought the brother must have made contact with him but I didn't like to mention the brother and the car waiting for him before he did, so I said: 'Maybe, kid, it would be better if you waited till night-time. You'd have the whole night before you then.'

'No, I wouldn't. There's a watchman goes round, winding a clock every hour. They'll expect me to make for the main road, but I'm away ahead of them there, Paddy, you'll see.'

The brother, I supposed, but his arrangements were his own. 'Well,' said I, 'the best of luck.'

'Thanks, Paddy, you're a decent fellow. More than I can say for these other sods. Some poeple don't like the Irish — I do.'

'They're very popular with themselves,' said I.

He gave a little sad smile. 'You're a funny bastard, Paddy.'

We went on working, though Ken wasn't going very fast.

'If we don't let out a bit, Ken, the screw might tumble you.'

I was really thinking that I should get a move on myself but it didn't seem polite to go on ahead of him; especially as we were parting.

The screw shouted down the rows, in the shrill and mincing sergeant-major's accent all the screws used for shouting (though there was no harm in it): 'Kim on, yew shower, bend those becks, laike a leetle jeck-knaife,' and in his ordinary serious voice: 'You two, down there! Hey, Paddy, what's keeping you?'

'Sodding Lancashire,' muttered Ken.

I worked on a bit quicker, till I was well past him, and then I reached in my pocket for a few papers and bit of snout, and threw them back at him when the screw wasn't looking. He might need a smoke waiting for the brother — or if he didn't find him.

He took them quickly and got back in his own row. 'Thanks, Paddy, I've got a couple of matches, but I didn't like asking you for the makings. You were decent enough yesterday.'

'Yerra, 'tis nothing,' said I, jovial and Irish, but making every move to work on a bit more.

'You're a good bloke, Paddy,' said Ken from behind me, 'and first chance I get, I'll work you something from the outside. I've got a few good jobs lined up for when I get out. When I get back to the Smoke.'

'I see the screw looking at his watch, Ken. Must be getting on for break.'

'Yes, it must.' I looked round under my shoulder at him. He smiled, the grief of the world on his face, and said, 'Well, good-bye, Paddy.'

'Good luck, Ken,' said I, 'and God go with you.' It was so sad, like seeing someone off to America.

He swallowed his spit a few times and got out a shout at last.

'Fall out, sir?'

I could hear the whole of his misery and despair in that cry, but the screw only nodded his head.

Ken put down his fork and ran through the orchard. The screw remarked on it.

'Can 'ardly wait to get there,' he said to the boy nearest to him.

'Must be that sea-pie we 'ad yesterday,' said the boy and the screw nodded, laughed with him, looked at his watch and shouted, 'Break!'

Charlie sat down beside me and we rolled our rake-ups.

The screw held a lighted match and we each went up to him, lit up and said, 'Thank you, sir.' I was sorry that it was from his party Ken had to scarper.

He shouted at the last fellow, 'Come on, look sharp. Do you want to burn the bloody finger off of me?' then he turned to the bloke who'd been in the East Lancs and they started another conversation about the Army.

'Well, how's the college boy this morning?' said Charlie. 'I see him falling out just before the break. Why doesn't he have his pony and trap in their time?'

'Maybe he didn't know the time, or maybe he was short taken. Wonder how Joe's getting on with the navvy gang?'

'Well, last night he seemed to think it was all right. Remember he was talking about it at tea-time. A lot of the London boys are on it. Ickey Baldock from the Elephant, and Shaggy Callaghan, and Nardone, he's a Wop like Joe, he's from Southgate, and there's Tommy Carr from Notting Hill. He says it's dead funny working on it. They're a rough team.'

I said nothing, but those I'd seen of them looked it. Still, the part of North Dublin I came from was as tough as any, or at least other people thought so. I didn't; being used to it, I suppose, and not having known any place else. I sup-posed it was the same in the Elephant and Poplar and all these other joints. Still and all, they were all together. Although I'd have liked to have worked with the Engineers — building was what I was used to. I didn't understand farming or vegetable growing very much. Though my mother sang songs about the Land War and the 'Rake up in the Rafters' and 'The Bold Tenant Farmer', the only land my own family ever had as far back as anyone could remember would fit in a window-box. My old man said that they sang those songs to give the country people a bit of a jee up when they were fighting the landlords.

'I'm more used to that kind of work than I am to this,' said I, pointing to the fields about me. 'All my people are in the building trade.'

'Yes, everyone knows Irishmen are good navvies,' said Charlie.

'They're good building workers all round,' said I, for though I wasn't a snob, a painter or a carpenter or a bricky or a plasterer is a skilled man.

'There's an Irishman on the navvy gang, too,' said Charlie.

'You mean Liverpool-Irish or London-Irish?'

'No, I mean Edgware Road Irish — Irish from Ireland, same as you. He's from Kerry or Derry or some place. His name is Parry.'

'Sounds more Welsh, don't it?' said I, though I knew there were Parrys in Ireland.

'No, he's Irish all right. Proper mad bastard. He was transferred from Lowdham Grange to Sherwood before he came here. He near wrecked Lowdham Grange. He done three months in Sherwood Forest. Three months' penal class till further orders. So they sent him here for a last chance. If he buggers about here he goes back to Sherwood to finish his full three years.'

'That Sherwood,' said I, 'is a good place to keep out of.'

'Dead right. What's happened to your china with the old school tie?'

'What about him?'

'He'll shit himself blue. He hasn't come back yet. Where's he gone?'

'I haven't got him in my fughing pocket.'

236

'You *are* a leery bastard. No need to take the needle over nothing.'

'I'm not taking the needle but you keep on about this bloke, and the way he speaks. I'm not responsible for the way he speaks.'

Charlie shook his head in temper. 'Oh, fugh off, you, you just about get me brassed off. A bloke can't ask you a simple question. Fugh off with your fughing college boy china, then, and 'ave 'im for a china and fugh you!'

'And fugh you, too!' said I. 'And your friends in America and double fugh you!'

Some of the blokes were beginning to look round at us. The screw, however, shouted just then 'Break up!' and we went back digging.

Then the screw looked doubtfully at the row next to mine and came down to me.

'Where's your mate, Behan?' he asked.

'You mean the lad that was working beside me, sir? In the next row, there?'

'Yes, and don't you come the old soldier, Behan; you know bloody well who I mean.'

'He fell out before break, sir.'

'"He fell out before break, sir." I know bloody well he fell out before break, but where the hell is he, now? He's been gone over twenty minutes.'

'I don't know, sir. I just fell out and had my break with the rest of the lads. You saw me over there yourself, sir.'

He drew a deep breath, nodded to me, and walked away. He went in the direction Ken had gone, shouting, 'Jones, Jones.' And louder, 'Jo—o-ones.'

Honest to God, I was sorry in a way. And a bit ashamed of being sorry over anyone getting out of the clutches of the British Government. But these weren't such bad clutches as clutches go. Now if it had been Walton, I'd have laughed myself sick over the old Chief, the turkey-faced bastard nearly exploding, and even the screw getting half-sheet over it would have been enjoyable.

'Jones,' shouted the screw, 'Jones. Hey, Jones.'

No Jones. 'Right,' shouted the screw. 'Fall in the lot of you.'

237

We ran up to the top of the field and fell in while he counted us. 'One off,' he muttered, taking a whistle from his pocket and blowing a long blast on it.

The boys muttered in excitement: 'Scarpered,' 'taken a powder,' 'fughed off,' 'blown town.'

Some screws came running into the orchard and the elderly Principal Officer came in, leading his bicycle, shaking his head and talking to himself.

'Oh, bejasus, and we're all caught,' said I. 'Here comes Head-the-Ball.'

The fellows in line nearly burst out laughing and that was his nickname from that good day forward. Even the screws took to calling him Head-the-Ball, though not to his face. He was a decent old sort, and we might all live to have worse ailments than head-wagging and talking to ourselves but I was far from considering that.

Head-the-Ball stood amid three or four screws and they all had a bit of a conference with our screw but there wasn't all that excitement and, after a minute or two, they split up and went different ways and our screw came back to us and said, 'Get back down on your rows, take up your forks and let's have some production.'

When I finished my row and went to get another one, Sullivan, the screw, put me on Ken's row and told me to finish it.

He stood looking at me and asked me, 'Did you know Jones was going to scarper, Paddy?'

I looked him straight in the face and said, 'As true as God, Mr Sullivan, I did not.'

He smiled and nodded his head. 'I believe you, Paddy, lad,' and repeated reassuringly, 'I believe you.' Then he walked back to the top of the field.

At one o'clock he came down to me and told me to take the other fork with me to the tool-house along with my own.

On the way to the tool-house Charlie marched beside me, and said he was sorry for having been so leery in the morning. 'You knew he was scarpering, Paddy, didn't you?'

'Of course I knew,' said I. 'But I couldn't tell you and the screw only a few yards from us.'

'You were dead right. I wouldn't like to grass on a bloke, neither.'

At lunch Joe was very interested in Ken scarpering off our party.

I could just see him myself, maybe lying down in the car while his brother flashed his officer's papers, or maybe he was in his uniform, and the cops would just salute and let him pass, without even stopping him, but then how were they to know that a commissioned officer would be helping a Borstal boy to escape?

Joe told us about his own party that morning, the navvy gang. Ickey Baldock rose a shovel to Tessie O'Shea, the screw.

Tessie O'Shea was six foot and weighed seventeen stone. Ickey was about five foot three and weighed about seven stone, even if he was all muscle. I personally thought him a little ballocks, but I pretended to be impressed by the story, but Joe wasn't.

'Bloody little short-arsed —t. Old Tessie just looked down at 'im and pisses 'imself laughing.'

Then they discussed Ken's chances of getting to the Smoke and stopping out for a few weeks. I thought it would be evens that he was in London at that moment. A fast car could do it in two hours, what with the brother being the sort of young officer driver I could just imagine. But I decided not to tell them anything about it till later. Joe and Charlie and poor old Chewlips were OK, but you never know how these things get out, and even when Ken was safely delivered to wherever he would be hiding out, it would certainly mean a court-martial for the brother if it came out.

'I suppose he goes to that bleedin' Sherwoood Forest if they get him?' said Charlie.

'No,' said Joe, 'not 'im. I 'eard them talking about it on the navvy gang. He'd be sent to Chelmsford. He's doing HMP.'

'He's doing what?' said I. 'He's in for screwing.'

'He's not, you know,' said Joe, 'he's doing HMP. One of the lucky ones. The judge said he'd have 'ad 'im topped only for 'is age. Most brutal murder and all that lot. He pushed

239

his crippled brother's bath-chair over a cliff. With the brother in it. Paralysed he was or something, from birth.'

'Well, how many brothers had he?' I asked Joe.

'Ow the 'ell do I know? Only the one I reckon, but I didn't know the family. Shouldn't fughing want to, neither.'

I was just as glad that I hadn't said anything about the brother being an officer and about the fast car.

In the afternoon we saw two station wagons go down the road. Some of the fellows at the three o'clock break said he would be caught before nightfall.

Charlie asked me my opinion and I said I didn't know because I didn't know the country well enough to give an opinion.

He wasn't caught that night. God help him, I thought, maybe it would be better for him if he was. I never saw such a night for rain. As I lay, warm and dry in bed, I thought of poor Ken, alone with himself and the torment of his thoughts out in that bloody miserable-looking bog.

Charlie whispered across in the dark, as the rain pelted off the windows, 'I wonder how old Jonesy is making out, Pad?'

'I'd sooner it was him than me, kid.'

'Maybe he'd go in a barn.'

'No, these old swede-bashers sit up all night with shotguns looking for scarperers. So I heard one of the blokes say.'

'Shower of sods.'

'It's a kind of sport with them. Like hunting animals. Breaks the monotony.'

'Are country people in Ireland like that, Paddy?'

'No, by Jesus, they are not. They have their faults. But even if they didn't help a bloke on the run, they'd not chase him. And if one of them did, he'd get no peace from his neighbours for the rest of his life. No, nor one belonging to him.'

'Do they 'unt foxes in Ireland, Paddy?'

'It's supposed to be the home of it, but I've only seen a fox in the Zoo in the Phoenix Park. I suppose the big shots hunt foxes, same as they do every place.'

'Hey, kip in there, you fughers,' muttered a weary voice. 'I'm on with cows at six.'

240

'It's that bleedin' farmer's boy again,' said Charlie.

The farmer's boy sat up and swore at us from a height, and some other blokes started muttering and waking up.

'Shut up, Charlie, and we'll give the bloke a chance of a sleep.' I wasn't frit of the farmer's boy, a big lump of a lad that told me he came from Itching, which I thought was a funny name for a place, but he was an inoffensive and harmless chap and besides I didn't want to tangle with the whole bloody dormitory.

'Oh, sod you!' said Charlie.

That's all fine and large, said I, in my own mind, but if one of these sods came over and gave you a dig in the snot, it's me or Joe you'd expect to get up and bundle for you. For you couldn't rise your hands to bless yourself, so you can be as needled as you jasuswell like.

But in a second or two, when everyone was settled down again, he said, very softly, 'Hey, Pad.' I could see his face mostly hidden in the blankets and lit in the glow of a dog-end. He reached over and I caught it from his fingers and put in my mouth. I blew into the dark above me and whispered, 'The farmer's boy's gone asleep again; counting his bloody sheep.'

Charlie shook with laughing in the bed and put the blankets into his mouth so as he wouldn't be heard, but at last, thank Jesus, he subsided and said, more softly still, ' 'Night, Pad.'

I whispered good night to him, and drew softly and invisibly on my dog-end, listening to the rain and the wind outside.

Poor Ken, lying out under that. He didn't look like he was suited to that kind of freezing and drenching. Not like if it was one of those Richardsons — the Geordies. It would roll off them, all right. They'd get rusty before they'd get pneumonia. Poor old Ken, he must have been frightened out of his mind to do it. Though people might think it's the terrors that go scarpering, it's mostly not. Mostly the likes of Ken, a sensitive sort of fellow, and amiable enough if he was left to it. Of if he gave the other blokes a chance to get to know him, they'd be amiable with him. There were a few all right that you'd never get on with but you'd get them anywhere.

That Ickey Baldock, now, that was the heart's blood of a canatt if he was let away with it, but by Jesus, I knew one citizen that would not let him away with it.

The watchman was coming. I heard him winding his clock in the corridor. I rolled the tiny dog-end up and flicked it away from me. The watchman came up flashing his light and looking at the blokes asleep.

The light shone on Charlie's face, fast asleep, and I shut my eyes and let on to be asleep till he passed, when I did go asleep.

From the first meal I had in the dining-hall, I had noticed that at Rivers' table the blokes always carried books with them and read while eating. I thought this was a great thing and wondered when I would be able to do it, or at least to take a book with me in the evening-time to read.

There was nothing more to getting a book than going into the library and giving your name to the bloke on duty, but you were supposed to read it there. I looked in the first day I came from work and the place was jammed to the doors with fellows sitting at the tables reading and other fellows standing as near to the fire as they could without getting into it altogether, and smoking and chatting and having an easy minute for themselves. But I didn't see any other reception there, so I was shy about going in. For I declare to Christ, in that library they were like one of those clubs in London you'd read about, with old bishops and colonels and other manner of tail-waggers discussing a letter to *The Times*, and I felt like the bloke that would call round the back for the pig-feedings, so I shut the door and went down the corridor in a hurry.

The centre and O/C and Director of Operations in the library seemed to be a fellow with a thin common face who sat at the desk. His face was common, I thought, but I don't mean that he was not an intelligent-looking bloke, because he was. There's many a one with a head like Solomon and a brain like a turnip, but this fellow had straight dirt-coloured hair, a sharp face and a Liverpool accent, and he was one of the four book-carriers at Rivers' table, and why shouldn't he be, seeing as he seemed to own the library? I was always hoping to get into chat with him, for I wanted to get a book, and he had them.

After lunch this day, Charlie and Joe and Chewlips went off to change their shoes and put their working boots and gaiters on, and I stalled there, finishing my lunch, because myself and some other blokes had wheeled a handcart of wooden posts for fencing down from the tool-house to Long Acre and the screw told us we could make up a quarter of an hour of the time at our lunch hour, though the job had only taken us ten minutes of our own time.

While I was finishing my cocoa, there was only myself left in the dining-hall except for these book-carriers at Rivers' table. Rivers spotted me and shouted up to me, 'Hello, Paddy, come on down to us a minute.'

I sure will, said I in my own mind, and took my cocoa and went down to them.

Besides Rivers and the sharp-faced librarian, there was a tall fellow of about nineteen, and he had the same name as a famous English novelist, I had never spoken to him before and took the opportunity of asking was he a relation, and it turned out that he was a nephew of this novelist. Another claim to distinction that he had was a cigarette holder and a civilian silk tie of rose colour. He spoke with a languid elegant accent and, through being Number Two labour, worked with some other delicate subjects making stockings with Miss Vasser. He was altogether as decadent as our frugal means allowed. He was doing his best anyway, and not badly under the circumstances.

The fourth man was also introduced to me for the first time; his name was MacCann and he said he was Irish, though he had an educated English accent. His right name, and I wondered did his old man ever tell him, was O'Kane or O Cahawn, which was the name of the ancient Irish chiefs of Antrim and also of their lineal descendants, who were the principal Catholic undertakers in Belfast, with the monopoly of burying fallen IRA men.

The librarian's name was Robin Jones and he was, as I thought from Liverpool.

The novelist's nephew's book, I was not so surprised to see, was the *Life of Oscar Wilde* by Frank Harris.

I knew Oscar Wilde's mother was 'Speranza' of the *Nation* newspaper in 1848, the time of the Young Irelanders. We learned some of her poetry at school. I knew Oscar was sent to jail and for a long time I thought it was because he was a rebel too, and I wondered what songs they had about him. But by this time I had a kind of an idea it was about sex, for once I'd asked my mother what he was sent to jail for and she just muttered, 'His downfall — they brought him down the same as they did Parnell.'

I had often heard of Frank Harris, too, because my father had his books, which were published in France, and in the first one, about his childhood, Harris told how he was a bit of a rebel, too. His father had taken him away from Portora School in the North because he'd come on a visit and the first thing young Frank asked was whether the English had caught James Stephens, the Fenian Head Centre, yet after he had escaped to Paris from Richmond Prison with the help of Breslin, the Chief Warder, who had to go off to America himself?

Didn't old Bishop Moriarty condemn the Fenians, and say that they were in league with French Freemasons and the Italian Carbonari, and that they were not to bring atheism to the country, and that hell wasn't hot enough nor eternity long enough to punish them?

But my old man said that maybe a little atheism wouldn't do the country that much harm at that; a little, but not too much.

Wasn't there one of the Fenians, a man that recruited five thousand British soldiers — Irishmen they were in the British Army — called Pagan Pat O'Leary, and when he was arrested and put into Mountjoy, he said he was an Irish Pagan, and they said to him that he had to be either a Catholic or a Protestant, and Pat replied, 'I'll be neither a beggar nor a thief'? Bradlaugh, a Free-thinking MP, asked a question about him in the House of Commons.

And wasn't my own uncle, a former member of the Supreme Council of the Fenians, later on, before 1916, the man that made the best song of all about the Fenians?

Some fell by the glenside, some died 'mid the stranger,
And wise men have told us their cause was a failure,
But they stood by old Ireland an' never feared danger,
Glory O! Glory O! to the Bold Fenian Men.

All this I knew but I didn't say it at Rivers' table, only: 'I
was born a few hundred yards from where Wilde was born.
His mother was a great old rebel, and Frank Harris was a
bit of a rebel too. I used to think that Oscar Wilde was sent
to the nick for being an Irish rebel but I believe now that it
was over sex.'

'So you thought Wilde was an Irish rebel, did you?' asked
the novelist's nephew, with a kind of a thin-lipped Black and
Tan officer's grin on his puss; all that he was short of was
a swagger cane and a toothbrush moustache. 'And you don't
know really what he was in for?'

'Well, not exactly,' said I.

'I'll tell you exactly,' said the novelist's nephew, with his
grin, and he did tell me exactly. 'What do you think of your
Irish rebel now?' said he.

'I think,' said I, 'that every tinker has his own way of
dancing, and I think that if that shocks you, it's just as well
ordinary people didn't hear about it. Because, bejasus, if it
shocked you, it'd turn thousands grey.'

Robin Jones, the librarian, looked up and said, 'There's no
need to do your nut over it, Paddy.'

'And when I'm finished you shall have a loan of the book,
and then read the life of your distinguished fellow-Patrick by
another distinguished fellow-Patrick, shan't he, Robin?'

'Yes, certainly,' said the librarian, and to me he said, 'that's
a County Library book, Paddy. They send them in here on
the recommendation of the Padre.'

'Yes,' said I, 'the housemaster told me so.'

'Yes,' said Robin Jones, 'but he didn't tell you that you
could have Frank Harris's life of Wilde. I got this book and
other books in while making up the Padre's list. He has other
things to do, poor man, and sometimes leaves that job to me.
Now, you shall have a loan of this book when he's done with
it, and make sure you return it to me personally, and any

other books you want I'll get them from the County Library for you, if you're a good Patrick and sing "Land of Hope and Glory" for me three times. And in our own library we have plenty of books you'll like. Call in to me this evening.'

'Thanks very much indeed,' I said to him, very sincerely and smiled to the others and ran off to work.

I looked forward to reading the Wilde book and finding out at last about his case, and the whole ins and outs of it.

The screw looked at me reproachfully when I came up and said, 'I told you to make up quarter of an hour at your lunch, Paddy, not to take the whole bloody afternoon off.' I was sorry to have seemed to take advantage of him, but I was glad I'd got myself well in with the librarian.

During the afternoon we took more fencing posts, dozens of them, but this time, instead of a handcart and four of us pulling and pushing, we had one of the trailers off a tractor, and the whole party was put hauling it.

On the way down the road we drew to one side to let a station wagon go past, and who was in it but Ken, sitting between two screws at the back? I smiled at him and some of the fellows waved to him and the screws took no notice one way or another.

It wasn't like escaping from Walton or some place like that. We were waving and smiling to him, because we were sorry for him, not to congratulate him.

While we were piling the posts on the trailer our screw told us about Ken. He just talked about him, the same as us, as if he was sorry for him, and you'd never have thought it was off his party that Ken had scarpered.

He was caught on a bus outside some village twenty miles away.

After spending a night in hiding, getting soaking wet and cold, and another night on the road, he came out in the morning and got on a bus. He paid a shilling fare and sat resting himself as the bus travelled on, unaware that his description had been circulated on the BBC news. The conductor spoke to the driver and the next thing was the bus pulled up at a police-station and Ken was taken off and locked in a cell.

The screw said he hadn't pinched anything while he was out

there so he was only being kept in detention, which was three cells up the stairs beside the hospital, till the Governor would try him in the morning.

If he'd pinched anything it would have meant a fresh charge and he'd had to wait for the visiting magistrates.

So we loaded our trailer and all thought, well, it might have been worse for poor old Ken, and it might have been worse still; it might have been us.

I sometimes saw a fellow wearing overalls and walking round very much his own master, carrying brushes and paint and sometimes glazing tools; hacking knife, glazing knife, toffee hammer, pliers, glass-cutter and rule.

There were about eight lads in the Painters' Party, I was told, but most of them were employed on the building of the new camp — the new house. But this one went round the place doing odd jobs of painting and glazing.

I envied him and admired his casual walk around the place and I would have liked to have been one of his seven mates even, for a start.

I watched another of the Painters' Party putting in a pane of glass in the dining-room door one day, after a cook broke it taking in a stool he'd been washing and had left out to dry.

It was an emergency job, so as the blokes sitting there eating their tea and dinner would not be perished with the draught, but might eat in a bit of comfort after slogging all day through muck and cold.

So I suppose this fellow they sent over to do it was the handiest one in a hurry. All the blokes looked up from eating their scoff to look at him, hacking out the old putty and then running in the fresh bedding putty.

They looked over at him with great respect, but I was not very impressed. My eldest brother, Rory, could run putty with his two thumbs, beginning the middle of the bottom, and meeting at the middle of the top, and could glaze half a housing scheme and be over in the boozer drinking a pint before dinner-time.

But all over the place I'd noticed bad paintwork. Joints in

247

ceilings where the fellows weren't fast enough to complete a stretch before the edges of the preceding one had dried; doors painted without going in the direction of the panels, muntels and styles; cracks left unfilled and holes unstopped.

They were all enjoying this fellow glazing the dining-room door while they ate.

'Ain't 'e neat?' said Charlie.

'Neat me knackers,' said I, 'he knows as much about it as my arse does about snipe-shooting.'

'Maybe you could do better?' said Charlie.

'I could do better than him when I was twelve years old.'

'Oh, kip in,' said Joe, 'it's a lot of perishing odds, isn't it? Keep out the wind and the bloody rain, won't it? That's all it's wanted for.'

Jock Smith, a tall, fair bloke from Glasgow, spoke across to us from the next table. 'Paddy's dead right, you know. That bloke doesn't know the first thing about it. My old man's a plumber and I was serving my time to it outside and plumbers do glazing, too.'

'That's right,' said I, 'my uncle's a plumber, and I often went down with my cousins to pay his card, and it said on it, "Plumbers', Glaziers' and Domestic Engineers' Trade Union".'

'That's it, Paddy,' said Jock, 'and it's a bloody shame that blokes that's serving their time to a trade before they came in here, shouldn't be put to their trade and given a chance to keep up to it.'

'Well, what about me, then?' said Joe. 'Why ain't I given a chance to follow my trade in 'ere, eh?'

'Go away, you registered ponce,' said I.

'And a better fughing trade than yours or Jock's,' said Joe.

Everyone laughed and told the joke to other fellows at the tables, and Joe shook his head and set his lip. 'It's a diabolical liberty. Geezers get no chance to follow their trade. 'Ere's me, I get no chance whatso fughing ever to keep my 'and in.'

'You mean your —k in,' said someone, and they all laughed more.

But Jock and I got together and talked seriously about getting on the Trades' Parties and we agreed that the best thing would be to see the housemaster and look for a transfer from the Gardens to the Engineers.

We were all delighted to be on the Gardens first, and it was like coming back to life to be open, and in the air, with the green grass and the trees. I was fed up with the fork and that old East Anglian bogman telling me that I should shake the sods out some more. So Joe and I made application to the housemaster for a change of labour; from the Gardens on to the Engineers.

The housemaster said that it was on my file that I was a fourth-year apprentice to the painting trade and that I'd been two years in the Day Apprentice School in Dublin. He said he personally thought that I would be useful on the Painters' Party and though the decision did not in any way rest with him, he would see what he could do.

When Jock went in he told him he would do what he could to get him on the Plumbers and told us both in our turn that in the meantime we were to do the best we could where we were.

Charlie was very hurt when I told him about Jock and me looking for a change of work. He said to go and work with Jock and I could get Jock to put his kip next to mine and all, for he was going to move his to the other end of the dormitory.

I thought maybe he'd snap out of it, but he did not and days afterwards was as surly as ever. So, I said in my own mind, what can't be cured must be endured, and one morning, a week after our interview with the housemaster, Sullivan called up Jock and me to the top of the orchard. 'I hear you two fellows want to leave us.'

'That's right, sir,' said I. And Sullivan seemed a bit hurt over it, and all.

'You don't like it here on my party?'

'Well, sir,' said I, 'it's not that. But we're more used to building work, sir. It's not that we don't like working with you.'

He smiled with his cross eyes. 'The old blarney, Paddy.' Still, it seemed to please him. 'Well, fair exchange is no robbery. We're getting two lads that wants to be transferred to

249

the Gardens and they'll be coming to us and you two will be reporting to the Engineers' yard in the morning instead of reporting to the Garden party. OK, get back to your digging. You'll know where to go in the morning?'

'Yes, sir,' said Jock.

'We do,' said I, 'thank you, sir.'

He smiled and said, 'Don't thank me, Paddy, lad, thank the Lord.'

Jock and I were very excited over the idea of getting into overalls again, and going to work at our trades on a real building job, just like outside.

'Well, it's nearly the same as being outside,' said Jock. 'Old dolls up in the Quarters, screws' mothers and wives making cups of tea for you, and all that. And there's two young maids in one big house we'll be going to. They'd eat it.'

'Would they, bejasus?' said I, and very interested.

'Yes, a bloke called Yorky Turner got done over one of them before you came here. He got six months in Chelmsford from the visiting committee and lost all his remission.'

'They might as well have left him alone,' said I, 'for nature breaks out through the eyes of a cat.'

'It broke out in him anyway,' said Jock. 'They let no one near the big house now, only the plumber or the painter.'

'Good openings for willing lads,' said I, singing:

'. . . Oh there was the plumber in the Servants' Hall,
   D'you think oh, me dear, he's going to solder us all?...'

'You're a comical bastard, Paddy, and no mistake,' said Jock.

I told Charlie on the way down to the tool-house about us going on the Engineers the next day and he didn't answer me. I let on to think that he hadn't heard me, and told him again.

'You go anywhere you bloody like,' he muttered, and turned away, 'you and that bleedin' Jock.'

I looked round but Jock hadn't heard him, being too busy telling some bloke about it himself.

At night-time, Charlie when up to Rivers, and asked if he could change his bed the other side of the dormitory. Rivers said the side we were on was the side all Receptions went on when they came first, because it was the coldest, but that 440 Smith was going out in a few weeks and that Charlie could wait until then and ask the new dormitory leader about it, because he, himself, would be gone out before then.

He sat in silence at the table in the dining-hall, and when I joined in the conversation he stopped out of it. I had to tell Joe that he had the needle, in case he would take the piss out of him, and have him start a row.

After tea Chewlips and Joe went off to see if they could get a game of billiards, or get on the queue anyway. They had their names down for a game for a week and it was coming up near their turn, and I went up to the library.

There was Shaw and O'Casey there. *John Bull's Other Island* and *Juno and the Paycock* and *The Plough and the Stars*.

These were like a visit from home. I knew Juno, and I knew Fluther Good in the *Plough*. The preface in *John Bull's Other Island* I knew almost by heart, and I found another book by an Irishman. It was called *The Silver Fleece*, by an ex-Irish Rugby International called Robert Collis.

Rugby was a game I'd always connected with the English or with the upper-classes. There was a Rugby pitch on the grounds of the huge Gaelic football and hurling stadium of Croke Park, separated from it by a concrete wall, at the bottom of our street. We used to see the boys from Belvedere Jesuit School, and from Mountjoy Protestant School, going down there on Wednesdays. We persecuted them without distinction of religion. Sometimes, when they were racing through on bikes, we threw stones at them. And if we caught them in small groups on their own, we beat them up, to such an extent that the Guards stood at our corner to see they got through safely.

We only knew they were rich kids and even I, who was usually amiable and too easy-going to fall out with anyone, thought it was a holy and a wholesome thought to give them as bad a time as we could. They were toffs, college boys, and toffs' sons.

251

I certainly never thought of Rugby football as having anything to do with Ireland or with Dublin. If I thought of it at all, I thought of it as a mucky version of cricket, which I found completely and absolutely incomprehensible.

Sometimes in the street we played a version of it under the influence of the *Wizard* or the *Rover* with a chalked wicket and a hurling stick for a bat, but it was more for skit and diversion than anything else and fellows would shout, 'Hefter yew, Algy old boy', or 'Mind your balls, Marmaduke'.

But reading Collis' book was like meeting someone from home, and I could see Rugby football not as a winter meeting of cricketers, but as a battle fought in the churning mud and myself in the forward line charging for Ireland.

At home we played soccer in the street, and sometimes a version of hurling, fast and sometimes savage, adapted from the long pucking grace of Kilkenny and Tipperary meadows to the crookeder, foreshortened, snappier-brutality confines of a slum thoroughfare.

Later, when the time came to think about getting on our minor soccer team, I was made nervous on the one occasion I played with real boots and jerseys, by the presence of my father, uncles, step-brothers, step-uncles — all veteran soccer players, some of them former professionals, and I covered up my embarrassment at their presence, and my shame in letting them down, by gamming on to a total lack of interest and boredom with any kind of sport except swimming.

The memory of that day at the Thatch football ground, when I was eleven and the worst outside-left that ever disgraced NCR.(boys), and better left outside as I heard some of my disgusted relatives remark, I washed out, or tried to wash out, in the canal, in the Irish Sea, and in the Liffey; I was a strong swimmer and a courageous diver and thought nothing of going off the top of a fifty-ton crane.

Now, at seventeen, when I'd have thought it was odds on against taking up any new sport, by this book, *The Silver Fleece*, I was reminded of what at the time I'd only noted with faint contempt; that Rugby would be starting here in September.

There was a dour-looking creature in Jones' place at the

desk, and when I went to take down the book he called me and said, 'Eh, you, you've no card.'

He took my name and number and wrote a card and put in in his files. I took my *Silver Fleece* and thought I'd sneak down to the dormitory and have a read of it, but this sorrowful-jawed bastard called me back and said I could only read it in the library; there or not at all.

Jones was at the fire, I noticed then, and he came over and said that it was OK, that I could have it.

'It's all right, Paddy,' said Jones, 'you can have it with you and read it. My assistant here is very conscientious, and it gives him something to do and saves me a lot of work. He's a Jehovah's Witness and very strict. Just as well, too. There's a few morons here, and they'd think nothing of using a page or two, in the cawsy, if they were stuck for paper. But you can take your book with you. What is it, by the way?'

'*The Silver Fleece,* by Robert Collis,' said I.

'You reckon it's good?'

'Sure,' said I, my mind already full of mad charges in the muck, the roars of an Irish crowd at Twickenham or Murray-field, the grunts and shoving. 'Sure,' said I, 'it's good. Good for what ails me.'

'Not much, I'd say by the looks of you.'

'Thanks for letting me have it, Jonesy, down to the dormitory, like.'

'That's all right, Paddy, always glad to do something for the enlightenment of the lesser breeds.' We smiled and I went with my *Silver Fleece* to the dormitory.

There were a couple of other blokes lying on their beds reading. They were fellows that worked from about four in the morning on the boilers for the greenhouses and I had never seen them before, except when I was half awake in the dim half-light on the one lamp they switched on to dress themselves with in the small hours of the morning

One of them I knew was a bloke call Cragg. He was about twenty and looked even older. He was big and heavy and a bit scarce of hair even, and looked like a middle-aged man.

He had a rake-up up to his face while he read his book and took a pull from it, without taking his nose from the pages, when I was going past him to my own bed. 'Want a spit?' he said, without looking up.

'Thanks very much,' said I, and took the dog-end from him. I looked over at the other fellow and said to Cragg: 'What about him?'

'Oh, Ah don't like 'im,' said Cragg. "E's a criminal. Been in trouble with the police.'

Jesus, said I, in my own mind, are there many like you at home? For once in my life I did not know what to say.

The other fellow said: 'Oh, kip in, Cragg, you daft bastard. He's barmy, Paddy; 'e believes the earth is flat.'

'Well, not altogether flat,' said Cragg, 'there's bumps like, where there's mountains, but it's mostly flat. What d'you think Paddy? 'Course it's all bloody bumps where you come from.'

'He's an atheist, too, Paddy.'

'That's years ago, you silly-born bastard, when I was in Durham Prison,' said Cragg, 'the Padre wore robes at service and he came into the condemned cell and asked me if I knew the significance of the different colours, I said I didn't but 'e should keep with the violet ones, they suited 'im; 'e did look well in them though, that's jannock. My wife came on a visit.'

"E's a wife all right, Paddy; two nice kids. Don't know what she ever saw in that dossy bastard. She comes two 'undred miles 'ere every month to see 'im, and all.'

'Even though I croaked 'er old man,' said Cragg, from behind his book.

'Go on with what you were telling Paddy about the Padre in Durham.'

'Ah', said Cragg, looking round his book again, ' 'e asks me 'ow I was getting on with my wife? so I said like that Pierrepoint was going to give us a decree neezy soon, but that we were getting along champion, and I asks 'im 'ow 'e was getting on with 'is and was 'e keeping 'er off the old rum bottle? and 'e looks at me like I should 'ave been 'ung, too, and maybe I should, and I wouldn't 'ave minded neither, only it's so bleedin' painful.'

He sighed and I took a drag on the dog-end which was nearing its end, not knowing what to do.

Then Cragg looked at us from over his book, and said, 'Ah, well, Ah better get on with improving me mind.' He turned his eyes down on the pages and read in a mutter . . . 'such was the depravity of the times, that she preferred the timorous touchings of the eunuch to the ponderous ballocks of the Roman Emperor . . . '

I went down to lie on the bed and read my book, and Cragg's, I noticed as I passed, was a volume of Gibbon's *Decline and Fall of the Roman Empire*. I'd heard it was on the Index, but that is not always a recommendation, I'd discovered, for so was *The Cricket on the Hearth* and I hadn't thought *The Decline and Fall of the Roman Empire* had interesting things like that in it. But maybe Cragg was after making that up himself.

I decided I'd find out, after I'd finished my *Silver Fleece*.

The next morning Jock and I went over to the Engineers' yard. The big screw they called Tessie O'Shea was falling in the navvy gang.

'We don't go there,' said Jock, 'we report to the plumber-in-charge and the painter-in-charge.'

'That's right,' said I, 'we better find out where they are to be found.' I looked over again at the navvy gang and said in my own mind, thanks be to Jesus, I'm not going with that bunch.

Jock went over to them and asked where we might find the painter-in-charge and the plumber-in-charge?

'What do you want them for?' asked one of the navvy gang, before the first fellow answered.

'Well,' said Jock, 'me and Paddy are working with them and we want to get our tools and brushes.'

At this, and as sudden and unexpected, the navvy gang let out a roar of laughing as if Jock had said the funniest thing that ever came out of a human mouth. They spluttered and laughed and screeched and said, some of them holding their sides and leaning on each other, as if they'd drop down dead from the laughing, 'Oh, blimey', 'Stuff me!', 'Did you 'ear that?', ' 'Ark at 'im', 'I'm bloody choked!', 'Did you 'ear 'im?' till I thought they would get altogether hysterical.

Jock got red in the face and swallowed a few times and tried to laugh as if he knew what the joke was, and I was thanking Christ in my mind that it wasn't me that had asked them the question, and thinking to myself that, anyway, it was five after eight and they'd soon be gone to hell out of it and up to their work and we needn't even see them for the rest of the day, when the next thing is big Tessie O'Shea comes out of the office with a list in his hand.

He let a roar at them, and they got silent immediately, as if they were switched off and struck dumb by the flick of a switch.

He looked at Jock and me and roared, 'Where the bloody 'ell do you pair think you're wandering to?'

'We — we're looking for the painter and the plumber,' said I, for I thought that poor Jock had done his share and he was demoralized for any more questions or answers.

The fellow Jock had asked for directions shouted from the navvy gang, 'Please, sir, the Jock says they're looking for their tools and their brushes.'

Oh, good Jesus, if they didn't all fall into explosions of laughing again, even worse than the first time and they were all shouting and saying things and big screw going mad with temper, and shouting himself to them to shut up, which they did for a second, till another of them shouts out, 'Tell them they can 'ave a loan of mine,' and they burst out laughing again and this time big Tessie O'Shea even couldn't control them, till he went towards them, his face flaming with temper, and their fright overcame their hysterics and they fell quiet.

'And keep shut, you shower, for the last time,' roared the screw, and turned to us. 'You'll get your tools out of the box like anyone else; a pick and shovel, and—'

'—a bloody big barrer,' said one of the navvy gang, and old O'Shea looked over at them and said:

'I've warned you shower for the last time,' and he turned to us and said, 'get in line there. I've got your names here. Which is which — which is Behan 537 and which is Smith 512?'

'I'm Smith, sir.'

'I'm 537 Behan, sir.'

'Well, get bloody well fell in there, and I'll fix you up with tools. Brushes, and tools,' he glared at us. 'A wet day in the place and you think you're going to walk into a detached job. Wonder you don't get after the Padre's bloody job, now that you've been here long enough to get your name dry.

'It depends on me whether you get a detached job, if ever. You shift enough shit out of this bloody big 'ole we got up here and throw down enough concrete and barrow enough earth and have a bit more manners than this bloody shower' — he glared across at them — 'I've got already, and we'll see

257

about it, in six months' time, maybe. Fall in there now,' and he roared at everyone. 'Right, up to the job, and you there, Parry, at the back, put out that dog-end. It's past eight o'clock. Put it out or I'll put your bloody lights out. Quick march!'

The navvy gang took the piss out of me more than they did out of Jock. He was eighteen and had a hard Scots' face, more like an Irish terrorist's than mine. And they didn't even give me too bad a time, except for asking me had I got my tool or my brush? — except for Parry, the Irishman.

He had an Irish country accent, heavily and deliberately overladen with imitation Cockney.

'So 'oo taught 'oo was going to git detached job strai' awye, did you, Pah'y?' He tried to leave out his consonants like some Cockneys do. Anyway, I didn't like another Irishman calling me 'Paddy'. ' 'Ow's all the pigs an' pray'ies a' 'ome, Pah'y?'

'You'd know more about them than I would, you coming from the bog,' said I back to him. 'The only place I ever saw pigs or praties was on a plate.'

'Oh, the Dublin jackeen for your life,' said he, and I could see he had the spike, so I decided to get it up for him a bit more.

'That's it,' said I over my shoulder to him, 'you're coming on a very bright boy — for a Culchie.'

'Don't 'oo call me a Culchie,' said Parry between his teeth, and ferociously, but he could have said it from between the two cheeks of his arse, and twice as ferociously at that stage of the game, for all I cared. Because I had him weighed up and it was clearly a case of have him now or be persecuted by him for as long as I'd be within reach of him. Now, it was, or never, as the man said; die dog or shite the licence.

He was older than I was by two years, but a couple of inches shorter, but like that again, he was very stocky, and strong, and had his hair cut in the BBB crop — the haircut they give Bad Borstal Boys at Sherwood Forest. But the hair style didn't frighten me, for he was long enough out of Sherwood for it to have grown again, and he must be keeping it that way, to scare people; which it did, but not this citizen.

'The Paddies are going to have a bundle,' said someone in the ranks, very excited.

My stomach was trying to get rid of my breakfast and a cold sweat broke out on me. Christ, said I in my own mind, no wonder Ken Jones tried to scarper. I was a fool ever to come next or near this god-damned navvy gang. Wasn't I happy enough where I was, on the Gardens with Charlie and the other blokes, mostly blokes that came in with our lot? And if I put the boot in real quick and destroyed Parry's marriage prospects, maybe he'd be that badly injured they'd send me to Chelmsford or Sherwood Forest or Wandsworth, in solitary. Walking up that road to the site, I'd have given a lot to be in solitary. Even looking at the bare slate floor, and the barred window that looked out at a basement wall three inches away and the blank eye of the cell door, and the smell of the piss of ages, I would be there and in peace on my own, and not be put to the trouble of marching up here as if the guts weren't twisted in me, and keeping my gaze straight in front of me so as not to have to look any of them in the face.

We got up to the building site. Some of the buildings I noticed were nearly finished. They were long single-storey structures of corrugated sheeting raised on a concrete base, like army camps. They looked modern and neat but my interest was not in architecture just then.

We went over to the tool box and when the screw opened it and lifted the lid we took a shovel each from it.

Some fellows were being sent to the concrete mixer, and though I knew it was only postponing the heave, I hoped that I might be sent there, or that Parry might be, or that we might be sent to separate places anyway. But we were sent in the one team, digging out a trench. I got down at the far end and Joe, whom I hadn't seen all morning, came over, looked at me, winked, and got down beside me. Jock looked round to see where I was and he came over and worked beside us. None of us said anything. I looked to see where Parry was and no sooner did I look up but there he was, on the edge of the trench, his teeth clenched, like something in a dog show. He took one look and jumped down straight at me. This, in the language of the poet, is where he dropped a ballock. I jumped to one side and before he could rise properly gave him a kick from each boot into the guts. I could not get the side of his head because the bastard was cute enough to have that above the level of my boot. Then I struck him with my head in the face as often as I could, for this was my only chance with this fughpig. He tried to rise and got his arm around my neck and threw me with me under him and tried to get his knee in but my thigh was covering my balls. This, said I, in my own mind, is where Brendan goes down for the third time, and if he does he does not come up.

'Up, up! Out of it, you pair of bloody savages.'

Tessie O'Shea, me life on you, sweetest voice in the land of Erin, or East Anglia or any goddamn place.

He came down into the cutting and pulled Parry up. He got in a last dig at me as his grip was loosened, and I went for him with my fists, letting on there was still fight in me.

The screw (that he may be blessed now and for ever more, amen) caught the two of us by the scruff of the neck — or the scruffs of our necks, for now that it was over and Parry damaged a little bit, I was lightheaded and happy — and he said, 'You dirty pair of animals.'

Parry I was glad to see wasn't standing up too well and his face was bruised and, to crown that lovely spring morning in the English countryside, Tessie O'Shea asked him, him, not me, 'You all right, Parry?'

'Uh huhrhuhr, suhr,' or something like that he said, as well as he could.

If you're half right it's too good for you, you jackamanape's scourings of a lock hospital piss-pot, said I, in my own mind.

He looked down at me, where I stood, sullen and breathing heavily and letting on I was defiant and did this exercise every day in the week. 'Behan, you'll behave yourself while you're on my party. I realize you were at your place of work when Parry attacked you, though it doesn't seem to have done him much good' — he turned, oh, cause of our joy, Gate of Heaven, Ark of the Covenant, Morning Star — 'does it, Parry?'

Parry grunted some more 'huhr huhr huhr' in a very insulted and aggrieved fashion, and Tessie O'Shea chuckled, yes, chuckled. I never heard anyone chuckle before but that is what he did. Then he unchuckled and turned to me again. 'If you want to fight, Behan, get fighting that trench there. The bloody idea. Fighting at labour on my party. Don't come any of your Irish larks here, for by God, you're on the wrong ship, Behan, and you won't be much older before you find that out.' He pointed to my place at the trench and I went back to my digging and listened to Joe whispering.

'Good boy, Paddy,' said he, 'a Chief's report, that's all you'll get, if that. You did all right, kid. Someone's going to do that Irish bastard yet.'

I didn't mind what he said about Irish bastards; I knew what he meant.

We talked quietly while we worked. I was delighted, of course, everything had gone so well, though it was more luck than good management.

I thought this Parry could use himself, in a bundle, but I knew another thing. A bloke that starts a fight when he knows a screw is nearby is not starting it there because he does not care about the screw, on account of his rage overcoming him, but because he knows the screw will stop it before it goes too long, and he can be dragged away, struggling to continue a battle he knows very well he won't be let continue.

But maybe this screw was one of the hearty old coves that would make us have it out in a stand-up toe-to-toe bundle.

'No bloody fear,' said Jock, 'Tessie O'Shea reckons there's only one bloke entitled to do any bashing round here, and that's himself. Besides there was one young screw, he came into the screws from a college because he liked the work, he said—'

'I know what he liked,' said Joe, automatically.

'—and he said he liked fair fight, and he caught these two blokes bashing each other, and he put them up to fight after work, and he got a half-sheet, and the Chief asks him how he would like to go back to the Boy Scouts? — so that lark is out.'

'You got that Parry properly frit,' said Joe, 'you'll see.'

And so I did.

At break-time I sat with Joe and Jock and smoked with them. I said nothing to the other blokes who looked at me with great interest, only to Shaggy, who came over from another team he'd spent the morning with. He waved and shouted, ' 'Ello, young Paddy,' and I waved back to him as he sat down.

The other blokes looked at me with interest all right and I enjoyed the impression I'd created for as long as it would last, for nothing lasts but only for a time.

Then I heard a voice behind me, 'Is this a meeting of the Sacred Heart Sodality, or can anyone sit down?' Parry stood beside me with a big smile on his face.

'Sure, sit down,' said I, much relieved.

'The old temper,' he said, holding out his hand, and making sure not to shake mine before he got the attention of the multitude, 'the old temper — sure we can't help it. We brought it with us from the old airt.'

I declare to Jesus I couldn't have done it better myself.

I smiled and shook his hand and gave him a light off my dog-end, and he sat down. I had him weighed up all right, but there was no real forgiveness in my handshake — only tinkers and tramps fight and make up — and young English gentlemen, of course.

Joe looked at him, without any expression on his face.

When we got back to the trench Jock said that he didn't think old O'Shea would even report us now that it seemed to be all over, so I sang a little song to myself:

'Pat may be foolish and sometimes very wrong,
Paddy's got a temper but it won't last very long,
Pat is fond of jollity and everybody knows,
There never was a coward where the shamrock grows.'

Pat couldn't afford to be a coward those times, the battle of Waterloo, the Peninsular, and the Crimea, and the Boer War, not to mention Trafalgar and Port Royal before it. Not when it was a choice between starving at home, or getting fourpence a day in the Army. The same with 'our dear High-landers'.

Parry belonged to that old Victorian Ireland. Me? I was saving up to be a coward and if I'd fight for anyone it'd be for myself. I suppose from the imperial point of view I was a more sinister type than Pat and Mike Parry.

But like that again, from my point of view I was as comic as I was pathetic and as comic as I was sinister; for such is the condition of man in this world (and we better put up with it, such as it is, for I never saw much hurry on parish priests in getting to the next one, nor on parsons or rabbis, for the matter of that; and as they are all supposed to be the experts on the next world, we can take it that they have heard something very unpleasant about it which makes them prefer to stick it out in this one for as long as they can).

On the way back to lunch, Shaggy Callaghan called out to me, 'Well, and how's the body, kid?' He'd heard me say this to someone, and took it up as an Irish greeting.

'Fit to burst, Shaggy,' said I.

He nodded over his shoulder at Parry. 'He'd be a bit too seaside to come that caper with me.' He looked round and straight into Parry's face and said conversationally: 'Wouldn't you? You know it'd be your lot, if you did. That I'd —ing kill you.'

Parry tried to laugh it off as a joke, and just shook his head.

'Well,' said Shaggy, 'so long as you never give me the trouble.' He smiled pleasantly at me and said, 'You're a game kid, Paddy.'

I laughed and was really pleased.

Joe told Charlie about the bundle. The boys were talking about it at the other tables, but Charlie pretended not to be interested, and the minute he had his scoff eaten he went out.

'Well, and he's the surly bastard and no mistake,' said I with bitterness.

'Oh, he's only needled,' said Joe, 'because you could go and work on another party and spend the day away from him. That kid thinks so much of you, Paddy, that if Parry had done you today, Charlie would more nor likely have gone after 'im with a razor blade and shivved him. It's only 'is feelings are 'urt. That's the way 'e is.'

But that didn't make me feel much better.

The work on the navvy gang was hard, but to me it was less monotonous than the Garden party, and I was more interested in it.

We had a free labourer called Fred and he seemed even a bit more thick than Reuben on the Garden party, but in a vacant good-natured way. He had red hair, wore a cap straight down on his head and looked like the village idiot. He was by no means any way mad about killing himself with hardship and his wife brought a snack to him every day at ten in the morning and at three in the afternoon, the same times as we would be having our break.

O'Shea said the break was for a smoke and not for a meal, and he said it took Fred fifteen minutes each break to have his snacks; but Fred said it was his own time and he could eat in it, that he could smoke all he wanted in their time and, if the screw didn't like it, there were plenty of jobs to be had in the aircraft factory at Norwich.

I said that Fred might get a job as a test pilot, and Shaggy spoke to Fred in his own dialect and said that that be the way to speak to these Government varmints. He made out to Fred that he originally came from Yarmouth and Fred said he'd have known him for a real Suffolk punch. Then Shaggy asked him be he vexed with the heat? And Fred said he was a little, and Shaggy asked him, ' 'Ow dew yew a reckon on your turnips, Fred?' and Fred was all for telling him about his turnips till Tessie O'Shea, who had turned away to hide his laughing, would straighten his face and turn round to tell us to get on with our work, to hell out of it.

We invented Fred's love-life for him and Shaggy acted Fred and his wife in bed, discussing various matters in what the other Cockneys called swede language; country talk.

Fred, as I remarked, was by no means as green as he was cabbage-looking and was well paid for the amount of fun we got out of him. The engineers, in their own spare time, and with cement, timber, glass, and paint obtained one way and

264

another, built Mr and Mrs Fred a greenhouse with a concrete base, with ten opening windows on either side of the ridge, and with five hundred panes of glass, leaving out gables, and I know the number, because I helped to put them in and likewise to obtain them.

Ickey Baldock would look at me occasionally and, though the others were laughing, he never seemed to be amused. He was at Mayford Approved School with Shaggy, and was fond of talking about it with Shaggy, so as the rest of us would know it. He resented anyone else talking with Shaggy. Not that he liked anyone. There was no humour in the little bastard nor the inclination for it.

But time passed well in the navvy gang and I was getting used to it, though old O'Shea roared now and again; once you did the graft, you could always have a bit of sport during the day and I had little to say to Parry, though polite enough to him, and hardly anything to say to Ickey Baldock, not that anyone else had, either. But all in all, I was working with Joe and Jock, who were my graft chinas, and I also had a bit of laugh with Shaggy about Fred-in-bed and so forth.

It was announced in the first week of April that we were to have an Eisteddfod in May. The Eisteddfod had nothing to do with Wales or any place else, for the matter of that, only ourselves.

The Old Man told us the history of it when he made the announcement. He founded our place, one of the first open Borstals in 1938, with fifty fellows from Camp Hill on the Isle of Wight. They walked to our place, from where they came ashore: all the way from Hampshire across the country, camping out on the way. The Old Man had boasted to the Prison Commissioners that he would not lose a single man in the transaction, and he didn't. Indeed one of the screws who had been on the march told us that at one stage of the game they had one boy over at the end of the trip and thought they must be breeding. But it turned out to be a mistake in counting.

All the fellows in the dining-hall cheered this announcement because they looked forward to an extra day's holiday from hard graft and also because most of the time we liked the Old Man − the Squire, as he was also called.

He was known to be a fair man and, though they were afraid of him to an extent, they knew that, no matter what they did, he would do anything rather than send a bloke to Sherwood Forest or Wandsworth. Other governors they spoke of got rid of trouble by sending a boy off to the local jail, which was easily done, or transferring him to Sherwood, and there were fellows with us who had been accepted by the Squire from Sherwood, when they'd completed their punishment there and when their original BI refused to have them back.

There was to be, at this Eisteddfod, a sports, a boxing tournament, a cross-country race, plays in the evening, a concert, prizes for gardening and handicrafts, and an essay competition on the subject, 'My Home Town'. One hundred Player's was the prize and that, I said in my own mind, is my hundred Player's.

So after that, when Charlie got up from the table, as soon as he'd eaten his scoff, I was gone in front of him and writing away in the library. The fellows taking part in the boxing tournament were picked from those who had boxed in competition previously. This made sure of fairly good fights but kept us later arrivals out of it. This did not upset me. The Deputy Governor organized it.

He was young for a deputy governor, and he was a very good talker, one of the few lectures I've ever listened to with pleasure. He caught me in the corridor this evening and said that he'd heard that I was a good singer.

'The divil a better,' said I.

'Well, that makes it a lot easier for me, Paddy. I'll put you down for the concert — Irish ballads, eh?'

'I'll give you a song about burning all the Border Customs' huts, both sides, on Coronation Day, if you like.'

'That'd be splendid, old boy, thanks a lot.'

I had to put down my name for the essay competition with the housemaster for we had to use special foolscap sheets of paper for the finished job. I told him of my encounter with the Dep, and how it hadn't taken a feather out of him when I offered to sing the 'Bonfire on the Border' at the concert. 'Probably his public-school training,' said I.

I worked very hard at my essay nearly every evening in my exercise book; writing a first draft and a second before I'd put it down on the foolscap.

The exercise books were those supplied generally to Borstal boys and long-term prisoners. They had a list of rules inside them saying that they 'were issued at the discretion of the Governor and/or the Chaplain and could be withdrawn any time' if it was brought to the notice of either or both that the exercise book had been used to write down 'any original composition in verse, prose or in music', but of course I wasn't expected to take any notice of that.

I could write for ten miles about my native city, but its songs were either seditious or indecent; like the one about Phoenix Park:

> Oh, I went up there on my honeymoon,

She says, 'Me dear, if you don't come soon,
I'll have to get in with the hairy baboon,
Inside the Zoological Gardens.'

That wouldn't look very choice in the winning essay, so it wouldn't. But I had plenty to put in and it wasn't a matter of what I'd put in but what I'd leave out. I could put in it a bit about James Joyce because, in one short week as a dairy boy, at the age of ten, I delivered milk to his sister in Mountjoy Square.

And Yeats and O'Casey and Richard Brinsley Sheridan, whose house in Dorset Street I passed every day on the way to the Tech, and Wilde and Shaw. But I couldn't put in about Shaw telling the judge it was himself was the coward, when sentencing Dunne and O'Sullivan to death for shooting Sir Henry Wilson, when he took the opportunity of blackguarding them in the dock from the safety of his bench in the Old Bailey.

Nor could I put down the story of Yeats and the old fellow in the Coombe, when they were listening to the loud pealing of the bells of St Patrick's.

'Wonderful, wonderful, don't you think,' says Yeats, 'to hear those chimes that once rang on the Dean's own ear. That Emmet listened to, and perhaps timed his mixtures by, as he laboured making gunpowder and shot for the Rising of '03, in Francis Street behind us. That Thomas Moore, the other side of us in his father's house in Aungier Street—'

The old fellow puts his hand to his ear and says, 'What's that you're saying, mister?'

'I was saying how strange a thing is time, or I should say a concept, that those same chimes, in the time of Wolfe Tone and Matilda, Lord Edward Fitzgerald buried close by in St Werburghs, those same—'

'To tell you the truth, mister, I can't hear a word you're saying for the noise a' them bleedin' bells.'

I had written and published pieces in verse and prose, in various illegal and semi-legal Republican and Left Wing papers and magazines, since I was twelve and I was quite confident I would win this essay competition. So far as I was concerned I was home and dried, but naturally I did not say this to Joe or Jock — I'd let it be a surprise to them. Charlie I could not tell it to, because he still had the spike for me over changing my party and leaving him.

I was even enjoying the navvy gang, and content to wait my turn with Jock till there were vacancies on the Painters' and the Plumbers', when this day I sees a long skinny bloke with a beaky nose that's only come in a week before with a lot of receptions, and he's put on the Painters' straight away. Now, I thought that that was a bit of a liberty and I hear that it's because he's a forger.

He's been done for forging pound notes. Well, that's nothing to do with me, but I don't see why that entitles him to get a staff job before anyone else and on the Painters', too, but I hear them saying that it's because they wanted someone to do sign-writing in the C of E chapel, and he's very good at it. Well, I passed the London City and Guilds — in the Day Apprentice School in Dublin, of course — examination in Painter's Work which includes lettering, and my father is a top letter-writer and my uncle on my mother's side and my granny even used to letter and gild the backs of the law books in Temple Bar, down opposite Dublin Castle, so I don't see why I didn't get the chance. So Jock and I said that we'd sneak into the C of E and have a look and see what sort of a job he's making of it. After all, sign-writing is a trade, where forgery is a gift.

But when we had a look at the scroll he'd written over the altar, I knew I wasn't even in the field with this fellow.

He had written in gold leaf, in ecclesiastical type, 'Jesu, My Lord and My God', and it was perfect — lettering, sizing, and gilding.

'But he's spelt it wrong,' said Jock in a consoling whisper, 'he's left out the "s" in "Jesus".'

But, no, I had to deprive myself of that consolation, for it was often spelt like that.

The day of the sports and the Eisteddfod began with a fine May morning, and the cross-country race.

What happens but the bloody forger is in that and the long forger's legs of him and his beaky counterfeit nose brought him before anyone else, also due to the conservation of his energies behind the incinerators, where he slyly hid and rested himself while the other honest poor bastards — well, by comparison, poor simple robbers and rapers and murderers — went round the second time. Because I met a fellow that saw him as he lurked there, waiting to join the panting throng.

So he won it — the honour and fifty fags to boot, and this lad reports to Cragg, who is a steward, about the forger only doing one round of the course.

'They used to cut the 'ands off forgers,' said Cragg, 'in olden days. Ah reckon it's the fughing legs they should 'ave cut off of 'im.'

But it was no dice; he still got the glory and the prize.

The sports were held in a big field near the greenhouses, and Sullivan, the Garden Party screw, was in his element throwing weights. His wife was there and another athletic screw called Farrar, with his wife. The two young wives stood together talking, and Joe said they were comparing the athletic feats of their husbands.

Joe won a race and Jock jumped and came third in something.

'What are you good at yourself?' said I to Cragg.

'The Long Spit,' said Cragg, 'and I 'ave you down 'ere, Paddy, for the tug-o'-war against the staff. It's after gymnasts.'

Sullivan and Farrar had two teams of acrobats and they barked at them like dogs while they jumped this way and that.

The Governor rambled round like any good-quality Squire should, shouting advice to all and sundry, and the divil a one taking much notice of him for once in a way, and at this stage of the game I must state that if I give the impression that these sports were anything less than highly efficiently done it's my fault and not the fault of the organizers or the participants. I am normally not anxious to be anywhere there is a sports but I'd have been sorry to have missed this one.

Then the tug-o'-war came on, and all the boys cheered us and the screws' wives and kids cheered them, but we pulled them over.

This was a surprise and had not happened before. The Squire stood leaning on someone, moaning and grunting and vowing that he'd never be the same again. 'How the devil could it have happened that you beat us?' he asked. 'We were far heavier.'

'Ah,' said Cragg, who was heavy as anyone on the staff team, 'you were fatter but we were fitter.'

'By God, you may have something there,' said the Squire, looking round, and wondering in his own mind, I suppose, whether he could slip in for a quick one unbeknownst.

His wife, a delicately built young woman, and a painter, stood at my shoulder and said to me, 'I'm Mrs—'

'I know who you are, ma'm,' said I, 'and I hope I see you well.'

'Very well, thank you, and your name is — please don't tell it to me with your number on it. It makes me feel as if I'm speaking to a telephone.'

'Behan is my name, ma'm.'

'Oh, but that's not what your mother calls you — or your girl friend.'

'I don't know whether I have one or not, ma'm.'

'What — you don't know whether you have a mother or not?'

The Squire looked from me to his wife. 'Most preposterous conversation I ever heard in my life. . . . Besides, he has a mother. In perfect working order, not sick or dead, thank God. I saw a letter from her only last week.' He walked away to talk to Cragg.

'No,' said I to the Squire's wife, 'I don't know whether I've a girl friend or not. I had one before I came in.'

'You mean, she gave you up because you were sent to Borstal?'

'Well, another fellow was after her and I got Borstal: he's been sentenced to fourteen years by the military court in Dublin. It kind of puts me in the shade.'

'Oh, of course,' said she, 'you're the Irish boy that was in the RI — I mean, the IRA. And the girl thinks this other fellow is a better patriot than you, because he got a longer sentence?'

271

'That's it, ma'm. That's about the height of it.'

'But you don't let it worry you?'

'No, ma'm, I'd nearly forgotten it till you mentioned it.'

'And you haven't told me your first name yet.'

'It's Brendan, ma'm.'

'Well, you have a lovely head, Brendan, and you must sit for me, sometime.'

'Thank you, ma'm, I'd love to. Anytime you like.'

We parted then, and smiled at each other and she went off, and the next thing I saw her chatting with Chewlips, who nearly had the two jaws ate off of himself before he setteld down in conversation with her.

Another well-known citizenness amongst those present was our matron, Anne Lafeen. Miss Lafeen was wearing a summer dress, that looked very pretty with a hat on her head; she also had her usual Rothman's Pall Mall cigarette, the dog-ends of which were much favoured for size and beauty by her numerous charges and followers.

She was surrounded by cups of tea brought to her by the faithful of St George's House, headed by her only acknowledged favourite, a black boy from Tiger Bay, Cardiff, that was doing HMP because he chopped the right arm off of a Norwegian sailor who collpased and died. His name was Christian.

Miss Lafeen had to drink all the cups of tea, because it would have offended some of her clients if she didn't.

There was another matron there, too, from St Andrew's House, and her name was Ellen Constantine; though she was not my own matron, like Miss Lafeen was, being of another House. She lent me the *New Statesman* every week, and I could read, amongst other things, the essays of YY who was Roibeard O Fhloinn, or Robert Lynd, and old Protestant Republican from Ulster and a great friend of my family's in what they called 'the old days'.

And there was the Padre and his wife; a tall man he was, and she a proud-featured woman but not aloof. He looked the dead spit and model of the parson that they use on the Three Nuns advertisement.

And there were housemasters and their wives and children

and screws with their wives and children, and old O'Shea came down the field, red-faced after the tug-o'-war, with his jacket back on him and his wife on his arm and followed by his family who were all nearly grown up.

He smiled at his workpeople, but shyly and nervously.

Joe and Jock and I saluted him and he nodded quickly and smiled ingratiatingly.

''E thinks,' said Joe, 'that some of us might shout, "Right, you shower, 'ow about some graft? Come on, you idle lot of bastards, let's 'ave you. Take your finger out of your arse-'ole you, and get digging." Nice things for 'is wife and kids to 'ear, eh?'

At tea we got bread and jam, treacle duff, sweet cake, and a half ounce of Ringers A1 shag tobacco and a packet of AG cigarette papers each. We queued up at the hatches in the dining-hall to get the tea and scoff and carried it to the tables which were all joined together to make it easier to shift them for the concert.

'We'll push down over 'ere,' said Joe to Jock and I, who were behind him, and in a general way to Charlie who happened to be standing near us.

'I'm going to have my tea with some St Andrew's blokes— they're from Croydon,' said Charlie.

''E can 'ave 'is scoff up on the perishing roof for all I care,' said Joe. 'Come on, Paddy, we'll shove down 'ere with Jock.'

After tea the kitchen orderlies cleared us all out double quick, and under Cragg's direction they started getting the dining-hall ready for the concert. Only the blokes in leader grade were allowed to remain and help them. The rest of us got drummed out to walk around and smoke and talk, which was not a bad fate, or kick a football round the back of the buildings.

These Croydon blokes were amongst the kickers and Charlie with them, and I'll say for him that he had the use of his feet, real Dixie Dean style for he took the ball and kept it glued to his feet for the length of the field.

Joe and Jock and I rambled round, and we were talking and stopping every now and then to roll a fresh rake-up or to get a light and smoking like lords' bastards on the buckshee half-ounce, when who should I see out of the corner of my left eye but Ken Jones, the scarperer, and two other blokes.

I went over to him and said, 'Well, Lamb of Jasus, if it's not yourself.'

He shook hands with me and said, 'Hello, Paddy, it's nice to see you again.'

'The dead arose and appeared to many. Where did you drop out of, at all?'

'I was up in chokey all the time. Our punishment cells were upstairs. I got two months PCTFO, for scarpering, and I've been up there all the time. You never saw us because we exercised at the back of the buildings when you were all out at work. We were looking from our cell windows, and one of these chaps' — indicating the two fellows beside him — 'shouted from his window that there was a sports or something going on. I could only hear the cheering and, Christ, it felt awful to be stuck up there, on our own, and all you blokes out in the sun, enjoying yourselves. Then about an hour ago, they brought up a smashing tea, and I said to myself that we haven't been forgotten with the scoff anyway, and just as I was finishing mine the Governor had our doors unlocked and came in to each of us in our turn. He gave each of us half-ounce of snout and a packet of papers and told us to get to hell out of it, and come down here quickly or we'd miss the concert and he said we were to keep out of his way for the rest of our time here, or we'd stop in chokey till our hair fell out.'

'Well, glory be to the old Squire,' said I. 'I saw him going off quietly and I thought it was into his house for a bevy he was gone.'

'Well,' said Joe, ''e's a bloody old toff.'

'He's all that,' said Jock. 'What were these other blokes sent up for?'

One was a fair kid of about sixteen and the other was a tall dark lad, and a year or so older.

Ken glanced at them to see if they were listening and said quickly, in a low tone, 'Ring.' Then he said in a louder tone, 'Will I walk round a bit with you fellows?'

'Sure,' said I, 'come on.'

274

'See you later,' said Ken to the two other ex-chokey blokes and we moved off.

'Oh, I heard about them two,' said Jock. 'The night-watchman caught them kipped in together.'

'That's right,' said Joe, 'they fell asleep on the job.'

'By the same token,' said I, 'how did you make out that night, Ken?'

'Well, I went off that time when I fell out and I hid behind some bushes, as if I was going to have a crap. Then I wheeled around and went up to a ditch and hid in it until dark. I heard them calling me in the distance, and I thought that he would be down asking you where I was gone.'

'He did, too.'

'But I knew you'd say nothing.'

'Oh, the divil a fear of me.'

'I knew that, Paddy. I waited in this old ditch till dark and then made towards the place I told you about, where I had the overalls and the scoff parked. I'd to cross the road to do it and I nearly ran into the screws. Later than night I wished to Christ I had, for it pissed rain. I lay there soaked and shivering till coming on to morning. Then I started moving south or south-west across the fields and I must have covered about fifteen miles that way by the time it was bright. Then I lay down and had a sleep for a while. I was out all that day, and ate my scoff and I pinched some leeks out of a field — it was the only thing I could find, and was out again that night. I passed the night some way and staggered on and thought what a bloody fool I'd been, not to be safe and sound in my warm bed like everyone else. But I cheered up in the morning and thought that I'd shaken them off my tracks and that I'd be OK when I got to London. I waited along till I came to a bus stop and waited there, till the first bus came along and I got on that. I thought that with the overalls on me, and the big boots, the conductor would have taken me for a farm labourer.'

Ah, sure, God give you sense, says I, in my own mind, is it for anyone to take you for a farm labourer — there'd be as much chance of them taking me for the Marquis of Salisbury.

'I looked along the list of fares and picked a place that was marked a shilling. It was called Berry — Berry — something. I've forgotten the name of the sodding place.'

'That doesn't matter,' says Jock, 'we wouldn't know it, anyway.' Joe and I shook our heads too.

'Then the conductor came along and told me the fare had been increased since they printed that notice, and I didn't know what to say, so I just gave him the shilling and told him to take me wherever that would bring me. So he brought me to the cop-shop.'

'He had you tumbled all the time,' said Joe, 'it was on the nine o'clock news.'

'So I heard. The coppers weren't bad. They took my clothes off and dried them at the day-room fire, and put me in blankets in the cell where I fell asleep till the station wagon from here came to fetch me. The coppers gave me some scoff and a smoke.'

'They were so pleased out in the country,' said Joe. 'You were probably the first cop they'd made since the time of the —ing footpads.'

'When I was brought back here, they put me up in chokey and I was brought before the Governor in the morning. He sat at the desk, asked my name and number — and — and why I'd scarpered.'

None of the three of us asked him what reason he'd given the Governor for scarpering, nor did I mention anything about him telling me he was being picked up by this brother with a fast car. He might even have forgotten what he'd told me; liars need good memories, but don't often have them, as I know and everyone else knows from personal experience.

'He sentenced me, as I said, to two months' PCTFO, and I was marched off and put in chokey. I got the same scoff as you, of course, and an hour's exercise a day; but only they changed our books three times a week, I'd have gone barmy.'

'What did you read?' I asked him.

'Well, I got some by Hugh Walpole. The others couldn't read it. I slipped one in to them, and they said it was a lot of ballocks about old parsons and their wives, but I read them, and liked them.'

'He'd be a good man and you in chokey all right,' said I, 'and Galsworthy. When I was in Walton I got a bloody great book of his, *The Forsyte Saga*. When I was starving with hunger, and perished with the cold in the old flowery dell all alone, it was like having a feed of plum pudding and port wine.'

'Did you know,' said Joe, 'there's a book called *Crime and Punishment* — it's about a geezer that kills an 'ore with an 'atchet.'

'It's by a Russian called Dostoyevsky,' said I. 'Did you read it?'

'No,' said Joe, 'can't say as I did. But I 'eard a bloke tell it once. You know the way you tell a film. It was double good. But the best book I ever saw in the nick was the Bible. When I was in Brixton on remand, I 'ad one in the flowery. Smashing thin paper for rolling dog-ends in. I must 'ave smoked my way through the book of Genesis, before I went to court.'

It was six o'clock and the sun shining away was bright as at noon. It was even warm, except for a breeze springing up.

Then Cragg roared out that in an hour we'd be going into the concert.

'Smashing weather today, wasn't it?' said Ken.

'Yes, it was,' said Joe, 'you don't get weather like this outside.'

The first part of the concert was a one-act play called *The Bishop's Candlesticks*. The novelist's nephew was the Bishop and Rivers was the convict. Our matron, Miss Lafeen, was the housekeeper and she was the best of the lot of them. She seemed to have acted before.

When they finished the play they got a big hand, the Matron the most of all, because she was a woman, and also because the boys all said she was damn near a Borstal boy herself. Rivers got a great hand too because he was going out on Monday.

We singers and other entertainers were kept at the back of the stage till our turn came and, at the interval, the Dep came and told us to go into the hall, till the speeches were over, and to make sure and be back in time for when the concert went on.

I noticed Cragg carrying a trumpet.

'It's 'ereditary like,' he said, 'my old dad used to play this in works' band and 'is dad before 'im — my old grandad that were — and one day 'e were playing "Land of 'Ope and Glory" for the Boer War or summat, and 'e blew and 'e blew and 'e blew is bleedin' brains out. A very patriotic man, Paddy, was my old grandad.'

'Hey, Cragg,' said the Dep, 'get on out there, will you? I told you they're about to start the speeches.'

'What am Ah to do with me instrument?' asked Cragg.

'Leave it there. It'll be all right,' said the Dep, 'leave it under a stool.'

''Ow would you like to 'ave to leave your instrument under a stool?' asked Cragg.

'Put the bloody thing down and get out there,' said the Dep. 'Colonel Craven is getting ready to speak.'

Colonel Craven was a big landowner round the place, and originally was the leader of the local opposition to having a Borstal Institution in the district at all. He was eventually soothed by being put on the visiting committee with the powers of a magistrate. According to legend amongst the blokes, in the early days of the place he was encouraged to sentence fellows to the most savage terms of chokey and bread-and-water; the offender was led off in despair to the dungeons and sometimes released after dinner, only to be hurriedly locked up again, if the Colonel showed a tendency to walk round the place after lunch. But everyone understood that we had to keep the right side of the Colonel.

'Colonel Craven,' said Cragg, 'Craven by name and Craven by nature. Took 'is perishing clothes off, and shaved off 'is moustache time the *Titanic* went down, and pinched a woman's night-dress. When they shouted "women and children first" 'e comes runnin', wearin' a shift, carryin' a bundle and screamin' "Save my little babby". When they'd landed safe and sound they discovered it was two bottles of Scotch wrapped up in a face towel.' Still muttering he led us to the back of the darkened hall.

These were lies fresh-minted from his own head that Cragg was muttering about the Colonel, who wasn't a bad old skin at all, now of latter days, and since he got to know us. He got a great clap anyway from the boys when he stood up.

'Force of 'abit,' muttered Cragg. 'When we came 'ere first the boys was threatened with three days' Number One each if they didn't clap the old bastard.'

The Colonel spoke for a while about our traditions. He used to get us mixed up with old public school, and spoke from what I'd have thought was a set speech he'd used previously, at some other venue, but the majority of people listening to a formal speech of that sort just regard it as a recitation, like the prayers at a religious service, and so much of what the Colonel said passed unnoticed, and much of it was appropriate to a school or a BI anyway.

'. . . and my dear boys, my dear young men, there are some of you who have come from your preparatory schools, perhaps, a trifle awed by this great world of masters and prefects, down to the boys in the lowest forms, who, though lowly in the hierarchy of school life are yet, to you, as ancient and settled inhabitants, accustomed to the usages of schools and their own small privileges.

'May I say that everyone experiences this feeling of loneliness, of not belonging. Wondering anxiously if they ever will belong, and wandering round for a day or two with other new boys, for comfort's sake. May I say that I myself, on my first day, in this old and worthy foundation, hard though you, sitting there listening to me, may find it to believe — may I say, that I too in my time, forty, fifty years ago' — he smiled shrewdly and said — 'I'll not give away my age or that of my contemporaries any more exactly. And my dear boys, I'll tell you a secret — that a very great Minister of State' — here he grew solemn — 'one who at this grave hour of our country's history, at this time of peril' — he lowered his voice — 'and glory' — there was a pause and we all clapped like mad, till he put his hand up and bowed his head several times like a Sinn Fein speaker after saying 'nineteen-sixteen' — 'one who is only prevented from being with us today by the manifold labours of great power, high

279

office and grave responsibility. I saw this great man, a little boy as you new boys are tonight, this great public figure, for whom the Prime Minister thanked God' — there was more clapping and a few cheers and Cragg shouted, 'Good old God!' — 'at this present perilous but glorious time in our island story — I saw that great man sitting there where you new boys are sitting now, a nervous shy fellow, just sitting between myself and the future Bishop of Rochester.'

Then the Colonel was handed a list of the prize-winners at the sports; they were called up in their turn and he presented them with their prizes. Cragg was presented with a bundle of cigarettes, ten each for the tug-o'-war team, myself included.

At last the Governor stood up and said that the Major, who was a man of about thirty years of age, in uniform and sitting beside him, would give judgement in the essay competition. The Squire said we were fortunate to get the Major, a personal friend of his own, and a well-known literary critic in civilian life, to judge our competition.

The Major got up and said that there was one essay he had no trouble at all in recommending for the first prize. It was about 'the sad and beautiful capital of that sad and beautiful island . . .' and with that there was a great burst of applause, led I noticed by Shaggy Callaghan, with Jock and Joe adding their piece, and Charlie, with his face lit up and his eyes near out on his jaws with excitement, clapping away like mad. Cragg, beside me, was stamping his feet.

MacCann put his hand up from the front seat and waved back to me. Then my name was called and up I went to the stage and was shouted, at, 'Good old Paddy' and 'Good boy, Pat', all the way up through the hall.

Our Matron who was sitting in front took her Rothman's Pall Mall from her mouth and said, 'You are a good boy, Brendan, and a credit to us,' and the other matron, who lent me the *New Statesman*, smiled and waved a half-knitted sock at me.

The Major spoke to me, and I said something, and thanked him and went off with my hundred cigarettes. I got back and by that time they were cheering someone else, though not as much as they had cheered me. What surprised me was the generality of the applause, for I did not think I was so well known.

When I got back into my seat, I passed round a packet of twenty to the blokes either side of me. Cragg took one of my hundred and handed me in return my ten out of the tug-o'-war prize.

All this passed off very civil and, as the last prizes were being handed out, the Dep signalled us from behind the curtain and Cragg led us back-stage again, where we sat smoking like lords' bastards, till our turn came to get up and go into our routine.

One of the screws did conjuring tricks and then Charlie Garland, the civil Geordie, came out and sang the 'Blind Boy' and two songs of Vera Lynn's, 'We'll Meet Again' and 'Yours'.

Of course this went down like a dinner with all and sundry and the citizens clapped their hands off, which they were lawfully entitled to do, seeing as Charlie Garland was a smashing singer, and those Vera Lynn songs all had that sob in them, which Charlie Garland could do nearly as good as Vera Lynn herself; and which no one enjoyed more than the Colonel, who clapped enthusiastically, and croaked in his old gravelly tones, 'Encoah, onk-awh!'

There was then to be accordion solos but the Dep said regretfully that the bloke who was to play it was with a sick cow, on the farm, and refused to come.

'It must be that farmer's boy,' said I to Cragg, but it wasn't. It was a Cockney bloke who had never seen a cow till he came inside. Cragg said it took some blokes like that, and city fellows are the worse. He said he remembered a bloke who was going out spending his last day, which was Sunday, going round the farm in tears, saying good-bye to the beasts.

'He was HMP bloke and all,' said Cragg. Jesus, it was nearly out of my mouth to say that that accounted for it, because everyone knew that HMP blokes were all barmy, anyway, when I remembered that Cragg was a HMP bloke himself, in the matter of his late father-in-law. 'Of course,' said Cragg as if he was reading my mind, 'he might have been a bit round the bend, like. He was a reprieved bloke same as I was and maybe I'm a bit round the bend myself. They used to 'ave religious texts on the wall of the condemned cell in Durham, that Chaplain 'ad put there. One of 'em said, "Today is the morrow you worried about yesterday and nothing's 'appened." It was the last thing a bloke saw as 'e went out towards the 'ang-ouse.' He was going on to say, I suppose, that it was no wonder for HMP blokes to be mad, when the next thing was that he was called to go on the stage with his trumpet.

Before he came out on the stage even, they were laughing. He made some low noise with his instrument and began playing. I knew a lot of heads in Dublin, or dance-band musicians, and I thought he was a pretty good trumpet player. He played 'Dixieland' tunes and finished amid the roars and acclamations of the multitude. I noticed, after all his lies about the man, he blew a special long note in the direction of the Colonel, who was one of his most vociferous supporters.

For his second piece, Cragg tapped spit vigorously from the mouthpiece of his instrument and having looked through it a couple of times, he began playing Purcell's 'Trumpet Voluntary' and, as far as I could judge, in a straightforward and very exact fashion; he finished it, stood for a moment, bowed, and walked off the stage without looking to the right or left, and without further acknowledgement of the tremendous applause they gave him.

One of the screws came out and recited a long piece about Marshall Hall, some big English lawyer, and though the blokes didn't seem to know any more about Marshall Hall than I did, the other screws and the visitors — especially the Colonel — went for it like fresh bread. And he gave a monologue then about a soccer referee which went down like a dinner with everyone.

Cragg went into a routine again, but this time he was only an assistant to Sullivan, the Garden party screw, who stood under a light on the darkened stage, in a white vest and flannels, to do strongman tricks, while Cragg, as he said himself, gave him up his weights and measures.

Sullivan bent bars and lifted weights, and then took a pack

of cards to tear them in half. He seemed to think this was dead easy, and smiled at first when they didn't tear at the first go, but later got worried and embarrassed and in the dim light I could see his wife looking anxiously up at him. He gulped a few times and sweat stood out on his forehead. There was a sympathetic silence, except for a few nervous titters.

Then Cragg went up on the stage and took the pack of cards from Sullivan's hand and removed one of them, tapped it on his heel, where it clanged like a piece of metal, amid the laughter of the audience and a relieved grin from Sullivan and took it away off stage with him.

He showed it to us — a piece of sixteenth of an inch steel, in the shape of a playing card, and painted by the forger — who else? — to represent the Knave of Spades.

By this time Sullivan had torn his pack of cards right across and in several bits to the acclamation of the multitude.

After that I went on the stage to sing a song.

I sang the 'Coolin' in Irish. It is a song that is about six hundred years old, about Poynings' Law, when he forbade the native Irish to keep up their own language and customs, and tried to stop the men wearing their hair in the Gaelic style, straight back and with no parting. There is the girl and she is singing to her sweetheart and his 'cuilfhionn', 'his fair poll', and I can sing it, by Jesus, and put love and defiance into it.

They gave it great applause and in the sea of faces, I could pick out Charlie's face looking up at me, his resentments forgotten, his lips parted in delight.

I sang, then, a mixture of verses to an English air, and some of them by an English poet, and all put together by my mother:

'When all the world was young, lad, and all the fields were green,
And every goose a swan, lad, and every lass a queen.
I would get up on my big horse, and gaily ride away,
For youth must have his fling, lad, and every dog his day.

When all the world is old, lad, and all the leaves are brown,

And the big high hopes you cherished, lad, come trembling,
   tumbling down,
Go, go you, to your corner, lad, the old and maimed, among,
God grant you'll find one face there, lad, that you loved when
   the world was young.

With rue my heart is laden, for golden friends I had,
Bright youth and rose-lipped maiden, and many a light-foot
   lad,
By brooks too broad for leaping, the lightfoot boys are laid,
And the rose-lipped girls are sleeping, in fields where the
   roses fade.'

They roared and clapped, till a while after I'd gone in off
of the stage and as I jumped down into the dark, Cragg said:
'Paddy, that was lovely. You've a great 'eart.' He recovered
himself, and added to those standing round, 'Best bloody
singer in the 'ole hI. hoR. hA. is our Pat.'

I excused myself and slipped down to the cawsy. I wanted
to be alone for a minute; I did not want to insult my friends
and I did not want to stand for 'God Save the King'.

We did not get to bed till nearly eleven that night. The
screw came round and counted us and told us to get kipped
in double quick, or we'd not be able to start our day's graft
in the morning.

But sure with the day's excitements and all that snout flying
round he was only out of the dormitory when we started looking for a rake-up and a light.

I opened another of my packages of cigarettes and brought
it round the dormitory.

Charlie was sitting on Shaggy Callaghan's bed talking to
him. I held out the box and Shaggy took one and thanked
me, but Charlie held up the lighted rake-up he had in his hand
and said, 'I'm burning, thanks.' Shaggy went to say
something, but I had passed on to the next fellow.

I talked a bit with Joe and then lay back on my pillow,
putting the day through my thoughts. It was all very good,
and the blokes were real good-natured, cheering like that
when I won the prize. I looked over to Charlie and caught

his eye, but he turned his head and went on talking and laughing with Shaggy till the lights went out and then came over and got into bed, and said 'good night' to Joe.

''Night, Charlie,' said Joe, ' 'night, Paddy.'

'Good night, Joe,' said I. I sat awake looking up at the ceiling, lay down, turned over and went asleep, as they say in Irish, to die and be born again, and deprive my troubles of a night's growth.

I heard through my sleep someone calling, 'Paddy, Paddy, hey Paddy,' and louder, 'Paddy.' I sat up and looked round and heard it again, 'Paddy.'

It was Charlie, and wondering if he was talking in his sleep, and half asleep myself, I got up and went over to his bed. There was someone at his bed.

'Oh, Paddy,' said Charlie again.

I went towards the other bloke and said: 'Fugh off, whoever you are!' The other bloke straightened up and I threw a left at him. 'Threw' is right. The next thing I felt something come at me in the dark and smack into my jaw. Down I went, flat on my back, came to and put my hand to my face for fear of another one. One of the lads put the light on, and I looked up. Charlie was sitting up in bed, and Shaggy stood over me. He was wearing only the top of his pyjamas.

'You all right, kid?' said he.

'I am, Shaggy, what's left of me.' I tried to laugh but I couldn't.

'Get back into kip quick, before they all wake up,' said he. He gave me a hand, and Charlie came over to help me up.

'You all right, kid?' said he.

'Ah, sure I'm hardly dead,' said I.

He said to the bloke that put the light on to put it out, and they sat for a moment beside my bed in the dark.

'I put it on you, Paddy,' said Shaggy, 'I didn't mean to, though.'

'You put it on me, all right,' said I, 'I was out — like a fughing light.'

'I'm sorry,' said Shaggy.

'That's all right, a-vic,' said I, 'it's nothing.'

'I'll look after him,' said Charlie, 'you can go to bed.'

'I will,' said Shaggy, 'good night.'

Charlie lit up and gave me a smoke out of his dog-end and then said, 'You all right, Paddy?'

'Sure, kid, I'm all right. You best get into bed before the screw or the watchman comes round. Good night.'

'Good night, Paddy,' said he and he hopped into bed, 'you're a good kid.'

'We're all good kids,' said I. 'We're all the kids our mothers warned us against.'

In the morning my jaw was a bit sore but that was all.

I went down to the ablutions and there were fellows washing and shaving and some standing in their pyjamas, yawning or smoking dog-ends. Cragg was pissing in one of the bowls.

The Jehovah's Witness glared at him and said, 'Eh, Cragg, I might 'ave to use that bowl after you.' I think it was mostly the exhibition of flesh he objected to.

'And too bloody good for you, you parish-bred bastard,' said Cragg, with his usual good humour.

I sang as I washed myself:

'Oh, there are people at fair and market who make arithmetic
    in low delight,
And then go praying, all hope delaying to see us burning in
    death's long night,
But hell or God, my native sod, is here below, and we'll
    chance the strife,
Or anger after, with love and laughter, or death's disaster—
    Still, more power to Life!'

'Good on you, Paddy, lad,' said Cragg. 'I'd call one of me kids after you only they're named already.' He turned to the Jehovah's Witness. 'There, get an 'earful of that, you miserable-looking bastard.'

Cragg's china, whose name I never knew, nor no one else because he was never called anything else but 'Cragg's china,' said, ''E got old Craggy done last Sunday for reading the *News of the World* at the Methodists' service.'

286

The Jehovah's Witness turned from the bowl and said in his mournful voice, ''E'd no business being there, 'e's C of E, 'e only came to mock.'

'You're a bloody liar,' said Cragg. 'I wasn't 'eeding the thing at all. I fell in with the Methodists only because I wanted a read of the paper and the screw 'ad me taped in the C of E. I only get the loan of it Sunday mornings, from a bloke in Andrew's till church is over.'

The Foreman engineer sent for me one day and told me that he was thinking of putting me on the Painters' Party.

He was a squat man and built in the shape of an Oxo cube.

'I don't suppose you know that I am half Irish,' said he.

In normal circumstances I'd have said no, and what's better still, I don't give a fish's tit what he was. But he seemed a decent old skin and in any event he was giving me my detached job on the Painters' and I didn't want to offend him, so I just said, 'I suppose it was your ancestors were Irish.'

'My mother was Irish — she was an O'Carroll from Longford.'

'A lot of people I've met inside seem to be of Irish descent, sir.'

'It doesn't seem to interest you very much,' said he.

'Well, to tell you the truth, sir, it doesn't. When I was in Walton a lot of the screws were of Irish descent — Lancashire-Irish, they were and to prove that they were as British as anyone else they were worse to me than anyone else. A Jewish fellow told me it was the same with them, only worse, as they mostly met other Jews who were judges or magistrates.'

'Well, anyway, it's something we have in common. We both had Irish mothers — can you serve Mass?'

'Yes, sure I can. But I'm excommunicated. I'm not allowed to the Sacraments.'

'You don't have to, to serve Mass. The present fellow goes out in a week or two and it's not always easy to get a server.'

So even the excommunicated will do, when it's not easy to get anyone else. When all fruit fails, welcome haws.

'It's a long time since I served Mass, sir.'

'I can get you the loan of a missal. You can read Latin, can't you?'

'Church Latin, I can.'

'All right, from next Wednesday — there's Mass that

288

morning — you can start serving and, now, get in there and report to the painter-in-charge.'

The painter-in-charge was a free worker called Reub Marten. He was a small man and a local from round the district. When I reported to him he listened to my accent with uneasy amusement.

'You're not a London boy, Be-ee-hann?'

'No, I'm Irish.'

'I see. We used to 'ave lots of Irish 'ere, years ago, working at 'arvest time, and pickin' taters. Funny crowd they were, they used eat taters without washin' 'em. Very 'ard to understand 'em— blowed if we could. They didn't speak English much.'

'Well, I speak English and about washing potatoes, I never saw a lavatory without water till I came to England, and then only when I came to this part of it.'

'I dersay, Behan, I dersay,' he said and added hurriedly, 'well, now, you be agoin' up to the New Camp, and the 'ead boy there'll give you paint, and you'll go priming doors. That's putting on the paint we put on first.'

'I know; I was serving my time to the trade outside and my father's a painter, and so was my grandfather and his father and his father's father before him.'

'Well, never mind that for now, Behan; just listen to me. You'll get a pair of overalls from the Part-Worn Stores: 'ere's a chit for the officer there. I 'ave it all made out and everything. You're to wear your overalls only when you're at work, and every night you're to bring them to me and not down to your 'ouse. Do you understand that?'

'I do, Mr Marten.'

'And you'll wear your working boots every day and not your shoes. Some of the fellows seem to think that when you're on a detached job they 'ave to be "flash", as they call it, and they go wearing their shoes.'

'Right.'

'Here's the note now and hurry back here.'

I went over to the block in good humour. The day was fine, the sun shone high in the sky, and I had a detached job; there would be no more of that god-damned navvy gang, wondering every morning who you'd have to fight before the day was out.

On the way out of the engineers' yard I met Jock. He waved a note at me. 'Going over to the Part-Worn Stores?'

'I am, that,' said I.

'I'll be over with you, I'm going on the Plumbers', myself. What's your bloke like? Is he a screw?'

'No, he's a free labourer.'

'I'd sooner a screw than one of these bloody swede-bashers.'

'You would, if you saw the little —t I'm with. Miserable-looking little sod with a disagreeable face.'

'My screw is all right. He was years in India and hates black men, that's all.'

'Maybe the black men weren't out of their minds about him, either.'

'Well, it seems as long as you let him go on about black men, he's all right.'

'I suppose you're right. He might as well rave there as in bed.'

'Let's go in the cawsy for a burn, Paddy. No need to hurry, it's all in the boss's time.'

'We'd have a better chance of swinging the lead on the way up to the job, if we got the overalls first.'

'That won't stop us having a kip-in here, too.'

We went into the lavatory and sat smoking in opposite compartments, facing each other.

There was a bloke working cleaning up the place.

'Tell that reception to keep the nick in case the screw comes,' said Jock.

I will in me ballocks, said I, in my own mind. I didn't fancy giving the bloke orders, as if we were house captains or something. 'Call him yourself there, Jock. He's over your side, I think.'

'Hey, there,' said Jock.

'Hello,' said the kid, coming down to us. He was a boy of sixteen, and he didn't seem very frit of anything for a new bloke. He stood in front of Jock with his yard bursh in his hand. 'Want something, mate?'

'Yes,' said Jock, 'come in here for five minutes.'

'Sod off!' said the boy indignantly, taking up his brush to go off.

'He's only jeering you,' said I, from behind him. 'We want you to keep an eye out there for the screw while we have a burn, and you can have the dog-ends after us.'

'I don't want your dog-ends, mate, I got some of my 'alf-ounce left, but I'll keep the nick all right.'

'Thanks,' said I.

''s all right, mate,' said he, and went on with his cleaning. When we had finished our smoke, I smiled and thanked him for keeping the nick for us.

''s all right, mate,' said he, 'you can do the same for me some time.'

'Sure.'

The screw and his boy seemed to be in good form this day. Geordie was at the desk and shouted down the store, 'Here's old Paddy come to see us.'

The screw came down and said, easy-going and pleasant, looking at Jock, 'This an Irish invasion, Paddy?'

'No, sir, Jock here is from Glasgow.'

'Well, he would be, if he's called Jock, wouldn't he? What are you two Celts after today?'

We showed him the notes. 'So you're getting a detached job, Paddy?'

'Yes, I'm going on the Painters' and Jock is going on the Plumbers'.'

'Good-oh. Geordie, reach me down a couple of pairs of overalls for old Paddy and his china, will you?' Geordie went to a shelf. 'No, not those. There's a new lot there. Fetch 'em some of those. Only the best is good enough.' He took the notes and gave me the overalls. 'There you are, Paddy, service with a smile.'

'The blessings of God on you,' said I, 'and may the giving hand never falter.'

'When were you ordained?' asked Jock, as we went down the stairs. 'Going round blessing people like a bloody parish priest.'

'Ah, sure, that screw would take the like of that very

seriously,' said I, 'and didn't he give us a new pair of overalls each?'

'Well, I didn't like his carry-on when we went in first. "What are this Paddy and Jock after?" or something, he says. 'I know what he's after.'

'Well, that's his business, and no skin off your nose or mine. Besides, didn't I hear you a minute ago saying to that young Reception to come in the cawsy with you?'

'Ah, but for Christ's sake, Paddy,' said Jock indignantly, 'that was only joking — everyone makes jokes like that.'

'Well, for all you or I know, sure it may be all joking about your man, too.'

'Would you catch yourself on, for Jesus' sake,' said Jock, with a scornful laugh.

'Well, they're a good pair of overalls he gave us anyway.'

'They are that — dead flash,' said Jock, going back to London talk as we got near the site.

We reported to our Trades' Parties and put on the overalls. We met outside the Painters' colour shop and walked round the job together to our places. The navvy gang looked up from their trenches and roared and shouted, and jeered us.

'We have the best of it, anyway,' said Jock.

'The divil take the begrudgers,' said I, 'we have and all.'

The work was a great deal easier than navvying and what was better, it was more interesting. I slapped into it and primed a big number of doors that afternoon. A good start is half the work, and if you get the name of an early riser you can sleep all day.

The painter over me was a thin red-haired boy from Blackpool called Tom Meadows. My pile of doors was at one end of a half-built room and he was cutting glass on a bench at the other. When we introduced ourselves and talked for a bit (he was from Andrew's and I'd never met him before, though I'd seen him round the place doing jobs on his own), he brought his bench nearer to my doors, to save us the trouble of shouting down the whole length of the place.

He was a painter outside, too. A fifth-year apprentice and two years ahead of me. He'd been in the Tech in Blackpool, and did the Second Year City and Guilds examination the year I did my first. He was born in the pot, like myself, for his father and his grandfather were painters. He was a good singer like most painters, my own family included, and the first book he'd ever heard tell of was the painter's bible, *The Ragged Trousered Philanthropists* by Robert Tressall.

We had a great talk about the poor apprentice kid, 'The Walking Colour Shop', Nimrod, the old bastard of a walking foreman, and the charge-hand that was getting free drink off of most of the men so as he'd keep them on, and Slyme the craw-thumper, and Holy Joe, that scabbed it, who wouldn't join the Society, worked under the money and tried to rape Ruth, the young painter's new wife when they took him in as a lodger to help them keep their new house; we spoke of poor old Jack who was old and worn-out and got sent up the sixty-foot ladder, and was afraid to refuse in case he'd be sacked and himself and his old wife put in the workhouse, so he goes up, the poor old bastard, and falls off and gets smashed to bits, and his wife gets thrown into the workhouse, anyway.

It was our book at home, too, and when my mother was done telling us of the children of Lir and my father about Fionn Mac Cumhaill they'd come back by way of nineteen sixteen to the *Ragged Trousered Philanthropists* and on every job you'd hear painters using the names out of it for nicknames, calling their own apprentice 'The Walking Colour Shop' and, of course, every walking foreman was called Nimrod, even by painters who had never read the book, nor any other book, either.

Talking to Tom Meadows was like meeting somebody from home, not only from your own country, but from your house and family, only better because he was more intimate than a friend without being a blood relation.

Tom took the IRA very seriously and was very much against it. But he said to me that he was also against the British upper-class and the Royal Family.

Jesus, it's hard pleasing you, said I in my own mind.

But I knew what he meant and agreed with him when I took time off to think about it.

He said it was the fault of the British boss-class that the

Irish were forced always into terrorism to get their demands, which he allowed were just and right. He was, of course, dead set against the Catholic Church, which he regarded as a tool of reaction. He said it was a disgrace to put me into Borstal among a lot of scum.

Well, fair is fair, and while I knew what he meant and it is the usual hypocrisy of the English not giving anyone the political treatment and then being able to say that alone among the Empires she had no political prisoners, I also knew that the IRA prisoners in Dartmoor and Parkhurst were getting a bad time, with the screws putting the lags up to attack them on the exercise yard — five hundred British sportsmen on to twenty of our fellows, and our fellows getting bread and water for assault when they fought back, as best they could — still, and all, I could not say that the blokes had been unfair to me, nor could I say that the Borstal screws treated me any different to anyone else.

I did not like hearing Charlie and Joe and Jock and Chewlips being called scum, but I only said 'Ah, sure the blokes are only working-class kids the same as ourselves, Tom.'

'They're not,' said he, with such indignation at the suggestion that I said in my own mind, thanks be to Jesus you're not on the bench at the Old Bailey, for it'd be a poor day for the punters in the dock. 'They're not working-class blokes. They never worked in their lives and no one belonging to them ever worked. You're a worker's son, and so am I, but most of this lot, ninety per cent of them, are a lot of bloody lumpers. They're reared up to thieving and stealing and living off prostitutes the same as the boss-class. And they know it. If you ever hear them talking of any heroes, outside the nick, it's about the way Anthony Eden dresses, or the way the Duke of Windsor ties a knot in his tie. Haven't you noticed nearly all thieves are Tories?'

I suffer from a weakness of character that I can't keep up indignation about things like that, only when there is something happening before my two eyes like a baton charge or something. And Tom was nearly frothing at the mouth like a Redemptorist preacher.

'Maybe,' said I, 'it's because all Tories are thieves.'

He laughed, and licked back some of the froth off of his jaws, and then said seriously: 'You're a couple of years younger than I am, Paddy, and I was younger than you when I came inside and I know more about these bloody lot than you do. They're a dirty degenerate lot of scum and you have nothing to do with them. When your old man was coming 'ome after 'ard day's work, theirs was putting 'is jemmy or 'is stick or whatever they call it, into 'is pocket to start 'is night's thieving. And when your Mum was sitting down to darn a few socks at the fire, theirs was loosening 'er drawers to go off down the town, on the bash. I been inside nearly three years now, and I should know them.'

I nodded my head in sympathy and went on priming my doors. If he was in three years he must be a HMP bloke. They didn't keep anyone else in that long. And that accounted for his giving out about the other blokes. 'I suppose you're right, Tom, when all is said and done,' said I. 'They must owe you a good many back days, here, now.'

Back days are the Friday and Saturday of the first week a painter starts work and which are not included in his first pay packet but are paid to him when he goes out.

'Reckon they do,' said Tom, 'and me 'oliday money. Well, I shouldn't grumble — it's constant employment — I can't be sacked only by 'is Majesty the King.'

He was telling me that it was HMP. We both laughed, and I asked him, 'You know the old saying about the skin?' 'Skin' is a slang term for painter. 'Cover me up to the First of March?'

'Should do,' said he, 'been 'earing it every winter since I was born.'

'Well, they have a song about it at home, and it goes like this:

'"Get me down me hacking knife, get me down me stock,
    Get down planks and ladders, there's a big job in the Lock . . ."

'That's the pox-hospital, and had to be done up more often

than any place else, I suppose, but the old painters used to say that there was nothing poxy about the money.'

'It's a good song that, Paddy, I must get that one off you.'

'Certainly, and my old man had a recitation for the beginning of the slack season in November, and it went:

> '"Now, Autumn leaves are falling,
> and the light is growing dim,
> The painter wipes his pot clean down—
> and —ks his brushes in!"'

He burst out laughing and put down his glass cutter. 'That's a right good 'un, Paddy. My old man would love to 'ear it. Your Dad and mine would get on like an 'ouse on fire.'

Well, it wasn't his old man he'd croaked anyway. He was a lonely poor old bastard, whatever way you looked at it, though everyone in the place thought he had a great time and they looked up to him more than they did to a screw when they saw him going round the place with his brushes and tools.

We sang Vera Lynn songs together, and worked away with a will. I never primed doors so quickly in my life. The pile of raw dry doors was going down and the pile of fresh, pink ones going steadily up, in time to the singing.

'You know,' said I, 'it was an Irishman that wrote the *Ragged Trousered Philanthropists*.'

'It's not an Irish name, though, is it? "Tressall."'

' 'Course it's not,' said I, 'it's not a person's name at all—'

'No, it's the name of a bloody — a bloody trestle, 'n't it?'

'That's it,' said I, 'his right name was Robert Noonan.'

'Well, that's Irish enough, all right. Well, I must put that in letter 'ome. That'll be summat to tell the old man. That was Tressall 'imself in the book, Frank Owen, wasn't it? He certainly knew his trade — a man with 'ands like 'is and the bloody boss — old Sludgem — couldn't whitewash a shit-'ouse wall, like all the bloody bosses — ah well, the world's changing, Paddy, you'll see.'

So on the head of that we sang the 'Red Flag', which not

liking to be too conceited I did not like to mention was
written by Jim Connell — another Irishman.

In the lengthening evening we sang, with Tom singing in
seconds, like a Welshman:

> '. . . It looked around our infant might,
> When all beside looked dark as night,
> It witnessed many a deed and vow,
> We will not change its colour now. . . .
>
> Then by this banner swear we all,
> To bear it onward till we fall,
> Come dungeons dark or gallows grim,
> This song will be our parting hymn—
>
> Then raise the scarlet standard high,
> Beneath its folds we'll live or die,
> Let cowards mock or traitors sneer,
> We'll keep the Red Flag flying here!'

'Good lad, Pat!' said Tom, more life in his face than I'd
seen before.

I felt fairly good myself. 'You've a lovely way of singing
seconds, Tom. Was your mother Welsh?'

'No, Paddy,' he smiled, 'I learned to sing like that in
chapel, believe me or not.'

I believed him all right. 'Do you remember the hymn the
young painter sings in the book?'

He put down his tools and looked over at me. 'I certainly
do, Paddy,' and turned his face to the window and sang,
'Work for the night is coming . . .' and I joined him, '. . .
when Man's work is done.'

That was the last we sang that day for the whistle went to
knock off for the night and Tom and I packed our traps, and
went down to the yard together.

At tea-time, Joe and Charlie and Jock and I talked about
the detached jobs.

Said Jock: 'Paddy and that head boy on the Painters' had a bleeding choir practice. Singing the whole evening they were.'

'Ginger-'eaded bloke,' said Joe, 'doing HMP for croaking 'is judy — with 'er own stocking. She was going with some other bloke in 'er offtime.'

'Well, he wasn't married to her,' said Jock. 'It was bloody savage. She was only seventeen and all.'

'It was a bit stern all right,' said I.

'I don't know,' said Charlie.

'Hey, Paddy,' said Jock, 'look who's sitting at Shaggy's table.'

It was the reception that kept the nick for us in the cawsy when we were smoking. They were sitting and laughing and talking together while Shaggy rolled a rake-up.

'Oh, I know that kid,' said Charlie. 'His name is Leslie Banks and he was doing the training ship at Deptford but he scarpered that many times they had to send him to Borstal. He's a Croydon boy.'

'Lots of puffs live out that way,' said Joe.

Charlie flushed and bit his lip. 'In bloody Soho, you mean, that's where the fughing puffs come from.'

Joe laughed and put his hand up to his mouth. He did not understand that Charlie took remarks like that seriously.

'He's only getting it up for you,' said I.

'That's all,' said Jock.

'I'm only what?' asked Joe. 'Why don't you pair of foreign-born bastards speak proper English?'

'Take no heed of the eedgit,' said I to Jock and Charlie, though I was glad to see that Joe's humour was now directed at Jock and me, who were better able for it than Charlie.

Joe put his hand to his ear, and waved at me. '"Eeedgit". You silly born Irish bastard, why can't you learn to speak English properly?'

' 'E won a prize for it with his essay at the Highsteadvote, more that you could do. Anyway, Irish and Scotch ain't foreign— not real foreign, like Wops,' said Charlie, with venom.

'And the best English in the world is spoken in Dublin,' said Jock.

'Well, it's given up to be the third best, after Oxford and Inverness,' said I with serious modesty.

'The best English is spoken in bloody London,' said Joe, 'and bloody Oxford and Dublin and — and — that other gaff you mentioned. I can't even pronounce the bleeding name of it. And my young sister, she can sing "God Save the King" in backslang.'

'Give us an old stave of it,' said I, by way of amiability, 'if you can remember it.'

Good singers have to be coaxed and Joe smiled shyly. 'Well, I wouldn't like to, not 'ere, I—'

'Ah, go on out of that,' said I, 'for Jasus' sake. Sure the other fellows are taking no heed of us, and they're nearly all finished their tea anyway, and rolling up dog-ends to have a smoke when they go out.'

'Awri',' mumbled Joe, putting his head down between his hands and growing confident from a shaky start:

> 'odGay avesay roway aciousgray ingKay,
> onglay ivelay roway oblenay ingKay,
> odGay avesay roway ingKay. . . .'

'Go it, Davvy,' said Charlie.

'More power to you,' said I.

Jock said nothing, but looked at me, and at Joe with interest, and some of the blokes at the other tables looked over. Joe stopped and muttered, ''s only to give you an idea of 'ow she does it.'

'Begod and the next concert,' said I, 'you'll have to get up and give us a stave or two in backslang.'

'My young sister, though,' said Joe, 'you should 'ear 'er,' and looking up from a bit of bread, when we finished the tea, he said, 'Come on, down the dorm, I'll show you.'

As we were going down to the dorm, Jock looked at me, but I said nothing and did not look back at him.

Joe went to his locker and took out a picture. 'I'd like to show this to you and Jock,' he said to me, 'because you're RCs, and I don't mind Charlie seeing it, too, because we're all chinas.'

'True for you, Joe,' said I, real serious.

'There,' said he. It was a photograph of girl of twelve or thirteen, in a white silk dress, wearing a veil and wreath and carrying a bunch of flowers. She was well developed, ripe and Italian. I was going to say that the first girl that ever attracted me — she was the second really — was an Italian kid, Gloria Bartoli, from the local chip shop, at home, on the Northside. But I thought it better to say something else.

'She's — she's lovely,' said Charlie, 'but Joe, ain't she a bit young to be—'

'To be getting married?' said Joe, laughing. 'She's not getting married.'

'No,' said I, 'she's making her confirmation.'

'That's right, Paddy. She was thirteen and a half when that was taken.'

'God bless her; she's a pure little angel,' said I. 'Like Blessed Maria Goretti.'

Joe nodded, and smiled with pleasure. 'You may fugh about and all, Paddy, and swear and that, but you're a good RC all right.'

Jock said nothing but looked at me and at the picture, and nodded and looked at me again.

Joe put his picture back in the locker, and we walked down the corridor again. Jock stopped to get a light, and the others walked on.

'Well, holy Jesus,' said he, twisted with the laughing, 'stuff you, and your pure little angel, and 'er brother the biggest young ponce in the West End, and 'er brothers and uncles. And you're blessing that old sod up in the Part-Worn Stores. Paddy, you'd say anything. You'd say Mass if you knew the Latin. Oh, Jesus,' said he, laughing some more, 'and Charlie taking it all so serious. Oh, Jesus!'

I said nothing but looked at him, as he had looked at me.

'The bloody English are good value all right,' said Jock. 'Regular art galleries of Mum and Dad and our kid. And maybe "our kid" is forty-five years of age. And Davvy is not even real English.'

'He was born and reared here — that makes him English.'

'Well, you never see a Scotsman or an Irishman go in for

300

that slobbering carry-on with pictures of Mum and Dad —
and me dear little sister — they might have the pictures, but
they don't make a bloody art gallery out of them, showing
them to everyone.'

'No, they're too dead in themselves, only when they're
drunk.'

'Paddy, I think you like the bloody English.'

'Well, the English can love people without their being
seven foot tall or a hundred years dead.'

'But I heard you giving out about what the English did on
the Irish, and on the Scots, and on the Indians and the blacks
out in Africa.'

'That's only the British Empire — that's a system. And
some of the worse bastards running it are the Irish and the
Scots. But judge them at home. How easygoing they are if
people are living together without being married.'

'In Scotland, all the old dolls in the place would be talking
about them, right enough.'

'And in Ireland, down the country anyway, if a girl got put
up the pole she might as well leave the country, or drown
herself and have done with it — the people are so Christian
and easily shocked.'

Shaggy and Leslie Banks came up the corridor, and said
'Hello.'

'Hello,' said Leslie.

'Hello,' said Jock, and I said, 'Hello, Mac.'

'His name is Leslie,' said Shaggy.

'Well, hello, then, Leslie, and how's the body?'

''s all right,' said Shaggy, laughing. 'Paddy says that to
everyone.'

Leslie looked at me seriously and then decided to smile.
'It's all right, Paddy.'

'We're going to the gym for a spar,' said Shaggy. 'Would
you and Jock like to come?'

'So long as you're not asking me to mix it with you. I get
my exercise,' said Jock, 'at night-time — in kip.'

'You're a coarse bastard, and very much in need of Borstal
training,' said I. 'Come on.'

Sullivan, the Garden party screw was there, and delighted

to get a few customers. He gave us singlets from a basket, and said we were to go down and get our gym shorts and shoes.

'We're all in the one dormitory,' said I.

Jock turned round, and was going to say to Leslie, 'You go—' when I said, 'I'll go down and get them.'

Leslie looked up from his serious study of the floor and said: 'Oh no, I'll nip down and get them. I know where all your kips are.'

He went off, good young Leslie.

'He's a good young lad, that,' said Sullivan, 'though they couldn't get no good of 'im, it seems, wherever 'e was before. 'E's on my party now and 'e's as good as gold.' So you are yourself, said I in my mind. 'All depends 'ow you take a boy, I reckon.' He turned to Shaggy. 'I see you're looking after 'im, Callaghan. I'm glad to see that. I know you'll keep 'im right.'

'I'll do my best, sir,' said Shaggy.

'Ah, here he is,' said I, 'the man himself.'

Leslie came in smiling over his pile of shorts and shoes.

Jock and I took ours and went over to a bench at the wall to strip.

'Stuff me,' said Jock, 'did you hear the screw saying how Shaggy would look after that bloke? I know how he'll look after him. That screw must be away in the head.'

'"Is beannuigthe na daoine ata glan na gcroidhe: oir do chifidh siad Dia",' said I.

'We had one but the wheel came off,' said Jock. 'I'm not a fughing Highlander and I have no Gaelic.'

'The Gospel according to St Matthew, chapter five, verse eight.'

'I told you today, you're going round like a fughing parish priest,' said Jock. 'Blessing people and looking at Joe's holy pictures and giving out of you in bog-Latin about the Bible.'

'You and Jock going to have a spar?' said Sullivan.

'I thought I might have a spar with Shaggy, after he's finished with Leslie, sir,' said I.

'And I only really came to have a look, sir,' said Jock.

302

'Well, you can be going up on the bars while you're waiting,' said Sullivan, who'd have slept, ate and drunk on the bars, if he had the chance. 'But in the meantime, it'd be better training for you and Jock to have a bash together.'

'Fugh you, Paddy, if you put a hand on me, I'll murder you. I hate these perishing larks; I shouldn't have come in here, at all.'

'All right, all right, I'll not do anything to you.'

'You better not.'

'I'll get Sullivan to show us some Judo. He's a black sash, you know.'

'He bloody well looks it.'

'We'll get him talking about Judo, and he'll show us some holds.'

'He's not allowed to. It's against the rules for the screws to show a prisoner or a BI their tricks — make you as good as themselves.'

'I'll get you a set of gloves,' said Sullivan.

While he reached in the box for them, I said, 'I heard, sir, there was a grip you could use, even against a fellow armed with a knife.'

'Or a gun, Paddy,' he said grimly.

'Go on,' said I, looking only half-believing.

'Oh, it's jannock, Paddy. True as you're there.' He looked up from the box with the gloves in his hands.

'Begod, and it's hard to believe all the same — a fellow with a gun or a knife.'

Sullivan said, 'No one been threatening you with a knife or a gun, Paddy?'

Jock and I laughed at his joke. 'Well, no matter of that, sir, it's a bit hard to believe that a man with his bare hands can beat a man with a weapon. Say if he came at you with a shiv — like this.' I brought my hand upwards towards his groin, as if I held a knife, the way I'd seen Joe describe it.

He brought his weight down on my wrist, and I shouted, 'Oh, sir.'

'Dead easy,' he smiled.

'But say if he came at you from behind,' said I, and I made to plunge the imaginary knife into his collar bone.

303

He pulled me by the wrist over his shoulder, in what they called at home the Irish Whip.

'You want to go about it this way, Paddy. Now, supposing I'm trying to stick a knife into you.' He brought up his hand. 'Frontal assault met by unarmed combat. Attack me with your knife.'

I went for him with the imaginary knife, and he put his left arm across my right wrist, and brought his right hand up to clasp his left hand and pressed in on my wrist with both of them. I'd have to drop the knife all right.

'No matter how strong a bloke is, that'll fix him, Paddy.'

'Can I have a go, sir?' said Jock.

'Of course you've seen it, now,' said I.

'Won't matter a tuppenny,' said Sullivan, smiling. 'Come on, get cracking, up with your knife, this way.'

I sat on a form and looked at Shaggy and Leslie in the ring. Shaggy was showing him to keep his chin in his shoulder. He was a couple of years older than Leslie but Leslie wasn't bad at all. When he landed a blow on Shaggy, Shaggy laughed, showing all teeth, and the two of them belting round like fair hell.

After showing Jock his anti-knife trick, Sullivan said he was going to slip down to the screws' mess for a cup of tea. He said we were to get sparring and to hand him in the gear, when he came back. He went off and Jock sat down beside me and rolled a cigarette.

He bowed his head in the direction of Shaggy and Leslie in the ring, and shook his head at me. They were panting, and sweating, smiling intently and throwing lefts and rights, and right-crosses, as if they had a certain number of movements to make before the world ended in three minutes' time.

'I'll come in a minute,' muttered Jock, 'looking at them two.'

'Kip in, for Jasus' sake,' I whispered. Shaggy might hear him, and besides, I was watching the performance myself.

At last with a deep sigh, Shaggy threw up his hands. 'All right, you young bastard.'

'Good on yous,' I shouted.

They came over, Shaggy leaning on Leslie's shoulders, gulping contentedly. ' 'Ow long is three two-minute rounds on that bloody training-ship of yourn?'

'Same as any place, I suppose,' said Leslie. 'Coo, I ain't 'alf in a sweat, Shag.'

'We'll go down and 'ave a shower. Coming down, Paddy? — Jock?'

'No,' said Jock, 'we haven't been exercising ourselves all that much.'

'It's only dirty people has to wash,' said I. 'Besides, the screw said we were to wait here to give him back the gear, when he locks up for the night. You can leave your lot, and we'll hand it in for you, when he comes back.'

'Good kid, give me a hand off with this mitten, will you?'

I undid his glove and Jock undid Leslie's. Shaggy took off the left glove himself and threw it at me. 'Cop on, Pat.'

I caught it, and he turned to throw a left on Jock who dodged it, and said, 'Haven't you had enough for one fughing night?'

They collected their clothes and went off. 'Come on, Leslie,' said Shaggy. 'Leave those pair of idle bastards, and get down before we cool off.'

At the door, Leslie turned and moved suddenly. 'Race you down, Shag!' after landing a sudden blow on him.

'You young bastard,' said Shaggy, tearing down the corridor after him.

When Tom Meadows had a lot of glass cut he said he would take me glazing with him. I wondered how the painter-in-charge would take this.

'Right, Tom,' muttered the painter-in-charge, and then told me I was to wait until he came back with a set of glaziers' tools. Tom was the only one he called by his Christian name. In some ways they were like two foreman painters on a job outside. They sometimes argued over politics, when Tom savaged the boss-class and their peasant supporters, and called the painter-in-charge 'a bloody peasant' when he spoke respectfully of the gentry. For the painter-in-charge was like

305

the Cockney crooks he hated, a great admirer of Anthony Eden and the Duke of Windsor.

But he and Tom Meadows had the same attitude to work, and Tom was even a sterner taskmaster when he was left in charge of the party.

The Cockneys had a contemptuous attitude to work of any description, and sneered when Tom said they might find a trade useful when they went to earn a living outside.

They laughed heartily at the idea of earning a living, it seemed, and Tom, white with temper, turned on them, at least, turned on me, and attacked them for he thought that, in some way, I had sympathy with them, and said, 'I suppose they don't worry about earning a living, when they can steal or live off of brasses.'

But when they got on a Trades' Party or on the Farm, or some work they were interested in, they became very enthusiastic, took their jobs very seriously, and even competed with each other. People take to hard work as easily as to drink. It's a matter of getting used to it.

It didn't make them like Tom any the better, though they respected him for his skill.

I mated him on the plank when we flatted the ceiling of the C of E chapel. We were using a paint that dries very quickly, which meant that to prevent 'flashes' — shiny bits of 'joints' where the edge has dried before the plank could be moved for the next stretch — we had to work at great speed, almost throwing the paint on with four-inch flat brushes. We worked in a lather of sweat, and after each stretch barely got our breath before our four helpers, ready waiting, had shifted the plank on for the next stretch.

Proudly we belted on in silence till we came to the last stretch where we could take it easy because we were working into the wall. It was drying out evenly without a visible break in it, so we sang a bit of a song, now that we had the energy to spare for it.

Tom startd the third verse of the 'Internationale', and we sang it like trumpets:

'No saviour from on high deliver,

No trust have we in prince or peer,
But in our strong arm to deliver,
And free the earth from greed and fear,
For too long our flesh has fed the raven,
Too long we've been the vulture's prey,
But no farewell to spirit craven—
The dawn brings in a brighter day—
Then comrades come rally, and the last fight let us face.
The "Internationale" unites the human race!'

'Go it, Paddy, lad,' someone shouted, and when I looked down I saw there was a crowd gathered at the door of the chapel, admiring our work.

Then we sang the 'Adeste', Tom in English and I in Latin.

We had worked over the time, for the fellows at the door had finished work and had already changed their boots for shoes. Joe put his head round the door when we were singing the 'Adeste' and shouted up at us, 'Hey, it's a long way to Christmas yet, you know.' Then he sang a little chorus of his own:

'Glo—ooo—o—oria' only instead of '—oo-ria', he sang, 'Glooo-ooo-oooo—up your pipe.'

'Disgusting bastard,' said Tom, looking down from the plank, 'no respect for nothing.'

I laughed down at Joe but put on a disapproving look when I turned to Tom on the plank. He shook his head resignedly and wiped his forehead. I did not know whether Joe heard him or not, but I did not let on that I'd heard him say anything and, just then, they all cleared away from the door and the Padre came in with Marten.

Marten stood silent, but I could see he was proud of the job, and the Padre said, 'Wonderful, it's all dried out beautifully white and in one piece.' This was the most complimentary thing that he could have said.

'Just like it grew there, Padre,' said I.

'Like it grew there,' said he, 'yes, that's exactly it.'

'That's what the painters say outside,' said Tom.

'Indeed? Most appropriate. Quite the best way to describe it. How can I thank you lads enough? If we'd got men from outside, I'd have had to pay them some fantastic sum.'

'I'm glad you like it, Padre,' said Marten, and secretly I knew that he did not like C of E padres, but he was glad to see our job being praised. 'I must be agoing off, now, Padre. Good night.'

'Good night,' said the Padre. I said nothing, for he had not wished me good night, and neither did Tom. I thought Marten had a conscientious objection to being civil with me. 'Now, men,' said the Padre, 'I cannot thank you enough for the wonderful job you've given us and, as you know, our Lord preaches that the labourer is worthy of his hire. Go down to the canteen after tea and tell the Matron I sent you.'

'Thank you, sir,' said we.

'No, no, thank *you*. No London firm could have given me a better job. It's beautiful. And next Sunday, I'll have some of my outside helpers at the service and the local Vicar. And you can look up at the ceiling when they're admiring it and you'll have the satisfaction of knowing that it's your work they're admiring.' He turned and went to the door. 'God bless you both.'

'And you, too, Padre,' said I, after him, while he went out.

Though neither of us would be there on Sunday to admire people admiring our work, on account of Tom being a Methodist, and me being a Catholic — well, an excommunicated one; it still didn't make me a Protestant.

The Padre was well liked by the blokes. He was a very earnest man, and was very holy, too, and never damned or blasted to make himself popular with the boys. Neither did he embarrass them by using their own slang and, on the altar, so far as I could make out from Charlie, he talked about God and never about football.

He was in charge of the County Library and only once did he refuse to get me a book. It was called *Fanny by Gaslight,* and I think he must have judged it by its title, the same as I did, for later it was made into a film, so it must have been respectable enough. But in its place, anyway, he got me the *Irish Republic.*

Unknownst to himself, the Padre was famous for a row he'd had with a screw. He had a custom of giving special breakfast for his Holy Communicants, which was called 'Agape', the Greek word for love feast.

It was the boys' ordinary rations, with maybe a little addition of some kind from his wife and her lady helpers and anyway, no matter what they got, it was always served in cups and saucers of their own and he used to give the boys a cigarette after it; it was more for the occasion than anything else but they all enjoyed themselves, and it passed off very civil.

Till this day: the black boy from Tiger Bay, called Christian, that chopped the right arm off of the Norwegian sailor, is putting down his name for Holy Communion and a screw called Carbett said he was only going there for the snout.

Now Darky had his feelings, as good as anyone else, and he was very upset, because he was a genuine craw-thumper; he told his china, Val Conneely, who was a Lancashire-Irishman, and a Catholic, but that did not stop him going up and telling the Padre, although he said it was the only time in his life he'd spoken to a minister.

The Padre jumped on this Carbett like a ton of bricks. The screw thought St Paul's Cathedral was after falling on him and the Padre swore by this and said that if he didn't apologize to Darky, that he'd turn in the Padre's job and tell the whole world the reason why.

So, in the heels of the hunt the screw had to apologize to Darky, and the Padre was well known amongst the boys for it.

When we went to the canteen that night after tea, the Padre was after leaving an ounce of snout and two packets of papers each for us.

This morning, Tom said to me, 'There's a job come in, to repair a window in the Part-Worn Stores, and I'm sending you down to do it.'

I nodded my head in grateful acknowledgement.

'I've a couple of panes cut there and, if they're a tight fit, you can knock a bit off the edges with your pliers. Take your kit and go down there and it'll save me the trouble of leaving this lot, when I've the chance of finishing all the glass for this new camp in one bash.'

'And it'll give me the chance of a bit of an outing,' said I.

'Well, you could 'ardly call it an outing to be going down to the place where you live. The same building, I mean.'

'It'll be a ramble down on my own, won't it?'

'I suppose it will,' said Tom with a smile. 'So take up your kit and get rambling.'

I went out into the sunshine carrying my bag, and walked down from the new camp site to the Centre Block. It would be a walk of about a mile and a half, and the sun was high up, a white dust on the roads and the leaves strong and green.

I was never in the country much, except an odd time training with the Webley and Thompson on the Dublin hills with the IRA, and had never slept a night in any countryside except this. It was flat and foreign and I missed the mountains, for you can see them any side of you, even from the middle of Dublin but now, in the sun, this countryside was rich and fat and, walking down the road, I felt quite proud of it.

The orchards were shining, and the corn, and there was an odd glint of the sea in the distance.

It was like the front bit of 'The Midnight Court' we learned at school:

> Ba ghanth me ag siubhail le chiumhais na na habhann,
> Ar bhainseach ur 's an drucht go trom. . . .

> I used to walk the morning stream,
> The meadows fresh with the dew's wet gleam,
> Beside the woods, in the hillside's shade,
> No shadow or doubt on the lightsome day.
> It'd gladden the heart in a broken man,
> Spent without profit, vigour or plan.
> Let a withered old ballocks, but rich, in gall,
> View the trees' arms, raised, like ladies tall.
> The ducks smooth-swimming the shining bay,
> The swan all proud, to lead the way,
> The blue of the lake and lusty wave,
> Battering mad, in the gloomy cave.
> The fish for energy, leaping high,

To take a bite from the spacious sky,
The birds all singing, strong and easy,
The bounding grace of the she-deer near me,
The hunt with the horn loud sounding o'er them,
Strong running dogs and the fox before them.

Not but what they could have left the poor old bastard of a fox to enjoy the day like anyone else.

It's great to be on your own for a bit, in the sun, and in the country. That's one thing you never were in Walton. Nor in any prison, I suppose. For all their solitary confinement you were watched and your every movement — even at times when you'd give a dog a bit of privacy. What they call in Irish — 'uaigneas gan ciuneas' — loneliness without peace. John Howard, the Quaker, invented solitary, they say. He must have had terrible little to do. These religious bastards, they have empty minds on account of not going in for sex, or sport, or drink, or swimming, or reading bad books. And Satan will find work for idle hands. To hell with him anyway. I always get grateful and pious in good weather and this was the kind of day you'd know that Christ died for you. A bloody good job I wasn't born in the South of France or Miami Beach, or I'd be so grateful and holy for the sunshine that St Paul of the Cross would be only trotting after me, skull and crossbones and all.

So, whistling 'The Lark in the Clear Air', for myself, I rambled on down the road and past the orchards.

I saw some fellows sickling grass and I waved to them. Charlie looked up and came running, half bent so as the screw wouldn't see him. 'Well,' said he, getting his breath.

'You too,' said I.

'Got a fag-paper, Paddy?'

'"Guh a feg-poipah, Paddy?"' said I, imitating his accent.

'Come on, you old bastard, reach in your pocket; the screw will be along any minute.'

I reached in my pocket. 'Want a bit of snout?' and gave him some tobacco too.

'Ta, Pat, I better move back to my row.'

'Sure,' said I, 'I've to get a move on, myself. I'm going down to the buildings to put in a few panes of glass.'

'You haven't half got a kip-in job. Ta, Paddy, see you at lunch.'

He went running back over the field, fell on the grass, waved his sickle, and continued his sickling as if he'd never left off.

I went up to the Part-Worn Stores and told the screw I'd come to put in his windows. He was standing at the counter and shouted down to Geordie, who was sorting kit at the back of some shelves, to come and meet the visitor. Geordie put his head out and shouted that I was just in time for tea. They would be making it in a minute.

'And how's old Paddy this morning?' said the Part-Worn screw.

'If I was any better,' said I, 'I couldn't stick it.'

'It's just like those bloody Engineers. They let us freeze all winter and just when the summer is coming in, and we're getting a bit of ventilation through it, they send up to have it fixed.'

'That's dead right, you know, Paddy,' said Geordie from the end of the store.

Well, by God, there is great agreeing going on in this Part-Worn Store this morning.

'I sent over to the Engineers three times during the winter, isn't that right, Geordie?' said the Part-Worn screw.

Geordie said it was.

'Think they took the slightest notice of me, Paddy?'

'Ah, sure, that's the way with some,' said I, hammering the hacking knife and lifting out the old putty, clean and decent, 'and more with others. And do you know what I'm going to tell you?— it's worse it's gettting.'

'You're dead right,' said Geordie.

'Looks like you did a little of that before, Paddy,' said the screw.

'Repair glazing is part of my trade. I was a painter outside.'

'You're double good at it; but there's no need to tear-arse away like that. It's getting on for break, anyway. Geordie, how about the Rosy Lee?'

Geordie made the tea on an electric heater and the screw shared his cakes with us. Someone pushed the door but the latch was on, and he had to knock. The screw signalled to us to put our cups under the shelf, and went to the door.

It was Leslie Banks.

'Come in, come in,' said the screw. 'Now what the bloody 'ell do you want this hour of the day?'

'Please, sir, I'm working inside, and the officer said I was to come up and get my working shorts changed.'

'Well, you can tell the officer from me that you can't change anything during working hours.'

'Can't even change your bloody mind,' said Geordie.

'Come back here, at the proper time. After tea, any day except Saturday. And make sure you have the pair of shorts you want to change with you.'

'I can get the new pair and try them on in the dorm and come back, sir?'

'You'll bring the old pair up here and try the new pair on up here till I fix you up, right. What do you think the boys from Andrew's do? Run up and down nearly two miles with every pair until they get fitted?'

Leslie nodded. 'Right, sir,' and ran off.

When we finished the tea, the screw gave us a cigarette apiece, and we sat talking and smoking for a few minutes before I went on with the glazing. I finished and smoothed my putty and put back my sash, gathered up my bits of putty and glass, thanked them for the tea and talk and the bit of snout, and went back up the camp site, taking plenty of time.

Later in the evening, when the classes and gym were over, getting for half-nine, when we went to bed, I was standing in the corridor having a smoke before we'd be going down to the dormitory. Joe came up to us and said to me: 'Shaggy's looking for you. He ain't half doing his nut, and all.'

Jesus, what's all this about? said I in my own mind. 'Looking for me? What's he doing his nut about?'

'Oh, it's got nothing to do with you. It's only that he.

313

reckons you're a regular old stir-lawyer. He says you got
more common and education than any of these bloody college
boys.'

All fine and large. 'But what's it about, Joe?'

'It's about doing a screw, or getting him done — by the law.
Shaggy wants to know the right way to go about it. Getting
him cased the way they case us. It will be a lark, you know.
I've never 'eard of a screw being cased before.'

'No more have I.' Nor the devil a much casing did the
screws case us, for the matter of that, said I, in my own
mind. 'What are you going to have him cased over?'

'It's over that Leslie. That new kid from the training ship.
He went up to change a pair of shorts in the Part-Worn
Stores, tonight.'

I smiled and nodded.

Joe burst out laughing. 'Oh, Jesus, it's dead funny. You've
heard it already, you bastard.'

'No, I haven't. Tell us. I was smiling because you were
laughing.'

Joe choked with the laughing and tried to recover himself.

'For Christ's sake, man, it'll be lights out before you've told
us,' said Jock impatiently. Charlie looked at Joe with serious
interest.

'When this Leslie, when 'e, the screw, makes 'im change
'is shorts in the Part-Worn Stores, and oh, Jesus, this is going
to kill you,' he laughed weakly, and continued: 'When Leslie
'as 'is shorts off, and is standing there fumbling with the other
pair 'e's trying to get on, and covering 'imself up, at the same
time, the bleeding screw comes out from nowhere, with a
bloody great cane, and w'acks 'im over the arse with it, and
round and round they go, and round and round, and—' Joe
finished for the moment, too weak from the laughing to tell
any more, and leaned against the wall.

'Nark your laughing for a minute,' said Jock, 'here's Shaggy
and the kid.'

Shaggy looked grim; Leslie walked beside him, his face
white and his mouth working.

'Paddy, I want you to do something.' He stared me straight
in the eyes.

314

'Sure, Shag, anything you like. What's it about, like?' I looked serious.

'It's about — it's about Leslie here.'

Joe, leaning against the wall, was taken by an uncontrollable spasm of laughing.

Shaggy went towards him, like a madman. 'What are you bloody laughing at?' He caught Joe by the throat and drew back his left to killing distance.

I got between them. 'Holy Jasus, Shaggy, what's up, what did Joe do on you?'

'He *was* bloody laughing.'

'We were only having a yarn about something that happened in Feltham. Jasus, Shaggy, you can't do a bloke for that.'

He dropped his hand and said nothing to Joe, just turned away from him, and when I looked round again, Joe was gone.

'It's about Leslie, here. When he went up to change a pair of shorts in the Part-Worn Stores, the Part-Worn score, 'e tried to — he beat him with a cane, when 'e 'ad 'is shorts off. I was going to out it on him, good and proper, but I'd get five stretch in Chelmsford. I wouldn't mind that. I wouldn't mind the cat. I wouldn't mind getting topped for the bastard, but 'e might get away with it.

'Some of the boys said the best way to do him was the crafty way. Leslie can complain to the Governor and they'll give the screw a fughing 'alf-sheet. Anyway, Leslie said 'e wanted to change 'is shorts today and take 'em down to the dormitory to try 'em on and the screw wouldn't let him. He says you were there.'

'Oh, Jasus, that's right,' I said, remembering now. 'I remember. Today, it was, Leslie, when you came up. You'd been working in the building here. I was after being sent over from the new camp to put in a couple of panes of glass and the bloke that helps the screw in the Part-Worn Stores, he gave me a cup of tea.'

'Well, you can tell the Governor that, Paddy, and maybe add a bit on. You can tell the tale anyway, to help do the bastard good and proper. Come on, Les, we'll go down to the Orderly Room, and you put in your application to see the Governor. I'll wait outside.'

They nodded to us and went off. Jock and Charlie and I went into the dormitory. Joe was sitting in his bed, breaking up dog-ends to roll a rake-up.

Jock started laughing and Joe looked up, and he started laughing again. 'By Christ,' said Jock, 'that's the best yet.'

'It's good, 'n't it?' said Joe.

'It beats cock-fighting,' said I, 'and that beats Banagher, and Banagher beats the divil.'

'I don't see how you blokes think it's funny,' said Charlie, 'a boy goes up to change a pair of shorts, and that dirty old sod attacks 'im.'

'You're dead lucky,' said Joe, 'you got a pair that fits you. And they better do you the rest of your time, and all.'

'If he came that lark with me,' said Charlie fiercely, 'he'd get my boot in 'is balls, and perishing rapid, and all.' He stood proud and indignant, looking across at them.

I said over to him, while we untied our laces, and with a sober face: 'You're dead right, kid. Though God knows, it's hard not to laugh looking at Joe's face. He takes nothing serious.'

'He took it serious enough, when Shaggy was talking about it,' said Charlie, reaching for his pyjamas.

There was a roar from the steps, 'Right stand to your beds.' Big Carswell came round counting us.

He passed my bed and Charlie's and came to Shaggy's and then to Leslie's and made no comment on their absence, but went up the steps, shouting, 'Get kipped in, now. Good night.'

The blokes were all whispering about it, till Shaggy and Leslie came down the steps and got into bed, just before the lights went out.

Next day, it was all over the place about Leslie and the Part-Worn screw. There were rumours that he'd been shifted already to some other Borstal or prison and some even said that he was in Chelmsford Jail as prisoner himself. Most of them didn't know him, having only seen him once, on the day they came on Reception, and they thought it would be a good thing to see a screw in the nick, anyway, by way of a change.

I was expecting to give evidence, but nothing happened that day, and after dark, when we were having our tea, I heard fellows saying that he was still up there, in his stores, working.

The morning after that, at breakfast, when Big Carswell read out the list of Governor's, Doctor's, and Chaplain's application, my name was on the list of those to see the Governor. I knew it was about the enquiry and hastened down to put on my tie, and get ready to take my place in the queue outside the office.

Leslie was there, and Shaggy and Geordie, the Part-Worn boy. Geordie was standing a bit apart from the other two, and looked a bit nervous. They all turned and said, 'Good morning,' to me, and I saluted them, and tried to get up a whispered conversation, but Shaggy and Leslie did not want any part of Geordie and when I saw how the land lay I spoke no more.

Other blokes came and joined the queue, most of them ordinary applications and, when we were all in line, the Governor came through from his house. Carswell saluted and shouted, 'All correct, sir,' and the Squire nodded, and went into his office followed by the Chief.

Big Carswell came over the straightened my tie and told another bloke to tie his laces, till the Chief came in and began calling fellows in their turn. There were a number called and they went in and went out, and then came Leslie's turn. He was in a long time. We would have liked to have broken the monotony with a smoke, but Shaggy whispered to me that what we really wanted was a hit and miss. Big Carswell overheard him, and said that he should take a bottle of gin for his kidneys, but to fall out, and look sharp for Christ's sake, that he might be the next called in. He was back a couple of seconds only, when Leslie came out.

Leslie seemed nervous and upset and stood looking at the floor. Shaggy whispered something to him and he smiled and nodded and looked down on the floor again. Then Shaggy was called and was in the office for about ten minutes.

He came out and whispered to me: 'I think you're next, Paddy. Give it to the sod when you go in.'

I muttered something but not so grimly this time, for I was getting a pain in my ballocks with all this carry-on over fugh-all, though I still did not want to fall out with Shaggy, any more than anyone else.

Geordie looked at me as I made to go in and gave a forlorn bit of a smile. I winked at him, offside from the others, and marched on.

'Behan!' roared the Chief.

'Sir!' said I.

'Stand in front of the Governor and state your full name and registered number,' and he banged the door behind me, and stood beside me at the desk.

'Behan, Brendan, five-three-seven, age seventeen, religion, RC, Saint George's House.'

The Governor put his hand up, and said, 'Good morning Behan.'

'Good morning, sir, and I hope I see you well,' said I.

'Very well, thank you, Behan.'

'More of that to you, sir.'

'You have an idea why I've sent for you this morning, Behan?'

'Well, not wasting your time, sir, I suppcse it's about young Leslie Banks.'

'That's right, Behan. He alleges he was assaulted in the Part-Worn Stores with a cane, and that the officer-in-charge there assaulted him.'

'I wasn't there, sir, so I couldn't tell you whether he did or not.'

'No, but you were working there in the stores the day before yesterday, when this man came looking to change some clothing which did not fit him, were you not?'

'I was, sir, I was there, sir, when young Leslie came up, looking to change a pair of shorts.'

'And you overheard the conversation that passed, on that occasion?'

'I did, sir. Leslie said he'd been working inside and that the officer-in-charge of his work sent him up to change a pair

of shorts. The pants didn't fit him and the Part-Worn screw —
excuse me, sir, I mean the Part-Worn officer — told him that
it was a rule that he couldn't change any kit during working
hours and that he would have to come back after tea, any
evening except Saturday.'

'What else did the officer say, Behan?'

'He said nothing, sir, nothing at all, sir.'

'Did he say, for instance, that Banks could not take his new
pair of shorts to the dormitory to try them on, but would have
to try them on in the stores?'

'Not at all, no, sir.'

'Are you quite sure, Behan, that you heard all the conversation?'

'I am, sir, because the window I was repairing is just beside
the counter where the conversation took place, sir, and I
couldn't but hear them, sir.'

'You are positive of this, Behan? You heard all the conversation that passed between the officer-in-charge of the Part-
Worn Stores and six-one-four Banks?'

'I am, sir. I was nearer to them than I am to you, sir, and
I am not deaf, sir.'

'Nor dumb, either,' said the Chief behind me with a
chuckle, as it's called.

'You may go, Behan. Good morning.'

'Good morning, sir.'

'About turn,' shouted the Chief, opening the door. 'Quick
march.'

I was told I could now go to work and, as I passed Shaggy,
he gave me an enquiring look and I winked, and as I went
past Geordie I winked too, just to show no coolness.

When I got up to work I told Tom about it.

'They're all a bloody rum lot, Paddy, if you asked me.
Between the screws and the fellows here, a bloody rum lot.
I shan't be sorry when I get back again and out among decent,
honest folk.' He sighed. 'Whenever that may be.'

It was rumoured that the Part-Worn screw was brought
before the Commissioner, and enquiries made. He transferred to a local prison shortly after. I saw him, when he was
on his way to the station, in a station wagon, and it passed

near the camp site. I was walking along carrying a gallon of turps from the stores. He looked out and smiled and waved. I waved back, and the car went on. Then I looked round, hoping that Shaggy hadn't been watching me. The navvy gang were working on the road quite near.

On a Saturday morning the engineer said to me, 'You're serving a Mass tomorrow.'

'Right, sir,' said I.

'You'll be able to read the Latin all right?'

'Certainly. I won't say "Pate-er" or "Mate-er" the way the English do, but I don't suppose the priest will mind.'

'You're an impudent pup. What do you say, then?'

'"Paht-er" and "Maht-er".'

'You remind me of my mother. She used to say "Patterand Avvy", and I thought for years that it was all one word. You can have a run over the prayer book, beforehand. Get one out of the chapel, if you haven't one of your own, and look over the Mass this afternoon.'

It was a hot afternoon, and the sun shone in the height of summer.

After dinner we walked round or lay out on the grass. The blokes were too hot to kick a ball about.

Far away, I could see the sea, in the distance, the sun glittering off it. I am a strong and fearless swimmer, but the beach was out of bounds because of mines and we were forbidden to go within a quarter-mile of it.

Joe and Jock and Charlie and Chewlips and I sat behind the laundry. Joe and Jock were giving out the Mass, from the book, and I was answering it.

'Introibo ad altare Dei . . .' 'I will go unto the altar of God . . .'

'Ad Deum Qui laetificat juventutem meam . . .' 'To God Who giveth joy to my youth . . .'

'Confiteor tibi in cithara. Deus, Deus meus; quare tristis es, anima mea, et quare conturbas me?' 'To Thee, O God, my God, I will give praise upon the harp; why art thou sad, oh my soul, and why dost thou disquiet me?'

'. . . Introibo ad altare Dei . . . ad Deum Qui laetificat juventutem meam . . .'

Charlie was rolling a rake-up and looking at it, sulkily. He didn't like to be left out of anything I was in.

'That's enough of the piety for a while,' said I.

'I should say so, and all,' said Charlie, 'muttering there, like a set of bleeding witch-doctors.'

'Well, it's one thing,' said Jock; 'in our church, no matter, where you go, the service is the same.'

'That's right,' said Joe, 'you go in a Catholic Church anywhere in the world and it's the same language.'

'Well, they're all bleeding foreigners,' said Charlie.

'And at every minute in the day,' said Jock, 'somewhere in the world a Mass is being said.'

''Ow about the North Pole?' asked Charlie. 'I reckon that in the C of E at least you know what the bloke is saying.'

'Well,' said Joe, 'seein' as 'e's usually saying dam' all, that shouldn't be hard. The C of E ain't a religion at all. They allow divorces and every fughing thing. They only got started because they allowed the King to 'ave a divorce when the Pope wouldn't wear it.'

I said:

> 'Na thracht ar an mhinisteir Ghallda,
> Na ar a chreideamh gan bheann, gan bhri,
> Mar ni'l mar bhuan-chloch da theampuill,
> Ach magairle Annraoi, Ri.'

'More —ing Latin, I suppose,' said Charlie.

'No,' said I, 'it's Irish:

> '"Don't speak of the alien minister,
> Nor of his church without meaning nor faith,
> For the foundation stone of his temple,
> Is the ballocks of Henry the Eighth."

That's what a preacher said in Ireland four hundred years ago.'

''E must have been a lovely preacher,' said Charlie, 'to come out with language like that in church.'

Chewlips laughed a bit, quietly to himself, where he lay

322

in the sun. 'It's all ballocks, I reckon. Like what my old man said when 'e was asked about 'is soul. 'E thought it was 'is arse-'ole they was talking about.'

I rolled over beside Charlie. 'Jesus, I'd love a swim,' said I.

'I should like one myself, Paddy, not 'alf, I wouldn't.'

'I wouldn't mind a swim, either,' said Jock. 'It's a pity about the beach being out of bounds.'

'Yerra, who the fughing hell would know a ha'p'orth about it, if we just snaked down the five of us?' said I impatiently.

'Ah'm game,' said a soft voice beside me. It was 538 Jones, a young kid of sixteen from Stoke-on-Trent. He had a head of disorderly fair hair, and sleepy blue eyes, and I liked him because he was the next number to me.

'Who bloody asked you whether you were game or not?' said Charlie.

'You don't own the bloody North Sea, does you?' asked 538 Jones, setting his face.

'Now, for Jasus' sake,' said I, 'nark the arguments. There's plenty a water down there for everyone and the only thing is, how to get down to it, without being tumbled by the screws, and number two, how to get a swim, without being blown to shit by these mines when we do get down there?'

'I been down there drawing sand for the farm party and I know a place where there's no mines. We drove 'orse and cart over it, so there can't be.'

'Good man yourself,' said I. 'Let's snake off down there and off we go. There's no more to it. Jones, lead the way.'

'That's it,' said Chewlips, 'lead on, MacDuff.'

'First though,' said 538 Jones, 'can I go and fetch my china?'

'By every manner and means,' said I. 'Who might that be?'

'It's Leslie Banks.'

The rest of us, except Chewlips, who was still half dozing and anyway didn't interest himself in matters outside his own business, looked at each other in some surprise. 'Is Leslie your china, then?' said I.

'Certainly. We've known each other since we were eight

323

year old and on training ship together. We was reared together, you might say.'

'Well, it'd hardly do to get drowned without him. Go and fetch him and we'll wait here till you come back.'

'OK, Pad, shan't be a jiff.'

'That Leslie,' said Joe, ''e's the one got w'acked over the arse in the Part-Worn Stores. But 'e goes round with Shaggy all the time.'

'He's an innocent poor kid, that 538 Jones,' said I.

'He fughing must be,' said Jock, 'not to know about Shaggy and this Leslie.'

'Well,' said Charlie, 'Leslie and 'im was chinas when they came on Reception 'ere together, and they were chinas before they came 'ere; on the ship, like 'e said, till Shaggy got chinas with young Banks.' He set his face sternly and defiantly. 'And I think it's a bleedin' shame for Shaggy, and a double diabolical bloody liberty, for Shaggy to be interfering with young kids like that. Shaggy's over eighteen.'

'You're fughing well dead right,' said Jock, 'I think.'

'Me and all,' said Joe. ''Ere's young Jones now, but 'e's on 'is Tod; young Leslie ain't with him.'

538 Jones came along, slowly and sadly dragging his feet.

'For the love and honour of Jasus, get a move on yourself,' I roared to him. 'We haven't got all day.'

He smartened his gait of going a bit, at this, and said: 'Leslie couldn't come, Paddy. He's doing overtime with Shaggy, digging a garden up in the quarters.'

'What do we care whether he's coming or not?' said I. 'If that's their way of spending a hot day, it's all equal to me. Every cripple has his own way of walking. Now you go in front, Jonesy, and show us the way — you that knows it.'

He forgot his troubles and looked very important. 'We go this-a-way,' he said, like a bloke in a cowboy picture.

He brought us down through an orchard, and the leaves were heavy and glinted in the sun, as if they had a coat of synthetic green enamel on them.

It was dark under the trees till we came out on a sand hill.

'By God, I can smell the sea,' said I.

'We're nearly there,' said 538 Jones.

I sang a bit of a song:

> 'The sea, oh, the sea, a ghradh gheal mo chroidhe,
> Oh, long may you roll between England and me,
> God help the poor Scotchmen, they'll never be free,
> But we're entirely surrounded by water.'

Charlie put his hand on my shoulder and smiled. 'You're a rum bastard, Paddy.'

'Them,' said I, 'are the truest words you ever said.'

We walked over some more sand heaps and, at last, 538 Jones stood on the top, looking down at the sea, as if he'd made it himself.

We stood beside him and looked down at the sun on the water.

'Me life on you, Jonesy,' said I. 'You're like "Stout Cortez when with eagle eyes, he stared at the Pacific — and all his men looked at each other with a wild surmise, silent, upon a peak in Darien". By Jasus, this equals any fughing Darien.'

There was no beach, like Killiney, but a stony stretch of pebbles that would remind you of the people of the place, but the water, glittering and dancing, stretched away out in front of us, with no limit but the rim of the world and it was green and blue farther out; there was a bit of a concrete breakwater, that I picked for a dive.

I caught 538 Jones by the arm, and said, 'Long life to you, 538 Jones, and a bed in heaven to you, but you're a great young fellow.'

'Who's going to break the ice?' said Jock.

'Maybe Joe would go in first?' said I.

'I only came down 'ere for the pleasure of seeing you sods drown,' said Joe. 'The only time I ever 'ad a bath was with a young judy from Birmingham way. She was only a week in London. I broke 'er in.'

'I'm afraid we can't provide that sort of accommodation for you here,' said I.

'You're a filthy sod and no mistake,' said Charlie to Joe.

'You could 'ardly call me a filthy sod for 'aving a bath.'

'Whatever kind of a sod you are,' said Jock, 'we can't stand 'ere all day arguing the toss.' He took off his jacket.

'There's a little stretch of beach here,' said 538 Jones, 'from where we cart sand.'

We moved down to the sand and a nice little beach it was; we took off our clothes, except Chewlips, who said he was only having a paddle.

The sun beat down on us, naked, and we stretched our arms under our heads.

'You right there, Paddy?' asked Charlie.

'I'm going in off that bit of concrete. You and Jock and Jonesy go in first and see what depth it is. Joe can't swim, so he can follow the rest of yous.'

'I'm away,' said Jock, blessing himself and running straight for the water, till he stumbled into his depth and started swimming. He dived and came up treading water, and shouted, 'It's smashing!'

'Come on, kid,' said Charlie to 538 Jones, and the two of them ran down together and into the water.

I stood on the concrete and shouted to Joe, 'Now, there's your depth.'

Joe blessed himself and waded in, and stood when the water reached his thighs. 'I never know what to do when I'm this far. I'm like an 'ore at a christening.'

'Go on in out of that,' I shouted. 'I'll be in, in a second.'

He went out to where the others were, but slowly. 538 Jones was delighted with himself, coming up and diving straight down with his bare arse turning over on the surface, till he came up and Charlie and he were doing a sort of dance, treading water and laughing and shouting.

'You're OK, Paddy, you've got plenty of depth there for a dive.'

I looked out over the sea, and up at the sun and the sky, and over to where they were swimming, their shoulders over the water, as they waited for me to dive, blessed myself and balanced on the balls of my feet.

Introibo ad altare Dei,' shouted Joe.

'Ad Deum Qui laetificat juventutem meam,' I shouted, and dived.

I swam under water till I came up in the middle of them. I dived under Charlie, caught him and nearly threw him out of the water.

'Let go, you Irish bastard,' he shouted, spitting sea water into my face. I swam away and lay back in the sea, looking up at the sun, and laughing.

538 Jones and Charlie and I dived and swam under water towards Joe, looking towards each other, as if this was where we'd always lived, a world of naked, waving limbs and silent, open eyes.

We hadn't the breath to make it and had to come up before we reached Joe.

'Now, no buggering about,' he said, when we came over to him, 'or I shall get out and go bloody back.'

'You are a leery bastard and no mistake,' said Charlie. 'No one buggers about more, any other time.'

'This,' said Joe, 'is not my natural helement. So there' — and he suddenly pulled on Charlie's wrist and sent him tumbling arse over tip in the water. Charlie was too surprised to get up for a second, and before he did, Joe was after running up on the beach and stood there, laughing and showing his contempt for Charlie in an unmistakable fashion.

'You dirty bastard,' said Charlie, 'a dog has more manners.'

Jock was swimming steadily out, and then slowly back, and I swam out to meet him.

Chewlips paddled leisurely in the water, smoking a rake-up, and smiling with calm enjoyment of everything.

When we came out, Joe was lying on clothes, fully stretched out to the sun. As they say in Irish, belly upwards one arm shaded his eyes, and he held a rake-up in the other, which he smoked lazily.

Charlie looked down at him, and said, 'The greedy bastard 'as all the bleedin' clothes.' He nudged Joe with his toes.

'Turn it up,' said Joe, 'you can 'ave your bleedin' clothes.' He stood up while each of us got his shirt and shorts and jacket sorted out, and we all lay down to dry in the sun.

Joe passed the rake-up along and we each had a drag out of it, and lay half-asleep in the heat till Jock came up and stretched himself on his clothes beside 538 Jones, who came to, double quick. 'You're still bloody wet, Jock move over a bit.'

'Kip in, there,' said Joe, drowsily, 'I was just dreaming about something; it was double good and all.'

'We can see that,' said Charlie.

'Don't be so fughing personal,' said Joe, 'or I shall do you.'

Charlie muttered something, and stretched himself more comfortably.

We got back safely, and before we went in to our tea I said to 538 Jones, 'You'll have to take us down there again.'

'I will, Paddy, and I'll tell no bastard. We'll only take what lot was with us today.'

'Good man yourself.'

In the dining-hall, Leslie called across to him in an embarrassed way, 'What you do all afternoon, Jonesy?'

538 Jones looked across at him and said, 'Oh, I just mucked about the gaff.' Then he turned and winked over at our table.

''E ain't 'alf proud,' said Joe, ''e reckons 'e owns that seaside, now.'

'We'll leave him with it,' said I, 'for we'd never have had a swim today, only for him.'

''E's a good kid, anyway,' said Charlie.

'A vic-o,' said I. 'We're all good kids.'

In the morning the screw came round shouting at us to get up; to put two feet on the floor. I sat on the side of the bed, in my pyjamas, yawning and stretching myself. I looked over at Charlie and winked. 'Hello, kid, how's the body?'

'A bit burned from yesterday, Paddy.'

Some mouthy bastard was roaring, 'Rise and shine, the day is fine, the sun will scorch your balls off,' though, it being a Sunday, we weren't in such a hurry to get up and out.

I looked around at Joe. He had his face screwed up, and twisted his body like a young Italian black cat, if there is such a thing. He nodded, as much as to say that he had something to say to me. Joe did one thing at a time. Stretching himself awake would have to be fiinished before he could speak. Then, he scratched his head, and shook his finger at me. 'You're serving Mass, this morning.'

'That's right.'

'You got to go out a bit tasty, like. I'll lend you my flash outside tie.'

'Thanks, Joe, what you give to the poor, you lend to the Lord.'

'I said bugger all about giving it to you. I want it back as soon as we come from the chapel, but you can 'ave it to wear while you're at the altar. I'll put it on you, myself. You don't know 'ow to tie a proper knot.'

After breakfast, Joe and Charlie and Jock said I'd have to shave again. When I dried my face, Joe fixed the tie, which was scarlet silk with aluminium leaves, in a big knot, which he said was invented by the Duke of Windsor. I was going to say that these dukes must have some way of passing their time, but Joe thought it was so important that I said nothing except thanks.

I went to the chapel first, to fix the altar with the engineer. When it was ready, we stood outside, smoking, waiting for the priest. A rich Catholic family in the district drove him over.

'They're a very old Catholic family, the Anscombes,' said the engineer.

'They're no older a Catholic family than my own,' said I. 'And we've never been anything but Catholics since the time of St Patrick. Big thanks we get for it, though. I'm excommunicated, and the Bishop of this diocese won't let me have the Sacraments, because I question the right of his country to rule mine.'

'You should try not to be bitter,' said the engineer, sadly.

But I wasn't bitter. When I am in good humour, I could not be bitter about anything. It was different in Liverpool, where the priest was an active enemy. Here the priest had nothing to do with me, and I had nearly lost interest in Sacraments and whether I was deprived of them or not. Walton scalded my heart with regard to my religion, but it also lightened it. My sins had fallen from me, because I had almost forgotten that there were such things and, when I got over it, my explusion from religion, it was like being pushed outside a prison and told not to come back. If I was willing to serve Mass, it was in memory of my ancestors standing around a rock, in a lonely glen, for fear of the landlords and their yeomen, or sneaking through a back-lane in Dublin, and giving the pass-word, to hear Mass in a slum public-house, when a priest's head was worth five pounds and an Irish Catholic had no existence in law.

There were few Catholics in this part of the world and the priest had a forlorn sort of a job but Walton had cured me of any idea that religion of any description had anything to do with mercy or pity or love.

English Catholics had no time for the Irish, except when they were begging from them. They had no use for Paddy the navvy and Biddy the skivvy, beyond taking their money when a new church was being built. The aristocratic old English Catholics had some kind of double-dealt immunity from the penal laws, and the conversions only started when the Irish got the Emancipation and it became legal and safe to be a Catholic, and a lot of the English shop-keepers' sons gave up Methodism and became Catholics because the more romantic-minded of them thought it brought them into contact with the great world of Italy and France, which was atheist or Catholic, but always lively.

But the Irish fought and suffered and many of them died, and kept the Faith, though their last shelters in the forest were cut down to roof England's Universities, and let Newman, like a long threatening coming at last, think his way into the Church with a good Irish oak roof over him.

'During the first years of my residence at Oriel, though proud of my college, I was not at home there, I was very much alone, and I used to take my daily walk by myself. I recollect once meeting Dr Copleston, then Provost. He turned round, and with that kind of courteousness that sat so well on him, made me a bow and said, *Nunquam minus solus, quam cum solus.*''

But it was not Newman had yet the power to thrill me, but the memory of Gaelic Tyge O Sullivan, kneeling out in the wet grass, at a mountain altar in West Cork, fifty years before:

> Brightness of my heart, Your Heart, O Saviour,
> Richness of my heart, the gaining of Yours,
> If I have filled Your Heart, with my love,
> Inside my heart leave Yours, for ever.

'Here they come,' said the engineer, throwing his dog-end on the ground. I topped mine and put it in my pocket.

A car stopped in the yard, and the priest got out, with a lady, and a bloke of about my own age. I had seen them before, for the young bloke served Mass often.

The priest was a small round-faced man. I never had much to do with him, except when he sent my application to the Bishop to be readmitted to the Sacraments. He was always very civil, but I think he thought he had enough to contend with, in a hostile area, without gaining further unpopularity by identifying himself too close with me. But he was always friendly and I think he did his best for me with the Bishop and, though his efforts were unsuccessful, I was thankful to him for them.

'Good morning,' he said to the engineer and me. 'This boy is serving my Mass this morning, Mrs Anscombe.'

The lady, a big lump of an old one, looked over me. 'Have you served Mass before?'

'He's Irish,' said the priest with a smile.

'Oh, I see. Well, you'll kneel beside Cyril, and follow him. He won't be here next Sunday, because he's going away.'

Cyril was a fair-haired lad, a bit taller than I, but not so broad across the shoulders. He was bad-mannered in the way of the English upper-classes, or I should say thick and ignorant and not used to mixing with people, but we knelt together, and murmuring the responses, and thinking of my mother singing, 'In that dread hour when on my bed I'm lying', while she rubbed hell out of the washboard, and of my grandmother, snaking a pinch of snuff to her nostril, during the sermon in Gardiner Street, and of old Sister Monica, telling us to go asleep with our arms folded so that if we died in the night we'd have the cross on us, I forgot everything but what I was doing.

'*Introibo ad altare Dei.*'

'*Ad Deum Qui laetificat juventutem meam.*'

"Ow was 'e?' asked Charlie, when he came out of the C of E.

"E was smashing,' said Joe, 'nearly better than the priest. There was that young puff of a college boy, and Paddy 'ad 'im down every time. Paddy worked the priest the wine and all — the other bloke was only left with the water.'

'And too bloody good for 'im, and all,' said Charlie. 'You could show a lot of these bastards up — these bleedin' college boys we got 'ere and all. I often 'eard you talking with them about books and you'd fughing blind them.'

'And when you won the essay competition,' said Jock.

'They weren't 'alf choked,' said Charlie, 'only you will fugh about all the time, making jokes.'

'That's right,' said Jock, 'Paddy the fughing Irishman.'

'Well, ain't 'e Paddy the fughing Irishman?' said Joe. 'Look at the bloody big lip on 'im — like a bloody ape.'

'Go 'long, you Wop fughpig,' said I.

'Oh,' said Charlie to Joe, impatiently, 'you can take nothing bleedin' serious.'

Joe rolled a rake-up. 'Anyone got a torch?' said he.

None of us were lighting, and there wasn't a match between us.

'We'll go round the kitchen for a light,' said Jock.

Just as we got to the kitchen door it opened and a screw called Gunboat Smith came out. 'Ah,' said he, 'the Four Just Men.' If there had been three of us he'd have said, 'Ah, the Three Musketeers.' 'I just want four volunteers for spud-peeling — you, you, you and you.'

'Ah, turn it up, Mr Smith,' said Jock disgustedly.

'It's a fair cop,' said Joe.

Charlie smiled in resignation. Joe and he liked Gunboat who was a Londoner like themselves.

We sat down on a bench in the kitchen yard beside a big sack of spuds and started peeling.

One of the cooks came out of the kitchen, carrying a bucket, to receive the peeled potatoes. He was stripped to his singlet, but the sweat ran out of him in streams. He sighed when he let down the bucket.

'Why don't you sods do your own fughing spud-peeling?' snarled Jock. 'We been working all week at our own jobs.'

'You'll fughing eat them like anyone else, won't you?' said the cook. 'If you were in there all bleedin' day, and the bloody sweat running out of you, you'd 'ave something to moan about.'

'I was stuck up on that fughing camp site, digging all the winter,' said Jock, 'when you and those other sods were kipped in there.' He nodded in the direction of the kitchen.

'In the warm,' added Joe.

'I was working out in the weather myself, until a month ago,' said the cook. 'I was out on the farm.'

'Well, you are a silly old —t,' said Joe, frankly. 'Out frozen on the bleedin' farm all winter, and when the summer comes, you go in the kitchen.'

'You must be a greedy bastard,' said Charlie. 'I suppose you went in there for the scoff.'

'I'm no greedier than anyone else,' said the cook, with an injured look. 'It's just that I worked on a farm outside, and I fancied some other kind of graft. I forgot about the weather and the heat — it was January when I applied for a kitchen job.'

'You've made your bed and you must lie on it,' said I with solemnity and justice.

The screw was calling him.

'Go back in your Turkish bath,' said Charlie.

I'll say that much for him, that when he came out with the cook and baker, they were carrying two mugs of tea each.

The cook and baker was a screw called Tucker.

The boys called him Tucker the —er, but only because it was a rhyme, and they didn't like to see it go to waste, for he was known far and wide as a decent old skin, and a smashing cook and baker. He was a big old bloke with a waxed moustache, and did his full time in the Army, and

333

more with it. He was thirty years in Hong Kong but mostly he liked to talk about Devon, which is where he came from in the first place.

He handed me my mug of tea and said: 'There you are, like Guinness, ain't it? You're the Irish bloke, ain't you?'

'That's right, the blessings of God on you, Mr Tucker the tea is great like cider,' all in one breath so as the others thought I was going to say 'Mr Tucker the —er,' and Jock burst out laughing into his tea, and had to let on he was only coughing. 'It's like cider.'

Mr Tucker laughed fondly. 'Ah, the old scrumpy. Know the way my old Dad used to make it, Paddy?'

'I do not, then, sir. It's made from apples, isn't it?'

''Course. All cider is made from apples. But not everyone can make it like everyone else, or as good.'

'Stands to common sense, that does,' said I, 'like everything else.'

'Well, my old Dad,' said Mr Tucker, 'when 'e 'ad the juice of the apples all pressed out and casked like, before he closed the cask, 'e'd throw into the ten-gallon cask, a quart of brandy, seven pound of best beef, and a dead rat.'

Jock looked at him with more disgust, and moistened his lips. Joe and Charlie looked at him as much as to say that they wouldn't be surprised to know what his father would do — nor himself, if it went to that.

I looked at the matter scientifically and said: 'Well, I won't say I ever saw that. It must have been a recipe handed down in the family.'

'That's what it was, Paddy, 'anded down. 'Course it was skinned.'

'Jesus,' muttered Jock.

'Put them mugs up in the window-sill, when you've finished. I've got to get back to me soup.'

He went back into the kitchen.

' " 'Anded down",' said Joe. 'What was 'anded down — the bloody rat?'

'He's a disgusting old bastard, and no mistake,' said Jock. 'I hope he gets up to none of his larks with that fughing loop-the-loop, like putting a dead rat in the pot.'

' 'E doesn't 'alf like nattering about 'is —ing old Devon,' said Charlie, 'though 'e ain't been there for forty years.'

'Ah, well,' said I, ' "the savage loves his native shore".' One exile to another.

' "Savage",' said Joe, 'is dead right. 'Im and 'is fughing rats.'

Every Saturday we went down to the sea and had a swim at 538 Jones' beach. I called it 538's beach, because he was the first to bring us to it and it made him feel big in himself, without costing us anything. He didn't bother with Leslie, now, but attached himself to us, and went round with me and Charlie, and Joe and Jock, and Chewlips. Charlie got to like him and they grafted together on the Garden party.

That was till the autumn came on; then the fruit picking started in earnest and the overtime began, when all hands joined in the fruit picking. All us fellows from the works, from the farm, any who could be spared from the harvest, which did not get really under way till most of the soft fruits were in. And the blokes from inside, the kitchen staff, and even Geordie, the Part-Worn boy, and the blokes from the laundry, these all got the mike taken out of them for their pasty colour and were called the 'Palefaces', though after a bit they were as brown as anyone else. We all joined the Garden party after tea, and worked in the orchards till dark.

But the first two nights, it was a disappointment, because it had been raining and we could only sickle the grass, because the fruit could not be picked when it was wet.

So we all looked anxiously like old farmers at the weather next morning, and sure enough, it was bright and sunny and dry.

I said to Tom that night: 'Looks like a good night for the overtime. I hope we're picking fruit tonight. I suppose you've been on it before.'

' 'Course I been bloody well on it before.'

'Will they let us eat much berries?'

'Eat all you bloody well like, as long you pick your two chips. It's like the notice they 'ave in soap works, "Eat all, but pocket none".'

'Begod, and that's a good one,' said I, with a laugh.

' 'Course it was really in a sweet factory but they change it to soap works for fun, like.'

'It's a good one, all right.'

'Some greedy bastards can't be but they must go trying to get the stuff into the dormitory with them, though they can eat all they like when they're out there. I don't pick nothing.'

'No, I was wondering I didn't see you last night.'

'Well, you wasn't picking anything, and I 'elp screws with the checking. Three of us do, me and Cragg, and Cattrick.'

All HMP blokes. Cattrick was called 'Gordon-where's-your-horse' on account of his bandy legs; he killed his father with a hatchet.

'You've got some influence there, Tom, if I eat too much, and can't pick enough.'

'You don't need to pick anything, Paddy, if you don't feel like it. I can always mark you up a couple of chips, but you don't go telling every bastard that. I don't like encouraging these bloody thieves and ponces and I don't want to have anything to do with them, one road or another. Degenerates, that's what I call them, and lumpen proletariat.'

'That's very decent of you, Tom. For my first night's picking, I might be better at filling myself than filling my chip.'

At tea-time, that night, I told them, at our table, about Tom being a head buck cat at the overtime.

'That's right,' said Jock, 'they've got three HMP blokes on the party for checkers. It's only right that they should get the kip-in jobs when they're here longer than anyone else.'

'Especially when Paddy is graft chinas with the 'ead one,' said Joe, 'the bleeding Lancashire strangler.'

I very seldom heard anyone, Joe least of all, make reference to what anyone was in for, except in the casual way of describing him, like mentioning the colour of his hair or the part of the world he hailed from.

But I only said: 'I suppose he's got to have a reason for being here, like everyone else. Anyway, sure, he did fugh-all on you?'

' 'E did,' said Joe, and his face set. ''E called me a disgusting bastard. I may be a disgusting bastard, but what's 'e? I never croaked no judies.'

336

'What in the name of Jesus are you talking about?'

'You know bloody fine what I'm talking about.' He was right, too; I did.

'When you and 'im were painting the C of E ceiling. I put my 'ead round the door, and sang a bit of a Christmas carol, for a lark.'

'Yerra, don't be talking such balloxology. The chap wasn't referring to you at all. I'll tell you what he was talking about.' (As soon as I could make it up.) 'I doubt if he even saw you there. What 'e was referring to, if you want to know—'

Joe interrupted me and just as well, to give me time to get my lie ready. ''E called me a disgusting bastard, with no respect for nothing, and anyway, what's it got to do with 'im, 'o's got respect for nothing. 'E's a fughing Protestant.'

''E's not a Protestant,' said Charlie, indignantly. 'I'm a fughing Protestant. C of E is Protestant, ain't it? You sods are all the same. That HMP bloke is a Nonconformist.'

'Anyway, no matter what he is,' said I, 'Joe has it all wrong. What he was referring to, and I don't deny he used the words Joe heard, but what he was referring to was the way the ceiling had been painted before without being washed off when the other blokes did it before us. That's what he was saying, and I don't believe he even noticed Joe or anyone else there that day. He takes his work very seriously. I've known painters like him at home. My old man is that way about his work, and Tom has very good hands.'

'Double good,' said Joe, 'for fughing strangling.' But still and all, I think my story convinced him.

'Well, sod him, anyway,' said Jock.

'And his friends in America,' said I. 'Let's get on with our tea. We've a long night before us and an empty sack won't stand.'

We all fell in together in the yard, everyone in the place except the blokes in the hospital, for there was no one in detention then, and marched off to the fields singing, 'Hey ho, hey oh, it's off to work we go.'

Though it was half-past six, the sun was shining away and everyone was in good humour. But a little discharge bloke, wearing a leader badge on his coat, said to Big Carswell, who was walking alongside us, 'If they'd been marching off down that dike, last winter twelvemonths, they wouldn't 'ave been doing no singing, would they, sir?'

'Too right, they wouldn't,' said Big Carswell, but absently, answering him out of politeness.

As we went into the field, the HMP blokes distributed baskets.

' 'Ello, Paddy, 'ere's your chip. That door you burned off today in the quarters, you can coat it tomorrow; I made up a sup of lead colour, and it should be nice and hard for morning.'

'Yes, it should be, shouldn't it?' said I. 'See you later, Tom.'

'What's 'e bitching on about now?' asked Charlie. 'Ain't 'e got enough bleedin' painting for one bloody day?'

I looked round to see that Joe was listening to me. 'That's just what I was saying at tea-time — he thinks about painting all the fughing time.'

'Come on, then,' said Charlie, hurrying down a row of bushes, 'cop this row, before some other bastards get it before us.'

Joe and Jock and I hurried after him, and we met Chewlips and 538 Jones on the way and we all sat down to work, team-handed, the six of us, round our bushes.

'Now,' said Joe, 'we'll 'ave a burn.' He dug round in his pocket, and I produced a Player's packet and distributed cigarettes round our party. I got them doing a job in the quarters.

'Tailor-mades!' said Charlie, 'sod me!'

'Certainly,' said Joe, 'any time. Is that Player's I see there, Paddy?'

'Sure,' said I.

All poor old Chewlips could say was: 'On Wednesday. You certainly can use your loaf, Pat. You're a fughing jeanus, that's what you are, mate.'

A flint and tinder was produced and we lit up. I ate blackcurrants, while I smoked, sitting in the warm dry clay. I didn't bother killing myself with work because Tom would see me right.

338

I blew smoke through a mouthful of blackcurrant juice and said, 'The wicked prosper in a wicked world — thanks be to God.'

A bloke from the next row called over, 'Give us a spit, mate.'

'Get stuffed,' said Charlie, without turning his head.

'In a minute.' I waved to the kid, took a few more drags from it, and threw it over to him. 'Cop on.'

He caught it, and said, 'Ta, Pat, you're a bloody toff.'

'You're bloody barmy,' said Charlie, 'you'll 'ave 'em all looking for snout. 'E's only a bleeding Reception, anyway.'

'Well, we were all Receptions once,' said I, tolerantly.

I picked a few to put in my chip, but mostly ate them, while the others worked away and we all talked.

After a while Joe looked in my chip and said: 'Is that all you've got picked? Well, you are a lazy Irish bastard and no mistake.'

'If 'e 'adn't grafted 'ard on his own party today, you wouldn't be bashing the weed like you are doing tonight,' said Charlie. 'Be a long time before you'd work 'ard enough for anyone to give you twenty Player's.'

'I'd sooner do without 'em, than be threading every old woman in the quarters for a bit of snout. There's not one of 'em under fifty.'

'There's many a good tune played on an old fiddle,' said I, not, for what little I'd know about it, that I believed that.

'Forty ain't really old for a blow through,' said Joe, seriously.

'I've heard that a woman is at her best round thirty-five,' said Jock.

'Bejasus, and I wouldn't think so,' said I, telling my honest opinion for once.

'Nor I don't think so,' said Charlie.

'Well, what about when you're thirty-five yourself?' said Joe. 'I reckon you fancy tarts of your own age all the time. Even when you're forty.'

'I don't reckon I will,' said I.

Charlie shook his head seriously. 'Nor I don't reckon I shall, neither.'

'Well, cheer up,' said Joe, 'none of us ain't nearly that yet.'

'Except you and Jock,' said Charlie, 'you're nearly nineteen.'

'Well,' said Joe, ''ow about your old man and woman? I reckon they're over forty.'

'My Mum's thirty-seven,' said Charlie, 'she was twenty when I was born, and my old man's a year or two older.'

'And you don't think they're 'aving a bit of crumpet still?' asked Joe.

'You shut your bloody mouth,' said Charlie, in a bursting rage, his lips set stern, and his fists clenched.

I thought he'd go for Joe, and I spoke across them. 'When I was working at my trade outside, I got sent out to a little job on my own, to coat out a kitchenette, in a house in Merrion, a part of Dublin with a lot of old women. And this old woman, an old maid she was, and with a house full of holy pictures, she gave me a dollar to have a go at her. "Oh, my young love, it's lovely," she moaned, "if I'd have known it was like this, I'd have done it years ago."'

'Ahhr of it, you lying sod,' said Joe, with a wave of his hand, laughing. 'That 'appened me — not you.'

Jock laughed and said, 'That's how you're getting your twenty Player's, a bash up in the quarters — your fughing stud fees for threading old women.'

'You're a —ing sight worse than any of them,' said Charlie, without a smile.

'Come on,' said I, 'and we'll take up the chips.'

He walked up the field beside me in good humour enough.

'Ah, Pat,' said Tom Meadows. He took the skips of berries and weighed them, and wrote in his book, 'Be-han'. 'And what's your name, mate?' he said to Charlie. 'I knew you was Paddy's china, like I'm his graft china, but I can't put down "Paddy's China" in me book, can I?'

Charlie laughed and shook his head and told Tom his name, and he wrote it in his book, and we went back to our bush, well pleased with one another.

Everyone had handed up their quota of fruit and eaten enough so didn't bother with them any more, only to pick one or two and shove them into their mouths, idly, while we waited to go back. The sun was gone down and the light fading.

'Shan't be sorry to get some kip,' said a sleepy voice from the next row. It was 538 Jones, and he was yawning, half asleep already. The whole field was tired and silent, and their faces round their bushes, in the soft and gathering dark, reposed and innocent.

By the middle of autumn we were all in the middle grade, all of us that had come from Feltham together. When the rest of the fruit was ripened, we were all put on the picking all day and every day with only a skeleton staff left on the Engineers' and on the Kitchens' and laundry.

Tom Meadows was the only one left on the Painters', and Joe said he was the right one to leave on the skeleton staff because he looked like a bleeding skeleton.

Poor old Tom said he missed our talks and singing together and I did a bit, too, but not so much as I let on, because Charlie and Joe and Jock and I worked together and had the best of diversion all day in the orchards. 538 Jones was in our team too. I liked him and so did the others. He was a good upstanding kid and as happy as Larry just to work on the same row with us, though he wasn't really listening half the time to what we were saying. Once Charlie saw that he was not shoving himself forward, he got very friendly with 538 Jones and even left my side to go and work with him, while Joe and Jock and I were telling yarns.

When Joe was telling us about his judies, and debating about whether a man could ponce on more than one judy at once, he was serious and thinking about a serious problem. Jock would not exaggerate, and you knew, listening to him telling a story about trying to screw a mot on the top of a hill on a wet night, and the annoyance of slipping backwards away from her on the bad ground that he was telling the truth, though Jock more often listened to Joe and myself.

What I told was ninety per cent lies, and that's being more than fair to myself, for I was an able liar, but my stories were often funny, and Jock, being a truthful bloke himself, saw no reason to disbelieve them.

Joe laughed, but I knew his expert sense was not deceived. That was mostly what any of the blokes talked about, but when we talked of that, 538 Jones was bored. His interest in that ran to an odd wank, like everyone else, but he thought nor talked no more about it.

Charlie seldom joined in talk about that at all, but he sometimes listened without wanting to be noticed, if we were talking anyway seriously about that, and looked from one to the other of us, as if he wondered if he might learn something he had not known before.

Mostly when we were telling jokes about that, he would fall back and work alongside 538 Jones, and through our chat I could hear the two of them having their own talk. About whether a man could run a mile in four minutes, and whether the Navy was better than the RAF. About caffs they'd been in, and smashing feeds they'd had, about the films they'd seen. One would say, 'Tell us a picture', and the other would begin at eight in the morning, and maybe go on half the time till the break at ten o'clock, telling it.

A lot of blokes went in for this telling pictures, and if a crowd was working near him, they would all work on in silence listening to a bloke a few yards away, if the story was a good one.

It surprised me to hear Charlie, that didn't have much gab out of him as a rule, telling, to four or five rows of blocks, the story of a picture.

Joe nor Jock nor I told pictures or bothered about them much, though I'd seen as many pictures and more shows than anyone in the place, because I went to two shows a week since I was four for nothing, because my uncle owned a cine-variety house in the city and a picture house in Ringsend. Joe was in a picture, when he was fourteen, as an Arab boy, and claimed that a cameraman fancied him and chased him round the set one day, in and out of the Casbah.

All that August and until the end of September the whole of the works — Painters', Plumbers', Carpenters', Bricklayers', Fitters', the fellows from the blacksmith's shop and the navvy gang — were on the fruit picking.

After the berries came the first apples, the Worcesters, and after that the first plums, the Early River's and in the high season, the Victoria's, till we started on the pears, and in the last day of September we were all, everyone in the place, brown and tanned from working in the fields and orchards. On the face, and chest, and arms and legs.

Our team, Charlie and Joe and Chewlips and Jock and 538 Jones, were more tanned than any from our secret swimming.

We were brown and tanned all over, said 538 Jones, looking down with great satisfaction along himself, along the length of his body and his bare legs, except for a few inches kept covered from the sun.

It was a great summer, and we were sorry in a kind of way to see it finished, and the first cold of mornings, and the first shortening of the day.

But time passing is like a bank balance growing to a prisoner, and every day, week and month for pounds, shillings and pence. Though we were not thinking of discharge yet. It was a bit soon for that, but still, roll on.

By the time the season was over we were no longer receptions, but in our middle grade, and Jock was in his upper. We knew everyone and everyone knew us and the Monday morning we went back to our jobs, we met together like blokes back in a factory or to a big building job after a holiday — sorry it was over but all glad to be together again, and glad even to be back in the familiar routine.

The free painter gave me a nod and a grin when I went into the yard the first October morning. 'Meadows be waiting for you up at the site, Bee-hann. I reckon you know where to go.'

Tom was very glad to see me back. 'Hello, Paddy, it's like an age since we 'ad a bit of chat together. I missed you, you old bastard, I did. You can't talk to these other daft bastards, they're too stupid, and when they do 'ave owt to say, it's about filth and muck, when it's not shagging lies about all the millions of money they got away with, and 'ave stacked away for when they get out. One fellow was 'ere, also on the skeleton staff like, 'e were working with fitter, 'e was, 'e 'ad me near driven barmy, telling me about 'is spiv suits he wore, when 'e were outside, and about running about with 'ores in taxis. Regular bloody Raffles. Bloddy tuppence-'a'penny Raffles, if you ask me.'

I laughed, as if I had to, and said: 'By God, Tom, you never lost it. I don't think you care a damn what you say, but speak it right out of your mind. And do you know what I'm going to tell you?' I looked at him, suddenly serious, and he nodded. 'You're bloody well right, too,' I said.

He smile deprecatingly, and said, 'Well, Pat, we're blunt folk where I 'ail from.'

'I can see that,' said I.

'And, now, Paddy after those few words, we'll 'ave the collection — I mean we'll get cracking on those outside sashes. I've the colour made 'up 'ere.'

The morning was cold, but bright, the sun shone through the long shaded trees, not white like the summer, and no way hot, but steady, golden.

Jock was put on outside plumbing and had a fire going in a brazier for melting lead, and he went out to it every now and again to give it a little blow from the blast attachment, and said that he and his screw would be having a drop of tea later on, so I looked forward to that.

Joe was working down, digging with the navvy gang.

Beside the site was an orchard, and growing right to the edge of our muck and mortar, half bricks and broken slate, was the green grass; up to the barbed wire fence that divided it from the site.

Till a week or two after we went back to our own work, nobody had much interest in fruit. We had eaten plenty of it for weeks, and now we got a couple of apples or a few plums with our tea, but that stopped after a while and we began to fancy a bit of fruit again, and wondered why, when we were picking, we had not eaten twice as much, although how we could have done that I do not know.

Now, these shortening days, if you were going down the road for oil or turps, and there was a Garden Party bloke working near the fence, you'd be lucky if he was near enough to throw over an apple or a pear without a screw catching him, for it was dessert apples they were picking now, for the Christmas market, and the pears were nearly counted, anyway. The screws were very strict about it. Joe said it was because they had a hard time fiddling a bit for themselves, more than likely.

And on our side of the fence, Tessie O'Shea threatened to case anyone caught going near the orchard, and apart from losing remission, that would certainly mean losing our good jobs.

'They're the best bastard apples of the lot,' said Tom Meadows. 'Cox's Orange Pippins. They got a special squad picking 'em, and all. Mingy bastards wouldn't work one to their mates. 'Course you can't blame them. They get good wages on that. No man gets less than eightpence a week.'

'Sure, we get eightpence a week.'

'I know we do. I often got a shilling and one and tuppence, once, but we're tradesmen. They're unskilled. Eightpence is big wages to them. They're not detached like us, you know.' He smiled. 'Of course we can do the work.'

'Well, you can, anyway, Tom,' said I, sincerely.

He nodded gravely and ran the full brush down the edge of a sash. 'You're bloody well all right yourself, lad. You cut in lovely, and if you took a little more care with your stopping and rubbing down, you'd be champion.'

While we were talking I heard Joe's hoarse voice behind me, 'Paddy.'

'Well, avic?' said I.

Tom said nothing, for he didn't like Joe for being a dirty-spoken ponce, and a Cockney.

So he was, all three, but it would be hard to dislike him in his present urgency. Bent low, so that you first got a view of his black head till he straightened up, brushed the hair out of his eyes, and raised his face, his brown eyes looking gravely and his chin and jaws smudged at the edges with a week's growth, except where the white scar of his shiv mark ran down, he waved his hand impatiently and said: 'What you grinning at, you Irish—t? I got something to tell you before old O'Shea tumbles me being away from the Party. I only fell out to go to the cawsy.'

346

The cawsy on the building site was a corrugated iron shed built round a pit, with a piece of timber running along it for sitting on. Except in bad weather or cases of urgent necessity, the fellows preferred to go up into the grass a bit. Many of them complained of it, though I knew it was no worse than the average lavatory on a building job outside. Besides, it was handy for a smoke.

'Well, tell us,' said I. 'Tom here won't mind you.'

'I was standing there 'aving a burn, and Charlie whispers me from the orchard there. He's on that Party picking them Pippins and so is 538 Jones. If you can get to the far end of the fence he'll work you some apples.' He looked up at Tom. 'I can't go, because I can't leave the Party, but you can. Crack on you're going down to the yard for paint or something. 'E won't ask you anyway, you being detached.' He dodged off in the direction of the navvy gang.

'Well, I'll crack on I'm going down for thinners, if he asks me.' said I, putting down my sash tool.

'You can if you like, Paddy,' said Tom.

I looked at him. His face was set, real snotty, like. 'Ah, poor Joe is a decent-enough ould skin,' said I.

'It's all one to me whether 'e is or not,' said Tom, ' 'e's your china, not mine.'

Nor is anyone else your china, said I, in my own mind. And small blame to them, with your scrawny face and your red Anti-Christ's stubble on it, and the miserable undertaker's labourer's chat of you; wouldn't it be the eighth wonder of the world if anyone would go within the bawl of an ass of you, except for the judy that got within strangling distance, bejasus? Talking about a decent ponce, if he is itself, and has a dozen judies, it's not like the only one you had: I had no mother to break her heart, and I had no china to take my part, but I had one friend and a girl was she, that I croaked with her own silk stocking.

'Well, go on, if you want,' said he, speaking off the ladder without turning his head, but facing up with putty a tiny bare spot on the sash.

You're too bloody right I'll go, said I, in my own mind, and pass you no compliment, and the devil thump and thank you, and a terrible pity about you, you red-headed whore's melt.

. I put down my knife beside my pot and brush, and walked off towards the road. Tessie O'Shea took no notice of me and when I got round the corner and out of view of the site, I signalled Charlie.

He came through the shade of the trees with his shirt bulging, looking round him and smiling. 'Cop on, Pad,' he said, reaching inside his shirt, and giving me the apples.

I put them inside my shirt and they were warm from being next to his skin. 'Christ, there's a great lot there, Charlie. Thanks, kid.'

'Give some to Jock, he's working up there near you, ain't he? and try and work some to Joe. 538 Jones helped me get them. He's up there, keeping the nick for me.'

I looked up in the direction of his hand and saw 538 Jones waving to me from behind a tree, and I waved back.

'Got to get back, Paddy.'

'Sure, thanks, kid.'

He nodded, half shut his eyes, smiled and put up his right thumb. 'It's O.K., Pad, you better get back and all,' and went off through the trees.

I made my way safely back to the job and spoke up to Tom Meadows. 'Got them,' I muttered, preparing to unload my shirt.

Tom Meadows said nothing but went on working.

Still has the needle, bad-tempered-looking fughpig. And if I speak to him again and offer him some of the apples, I may be giving the ginger Judas-jowled get, the chance of telling me to sod off. Ah, sure Christ help him, for all that, every cripple has his own way of walking, and besides I've to spend nine hours a day with the sod, whether or aye.

But begod, I had it, and the Father of Lies, God bless him and the Mother of Lies, too, if she's still on the go, I had it. 'Charlie said I was to make sure and give you first bash at this lot, so come on and take your pick.'

Before he knew where he was, he turned round on the ladder and said, 'Did he, though?' with great pleasure.

'Begod he did. He said, "Be sure and give your graft china

first bash at those apples, for he was very decent to me when he was doing the weighing of the berries on the overtime".'
Liars need good memories, and I have one.

'Ah, that was nothing. 'E's a nice lad, is that Charlie,' but not giving in entirely. 'I can't say as much for that Wop, bloody ponce.'

'Sure, I suppose he is,' said I with a sigh, 'but if it's a crime to be black, well, there's thousands damned.'

'Ah, I suppose there's a lot in that, too, Paddy.' He examined an apple and took a bite from it. 'Bloody lovely, lad.' He was now praising the gift to make up for being surly. 'Champion. Wouldn't get them outside.'

'No, thank God,' said I, 'they're good enough for us. I wonder would Joe fancy one now?'

''Course 'e bloody would. Grafting in that bloody trench.' He came to a decision. 'Here, give me a couple 'ere and I'll 'op over with them. Screw won't take no 'eed of me.'

'Ah, sure, I'll snake over myself, Tom.'

'No, lad, I'll go over and show you 'ow it's done. Give 'em to me. I'll stick 'em in bucket as if I were going for water to make distemper.'

I gave him a half-dozen apples, and he put them in the bucket. Any traces of distemper in it were as hard as the hob of hell so it was clean. He stood up and went off with his bucket, and I said after him, 'Good luck now, Tom,' as if it was carrying a mine to blow up the Castle he was.

He turned and smiled his thin ginger smile. ' 'E won't tumble me, Paddy. I'm too bloody fly for that. Not the first time I slipped it across them.'

It was the first time he'd broken any rule, since I'd known him, barring marking me down for fruit I hadn't brought in. I watched him move over to the trench the navvy gang were working in. If old O'Shea caught him it was little enough he would do, except ask him what the bloody hell he thought he was on, but that would upset Tom more than three days in detention would another fellow. He was that law-abiding and respectable. The loss of remission couldn't affect the poor bastard because he had no remission to lose, because he was an HMP bloke.

'Well, back safe, mission accomplished,' he said, behind me, laughing as if he'd robbed a bank and had it off for a million nicker.

'You're as cute as a Christian,' said I, admiringly. 'By God, if you didn't go to school you met the scholars. I saw you going past old O'Shea and I even think you had the hard neck to pass the time of day with him.'

'Oh, I just said, "Fine day, sir," and what did you want me to tell him, that I was going over to deliver pinched apples to some of his party?'

'You've a neck like a jockey's ballocks,' said I, with a sigh.

'You haven't 'alf got some expressions, Paddy. Comes of kissing the Blarney Stone.'

'The very thing,' said I, 'but I'll bet Joe was very surprised at the rapid delivery of the message.'

'He was that. I just came alongside 'im with the bucket, and O'Shea walked away a bit, and I said down, "Come on, look sharp, cop on," and 'e didn't 'alf get a start. He near dropped his bloody shovel. I just dropped them at his feet in the cutting. Whole thing didn't take 'alf a tick.'

'I'll lay odds he didn't half enjoy the juice of that apple.'

'Yes,' said Tom, 'those poor bastards on the navvy gang, they don't 'alf get sweated. And that bloke, maybe 'e ain't a bad bloke when you get to know 'im.'

'He is not a bad fellow at all then, poor Joe, though I must agree with you,' said I, with compassion, 'he has a filthy way of expressing himself.'

'I always told you, Paddy, I can see you was reared decent like myself. Though I don't 'old with the IRA bombing where ordinary people got killed that knew nowt about Ireland, and was doing no one no 'arm but going about their day's work. Now if it was the big nobs that got it, no 'arm, but when all is said and done you thought you was fighting for your country, and it's a shame to 'ave you 'ere listening to all the manner of filth these fellows talks about, though they can't 'elp it. They're really victims of society.'

'Ah, now,' said I, candidly, 'I can use some choice language myself when I'm at it.'

'Ah, a bit of swearing like, when owt goes wrong, we can

all do that. But that there filth and muck they're always at
'ere.'

'Well, I must admit it, I have to give into you there. I can't
stand that sort of conversation. A fellow doesn't have to be
a saint to be disgusted by that sort of talk,' said I. 'Of course,
they can't help it. It's the rearing they got. But poor Joe isn't
the worst in the world.'

'The lad is all right,' said Tom, 'in 'is own way. But it's
a pity they don't make more distinction between the blokes
they send to these places.'

However, from that day forward, my snout chinas — the
team, Joe, Jock, Chewlips, 538 Jones, and Charlie — were
all quite friendly with my graft china, Tom, and he was a
kind of a member of our team, even though they didn't see
him that often, and they talked about him at meals and Tom
often asked about them when we were at work. And at
concerts, or when there was an announcement from the
Governor, when we all assembled together, five hundred of
us in St George's dining-hall, he stood along with us and was
with our team, and one of it, where before he had stood
anywhere, on his own. And once I heard him ask a bloke
to move out of his way, that he wanted to go up with his
chinas.

The autumn got weaker and beaten, and the leaves all fell,
and a bloody awful east wind that was up before us and we
on our way to work in the morning, sweeping down off the
top of the North Sea, which in the distance looked like a
bitter band of deadly blue steel out along the length of the
horizon, around the freezing marshes, and dirty grey shore,
the gunmetal sea, and over us the sky, lead-coloured for a
few hours, till the dark fell and the wind rose, and we went
down the road from work at five o'clock in the perishing
night.

This Friday night there was a notice on the board outside
the Orderly Room about starting Rugby football for the
season, and explaining that our season started later than is
usual on account of all the work on the Garden Party and

Farm during the autumn; would those interested come to the Library after tea.

I never heard that Rugby was a proper game for anyone except bank clerks, and nobody I knew had even an idea what way a Rugby team lined out. Because there was that much about it in the papers, I suppose, everyone round our street discussed Ireland's chances the day of an International, but none of them had even seen a match. It was the same with nearly everyone else in the place. None of the blokes knew anything about Rugby and very few knew anything about cricket. For instance I heard Chewlips asking what they wanted two wickets for?

Everyone from a town in Britain or Ireland knows about Soccer, because it is the game of the streets, where the ball is kept low and does not break many windows, and you are not often brought down on the hard asphalt.

I knew Welsh miners played Rugby and in Ireland, the Limerick dockers played it, but mostly it was Gaelic football and hurley with the countryman and Soccer in the towns.

Soccer supporters went to the big Gaelic matches, and understood the game and many of the greatest Soccer players of the age, like Jackie Carey, who went over to Manchester City, and led them when they won the FA cup, were Dublinmen who had played Gaelic football in their boyhood.

But Rugby, it was a game for the Protestant and shop-keeping Catholic, and I never thought it had anything to do with me.

That was until I read this book in our library, *The Silver Fleece*, by Robert Collis.

He was an Irish International, and played American football too when he was over there studying medicine, and I was quite sure he was an Irishman. I was quite sure he was some kind of a bloody man anyway, and the way that he wrote about the Irish forward line would set your blood pumping like 'Speeches from the Dock'.

Now, there was a lot of shoneen writing and playing up to the Herrenvolk by Rugby writers, one of whom described an Irish forward as going over the line 'festooned with Saxons' which is what the English call themselves, but this Collis

352

made up his own writing and the way he described an Irish forward rush would put you in mind of 'Fontenoy' by Thomas Davis:

> And standing in his charger, the brave King Louis spoke,
> 'Send on my Irish cavalry,' the headlong Irish broke,
> At Fontenoy! at Fontenoy! 'Remember Limerick,
> Dash down the Sasanach!'

We assembled in the Library and Shackleton, one of the housemasters, gave us a lecture about the game.

A few blokes had played it before and Cragg was one of them. He played Rugby League at full back, and said to the housemaster: 'Look 'ere, Mr Shackleton, I don't rightly know whether you should 'ave me or not. When I was laiking, it were for brass. I didn't know gentlemen Rugby players like you could 'ave owt to do with the likes of me. Say if your club finds out?'

'I don't expect you'll shop me, Cragg,' said Mr Shackleton. 'How much did you get anyway?'

'Ah got paid five bob for a draw, ten shillings for a win, and no tea and bloody well walk 'ome if we lost.'

Mr Shackleton winced slightly for he was religious, but kind too, so no one like to discommode him, and said: 'Well, Cragg, I can promise you the tea, only if you win of course. I'm afraid the kitty won't run to your other emoluments. Still, I hope you'll oblige us.'

When he explained the game to us, he took names and asked what position we'd like to play in. I said I'd like to play wing three quarter which was the only position I'd heard much about, but Shackleton smiled under his little scoutmaster's moustache and said that it was a cissy position and that he was sure I'd be better accommodated with the forwards.

The word didn't choke him, for he put me playing hooker the first trial we had. I was like a streamlined bull at it, and there I played ever after. Jock played second-row forward and my two props were a big lump of a reception, a half-black man from Pompey, and in for croaking a judy in an

353

air-raid shelter, by the name of Lascelles, and another negro bloke from Tiger Bay, called Christian, the one chopped the right arm off of a Norwegian sailor with a butcher's knife.

Sullivan, the screw, said that I was the whitest man in our front row.

We got teams going in each house and played on Sundays, because the Soccer teams used the pitches on Saturdays.

We were easily the best of the house teams and, after a bit, when it got under way properly we played outside teams. We went a few times to play a college on the far side of the county, and Shackleton said it was standard practice for Borstal boys playing games in colleges not to smoke at half time, because the college boys weren't allowed to. Mostly they were a dirty lot of bastards on the pitch and not at all what you'd expect. In the scrum one geezer tried to give me the head, and I had to warn him, when he went down again, that if he wanted any of that lark, I'd be glad to give him a lesson, and maybe the knee too, up into his marriage prospects if he didn't turn it up.

But in the showers afterwards they were just a lot of blokes like anyone else, and they had just as much low talk out of them, and low trick acting, and at tea afterwards they were a very decent lot of boys and tried to make us as welcome as they could. Also, though they weren't supposed to smoke they had stacks of snout, and always we got a packet from each of them before they went back. This hooker that tried to give me the head gave me twenty Senior Service when I was leaving.

We also played a match against the screws now and again, and they were a good-tempered example to anyone of how to give a knock and take one without doing your nut over it.

I was inclined to lose my temper sometimes and once I aimed a kick at this screw when I let on to be aiming at the ball; if it had been aimed at me, I'd have riveted the kicker with a dig between the two mincepies, but he just looked and said, 'Surprised at you, Paddy,' and I did not forget it.

I would be inclined to say that the Borstal screws were better gentlemen, in the way that word is used, than any of us, the college boys included.

Once we played the Highland Light Infantry, who were stationed nearby, and they were all officers except for a red-headed sergeant named Duke, and he was playing hooker. He had also been middle-weight champion of India. He was a bit rough in the scrums but I got him off the ball just the same, more times than he liked, so when we got in a line out and stood together for the ball to be thrown in, he gave me the elbow when I jumped, and there were screws playing on our team and one of them come over, in a blazing temper over Duke giving me the elbow, because he did it well, and I was twisted on the ground, and he told Duke he was a bastard and some other things and offered him a fight, and there was nearly bloody murder on the pitch, with us and the screws getting stuck into the officers and sergeant of the HLI, till Shackleton, who was doing ref, imposed order. But we all had a sing-song later and one of the officers gave me a slug out of a whiskey flask to sing him some Gaelic songs, and right rebel ones at that, and some of them bi-lingual, and the more insulting at that; the more transmutable they got the better this bloke liked them; till they went off to dinner with the Governor and we went to our tea, where we got a cheer from the boys, not because we won, because we didn't, but because there was nearly a bundle at the match, which I suppose, like every row that ever was, gave them something to talk about.

Our front row, when we played an outside team, was always the same. Shackleton was a good little sort, and refereed matches and coached us and told me off for cursing the scrum and shouting to them behind, to give me a bit of weight for Jesus' sake. I was still a bit surprised at Protestants objecting so strongly to cursing and taking the Name of Our Lord in vain, because I thought it only mattered to them as a piece of impoliteness, like shooting a fox or eating peas with a knife, but Shackleton was really upset by it, and I gave it up when he was listening, for he was a decent man. They said he was a Quaker, but whether he was or not, I did not wish to displease him, because he smiled and said, 'Good old Paddy, push him off it,' and all to that effect, till I became a dab hand at this Rugby, and a bull-shoving bastard at getting the ball back.

Charlie played Soccer on Saturdays but came along on Sundays to watch us; when we played in the inter-house League, or when we played an outside team, he was on the sideline shouting with the rest, and only shouting a bit more excited when I got the ball at my feet and went up with it. Charlie was a regular Dixie Dean to dribble a ball at Soccer but I was fairly handy at it, at Rugby, and I must have inherited something from my father and uncles playing Soccer, for they could dribble a ball as if there were hinges to their insteps.

There was another thing I was no good at, though my father and stepbrothers were very good at it, and my younger brothers and my uncle; that was billiards. But I liked to look at it, and Charlie and Chewlips were very good indeed. It was Chewlip's great thing and we went and watched him with bated breath taking his practice shots for a tournament he was in with Charlie. Chewlips, though, did not bate his breath, but just took the cue in his big awkward hands and looked at the ball with a mild and easy eye.

The screws came sometimes to watch him, and he was very proud, as well he might be, and we were all delighted, even Jock and I that couldn't play at all, because Chewlips was in our team, and a quieter, decenter poor old bastard it would be hard to find in a day's march.

So Charlie and Chewlips they got into a championship of the entire place, the final of which was being held up in Andrew's, and we were allowed to go up there with them.

It was strange to be out at night and going up the long road in the windy dark to the New Camp, and the noise of the North Sea constant with the wind and the trees, but not at all disagreeable, as the girl said to the soldier.

When we got to Andrew's, Tom was in the crowd, waiting at the door for us, and he acted very important with his chinas before the other geezers from Andrew's, who'd never seen him knocking round much with anyone up there, and brought us down to a store-room where he had a can of tea and some mugs parked. We were glad of the tea after the walk and he gave us all a bit of snout with it, so we smoked and drank tea till it was time for the game to start.

They were all astonished at Chewlips, and Tom said to a bloke standing beside him: 'And that there Charlie is a good'un, too. They're both in our team.'

The bloke said respectfully that Charlie was a good player. 'It's fugh-all to him,' said I, 'playing on a steady table. He's a sailor and he learned to play on a destroyer, with the balls rolling round the ceiling when the boat pitched or rolled.'

Charlie looked round at me while he chalked his cue and smiled. He seldom mentioned being in the Navy, but he was proud of it, I knew, and didn't mind people knowing it.

Charlie and Chewlips won, too, and got fifty snout each, and were brought for a feed into Andrew's kitchen. Tom Meadows gave Joe and Jock and myself more tea, and we sat in his store and a crowd of Andrew's blokes came up and got chatting us.

Tom Meadows was showing us off a bit and saw us off like the compere in a very successful revue, laughing and telling me at the same time that he had a grand drop of priming made up for the doors on the camp site, and it would be nice and hard for morning. Charlie and Chewlips gave him his ration out of the fifty snout each they got, which delighted him, because everyone at the door saw him getting them and Charlie said, '538 Jones couldn't come up, he's in a PT class but we got his here,' and Tom nodded and we all shouted good night to everyone at the door, and 'good night, Tom', to him, and I never saw a man so proud, as he smiled all over his face and said, 'Good night, Paddy, Charlie, Joe, Jock, and don't smoke 538's snout ration on him.'

Going back down the road I could see the moon, wild and hiding itself, behind an odd cloud, out over the mad grey sea, beyond the half-drenched marshes.

In the last week of November our Matron asked fellows she

357

met in the corridors to go down to the Library, where she was picking a cast for the Nativity play for Christmas.

Our Matron was a fine hardy woman, and was well got with everyone. She had been in Portland for years and her and Big Carswell made jokes of their own about the times they were there, and called each other by their first names like tough old sweats that had been through the mill together, though they were always laughing when they spoke to each other. Except when it was about religion; for Big Carswell was a real black Protestant, like a Methodist or something from Norfolk, and our Matron and the Padre were what they called English Catholics and she even came into Mass now and again. Joe said that I put on a special show when she did, and maybe he was right for we all liked her. She said the only thing she feared was being sent to a women's prison or a girls' Borstal. Though she loved boys and men.

And by Jesus, it must be lawfully admitted that she liked us all, so that one fellow would be disgusted with another that she'd have up to tea in her quarters, or that she'd give a bit of snout to.

She walked down in the morning with her dog, and all the fellows in the parties she passed would shout 'good morning' at her, and she'd wave back. It was said of her that she met two blokes that were after scarpering on the road some miles from the place and she threatened to box their ears if they didn't go back to the place, and they did. On the other hand she didn't shop them and say she'd met them so far from the place, and they got back and into the dining-hall for tea and were not noticed, it being a Saturday afternoon.

In bad weather when she walked between the buildings and her quarters, she wore a flying cap and always smoked a Rothman's Pall Mall cigarette.

The blokes all said that her bloke was killed in the First War, and she never said whether he was or not; but even if it was a lie, it showed what they thought of her, for they could make up very vicious lies too, if they didn't like a person; there was a screw they called One Ballock Barney, because they didn't like him.

The Matron's dog was called 'Bran', and I told her that that was the name of Fionn Mac Cumhaill's dog in the old stories, and she was pleased, for she grew up in the times of Yeats and James Stephens when the educated English liked the Irish for a while.

My mother worked in Maud Gonne's house on St Stephen's Green and my uncle was in the IRB with Yeats, and many is the winter's evening I spent after tea, telling her stories I'd heard from my father and mother and uncles about Yeats, Stephens and his lovely red-haired wife, and Maud Gonne, and AE.

There was a crowd used to gather there most nights, except when some bloke had heard that his brother was killed or lost at sea; once when a bloke was crying all day because his old man was being hanged the next morning. Then she would say to the rest of us, 'Out, you lot, Scapa Flow,' which means 'go' in rhyming slang which she spoke like a native.

There was this night and she's asking me about Yeats and AE and all to that effect, and I said: 'It seems strange to be talking about Yeats and Susan Mitchell in this bloody neck of the woods. This bleak and horrible old English marsh, and it full of half-made English bogmen, and they a bit worse than Irish ones, even.'

'Get along with you,' said she. 'Dickens drowned Steerforth just up the beach, and Edward Fitzgerald translated Omar Khayyám only a few miles away. This place has as many literary associations as any.'

'Well, Edward Fitzgerald was a descendant of the Mac Gearailt Mor and a relation of Lord Edward Fitzgerald, that was stabbed to death by the yeomen in ninety-eight, and your translator of Omar Khayyám was an Irishman.'

'Well, E. Arnot Robertson wasn't and isn't,' she said, for the Matron was a very sensible woman, though her own favourite book was *Precious Bane*, by Mary Webb.

So we went down a lot of us to the Library for the meeting about the Nativity play.

Ken Jones was there, down from Andrew's, and he must have given up telling people that he was in for screwing, for he stood talking with Tom Meadows, and another HMP bloke called Gordon-get-your-horse.

359

Gordon-get-your-horse croaked a soldier for offering his auntie a glass of beer and went round the place on his own, when he wasn't up on the heath minding his sheep. He was barmy, of course, but the blokes reckoned all the HMP blokes were a bit barmy.

But Gordon-get-your-horse ran out in the middle of the night during the blitz, and they thought he'd scarpered. But he was found in the morning up on the heath with his sheep all round him, where he'd been minding them from the bombs.

But though he was a very good shepherd, you couldn't have had him for St Joseph. He was as bandy as a barrel. You'd have thought he rode pigs to hounds, instead of minding sheep. They called him Gordon-get-your-horse, but I thought he looked more like Johnny Dines.

I was talking to Tom and to Ken Jones, and then the Matron called Ken over to her and told us he was going to act St Joseph.

Joe looked over at him and said, 'That there Kenneth—'e shouldn't be St Joseph—'e's a C of E.'

'You silly born bastard,' said Charlie, 'we got St Joseph and Jesus Christ, the lot, in the C of E church, same as you 'ave.'

The door opened, and Charlie whistled in a whisper.

'My, my,' said Joe, 'get on that.'

A girl of about nineteen had come in. Some of the blokes made room for her beside the Matron.

'She's the wife of Mr Hackbell, the young screw over the farm machinery,' said a Welsh bloke behind us. He was on a tractor himself. 'She is going to act the Virgin Mary.'

'I'll be the Holy Ghost,' said Joe.

The Welshman looked away, shocked.

I looked away from him myself. Not that I was shocked, God knows, but I was afraid I would burst out laughing and that we would embarrass the girl, who was among a lot of strange blokes and Borstal boys, at that. You wouldn't mind the Matron, she was a Borstal boy, herself, damn near, but it would be also letting her down before the girl.

'Come along, dear,' said the Matron, 'we've only just begun.'

The blokes stood up and made way politely for her, and murmured 'Excuse me,' as she went to the place where the Matron and Ken Jones stood.

'She's a smasher all right,' said Joe.

'She is that,' said I.'

Charlie looked at her and nodded and said: 'She's in the Nativity play. She's the Virgin Mary.'

'I know,' said Joe. 'I wish I could be the Baby.'

Charlie said nothing, but looked away, and then the Matron called us over to give the rest of us our parts.

Charlie and 538 Jones were shepherds, and Gordon-get-your-horse was the head shepherd.

He was delighted over this, but we had to explain to the matron that he would have no lamb available at that time, but that he would have a little kid goat that he was rearing. It was a little undersized goat born out of its time, and it was so small now that it wouldn't be any bigger than a lamb at Christmas when we put on the play.

The Matron said that that was great, and that he needn't bring this kid goat to rehearsals but only on the night of the play.

Chewlips and Jock and Tom Meadows were innkeepers and census-takers. Joe and I were picked for two of the Wise Men, and the third Wise Man, the Black King, was a real black bloke, who played in our front row at Rugby. He was the bloke from Tiger Bay they called Christian.

'That's all for now,' said the Matron, 'you can go now, except for Kenneth Jones, and Taffy Lloyd.'

Taffy Lloyd was a Welsh bloke that was singing a hymn in the play.

Going along the corridor, Charlie said to Joe, 'That girl would get a nice idea of us if she'd heard you.'

'Why, you fancy 'er yourself,' said Joe. 'Look at 'im blushing.'

'It's equal to you whether he fancies her or not,' said I. 'I suppose he wasn't got in a foundry any more than the rest of us; but you can fancy her without passing remarks on the girl and she good enough to come down amongst us and act in the play. Though I must admit that Ken Jones has a soft job.'

'He's kept back and all,' said Charlie.

'Probably practising clinching with 'er,' said Joe. 'Why didn't they pick me for 'er spouse? I am Joseph, anyway, and always 'ave been. In real life.'

'You'd have been a bit too much like real life,' said I, 'for a play.'

From the gym we could hear Sullivan shouting 'Ams raising sideways and apwards, begin . . . Passing for buckets — right weigh-eight for it!' and the thud of their feet off the floor.

'Well, one thing,' said 538 Jones, 'I'd sooner 'ave the Nativity play than that bleedin' PT class.'

'But, Jesus,' said Joe, ''ere's that Gunboat Smith. I bet 'e's looking for spud-peelers.'

'Well, well,' said Gunboat Smith, in his jolly way, 'fancy meeting you gentlemen, and me worn out going round the gaff looking for spud-peelers. Volunteers, of course. One volunteer is worth ten pressed men, you, you and you.'

But it wasn't too bad. We sat before the big range which was red hot, and peeled away. Mr 'Ucker was gone since teatime, and Gunboat Smith was in charge. He told the cooks to drum up, and we sat before the range drinking this tea, and it was worth it, even if we had to peel spuds.

When we were fininshed, Joe stretched himself, and said, 'I 'ope this 'eat keeps in till I'm in kip.'

'You blokes are all right,' said Gunboat Smith, 'what about me? I got to stop beside that bloody telephone in the Orderly Room till six tomorrow morning.'

'Well, after that you can get in kip, and you won't be long warming yourself, up at our 'ome sweet 'ome.'

'I shall clip your bloody ear'ole,' said Gunboat Smith; 'don't be so personal.'

'Well,' said Joe, 'I got nobody to warm me. Except I slip in beside old Charlie 'ere.'

'Oh, kip in sometime, for Christ's sake,' said Charlie. 'I reckon you're King Lear.'

'He's a fughing sex mechanic, I reckon,' said Jock.

'Could be,' said Joe.

362

'Don't heed him, Millwall,' said Gunboat Smith. 'Come on, you shower, all of you, down to your dormitories.'

Leaving the kitchen it was cold in the corridor. We went to the lavatory before going down to the dormitory and, before we left, I opened the door to have a look out at the night.

Joe and Jock, 538 Jones, Chewlips and Charlie stood behind me and looked out over my shoulder.

The moon shone hard on the marshes, and to the east, as far as the length of the horizon, on the sea, a broad bright steel band.

'Shut that bleedin' door,' a bloke shouted. Some of them had come down to the cawsy, already undressed and in their pyjamas, for a quick visit before jumping back into bed for the night.

'Oh, kip in,' said Charlie, contemptuously. They were either receptions or had, at least, come in after us. Besides, we were team-handed.

A bloke grumbled from inside a compartment. 'Reckon it's bleedin' cold enough without 'aving that bleedin' door open.'

'Oh, kip in,' said Charlie.

The bloke straightened himself and stood up, pulling up his pyjama slacks and tightening the cord as we passed. 'It's all right for you blokes, you got your clothes on,' he muttered.

'Get stuffed,' said Joe. 'You don't 'alf fancy the sea, Paddy. I reckon there's not a night you don't go down and 'ave a look at it before you kip in.'

'Remember the song you used to sing in the summer, Paddy, when we went down to the beach?' said 538 Jones.

I sang:

> 'The sea, oh, the sea, a ghradh gheal mo chroidhe,
> Oh, long may you roll between England and me,
> God help the poor Scotchmen—'

'That's it,' said Jock.

> '—they'll never be free,
> But we're entirely surrounded by water.'

363

Charlie smiled and said: 'Christ, they were smashing days down there. You'd never think now that you could be burned by the sun on that beach.'

'You would not,' said I. 'It's like a dream that we were ever warm. Still and all, we live through winter, and the divil wouldn't kill us in summer.'

'You're dead on, mate,' said Joe. 'Roll on Christmas till we get a bit of duff.'

At Christmas we had the Nativity play on Christmas Eve; the screws all brought their families to it; the Matron told us she was very proud of us, and so did the Squire.

On Christmas Day we had a big dinner, with duff, and old 'Ucker put rough cider into it, which was very decent of him, even though the blokes said he had a bloody great barrel of it up in his house that was sent to him by his brother, in Devon.

On February the ninth I was eighteen, and on St Patrick's Day, which fell on a Monday that year, Charlie and Joe and Jock went out.

Joe had a very smart suit on him, and Charlie stood in his sailor's uniform, very proud of it he was, and a lot of blokes looking at him, because he'd never boasted about being in the sailors, and Jock was wearing a blue suit and they were giving me last-minute instructions for how to find them whenever I went to Glasgow, Croydon, and Soho.

My own family never went a bundle on St Patrick's Day or on shamrock, because it was Easter that was the Republican feast, but someone had sent me shamrock and they were all delighted to get a bit. Charlie put a sprig of it into the ribbon of his matelot's hat; Joe and Jock had it in their lapels.

I smiled as they went down the steps and into the lorry, and waved and turned away and went back to the dining-hall to drink some tea. Then I went off up to work, hurrying up to get out glazing a greenhouse with Tom Meadows, going up the road, grown up now, like Ossian after the Fianna.

And the period of Borstal was reduced, and Chewlips and 538 Jones, and even Ken Jones, that was doing HMP, all went out; and then poor old Tom Meadows went out, and I thought he'd die from excitement, his hand shaking while he shook mine, and told me where I'd find an extra can of turps, if I wanted thinners. At the end of that summer the Squire went off to open some new-style approved school for the Home Office, and take charge of it.

The last order he gave us, was that there should be no demonstration or cheering or anything, because he'd heard there was something of that afoot, but he didn't think it fair to the new Governor.

This man was fair enough, only I suppose I didn't know him so well and then only the Squire, I suppose, could run a place the way the Squire ran us. I suppose that was why the Home Office wanted him.

So this October day, I'm walking up the road to the site, with a few panes of glass, when Gunboat Smith, out for a walk after his lunch, having been on the first shift that day, walks alongside me, and says, 'Remember your china, Paddy?'

'Which of them?' said I. 'Is it Charlie Millwall? He went out in March.' But I knew it was.

Gunboat handed me a cigarette and lit mine and his own, a thing a screw would never do during working hours. 'I'll walk up towards the camp with you, Paddy. Well, I just heard today in the mess. Millwall—'

'Is croaked,' said I.

'You knew? You'd heard already.'

'Oh, I just fughing guessed,' said I. 'Where was it? At sea, I suppose. Seeing as he's, was, a sailor.'

'Remember the convoy was attacked, and the *Southampton* was sunk a couple of weeks ago?'

'I suppose I do. I don't take that much interest in your bloody convoys, as a rule.' Gunboat let that go.

'Well, it was in the Straits of Gibraltar.'

'I'd have guessed it,' said I, 'that he'd have been croaked before it finished.'

'How's that?'

I said nothing but 'Thanks for telling us, Mr Smith, and thanks for the bit of snout.'

'That's all right, Paddy, boy,' said he, patting my shoulder.

I went on up the road to the camp site and did sod all for the afternoon but drank tea with the plumber's head boy, which he made on his charcoal burner. And I gave him some snout and we smoked and drank tea and I listened to him telling me what he was done for, and how he was done, and I wasn't minding a word of what he was saying, or giving a fish's tit about him, or what he was done for either, but saying, 'yes' and 'no' and 'go on'.

Till there's this day, and the painters are sent up to put anti-fire mixture on the rafters in the roof; the best way up to the roof is through a trapdoor in the detention, and we go in and see all the chokey blokes sitting outside their cell doors, in the pale wintry light, scrubbing buckets, and who do I recognize, and easy to pick him out, but Christian, the black boy? He winks at me, and I wink at him and, on account of knowing him, I slip a couple of dog-ends, and this dreary red-headed Welsh Methodist bastard of a screw — not that I have anything against any particular kind of bastards, but that's the kind of bastard he is, with a creeping Jesus accent of remembered starvation on him — tumbles me and, to cut a long story short, he brings me before the Governor.

Well, it will be readily understood that this Governor is not running a boy scout camp, so he gives me PCTFO, which is Penal Class Till Further Orders. This means that I can be kept in chokey for an indefinite period (till the Governor sees fit to let me out, in other words, though I am on full diet).

The boys in the kitchen are very good and I get very good scoff, and nothing happens but this Welsh —kpig brings up a bucket after tea and when we sit outside our cells, he works me this dirty old bucket and hands me a piece of glasspaper, and says, 'Now, Bee-hann, you'll clean this bucket till it's like silvair.'

'I will,' says I, 'in my ballocks — my big brown ones.'

'What is that you say, Bee-hann?' says he, gamming on not to get my meaning.

'I never saw a silver bucket in my fughing life,' said I.

366

So he lets on not to understand me, though he's shouting his head off and threatening a kid of fifteen from an approved school down the line, but by this time all the chokey kids are giggling and half-terrified but delighted to see me having this bastard on.

'I'll show you,' says he, taking the piece of glasspaper in his hand, starting to rub this old bucket and squatting beside me in very comradely fashion. I have him bitched, balloxed and bewildered, for there is a system and a science in taking the piss out of a screw and I'm a well-trained young man at it. 'There now, you try it,' says he, and I only smile in a very insulting fashion, and let him carry on for a bit, while he proffers his old bucket to me and silver or gold, I want it not. Out of being a silly born —t, instead of just banging me into my flowery and not be making a worse —t out of himself than God intended, he at last throws the bucket on the floor, and says: 'All right, Bee-hann, I've just 'ed enuv off yew. You're for the Governor in the morning.'

'I'm not, you know,' said I with an almost Cockney accent.

'You are for 'im, in the morning.'

'I'm not for him in the morning, or any fughing time, and sod him, and you too, you stringy looking Welsh puff.'

'Get in that cell!' he says, and goes over to ring a bell they have for calling more screws, in reinforcement.

So I look down at these kids while his back is turned, and grin, and they're delighted with a fearful joy, and I go into the cell, and start making up my bed.

In the morning I'm only opened up to slop and then locked up again, but I get my breakfast, as good as ever, and a little Welsh orderly that brings it up, but no kin to that ginger Judas-headed —t of a screw, tells me incredible news. 'You're going out in the morning, Paddy. We've known all week. The Governor took the opportunity of locking you up because he thought we'd give you a cheer in the dining-'all.'

Jesus wept, or danced or something, and well He might. But it was right. In the morning our good old Chief, that I'd always known, comes up and takes me down to the showers with his arm round me. 'Go in there, Paddy, and get cleansed, and then run up to the Part-Worn Stores and we'll

367

dress you and have you as smart as paint, for when your escort comes.'

I went up and took off my shorts and kit and put on a pair of long trousers for the first time in two years. They felt very awkward, though it was a smart outfit they got for me.

I was put into the Governor's office and we shook hands politely. Then I went into the next room where the Chief and Mac, and my housemaster were gathered. 'Well, Paddy,' says my housemaster, 'it's come at last.' And we all shook hands again, and the Chief brought me to the Orderly Room. Who was there but the sergeant that led the raid when I was pinched in Liverpool.

He smiled and said, 'They've made a fine man of you, Brendan.'

Well, I had to admit, except for my late differences with them, I'd been well looked after. I suppose even throwing my PCTFO in the scales, I'd probably got away with more than I was ever punished for.

'I've a document which I must read to you,' said the sergeant.

'I know what it is,' said I, 'I've seen them before.'

'I've to read it just the same,' said the sergeant, and cleared his throat, and read:

'Prevention of Violence (Temporary Provisions) Act, 1939. Notice of Expulsion Order.

To Brendan Behan.

Take notice that the Secretary of State has made an Expulsion Order against you under subsection two of section one of the Prevention of Violence (Temporary Provisions) Act, 1939, requiring you to leave Great Britain forthwith, and has given directions under subsection two of section two of that Act that you be detained in custody under that Act so long as you remain in Great Britain, and take further notice that the Order has been made by reason of your being concerned in the preparation or instigation of acts of violence in Great Britain designed to influence public opinion or Government policy with respect to Irish affairs.

Section 1 (2) of the Act empowers the Secretary of State to make an expulsion order if he is reasonably satisfied that a person is concerned in the preparation or instigation of acts of violence as described above, and that he is not a person who has been ordinarily resident in Great Britain throughout the last twenty years, or in the case of a person under the age of twenty years, throughout his life.

If you object that there are no grounds, or no sufficient grounds for the making of the Expulsion Order against you, you may within forty-eight hours of the service of this Notice upon you, send representations in writing to the Secretary of State stating the reason for your objection. If you make such representation, you will be detained in custody pending the reconsideration and disposal of your case.

If you do not make representations within forty-eight hours of the service of this Notice upon you, you will as soon as may be thereafter placed on board a ship about to leave Great Britain.'

My sergeant handed me this document after he'd read it, and I put it in the pocket of my sports coat, wished everyone good-bye, and went down the steps into the car with him.

I'd have thought our Matron would have been there, and was disappointed that she was not, but, all of a hurry, just as we started the car, she came rushing to the doorway and waved a half-knitted sock, and I waved frantically back, and that was the last I saw of Borstal. Though she wasn't given a chance of saying good-bye to me, not a bad picture was our Matron, to carry away with me.

The next morning I stood on deck while the boat came into Dun Laghaire, and looked at the sun struggling out over the hills; and the city all around the Bay.

. . . and I will make my journey, if life and health but stand,

Unto that pleasant country, that fresh and fragrant strand,
And leave your boasted braveries, your wealth and high
   command.
For the fair hills of Holy Ireland. . . .

There they were, as if I'd never left them; in their sweet
and stately order round the Bay — Bray Head, the Sugarloaf,
the Two Rock, the Three Rock, Kippure, the king of them
all, rising his threatening head behind and over their
shoulders till they sloped down to the city. I counted the
spires, from Rathmines fat dome on one side of St George's
spire on the north, and in the centre, Christchurch. Among
the smaller ones, just on the docks, I could pick out, even
in the haze of morning, the ones I knew best; St Laurence
O'Toole's and St Barnabas; I had them all counted, present
and correct and the chimneys of the Pigeon House, and the
framing circle of the road along the edge of the Bay, Dun
Laghaire, Blackrock, Sandymount Tower, Ringsend and the
city; then the other half circle, Fairview, Marino, Clontarf,
Raheny, Kilbarrack, Baldoyle, to the height of Howth Head.

I couldn't really see Kilbarrack or Baldoyle, but it was only
that I knew they were there. So many belonging to me lay
buried in Kilbarrack, the healthiest graveyard in Ireland, they
said, because it was so near the sea, and I thought I could
see the tricolour waving over Dan Head's grave, which I
could not from ten miles over the Bay. And I could see
Baldoyle, there, because it was the races.

'Passport, travel permit or identity document, please,' said
the immigration man beside me.

I handed him the expulsion order.

He read it, looked at it and handed it back to me. He had
a long educated countryman's sad face, like a teacher, and
took my hand.

'Céad míle fáilte sa bhaile romhat.'

A hundred thousand welcomes home to you.

I smiled and said, 'Go raibh maith agat.'

Thanks.

He looked very serious, and tenderly enquired, 'Caithfidh
go bhuil sé go hiontach bheith saor.'

'Caithfidh go bhuil.'

'It must be wonderful to be free.'

'It must,' said I, walked down the gangway, past a detective, and got on the train for Dublin.

Confessions of an Irish Rebel

Brendan Behan

The immigration man read my deportation order, looked at it and handed it back to me.

'Are you Irish?' he asked me.

'No,' I said, 'as a matter of fact, I'm Yemenite Arab.'

Two detectives came forward who were evidently there to meet me. 'Apparently he *is* Brendan Behan,' they said.

This immigration officer shook my hand and his hard face softened. 'Céad míle fáilte romhat abhaile.' (A hundred thousand welcomes home to you.) I could not answer. There were no words and it would be impertinence to try. I walked down the gangway. I was free.

First published after Brendan Behan's tragic death, *Confessions of an Irish Rebel* picks up where *Borstal Boy* left off. Not only is it the last instalment of a unique and unorthodox autobiography, but of a unique and unorthodox life that was as touched with genius as it was with doom.

'The best thing in Irish writing since Sean O'Casey'
Spectator

arrow books

Order further Arrow titles
from your local bookshop, or have them delivered
direct to your door by Bookpost

☐	**Confessions of an Irish Rebel** Brendan Behan	0 09 936500 6	£6.99
☐	**De Valera** Tim Pat Coogan	0 09 995860 0	£11.99
☐	**The Troubles** Tim Pat Coogan	0 09 946571 X	£10.00
☐	**Michael Collins** Tim Pat Coogan	0 09 968580 9	£10.00
☐	**Wherever Green Is Worn** Tim Pat Coogan	0 09 995850 3	£10.00
☐	**The Dirty War** Martin Dillon	0 09 984520 2	£6.99
☐	**The Shankill Butchers** Martin Dillon	0 09 973810 4	£6.99

Free post and packing
Overseas customers allow £2 per paperback

Phone: 01624 677237

Post: Random House Books
c/o Bookpost, PO Box 29, Douglas, Isle of Man IM99 1BQ

Fax: 01624 670923

email: bookshop@enterprise.net

Cheques (payable to Bookpost) and credit cards accepted

Prices and availability subject to change without notice.
Allow 28 days for delivery.
When placing your order, please state if you do not wish to receive any
additional information.

www.randomhouse.co.uk/arrowbooks

arrow books